JAFFA Shared and Shattered

PUBLIC CULTURES OF THE MIDDLE EAST AND NORTH AFRICA
Paul A. Silverstein, Susan Slyomovics, and Ted Swedenburg, editors

JAFFA
SHARED AND SHATTERED

CONTRIVED COEXISTENCE IN
ISRAEL/PALESTINE

DANIEL MONTERESCU

INDIANA UNIVERSITY PRESS
Bloomington & Indianapolis

This book is a publication of

Indiana University Press
Office of Scholarly Publishing
Herman B Wells Library 350
1320 East 10th Street
Bloomington, Indiana 47405 USA

iupress.indiana.edu

Manufactured in the
United States of America

Library of Congress
Cataloging-in-Publication Data

Monterescu, Daniel, author.
  Jaffa shared and shattered : contrived
coexistence in Israel/Palestine / Daniel
Monterescu.
     pages cm. — (Public cultures of the
Middle East and North Africa)
   Includes bibliographical references and
index.
  ISBN 978-0-253-01671-3 (cloth : alk.
paper) — ISBN 978-0-253-01677-5 (pbk.
: alk. paper) — ISBN 978-0-253-01683-6
(ebook) 1. Jaffa (Tel Aviv, Israel)—
Ethnic relations—History. 2. Jaffa (Tel
Aviv, Israel)—Social conditions—20th
century. 3. Palestinian Arabs—Israel—
Tel Aviv. I. Title.
  DS110.J3M65 2015
  956.94'8—dc23

                                    2015002896

1 2 3 4 5   20 19 18 17 16 15

The superficial inducement, the exotic, the picturesque has an effect only on the foreigner. To portray a city, a native must have other, deeper motives—motives of one who travels into the past instead of into the distance. A native's book about his city will always be related to memoirs; the writer has not spent his childhood there in vain.

—WALTER BENJAMIN

CONTENTS

ACKNOWLEDGMENTS

This book is the culmination of a personal and intellectual obsession with Jaffa that has lasted well over a decade. In my case this "Jaffa-mania" stems from my own quotidian experience of living in the city for almost three decades, prior to fieldwork, without being capable of, or particularly interested in, theorizing it. During that time, the history of my family since its arrival in Manshiyye in the early 1950s with the massive immigration waves was only that—my own personal family story. This changed of course with my increasing involvement with ur-ban activism and my attempt to critically situate the city and its subjects in time and space, history and context. Inevitably, therefore, I could not but write "a native's book about his city," as Benjamin puts it. However, in Jaffa, where nothing can be taken at face value, not least the question of belonging, I therefore remain, like many Jaffans, both a native of and a stranger to the city at one and the same time. In a city that prides it-self on being known as the Mother of the Stranger (*Umm al-Gharib*), I am no exception.

Writing from the perspective of alterity thus required disentangling myself from the city's webs and observing it from a critical and physical distance. In the last fifteen years I have been a recurrent returnee, and I wrote this book from this oscillating perspective of ethnographic re-cidivism. Many of the communications and miscommunications with my informants—some of whom I have known since childhood—that form the backbone of this book were in one way or another an exchange of reciprocal differences. While it is futile to thank a community as a whole without reifying it in the process, I wish to express my gratitude to my interlocutors for helping me chart the limits of personal and political alterity.

This odyssey would not have been possible without the support, guidance, and collaboration of a lifelong friend and three mentors. In Jaffa I wish to acknowledge the crucial input of Hicham Chabaita, my alter ego, a mythical classmate, and a relentless critic. The constitutive experience we shared at the Collège des Frères will always nurture and challenge my anthropological way of seeing. At Tel-Aviv University, Haim Hazan and Danny Rabinowitz have been, for almost two decades now, precious sources of inspiration and collegiality. The collaboration with Haim Hazan resulted in our co-authored monograph on the life stories of Palestinian and Jewish elderly people in Jaffa (*A Town at Sundown: Aging Nationalism in Jaffa*) and changed the way I understand both the personal and the political. Following in his giant footsteps and keeping up with his pace was a joy rarely attained before or after. Haim also deserves credit for many of this book's poetic moments and chapter titles. The collaboration with Danny Rabinowitz resulted in the first edited volume published on urban mix in Israel/Palestine (*Mixed Towns, Trapped Communities: Historical Narratives, Spatial Dynamics, Gender Relations and Cultural Encounters in Palestinian-Israeli Towns*) and in a co-authored article in *IJMES*. His unmatched talent in writing fine-grained history into cities and our ongoing dialogue continue to nourish my thinking on binational urbanism in Jaffa and beyond. At the University of Chicago John Comaroff has been a role model of intellectual rigor, integrity, and creativity. I will be forever indebted to him for transmitting the pleasure in theory-making and for his infinite generosity. In many ways, all four of these individuals can be considered implicit co-authors of this book.

The journey from Jaffa to Chicago and back again would not have been as fruitful without the support of Jim Fernandez, Saskia Sassen, and Rashid Khalidi. From their respective disciplinary and personal perspectives, each has offered me invaluable insight and advice. A very special tribute must be paid to Anne Chien at the Department of Anthropology for her unwavering kindness and unbroken resourcefulness. I am equally indebted to my companions on the European leg of this journey, my colleagues and students at the Central European University Department of Sociology and Social Anthropology, for their support and solidarity. Many have read parts of the manuscript but all were loyal partners in the research and writing process.

The Robert Schuman Centre for Advanced Studies at the European University Institute in Florence provided an idyllic working environment and a cultural adventure for three memorable years from 2008 to 2011. The Jean Monnet Postdoctoral Fellowship enabled me to meet Donatella della Porta, Pascal Vennesson, Laszlo Bruszt, and Heinz-Gerhard Haupt, and to join the members of the European Forum on Political Violence. Most of this manuscript was written in Florence with the support of a Marie Curie Intra-European Fellowship for Career Development and a Marie Curie Career Integration Grant within the Seventh European Community Framework Programme, which also funded this research upon my return to CEU. While my Europeanness remains an open question, it was a privilege to be part of the European research network.

It is a pleasure to acknowledge the generous support awarded by the following funding agencies and academic institutions: the University of Chicago (the Century Fellowship and the Council for Advanced Studies on Peace and International Cooperation Dissertation Fellowship); the Palestinian-American Research Center; the Lady David Fellowship Trust at the Hebrew University; the National Science Foundation (Doctoral Improvement Grant); the United States Institute of Peace (Peace Scholar Dissertation Fellowship); Le Centre de Recherche Français de Jérusalem; Tel-Aviv University (the Department of Sociology and Anthropology and the Herczeg Institute); the Dan David Prize; the Harry Frank Guggenheim Foundation; and the Josephine de Kármán Foundation (Dissertation Write-Up Fellowships).

I am indebted to Oren Yiftachel, Sandy Kedar, and the Israel Science Foundation for funding my research assistants as part of their project entitled "Israel's Land Regime, 1948–1998." I am grateful to Naor Ben-Yehoyada, Oded Korczyn, and Luna Barakat for their excellent assistance with the archival work. I also wish to thank the participants of the workshop "Ethnically Mixed Towns in Israel/Palestine," which I co-organized with Danny Rabinowitz and which first took place in 2002 at the American Anthropological Association annual meeting and reconvened in 2003 at the Jerusalem Van Leer Institute: Deborah Bernstein,

Glenn Bowman, David De Vries, Elizabeth Faier, Hagith Gor-Ziv, Ghazi Falah, Tamir Goren, Jasmin Habib, Laurie King-Irani, Mark LeVine, Hanna Herzog, Amalia Sa'ar, Salim Tamari, Rebecca Torstrick, Anton Shammas, Haim Yacobi, and Raef Zreik. Meeting the prominent figures in the field and engaging with their work at such an early stage of my research showed me how to view Jaffa in a broader comparative context.

I owe special thanks to Khaled Furani, who in the midst of my confusion rescued me from drowning in a sea of alternative titles for this book by effortlessly waving his wand and proposing what became the eventual one. In Jaffa, my field and home base, I had the privilege of conversing and arguing with the following individuals: Susan Loewenthal-Lourenço and Louis Williams, 'Abed Satel, 'Omar Siksik, Gabi 'Abed, Sami Abu Shehade, Kamal Aghbariyye, Nassim Shaqr, Moussa Abu-Ramadan, Muhammad Jabali, Eran Sachs, Jonathan Kunda, and many more. I am grateful to the members of al-Rabita for accepting me as a volunteer, and to the late Fakhri Jday, Rabbi Avraham Bachar, Naziha 'Assis, Subhiyye Abu-Ramadan, and Abu-Georges, as well as numerous others, for sharing their life stories with me. My sister Aurélie Monterescu has given me a much-needed dose of sanity and perspective that only an uninfatuated native observer could provide.

For their illuminating comments on this book at one or another stage of its unfolding, my gratitude goes to my readers and friends Roy Fabian, Nili Belkind, Josh Kaplan, Ariana Hernandez-Reguant, Yfaat Weiss, Ronen Shamir, Marina Peterson, Hadas Weiss, Alexandra Kowalski, Danna Piroyanski, and Benoît Challand. I especially thank Noa Shaindlinger and Miriam Schickler for bringing me back to the field yet again and for helping me to look at it in a new light, attuned to the intricacies of creative radicalism. In the last round of revisions Naor Ben-Yehoyada, with ingenious clarity of mind, has generously helped me to reassemble the pieces of the argument. I thank Moussa Abu-Ramadan for facilitating and attending the interviews with his aunt Subhiyye and with Fakhri Jday (narrated in chapter 6). Photographers Haim Schwarczenberg, Hicham Chabaita, Yudit Ilany, and Activestills' Oren Ziv have kindly permitted me to use their photographs.

Related versions of certain portions of this work have been published elsewhere, as follows: an earlier version of chapter 2 was published as

"The Bridled Bride of Palestine: Orientalism, Zionism and the Troubled Urban Imagination" in *Identities* (2009); a shorter version of chapter 5 was published as "To Buy or Not to Be: Trespassing the Gated Community" in *Public Culture* (2009); several sections of the introduction and conclusion were revised from "Reconfiguring the 'Mixed Town': Urban Transformations of Ethno-National Relations in Palestine/Israel," co-authored with Danny Rabinowitz and published in *IJMES* (2008); and parts of chapter 7 appeared as "Situational Radicalism: The Israeli 'Arab Spring' and the (Un)Making of the Rebel City," co-authored with Noa Shaindlinger and published in *Constellations* (2013). I am grateful to the respective publishers, editors, and reviewers involved in the production of these publications and the arguments developed therein, as well as to my various co-authors for the permission to use these texts.

At Indiana University Press I was fortunate to work with an experienced, committed, and highly professional team. My heartfelt thanks go to Rebecca Tolen, the sponsoring editor; her assistant Sarah Jacobi; and the series editors Paul Silverstein, Susan Slyomovics, and Ted Swedenburg for their support, skill, and patience. Thanks are due as well as to Michelle Sybert, the project manager; Eric Levy, the copyeditor; and Peter Brigaitis and Marie Nuchols at IndexingPros, for their excellent work during the production stage and for making the process so smooth, efficient, and enjoyable.

My final thanks go to my family, who have contributed to the making of this book more than I can possibly express. To my mother and father for teaching me to embrace Jaffa's contradictions. To my life partner, Roni, for her refined wisdom, and for magically carving out an island of sane solace wherever we go, while also working on her own research. And finally to my children, Hillel and Gaia, who still cannot answer the question of what their dad is doing for a living.

This book is dedicated to the memory of Yehuda Elkana (1934–2012), the founder of the Interdisciplinary Program for Outstanding Students at Tel-Aviv University, among numerous other remarkable accomplishments, for being a consummate builder, a free spirit, a courageous intellectual, and the first academic figure, some twenty years ago, to believe in me and to give me a chance to win an entry ticket into the labyrinth of academia.

NOTE ON TRANSLITERATION AND TRANSLATION

Some readers may not be familiar with the technicalities of scholarly transliteration. I therefore follow a simplified transliteration system for Arabic and Hebrew terms and phrases based on the style guide used by the *International Journal of Middle East Studies,* except for words that would be commonly recognized by English-speaking readers. I use no diacritics, including the indications of long vowels, except to mark the *ayn* ('Ajami, 'ir me'orevet) and the *hamza* (Yisra'el, ta'rikh). Also I use double Latin letters to indicate the gemination of Arabic consonants, in lieu of using the diacritic *shadda* (Al-Ittihad). For Hebrew I largely follow the Library of Congress transliteration system, with some modifications for the sake of clarity and consistency with the transliterated Arabic. In both languages, I privilege the colloquial over the literary spelling (for instance, Ramle and Manshiyye rather than Ramla and Manshiyya), to better capture how the name would be pronounced. Translations of all sources from Arabic, Hebrew, or French are mine unless otherwise noted.

JAFFA Shared and Shattered

Contrived Coexistence

Relational Histories of Urban Mix
in Israel/Palestine

"Me" or "Him"—
Thus begins the war. But it
Ends with an awkward encounter:
"Me and him."

—MAHMOUD DARWISH, *State of Siege*

AWKWARD ENCOUNTERS

On the eve of the Al-Aqsa Intifada, in what would be his last interview with an Israeli journalist, Edward Said proposed a highly perceptive reading of Palestinian-Israeli entangled histories: "When you think about it, when you think about Jew and Palestinian not separately, but as part of a symphony, there is something magnificently imposing about it. A very rich, also very tragic, also in many ways desperate history of extremes—opposites in the Hegelian sense—that is yet to receive its due. So what you are faced with is a kind of sublime grandeur of a series of tragedies, of losses, of sacrifices, of pain that would take the brain of a Bach to figure out. It would require the imagination of someone like Edmund Burke to fathom."[1]

The main protagonists in this dialectic "series of tragedies," namely, the Jewish and the Palestinian national movements, have long been vying for control over the contested space of "the Land"—its villages, towns, and cities. More than sixty years after the 1948 War, in Haifa, Jaffa, Lydda, Ramle, and Acre the struggle still goes on. In these ethnically "mixed" cities both Jews and Palestinians have been sharing one living space and competing over limited resources. Out of a condition of forced coexistence, an urban border zone thus emerged which brought to the fore the paradox of Palestinian citizens in a fundamentally Jewish state, while simultaneously suggesting, by the very spatial and social realization of "mixed-ness," the potential imaginary of its solution.

The term "mixed towns" (in Arabic, *mudun mukhtalata;* in Hebrew, *'arim me'oravot*) refers to the modern urban centers in Mandatory Palestine that were officially transformed into Jewish cities during the first years of Israeli statehood. The majority of the Palestinian population (95 percent) in Jaffa, Haifa, Acre, Lydda, and Ramle, including most of the local elite strata, were forced to leave during the hostilities of 1948. At the same time, Jewish mass immigration from Europe and the Middle East poured into Israel and settled in the emptied cities (Morris 1987). Today, 10 percent of the entire Palestinian population in Israel (approximately 130,000 people) reside in mixed towns, where they compose up to one-third of the population. However, despite their modest population size, mixed towns occupy a disproportionately important place in Israeli and Palestinian public discourse and national imagination.[2]

The politicized encounter between Jewish and Palestinian individuals and social worlds—which Mahmoud Darwish qualifies as "awkward" and Anton Shammas (1995, 31) labeled "one of the greatest blessings of this accursed century"—can be literally read from various public representations that cover Jaffa's city walls. A series of graffitis I photographed between 2003 and 2008, three to eight years after the outbreak of the Al-Aqsa Intifada, point to the persistence of a deeply rooted structure of ambivalence. In one (figure 0.1), someone has drawn a series of five misguided swastikas on a side street in one of Jaffa's mixed neighborhoods, clearly in an attempt to express frustration and anger, but has failed to draw the historical sign accurately, thus blurring the message. The result is an indeterminate signifier, which exposes the drawer's con-

FIGURES 0.1 and 0.2. (*facing*) Public signs of impossible love and hate: failed attempts to draw a swastika and a declaration of binational love ("Fuad Love OSNAT"). *Photo by the author, 2003.*

FIGURE 0.3a. Jewish attempts to (re)claim the mixed city.
Photo by the author, 2007.

fusion as much as it attempts to relay an ideologically coherent statement. Rather than an icon of nationalist enmity, which invokes an internationally identified symbolic code, the swastikas reflect the unsettled political context of urban mix from which they sprang. On the other hand, graffiti which reads in English "Fuad Love OSNAT" celebrates a romantic relationship between a Palestinian man and a Jewish woman on the walls of a mosque recently renovated by the Islamic Movement (figure 0.2). However, here too the choice to express their love in English, a foreign and "neutral" language, while insisting on exposing it to the public in what might be perceived as a controversial location, reveals a similar position of incongruity.

Clearly shaped by social and economic marginality, these public expressions of love and hate are culturally inarticulate and attest to the political, social, and semiotic difficulty of mobilizing coherent subject positions in Jaffa. The third graffiti (figure 0.3), located in the same mixed neighborhood as the first one, seems to correspond with the figure of the swastika. Stating, in English, that "JAFFO [*sic;* misspelled

FIGURE 0.3b. Fighting ambivalence, erasing ambiguity.
Photo by the author, 2008.

Hebrew for "Jaffa"] IS THE JEWISH CITY TOO," the graffiti invokes the
Star of David to make an ethnonational claim on the city. This claim
over space and entitlement, however, seems qualified ("JEWISH CITY
TOO"), and refrains from making an exclusionary territorial statement.
Again, here, more than it calls for a Jewish takeover of Jaffa, the writing on the wall reflects a cultural and political indeterminacy vis-à-vis
the city's identity. First photographed in 2007, the graffiti was altered a
year later and now sends an unqualified message of ownership: "JAFFO
IS THE JEWISH CITY." At the end of the day, however, the removal
of the qualifier "too," more than it succeeds in establishing an exclusionary definition of the situation, only amplifies Jewish ambivalence
and anxieties.

While these graphic representations express opposing emotions and
diverging political positions, which spring from a collective sense of
identity crisis in the Jewish and Palestinian communities alike (Shaqr
1996), they have in common a failure to convey a coherent message, thus
problematizing exclusivist narratives of identity and place. This inconsis-

tency within the two ethnonational factions that define difference and identity in the Palestinian-Israeli city disrupts a unified definition of the city as either Jewish or Palestinian. Such examples challenge both liberal and radical notions of coexistence. Addressing the politics of recognition, collective memory, and the future of the city, they illustrate the contested nature of binational urbanism in Jaffa and beyond.

How should these paradoxical representations and the social world that enabled them be understood? Answering Ann Stoler's call to "recoup the inconsistencies of these narratives," we must therefore "write a history that retains the allusive, incomplete nature of colonial knowledge" (1992, 183).[3] The methodological task that Jewish-Arab sociality and urban mix challenge us to undertake calls for making sense of such political inconsistencies and cultural reciprocities, without losing sight of the structural inequalities at play between these collectivities. Meeting this challenge, I believe, is of utmost importance for a historically grounded interpretation of the Palestinian-Israeli colonial encounter.

Cities like Jaffa have long been sites of opposing as well as complementary cultural and social processes. Folding power and class into spatial analysis, I offer a dialectical reading of the urban, national, and class scales of position and action that produce Jewish spaces within Arab spaces and Palestinian spaces within Israeli ones, rather than one ethnically homogenous urban space or two divided parts.[4] Beyond the barriers of religion, class, and nationality encoded in dualistic metaphors of East and West (as in Jerusalem) or North and South (as in Tel-Aviv), such cities problematize the concept of ethnic mix itself. Put differently, the intersection of urban spaces corrupts the correspondence between spatial boundaries (that would delimit neighborhoods) and social boundaries (of a certain class or ethnicity). In Jaffa as well as other mixed towns, the coupling between space and identity collapses.

Ethnically mixed towns in Palestine/Israel, such as Jaffa, Ramle, Lydda, Haifa, and Acre, occupy an ambivalent place in the Israeli and Palestinian political and cultural imagination. Under British colonial rule, cities like Jaffa and Haifa were important sites for the emergence of Palestinian identity (Khalidi 1997, 2007; Tamari 2008) and its modern project of national urbanization, only to become after 1948 the symbolic markers of its tragic failure (Monterescu and Rabinowitz 2007). Enacting the predicament of contrived coexistence in the aftermath of the *Nakba,* mixed urban spaces are currently sites of national nostalgia, historical claims, and violent conflict over lived and symbolic space (Tamari 2003).

These tensions have been reflected in the scholarly discourse. Some critics have rejected the very notion of mixed spaces as being "both exceptional and involuntary" (Yacobi 2009), while others have noted moments of "cooperative conflict" and "Jaffa's emergence as a space of (limited and localized) ethnonational cooperation" (Sa'ar 2006, 136). Against these debates, the concept of contrived coexistence seeks to incorporate the involuntary nature of binational cohabitation with the creative agency and survival strategies of its urban subjects. Going beyond essentialist urban dualities, I point to ongoing processes of production and contestation whereby Arab and Jewish spaces are constantly made and remade, shared and shattered.

A product of these intertwined urban histories, Jaffa has long been a city of acute social contradictions and political tensions that cannot be reduced to categorical dichotomies such as immigrants versus natives, hegemony versus resistance, or foreignness versus locality. An instantiation of what David Harvey (1991) termed "creative destruction," Jaffa inhabits a binational and colonial "contact zone" (Pratt 1999) that reproduces different forms of urban mix—Arabs and Jews, veteran residents and newcomers, Mizrahim and Ashkenazim, rich and poor. It encompasses a heterogeneous variety of historical neighborhoods and new residential quarters alongside gated communities and luxury projects often built on the ruins of previously demolished Arab houses. Jaffa is physically located at the center of the metropolis but in fact inhabits its margins. For its Palestinian inhabitants and working-class Jewish residents, its recent return to the center of public attention and neoliberal city planning is a mixed blessing, as it jeopardizes their "right to the city" (Lefebvre 1996).

Inextricably linked to the national scale, the history of Jaffa was tied to Tel-Aviv. The oedipal relations between these two rival cities unfolded through five distinct historical phases:

1. the founding of Tel-Aviv in 1909 as Jaffa's modern antithesis (a.k.a., "the white city" or "the city that begat a state");
2. the violent escalation of the conflict from the 1920s to the 1940s;
3. Jaffa's conquest in 1948 and its official annexation to Tel-Aviv in 1950;
4. the three decades of disinvestment and "slum clearing" up to the 1990s; and finally
5. the present neoliberal phase of gentrification and resistance to it.

The century-long relationship between Jaffa and Tel-Aviv thus reflects a tension between assimilation and distinction, cultural integration and spatial separation—a dialectical tension that has shaped Jaffa's identity to date.

Faced with Zionist expansion, Jaffa, the former Arab metropolis, underwent radical demographic changes: only 3,500 people (5 percent) remained of an Arab population that was estimated to have previously numbered 75,000. Jaffa, which had been a regional seaport and international trade center under late Ottoman and British rule, was transformed overnight into the notorious and dilapidated "Quarter 7"—Tel-Aviv's "Arab neighborhood." This radical urban transformation turned Jaffa from an Arab city with a Jewish minority of 30 percent (35,000 Jews out of a total population of 110,000 in 1947) into what it is today, a mixed city with a Palestinian minority of 30 percent (15,000 out of 45,000 in 2012).[5] Once the "Bride of Palestine" (*'Arus Falastin*) and hence Tel-Aviv's enemy, and then its disinvested "Arab backyard," Jaffa is now embraced by its "daughter-turned-rival" global city (Alfasi and Fenster 2005; LeVine 2005).[6] Heralding this rediscovery as a form of corrective historical justice, Tel-Aviv Municipality has recently launched a neoliberal planning policy of so-called affirmative action, which further depoliticizes its creeping gentrification. Ironically, the policy shift allowed Mayor Khuldai to declare in 2005, "We have taken the hyphen off Tel-Aviv-Jaffa." From the beginning of the twentieth century to the present, the troubled relations between Jaffa and Tel-Aviv exhibit a recurrent pattern of dialectic opposition that reflects Zionism's inability to come to terms with the unsettling presence of Jaffa's Arabness.

FIGURE 0.4. Graffiti in the gentrified 'Ajami neighborhood by the Popular Committee for Land and Housing Rights: "Jaffa Weeps [in Arabic]— Housing for the Jaffa Arabs!!! [in Hebrew]."
Photo by the author, 2010.

More than sixty years after the Nakba, the Palestinians in Jaffa still struggle to retain a collective Arab presence as they watch their city turn into a bourgeois space of consumption—"the darling of real estate investors."[7] In addition to producing a deep sense of alienation, ethnogentrification and Palestinian resistance to it push new social actors to the fore.[8] Instead of the liberal plea for equality, a new discourse of urban rights calls for the institution of an inclusive redefinition of citizenship, which replaces the "coexistence between the horse and its rider" (*ta'ayush*) with an assertive claim for communal "existence" (*wujud*). By mobilizing both Jewish and Palestinian residents, in Hebrew and Arabic alike, these actors engage Zionist anxieties and Orientalist fixations, thus creatively formulating alternative imaginings of state, nation, and binational partnership (figure 0.4).

The urban history of Jaffa replays persistent attempts by the Israeli state, the Jewish population, and the Palestinian community to establish respective definitions of the urban situation. By rescaling the binational encounter to the urban arena of everyday life, I show how these definitions were subsequently undermined and redefined by different spatial realities and political actors. A site of stubborn binational hybrid urbanism (AlSayyad 2001), Jaffa poses a political and theoretical challenge to the hegemonic ethnonationalist guiding principles of the Israeli state, which seeks to, but fails to, maintain homogeneous, segregated, and ethnically stable spaces. This failure results in the parallel existence of overlapping spaces in these towns, which operate through multiple and often contradictory logics of space, class, and nation. Analyzed relationally, these spaces produce peculiar forms of communal relations between Palestinians and Israelis, enacting cross-national coalitions that challenge both Palestinian and Jewish hegemonic identities. Embedded in the current realities of communal struggle, these urban processes should be read against the *longue durée* of ethnic mix in the Mediterranean, the Ottoman legacy of confessional sectarianism, and the enduring effect of British colonial rule (Rabinowitz and Monterescu 2008).

RELATIONAL REALITIES

Now more than ever, Palestinian-Israeli relations seem like a zero-sum game of blood and vengeance. Indeed, for more than a century Jewish and Palestinian national movements have been struggling to establish their collective identities as separate autochthonous nations with respective distinct cultural histories, and so were they analyzed by sociologists, anthropologists, and historians. Both critical and conservative scholarship have conceptualized Palestinian and Jewish projects of nation-building as antagonistic processes, each defined only by the negation and exclusion of the Other (e.g., Gur-Ze'ev and Pappé 2003; Massad 2005; Rotbard 2005; Yiftachel 2006). Implicated in this struggle for recognition and exceptionalism, however, under Ottoman, British, and later Israeli rule, Zionist settlers, Israeli citizens, and indigenous Palestinians interacted in a complex, multivaried web of relations. This included on the one hand land purchase, dispossession, and territorial feuds, and on the other hand commercial partnerships, class-based coalitions, residential mix, and municipal cooperation. Rather than a unidimensional conflict between primordial, self-contained, and largely monolithic entities, the two groups and their identities constituted each other in a relational dialectic of negation and recognition, authenticity and mimicry, segregation and mix. Historically and analytically, therefore, the Palestinian-Arab and the Jewish-Zionist political collectivities and cultural projects not only opposed each other, but at the same time created each other, albeit in obvious asymmetrical positions of power. The relations of mutual determination and the history of contact between these communities have often been rendered invisible in Palestinian-Israeli studies (Lockman 1996; Rabinowitz 2001; Stein and Swedenburg 2004).

The mutually constitutive relations and cultural encounter between the rival ethnonational groups and individual actors have been acutely marked in ethnically mixed urban centers, where both Jews and Palestinian Arabs reside. This twilight area and intercultural contested space is the analytical territory this book explores. The mixed city of Jaffa, which has been historically central to the development of both Palestinian and Jewish urban nationalism, will serve as my ethnographic point of departure. Home to Palestinian longtime residents, labor migrants, and collaborators (*'umla'*) relocated from the West Bank and Gaza, as well as Jewish immigrants from the Balkans and North Africa and recently also well-to-do Ashkenazi gentrifiers, Jaffa lays bare the open wound of Palestinian dispossession as it unfolds new potentialities for historical reconciliation.

This study grows out of my longstanding familiarity, both professionally and personally, with the binational realities in ethnically mixed towns. Born and raised in Jaffa, I was educated at the Collège des Frères, a mixed Christian-Jewish-Muslim school which caters to sons of resident francophone diplomats, to a number of Jews, and mainly to local Palestinians. This formative education in a trilingual (French-Arabic-Hebrew) cultural nexus, along with an engagement in grassroots activism, gave me firsthand access to both communities in the city. During two years of residential fieldwork in a mixed and gentrified neighborhood ('Ajami), I became involved in Palestinian organizations, as well as with associations of Jewish gentrifiers, veteran residents, and municipal officials. The intersecting webs of affiliation of different actors in the urban field illustrate how Palestinian and Jewish presence is constantly invoked and problematized in the collective imagination of the city. This study thus diverges from standard accounts of urban politics in Israel, which are overwhelmingly top-down and state-centric. By activating these ethnographic resources to describe and theorize the unique forms of relationality between Jews and Palestinians, I propose a personal ethnography and an analytical reflection on the future of coexistence in these cities and beyond.

A BINATIONAL GENEALOGY OF THE TERM "MIXED TOWNS"

One of the striking features of the public and scholarly debate on the social realities in mixed towns is the politically charged nature of the term itself. Like political and anthropological concepts such as "Mediterranean culture" (Herzfeld 2005), "Palestinian citizens of Israel" (Rabinowitz 1993),[9] or "Arab-Jews" (Shenhav 2006), the very naming of binational urban spaces calls for a historical qualification.

What distinguishes a "mixed" town (like Haifa in the 1930s and contemporary Jaffa) from a "divided" city (like post-1967 Jerusalem)? To decipher these urban realities, it is not sufficient to study their ethnographic specificities or institutional power structure. One also needs to reconstruct the discursive frame of reference, which made it possible to talk about "mixed towns" (*'arim me'oravot* in Hebrew, *mudun mukhtalata* in Arabic) as a distinct spatiopolitical category in the first place. Such genealogy sends us back to the genesis of the discourse on urban mix in Palestine under British colonial rule and extends to the present appropriation of the concept by the state and civil society (cf. Tissot 2007). The definition of a (Jewish-Arab) "mixed town" which I propose to use here is two-pronged (Rabinowitz and Monterescu 2008, 199–200).[10] One element of it is a straightforward sociodemographic reality: a certain ethnic mix in housing zones, ongoing neighborly relations, socioeconomic proximity, and various modes of joint sociality. The second element is discursive, namely, a consciousness-based proximity whereby individuals and groups on both sides share elements of identity, symbolic traits, and cultural markers, which signify the mixed town as a shared yet contested locus of memory, affiliation, and self-identification.

The term "mixed towns" has had a checkered history in Palestine/ Israel. It was and still is used by Israelis and Palestinians in diverse historical and political contexts, serving a number of discursive goals and altering definitions of the urban situation. The first significant mention of the concept was in the report of the Peel Commission (1937), formed after the outbreak of the "Arab Revolt" (1936–1939). The report puts forth the first plan for territorial partition as a possible resolution to the escalating national conflict. In the "mixed towns," however, the commission stresses that no absolute separation can be achieved. In order to guarantee the protection of minorities in these towns, the report recommends keeping these towns under "Mandatory administration" even after the partition plan is underway. In its inception, therefore, the concept enabled the colonial administration to demarcate spaces of control, while defining geographical categories such as "Arab towns," "Jewish settlements," and "sacred places." Sites of ethnic mix supplied for the British a source of friction and enmity, hence justifying the continuation of the Mandate, and exposing the colonial assumption of homogeneous spaces as the only feasible ones.

In its second phase, the term was adopted as part of liberal Zionist discourse in Mandatory Palestine. A survey I conducted of the main Hebrew and Arabic newspapers from the early 1940s through the present showed that the term was used in the early 1940s by the liberal Zionist establishment, and more specifically by Labor Zionist spokesmen trying to depict the peculiar situation of Jewish communities in predominantly Arab cities under British rule. The earliest mention of the term in Hebrew is in an article published on February 24, 1943, in *Yedi'ot aharonot*. The article, titled "The First General Employment Office Has Opened," quotes Aba Hushi, a prominent Zionist Labor politician who later became Haifa's longest-serving mayor. Hushi comments on the "unique circumstances" of Haifa as "a mixed town" (*'ir me'orevet*), a situation he obviously saw as a challenge to the Histadrut, the Zionist trade union federation of which he was the local leader. The task of the Histadrut, he says, is to "stand fast" and ensure that although Jews in Haifa are a minority, they will nevertheless get their share of employment in a labor market dominated by governmental, municipal, and industrial projects operated by transnational colonial corporations. His implication is clear: a "mixed town," as opposed to a "Jewish town" like Tel-Aviv, is an impediment to proper protection of the interests of Jewish labor, which presumably would have been better served by an exclusively Jewish municipal administration.

The debate about mixed towns that took place in Jewish and Zionist leadership circles in the 1940s was particularly concerned with whether Jaffa should have been defined as a mixed town. In an article from 1945 entitled "Jaffa: Ad Hoc Mixed City and Non-Mixed City" ("Yafo 'Ir Me'orevet ve-lo Me'orevet lefi ha-Tzorekh," *Ha-Tzofe,* December 3), the unnamed author bemoans Jaffa's ambivalent status:

> When is Jaffa considered a pure Arab city and when is it a mixed city? The authorities find it hard to decide. The mayor of Jaffa is in his element amidst this confusion. When convenient, he serves as the mayor of a pure Arab city, and otherwise—the mayor of a mixed city. Thus he attended the reception for the High Commissioner, while the mayors of other mixed cities (Haifa and Tiberias) were not invited. Suddenly, Jaffa's 40,000 Jewish residents vanished and Dr. Haykal appeared as the representative of a purely Arab city. This however did not prevent the Municipality from charging taxes from Jaffa's Jewish neighborhoods the very same day.

The undecided symbolic status of Jaffa posed a political problem for the Jewish leadership. As in the case of Haifa, here too the term "mixed city" appears to have been used in an attempt to properly account for the peculiar situation of a Jewish minority population under Arab majority rule. In a retrospective published after the 1948 war, entitled "The War of the Southern 'Neighborhoods' over Their Annexation to Tel-Aviv," the author puts the blame on the British administration for ignoring the interests of the Jewish minority: "We were used to considering Jaffa until 1947 among the mixed cities, for its overall population of 94,000 residents included 30,000 Jews. For more than a decade, debates addressed the problems characteristic of mixed cities—deliberations within the Jewish institutions, vis-à-vis the Arabs, with the authorities, etc. However the Anglo-American Committee of Inquiry (1945) said that Jaffa is an 'Arab' city despite government statistics mentioning that Jews make up 30% of Jaffa's population" ("Milhemet ha-Shkhunot ha-Dromiyot le-Sipuhan le-Tel-Aviv," *Yedi'ot Tel-Aviv-Yafo* 22, no. 1–3 [1953]: 28).

In the third stage of the concept's metamorphosis, in the aftermath of the occupation of these towns in 1948, the Zionist discourse focused on the need to turn the occupied cities into "Hebrew cities" or "Israeli cities." In the course of Jaffa's annexation to the city of Tel-Aviv the administration considered its condition as a mixed town merely a temporary one which would inevitably lead to its baptism as a Hebrew city: "The derelict, unruly and polluted Jaffa became a city where law and order rule. Whoever walks its main streets would not recognize Jaffa before the Israeli occupation. If this is a 'mixed' city and among its 50,000 inhabitants are 6,000 non-Jews—then the non-Jewish minority is almost unnoticed, and the visitor would find himself in a typical ingathering of the exiles who speak dozens of languages. But the language of communication of everyday street life is Hebrew" ("Yafo beshnat Tashya" [Jaffa in 1951], *Yedi'ot Tel-Aviv-Yafo* 22, no. 5–6 [1952]: 71).

Although Zionist institutions treated the annexation and control of Palestinian urban space as a signal of historical justice, ordinary Jews who had maintained business and social ties with Palestinians and other Arabs in the region prior to 1948 were more ambivalent. Some were surprised by the sudden transformation of a familiar town into a space from which they now felt alienated. A Hebrew guidebook to Jaffa, prepared in 1949 for Jewish immigrants about to settle in the town, reflects the incongruities associated with this rapid urban transformation:

> The massive immigration [*aliyah*] brought about the creation in Jaffa of a Jewish settlement [*Yishuv*] of fifty thousand or more—the largest urban community created by the current ingathering of the exiles. This New-Old Jewish city is like a sealed book—not only for most Israelis living elsewhere, but also for those living in nearby Tel-Aviv and even for many of the residents of Jaffa itself. . . . Names of quarters and of streets were revoked and changed in Israeli Jaffa to the extent that it now has a new face. . . . Jaffa has already become an *Israeli city but not yet a Hebrew city*. . . . This is not the normal process of building a new city. Here the empty shell—the houses themselves—were ready-made. What was left to be done was to bring this ghost town back to life. . . . Materially and externally, Hebrew Jaffa is nothing but the legacy of *Arab Jaffa* prior to May 1948. (italics added)[11]

Throughout the British Mandate period and five decades into Israeli rule, the Palestinian public discourse in Arabic yielded no mention of the term "mixed towns." A systematic reading of the Arabic daily *Al-Ittihad* from 1944 finds Jaffa, Haifa, Ramle, Lydda, and Acre referred to as "Arab" towns. It seems that Palestinian recognition of the existence of mixed towns as a discursive category did not evolve until the 1990s.

The fourth stage of the concept in its current Palestinian use emerged as the second generation of Palestinians born as citizens of Israel sought to define the position of what were effectively mixed towns vis-à-vis the state, the local government, and the Supreme Monitoring Committee of the Arabs in Israel (Rabinowitz and Abu-Baker 2005). This need was accentuated following the outbreak of the Second Intifada in the Occupied Territories and the violent events of October 2000 inside Israel, some of which took place in mixed towns (Jaffa, Acre).[12] These tumultuous events, in which many Palestinians felt that their personal security was breached, yielded an assertive position on mixed towns. Resorting to the language of collective rights, this position, which has since gained some visibility in Palestinian public discourse, demands that Arab populations in mixed towns be represented in the Supreme Monitoring Committee from which they are excluded, and calls for the unique needs of their residents to be addressed through negotiations and joint projects with local authorities and NGOs.[13] This new discourse of rights was clearly articulated by Buthayna Dabit, the head of the Shatil "Housing Forum" (First Public Manifest, November 2004):

> When we, the Arab minority living in the mixed cities, say that we have been suffering from discrimination and oppression for the last fifty years, *we've said nothing new.* When we say that our neighborhoods suffer from neglect of infrastructure and that our streets are dark and filthy, that our schools are deprived and our classrooms are overfilled with students, *we've said nothing new!*
>
> It seems that the next fifty years will be similar to those past, however, this time we refuse to play the role of the victim. We want to be in the position of the lawyer who protects our rights, who will not yield or compromise. We will not let go until we secure the future of our children with decent schools, clean neighborhoods, affordable housing, and public parks.
>
> *This is our goal and this is the path we will walk, step by step!* (italics original)

These sensibilities were brought to the attention of the Jewish public through increasing media coverage and public debate. A particularly visible example is a series in *Ha'aretz*, authored by Ori Nir and Lily Galili in late 2000, which looked at mixed towns in the wake of the October 2000 events. This debate, Nir and Galili argue, is important, as "mixed towns are a metaphor for the entire Israeli-Palestinian conflict. They are a microcosm which contains all of the possible variations on coexistence, a kind of a workshop from which solutions can be derived."[14] Fifty years after the establishment of the state and the destruction of Palestinian urbanism, Arab and Jewish public discourses of civil society reconstituted mixed towns as a marked category, deeply intertwined with the future of the State of Israel and its Palestinian minority.

As indicated by the media survey, the discourse on mixed towns was conducted not only positively but also negatively, by denying their very existence as such. A certain Palestinian nationalist and scholarly discourse thus rejects the very characterization of such towns as mixed (Bashir 1996), maintaining that they are nothing but figments of the Zionist imagination. In reality, this position claims, they are nothing but Jewish cities with marginalized Arab communities (Yacobi 2009). This critical view rejects the discourse of mixed towns as liberal, preferring to define such towns as "targeted towns" (*mudun mustahdafa*) or, in a rarer and more optimistic vein, "shared towns" (*mudun mushtaraka*).[15]

On the Jewish-Israeli side, discursive strategies reflect other forms of denial. As Dan Rabinowitz (1997) shows, local leaders in towns such as Natzerat Illit were known in the 1980s to suppress statistical data that indicated that their town, perceived and represented in their books as exclusively Jewish, had a Palestinian component meaningful enough to render it a mixed town. Instead, official local publications pushed an image of the city as exclusively Jewish and intensely Zionist. A decade or so later, the mayor did go on record admitting that the Arab minority accounted for 8 percent of the population, but he rejected the notion that Natzerat Illit was a mixed town. In his view, "a mixed city is a city in which between 10 and 20 percent of the residents are Arab residents."[16]

Presently, it seems that the concept of mixed towns has been by and large adopted by the leaders of the Arab communities in these cities. In 2006 the League for the Mixed Cities was founded in the Israeli Parliament, headed by MK Nadia Hilu, a Jaffa Palestinian. In a conference held by the initiative of the Abraham Fund under the title "Mixed Cities:

Laying Out a Multicultural and Egalitarian Policy in Israel," the activists likened the social and physical state of these cities to "an explosive
barrel which calls for immediate systemic treatment." This attention has
pushed leading NGOs (such as Sadaqa-Re'ut, Ta'ayush, New Horizon,
and Shatil) to promote a binational agenda and define ethnically mixed
towns as "shared cities."[17]

Such processes of simultaneous discursive constitution and negation
suggest that the concept "mixed towns" underwent a structural inversion
during the twentieth century. Originally coined to suit British problems
of population management, it was later invoked to describe the predicament of Jewish neighborhoods under Arab municipal dominance, and it
currently denotes the predicament of the Palestinian minority in towns
where the majority is Jewish. Whereas Palestinian discourse traditionally
constructed Jaffa, Haifa, Ramle, Lydda, and Acre as an unmarked category (an "Arab town"), thus symbolically erasing the presence of Jewish
communities in their midst, the effects of the Nakba and the Judaization
of urban space entailed the transformation of these towns into a marked
category that demands cultural definition and political mobilization.

The vacillation in the use of the concept of the mixed town, from colonial language to Zionist and now Palestinian ambivalent appropriation,
enacts mono- and binational definitions of the urban situation as either
Arab, Jewish, or mixed. Emanating from the external perspective of empire, the signifying act of naming urban mix was internalized in a series
of mononational discursive trajectories (Palestinian and Zionist), only
to emerge as a new binational site of shared existence when the term is
used by civil society organizations and political activists—a third space
of recognition which is neither Zionist nor exclusively Palestinian.

The unfolding vicissitude of the discourse on mixed towns encapsulates many of the pertinent issues in the history of twentieth-century
Jewish-Arab relations. This dialectic inversion corresponds to what
Juval Portugali (1993) has termed "implicate relations," denoting the
similarities in form and content that exist between the two national
projects.[18] The urban landscape is a dramatic vantage point from which
to observe how social exchange, collective memory, and political sensibilities evolved in a process of dialectical opposition and reciprocal
determination between the two communities.

PLURAL URBANISM IN THE MIDDLE EAST

Studies of Middle Eastern urbanism have traditionally been guided by a limited repertoire of tropes, which emphasized antiquity, confinement, and religiosity (Rabinowitz and Monterescu 2008).[19] The images of the old city, the *qasbah,* the *medina,* subsumed under the quintessential "Islamic city," have all been part of the West's longstanding fascination with the region (Weber 1958; Hourani 1970; Abu-Lughod 1987; Monk 2002; Slyomovics 2001). Accentuating authenticity and a concomitant cultural autochthony, the vividness of these images can breed essentialization and theoretical impasse. Observers have often been fixated by obscuring idioms such as stagnation and traditionalism (Said 1979), leading them to overlook or misrecognize the emergent urban configurations of Middle Eastern cities. Responding to this Orientalist bias, scholars in the 1970s began to approach Middle Eastern cities as instances of Third World urbanization (Abu-Lughod and Hay 1977). This comparative perspective focused on the colonial and postcolonial city as a site of class struggle, urban apartheid, imperial planning, and colonial architecture.

This revisionist framework in turn yielded three paradigms: the colonial city (e.g., Algiers under French rule), the dual city (e.g., Rabat under post–Morrocan independence), and the divided city (e.g., Jerusalem since 1967) (Fanon 1963; Abu-Lughod 1980; King 1990; Çelik 1997). Stressing political economy, colonial governmentality, and recently neocolonialism (Mitchell 1988; Yacobi and Shechter 2005), these idioms have their own myopic limitations—primarily their tendency to misrecognize intercommunal dynamics and to underestimate social networking across ethnic divides. They tend to foreground exclusion and disenfranchisement, and as a result are often oblivious to professional collaboration, residential mix, and other factors that nourish and vitalize plural urban societies.

In focusing on everyday spatialized practices such as cohabitation and gentrification in ethnically mixed towns, I seek to avoid the restrictive tropes of urban Orientalism and Manichean conceptualizations of the colonial and dual city. Mixed towns defy simple binaries and manifest both nationalist and colonial segregation while at the same time actively resisting them. This analysis examines demographic diversification, geographical and cultural expansion, and intercommunal relations in order to reconfigure the sociopolitical portrait of this city-form. Like scholars of the urban who draw on postcolonial theory, I recognize that ethnic segregation does not rule out cohabitation, and that the dialectics of oppression and resistance are often intertwined (Jacobs 1996; King 2003). This leads me to argue that mixed towns in Palestine/Israel are best characterized as emergent constellations, i.e., historically specific superpositions of earlier urban forms (Rabinowitz and Monterescu 2008, 196). Rather than treating them as essentialized primordial entities, I see them, following Nezar AlSayyad (2001), as unfolding manifestations of hybrid urbanism—an idiom resonating with imageries of mimicry and tense cross references between the colonizer and the colonized.

My proposed revisionist conceptualization of the urban colonial encounter makes visible, as Albert Memmi (1985) has noted, the dialectic *enchaînement* between the colonizer and the colonized that produces in the process multiple intentionalities, identifications, and alienations. The urban colonial frontier thus emerges not as a site of zero-sum conflict but rather as "a place in which the unfolding histories" of both dominators and dominated, center and periphery, "met—there to be made, reciprocally, in relation to each other." Beyond and beneath colonialism's black-and-white dualisms and "working essentialisms," the binational encounter did create an "awareness of ruptures at which local resistance was directed, and in which new hybridities could take root" (Comaroff and Comaroff 1997, 403). Similarly, from this perspective the city can be viewed not as a container for ethnic communities, but as a site of production, mediation, and transaction, a locus of interaction among form, function, and structure, where social processes and urban "things" get intertwined (Harvey 1997; Lefebvre 1996). The same reconceptualization applies to urban space and minority/majority relations between ethnic groups as well as to the national and local identities they produce. The perspective of relational urbanism thus revises the multiscalar links between the hegemonic logic of urban nationalism, the economic logic of neoliberal gentrification, and the social logic of ethnic cohabitation.

Another of my goals is to move beyond the paradigm of methodological nationalism, which can only describe binational spaces as historical anomalies, in order to trace a series of transformations in collective vio-

lence, nationalist narratives, citizenship configurations, planning ideologies, and everyday life in Jaffa from the end of British colonial rule to
the present. These transformations illustrate how the Jewish-Arab city
changed from a site of ethnic violence and social marginality—a radical
marker of cultural alterity in the postwar public landscape—to a symbol
of urban desire for liberal gentrifiers in search of Oriental authenticity
and spatial capital. Paradoxically, however, in the process of resistance
to neoliberal restructuring and gentrification the mixed town came to
produce scopes of agency for activists, artists, and residents seeking a
viable shared future often framed in cosmopolitan, transregional, and
postnational terms.[20]

❧ ❧ ❧

Borrowing from Brubaker's opus on the mixed town of Cluj-Napoca,
we can say that while this study was conducted *in* Jaffa, it is not simply a
study *of* Jaffa; it is a study of the everyday workings of ethnonational politics and urban capitalism in "a setting marked by sustained and highly
charged conflict, on the one hand, yet by traditions and expectations
of civility, on the other" (Brubaker et al. 2006, 357–358). The ensuing
urban regime that I term "contrived coexistence" reflects this paradoxical reality. Focusing on a specific city-form, the book thus diverges from
most urban ethnographies, which traditionally draw on "communities"
as their primary unit of analysis.

The book's structure reflects the organizing principle of the argument regarding relational urbanism. It thus offers a dialectical reading
of the simultaneous Palestinization and Israelization of urban space.
The argument follows three sites of urban conflict to outline a relational
theory of sociality and spatiality. Part I focuses on the collective struggle
and communal histories in the mixed city, showing that Palestinian and
Jewish collective narratives and modes of urban experience are not only
intertwined but are inherently mirror images of each other—though
uneven and distorted, to be sure. These refracted images reflect compa-
rable fears and longings for future coexistence and political recognition.
Part II follows the historical transition from centralist planning to the
neoliberal appropriation of space. Signaling new modes of exclusion, the
emergence of gentrification and gated communities became the main
event in the city in the 1990s and its mobilizing bone of contention.

Part III zooms in on phenomenological aspects of the everyday life of ordinary citizens and documents the dramatic clash between the collective narrative and personal life-stories. Between nationalist totalities and individual experiences lies an agonistic yet hopeful vision of the city.

Chapter 1 provides the analytic vocabulary needed to examine how urban space, Jewish-Arab sociality, and local/national identities have been both represented and produced in ethnically mixed towns since the establishment of the State of Israel. I proceed from an ethnography of the October 2000 events following the breakout of the Al-Aqsa Intifada to describe social processes such as demographic interpermeation, communal fragmentation, and intercommunal exchange that have created an unresolved spatial order on the ground. Outlining a theory of spatial relationality, the concepts of "spatial heteronomy," "stranger relations," and "cultural indeterminacy" are proposed to characterize the challenge raised by ethnically mixed towns to the Jewish state and to the ethnonational logic that guides it. On one level, cities like Jaffa personify the political conflict over space and identity as they evolved from confessional communities to modern nation-based collectives shaped by milestones of the Palestinian-Israeli conflict. On another level, they form political and cultural arenas that defy the binary logic of ethnonationalism and urban colonialism.

The next two chapters describe the indeterminate image of the mixed city as it has been represented in the Zionist and Palestinian historical imagination from 1948 to the neoliberal present. Vacillating between romantic historicity and political violence, the Israeli image of Jaffa poses a political and hermeneutic challenge to the territorial project of urban Judaization, which ultimately failed to define and establish the national-cum-cultural identity of this "New-Old" city. This failure results in a persistent pattern of semiotic ambivalence which, from the Jewish-Israeli point of view, positions Jaffa both as a source of identity and longing (in the distant past) and as a symbol of alterity and enmity (in the recent past)—an object of desire and fear alike. Identifying four distinct historical modalities of urban Orientalism, chapter 2 draws on archival research, daily newspapers, and popular culture to historicize the highly politicized image of the Jewish-Arab city and the discourse on its future. These discursive formations reconfigured the public space that enabled, paradoxically since the Al-Aqsa Intifada, new political claims for equal citizenship, binational cooperation, and Palestinian presence.

Echoing the Jewish inability to provide a viable discourse of rootedness in Jaffa, chapter 3 narrates the Palestinian image of a city trapped between romantic nostalgia and critical counternostalgia. In constant dialogue with the Palestinian discourse of diaspora, which views the city as a *lieu de mémoire*, for the living community in Jaffa the struggle over land and identity is an existential project of survival. While Jewish immigrants were engaged in a process of integration and normalization of the postwar city, the history of the indigenous Palestinian population under Israeli rule is an ambivalent story of *Sumud* (steadfastness). This chapter follows literary and quotidian tropes of estrangement, which reconfigure a simultaneous experience of dispossession and community building. Rather than isolated histories, the crystallization of Palestinian political consciousness since the 1970s was intertwined with circumstantial coalitions between Jews and Arabs, which shaped intercommunal relations for years to come.

With the advent of a new economic regime in the 1980s, the neoliberal city changed its face, altering in the process the constitutive relations between groups and individuals. Focusing on the sociological facets of this new cityscape, chapter 4 draws a composite portrait of five social types that perform as agents of gentrification and urban renewal. The chapter's title, "Inner Space and High Ceilings," thus reflects the cultural valorization of space, which redefines urban agency and reconfigures what I term "spatial capital." In contested cities like Jaffa, located minutes away from the Jewish metropolis yet marked by *sui generis* alterity, gentrification involves a double move of spatial and affective intentionality—away, but not quite, from one form of cold yet functional urbanity (in Tel-Aviv), and toward, but not entirely, an alternative form of quality space and social warmth (in Jaffa). The gentrified city is thus seen as a cultural matrix that enables an individualized horizon of creative possibilities for the new middle class. Drawing on in-depth interviews and archival research this chapter proposes a history of gentrification and a phenomenology of its actors. The narratives of these urban agents illustrate the transformation of the mixed city from a political anomaly to a sought-after commodity. In this force field Jewish architects, planners, real estate agents, students, artists, and activists all take part in rebranding the mixed town as a space of urban authenticity.

The shift from an ethnocratic property regime to the neoliberal appropriation of space is best illustrated by the emergence of gated communities, which signal new modes of urban exclusion and reshape previous forms of spatial distinction. Chapter 5 follows the unprecedented number of gated communities constructed in Jaffa since the 1990s by interrogating the *modus operandi* of the Andromeda Hill project and Palestinian resistance to it. The advertising slogan "To Buy or Not to Be" captures the zero-sum predatory logic of urban restructuring. In Jaffa, the gated community attempts to achieve the impossible task of positioning itself both within and outside local lived space and inhabited time. Operating as a neo-Orientalist simulacrum, such projects subvert, spatially and semiotically, the standard logic of urban representation and modernistic notions of segregation. The concept of spatial heteronomy is employed to address such dialectical strategies of spatial orientationality—circumventing the contested local urban space and projected onto a mythological plane of Mediterranean fantasy.

Formulated as a problem of being and belonging, binational sociality challenges the nationalist imagination. Chapter 6 relates the personal stories of elderly Jews and Arabs who reflect on sixty years of contrived coexistence. These neighbors inhabit two incommensurable existential planes: while the Zionist national story unfolds from Diaspora to immigration (*aliyah*), and from Holocaust to nation-building, the Palestinian collective narrative is one of traumatic passage from "the days of the Arabs" to the national defeat of the Nakba and its ensuing resistance (*Muqawama*) and steadfastness (*Sumud*). This dichotomous official narrative, which has been produced and reproduced by the national collective memory, creates a unidimensional narrative of "liberation" versus "victimhood" that nourishes the biographical narrative, which in itself can either adopt it, reject it, or alter it to suit its own needs. Revisiting hegemonic national scripts, a phenomenological examination of the personal life-stories of Jaffa's aged residents reveals a whole universe of contradictions and complexities: some of Jaffa's Arab residents reject major chunks of the Palestinian national narrative, while some of the Jewish residents do not see their own life-stories as the metonymic celebration of the Zionist nationalist project and often personally identify with the predicament of the Palestinians. Emerging from these critical reflections is a new outlook on the personalized performance of nationalist narratives and the creative agency of interpretive subjects.

Further exploring Jaffa as a space of (non)belonging, chapter 7 highlights moments of "situational radicalism and creative marginality." The 2011 social justice protests, which broke out in response to the Arab Spring uprisings, provide a rare historical occurrence of a momentary coalition of interests between the Palestinian community and Jewish activists. These efforts however were soon revealed as mere wishful thinking, which did little to improve the predicament of the Palestinian population in the city. Not without effect, the very marking of Jaffa as a space of political engagement reconfigured an alternative scene of creative marginality, political art, and binational memory activism. Examining the everyday enactment of alterity I show how marginality and exclusion become precisely the driving force behind one of Israel's most creative backstages.

The nexus of ethnos and capital in Jewish-Arab mixed towns reveals new forms of political and cultural agency, which situationally oppose or unite rival subject positions and require that we read power and class into spatial analysis. Educators, planners, real estate entrepreneurs, political activists, and not least ordinary citizens compose the fragile texture of cohabitation in what is increasingly becoming the internal frontier of ethnonational conflict in Israel. The history of "creative destruction," which brought about the demise of Palestinian urbanism in 1948, gave birth to the growth machine of the Hebrew metropolis in the heart of the new state. Palestinian presence, however, did not disappear without a trace. Decades later, these residual traces of communal life and memory now return with a vengeance to claim historicity and space. The concluding chapter formulates a research agenda for a new kind of relational anthropology by reassembling urban scholarship and reframing the classical models of social theorists such as Georg Simmel, Zygmunt Bauman, Henri Lefebvre, and the Chicago School. Mixed towns present a model of urban oppression intertwined with contrived coexistence in the heart of political conflict, as well as a model for sustainable social policies with far-reaching implications for the future of peaceful coexistence in Israel/Palestine and beyond.

PART ONE

Beyond Methodological Nationalism: Communal Formations and Ambivalent Belonging

ONE

Spatial Relationality

Theorizing Space and Sociality in Jewish-Arab "Mixed Towns"

> In the Mediterranean, birthplace of the City-State, the State, whether it
> be inside or outside the city, always remains brutal and powerless, violent
> but weak, unifying but always undermined, under threat.... Every form of
> hegemony and homogeneity are refused in the Mediterranean.... The very
> idea of centrality is refused because each group, each entity, each religion and
> each culture considers itself a center.... The polyrhythmy of Mediterranean
> cities highlights their common character through their differences.
>
> —HENRI LEFEBVRE, "Rhythmanalysis of Mediterranean Cities"

SITUATED VIOLENCE: THE OCTOBER 2000 EVENTS IN JAFFA

The large-scale protest demonstrations staged by the Palestinian citizens of Israel throughout the country in the first two weeks of October 2000, now widely known as "the October 2000 events," did not bypass Jaffa. For a few days in early October, Palestinian youngsters marched through the streets in solidarity with the casualties of the Al-Aqsa Intifada, destroying public symbols and state institutions including banks, post offices, and Jewish-owned stores.

Shortly after these events I met with my Jaffa-born sister, Aurélie, who lives in the heart of Jaffa's predominantly Arab 'Ajami quarter, and with Hicham, a Palestinian high school classmate from my own Jaffa days twenty years ago. Inescapably, the conversation turned to the recent upheaval and its implications for Jewish-Arab relations in Jaffa. I asked my sister how she had coped with the "riots," referring to an incident in which Palestinian youths burned down a lottery booth a block away from where she lives. Her answer surprised me, as it stood in sharp contrast to the biased and hysterical anti-Arab media reports and to the anxious responses of most Israeli residents of neighboring Tel-Aviv. Dismissing the notion that these events were in any way dangerous, she said dryly that all she had to do was detour to avoid whatever demonstrations were going on and go home from work another way. At the end of the day, she concluded, Tel-Aviv is more dangerous than Jaffa, if only for the fact that Jaffa, where many of the residents are Arabs, is immune to suicide attacks by Palestinian terrorists. She said,

> The whole thing was not a big deal. Nothing happened to me. They [the demonstrators] never reached my house. From the outside it looked much worse than it actually was. Some Jerusalemite Palestinians arrived to agitate and nationalize the atmosphere, and some youngsters from Jaffa went along. I know that for Tel-Avivans it looked awful, but I wasn't afraid. Friends suggested that I stay with them in Tel-Aviv, and some of them did not visit me for months. . . .
>
> I live in the ideal location, you see. They didn't enter the houses and there were no pogroms. They were not brutes like Sharon's people. They focused on expressing their protest—with no looting or rape. They didn't hurt civilians because so many of them are Arabs like them. They looked for external Jewish elements—people from Bat-Yam [a coastal town just south of Jaffa], for example, who never try to integrate with them. The post office represents the Jewish-Israeli establishment. But they did not think it through: damaging it eventually hurt them, since they are the ones who use it. For me, as someone who lives in the area, it wasn't serious. Tel-Aviv, with all those suicide bombs, is much more dangerous.

Proceeding with this surprisingly sympathetic view of the events, Aurélie described them in apolitical and non-national terms. Her description was of what might be called "collective effervescence"—a ritual of semi-spontaneous gathering involving in-group agents ("Jaffans") and out-group agents ("Jerusalemites") alike. Rather than a threatening and frightening occurrence, Aurelie's account of the October Events took a Durkheimian tenor, whereby Jaffans recognized their collective unity by means of a primarily social and quasi-ludic practice of opposition. In her words,

> The atmosphere was like a festival; people enjoyed the action. Evening comes and everyone goes out to the streets. The gutsy ones throw some

stones, but the driving force were those Jerusalemites. I told my friends
that it all took place at certain hours in the evening, around six or seven, as
youngsters come home from school or work. Jaffans are usually calm and
quiescent, but when the Jerusalemites arrived it made the locals finally feel
they were part of the whole thing, of the Palestinian people. Also you have
to remember in October the air outside is pleasant in the evening.

Disagreeing with what my sister described as the pivotal role of the
demonstrators from outside of Jaffa (the "Jerusalemites"), Hicham, who
took part in the demonstrations, insisted on the political dimension of
the violent events. Aurélie's association of the events with undisciplined
working-class and youth-based leisure practice was wrong, he thought.[1]
He said,

> Even though the demonstrations were pretty lame, the Israeli newspapers
> depicted Jaffa as a "ticking bomb." Most gatherings took place when we
> thought that people from Bat-Yam were about to attack Jabaliyye [a southern
> neighborhood in Jaffa]. At least two hundred people came out to defend the
> neighborhood's mosque. Luckily, the police stood between us and the Jews
> and after a few days the tension dissolved. What made most people happy—
> me too—is that they closed Yefet Street. It was a festive atmosphere, like
> that on Yom Kippur [when in Jaffa both Jews and Arabs fill the streets].
> An atmosphere of disorder and festival. We were happy that the Jews were
> afraid to enter Jaffa.

Referring to the *de facto* Israeli boycott of Jaffa in the weeks that followed, Hicham continued:

> Abu Hassan's hummus restaurant was already empty at ten or eleven in the
> morning, and people started going there more to prove to ourselves that the
> Jewish boycott was not getting to us. There was one day when Abu Hassan
> was really moved as Jaffan Arabs filled the place. We proved that he is not
> here only because of the Jewish market.
>
> These were strange months, with Jaffa completely empty on Saturdays. Then
> the situation gradually went back to normal. The following year the Rabita
> [Jaffa's national-secular association] spread flyers calling for a general strike,
> with absolutely no effect. October succeeded because it wasn't planned. Jaf-
> fans don't go to the streets when they are organized.

Hicham then gave two examples of what he called "the dynamic of
destruction": One was Ha-Sukkah ha-Levana (the White Sukkah), a
restaurant owned by a Jew and run by Sabbagh, a Christian-Arab. The

second was Ochayon, a Jewish Moroccan tailor who also owns a clothes shop:

> The demonstrations were not completely ideological. There was a dynamic of destruction and there was a separate nationalist dynamic that led people to attack stores owned by Jews. Had they demolished Andre's ice cream place [a Christian well-to-do business], I wouldn't be surprised—they are a weak family. Messing with the Kheils' restaurant is a completely different matter—no one wants to have to deal with that family. The dynamic was to break everything. They stoned Jews who had no strong backup. The White Sukkah restaurant is managed by Sabbagh—a Christian Arab. Everybody knows that. His place was totally destroyed, but Ra'uf's restaurant just across the street was left intact. Both Sabbagh and Ra'uf are Christians but Ra'uf is cool, he has many Muslim friends. The idea was to break everything, but some things are more easily broken than others.
>
> In Ochayon's case, although the demonstrators stoned his store, he showed up the next day and reopened soon after, taking this opportunity to renovate the place—and now he's actually doing better in a much nicer store. Ochayon sells expensive jeans and his store is often broken into. There are Jews in Jaffa, but no one thought of breaking into houses of Jews. It didn't occur to anyone. From demonstration to demonstration in Jaffa, Ochayon has been upgraded and got more and more successful. Ochayon is no gentrifier—he's been here for fifty years. It's the preferred jeans store in Jaffa. One hundred percent of his clientele are Arabs—everyone buys at his store.

In spite of their disagreement, resulting in part from their different ethnonational affiliations and their respective access to social networks in Jaffa, Aurélie's and Hicham's reactions both stand in sharp contrast to the flat and hysterical coverage of these events in the Israeli media.[2] Their accounts differ substantially from the stereotypical perceptions of most Jewish Israelis and the violent "counter-rioting" of the police.[3]

The October events illustrate the overwhelming power of nationalist forces but also their limits, and bring to the fore three levels of the constitutive tensions which characterize Jaffa. First, they reveal the complicated relations between the political and the social realms, namely, between Palestinian nationalist mobilization and non-national social dynamics stemming from the urban mix with Jewish residents and from internal dynamics within the Palestinian community. From the point of view of a Jewish resident who could have been a victim of this mobilization, the demonstrations were both legitimate and harmless. For

a Palestinian resident, these demonstrations reveal the social intervention of communal and non-national forces that determined the nature
of violence in Jaffa, such as mass behavior and internal clan-based power
relations and religious divisions. Power is woven into the social fabric
and is thus both structural and situational. In this relational approach,
"the concept of power is transformed from a concept of substance to a
concept of relationship" (Elias 1978, 131; also see Emirbayer 1997).[4]

Second, this case demonstrates the productive and dialectic aspect
of conflict *qua* social form which Simmel theorized almost a century
ago ([1922] 1955). Ochayon's increasing success with Jaffa's Arab clientele
and his determination to remain in town despite recurrent attacks on his
store show that the Palestinian demonstrations were not perceived by
veteran Jewish Jaffans to be personally targeting individual Jews.[5] More
precisely, the story illustrates that individual Jews were not targeted as
emblems of the Jewish state and remained social persons with relational
identifications with their Palestinian neighbors.

Third, it is striking that during the October Events and in their immediate aftermath, the farther one got away from the actual scene in
terms of social and physical distance, the more stereotypical the image
and representation of the conflict became, and the more it was narrated in dichotomous collective terms of "them" and "us." When one
got to the neighboring city of Bat-Yam one already had encountered
a collective melee of two armed crowds, set apart only by the police.
The October Events in Jaffa thus expose the relevance of "social distance" (Simmel [1908] 1971) and spatial proximity for political action
as well as its representations in ethnically mixed urban contexts. Such
moments of conflict and collective mobilization stand in diametric opposition to the perspective "methodological nationalism," namely, the
analytic bias which conflates social boundaries with state boundaries,
and allows national categories to seep into sociological analysis (Beck
2003).

In an attempt to interpret such ambivalent behaviors, the argument I
put forth is not a liberal argument of multicultural peaceful coexistence,[6]
nor is it an argument of urban ethnocracy as total exclusion (Yiftachel
and Yacobi 2003). Within this theoretical context I suggest a third alternative that perceives Jaffa as a relational field in which nationalism and

urbanism, identity, and place are simultaneously contested and confirmed in everyday interactions (Brubaker et al. 2006). My argument describes the *systemic complexity* embedding the "political" and the "social" which implicates nation and class in dialectic and contradictory ways. I deconstruct the reified notions of ethnically bounded "communities" and the politicized concepts of indigenous locals and alien immigrants in order to address inter- and intracommunal relations between different populations in Jaffa. The complexity of what Simmel ([1922] 1955) calls the intersecting "webs of affiliations" is one of the reasons for the relative lack of intercommunal violence in Jaffa, where networks and social relations between Jews and Arabs are intricately implicated by the mixed urban scene.

The argument proceeds in five steps to outline a dialectical theory of sociality and spatiality. The first section criticizes the "dual society" paradigm in Palestinian-Israeli studies (Lockman 1996; Shamir 2000), which posited the existence of two essentially separate societies with distinct and disconnected historical trajectories. As an instance of the broader analytic bias which Martins (1974) had termed methodological nationalism (also see Wimmer and Glick-Schiller 2002), this paradigm chained sociological analysis of ethnically mixed towns to the category of the nation-state and thus concealed much of their interstitial complexities. The theoretical perspective of relationalism (Emirbayer 1997) is proposed to address the deficiencies of current approaches to Palestinian-Israeli relations and thus change the focus of analysis from *a priori* relations of exclusion between reified communities to a space of social transaction and mediation where projects of exclusion operate and often fail in one way or another. Linking the concepts of spatial heteronomy, collective strangeness, and cultural indeterminacy, the following sections put forth three propositions, which locate the foundations of the spatiality-sociality-culture nexus in three sites of productive conflict: the spatial history of the city, the social relations it produces, and its contested cultural representation. Reformulating urban nationalism as a problem of mediation, the analysis concludes with the implications of this approach for the comparative study of mixed towns, toward a new understanding of scales of mediation and transaction extending from the city to the state and beyond.

RELATIONAL ANTHROPOLOGY VERSUS
METHODOLOGICAL NATIONALISM

While social scientists have been increasingly sensitive to the ideological and analytic reification of the category of the nation-state (Abrams [1977] 1988; Appadurai 2000; Beck 2003; Brubaker 1996; Wimmer and Glick-Schiller 2002), Mustafa Emirbayer (1997) has framed the critique of methodological nationalism within a much broader alternative theoretical perspective, which he termed "relationalism" (as opposed to substantialism).[7] Following a long list of social theorists from Simmel and Elias through Maffesoli and Bourdieu, "relational theorists reject the notion that one can posit discrete, pre-given units such as the individual, class, minority, state, nation or society as ultimate starting points of sociological analysis." He explains, "What is distinct about the relational approach is that it sees *relations* between social units and actors as preeminently dynamic in nature, as unfolding ongoing processes rather that as static ties among inert substances or structures" (287). It is the mutually constitutive relationship between individuals, political groups, and cultural categories that determines their nature, and not vice versa.

The theoretical implications of the relational approach are far-reaching, proposing a profound reformulation of social science's basic concepts such as power, society, and culture. Thus Strathern (1988, 13) ingeniously leads us out of the conceptual cul-de-sac of the reified notions of individual and society "imagined as conceptually distinct from the relations that bring them together." And as Brubaker (1996) shows, the concept of the nation-state changes, and instead of signifying a naturally bounded, integrated, sovereign entity, designates a figuration of power, namely, a complex intercommunal and intra-organizational network or, in short, a relational field. This interpretive paradigm also enables a revisionary conceptualization of the colonial encounter as a site of rupture and negotiation (Comaroff and Comaroff 1997; Memmi 1985). Similarly, it reframes the city as locus of production, mediation, and transaction between form, function, and structure (Harvey 1997; Lefebvre 1996). In examining the past, present, and future of urban mix in Israel/Palestine from the perspective of relationality, we can gain crucial analytical leverage for charting varying degrees of alienation, identification, and agency, revealing social formations as simultaneously enabling and disabling modes of action.

In the historiography of Israel/Palestine, ideologically motivated and methodologically nationalist scholarship has laid the basis for the model of the "dual society" (cf. Shamir 2000, 15). Institutional Israeli sociologists such as S. N. Eisenstadt have been particularly important in propagating this notion of conceptual segregation. As relational historian Zachary Lockman (1996, 12) argues, "The Arab and Jewish communities in Palestine are represented as primordial, self-contained, and largely monolithic entities. By extension communal identities are regarded as natural rather than as constructed within a larger field of relations and forces that differentially affected (and even constituted) subgroups among both Arabs and Jews. . . . This approach has rendered their mutually constitutive impact virtually invisible, tended to downplay intracommunal divisions, and focused attention on episodes of violent conflict, implicitly assumed to be the sole normal or even possible form of interaction."

Equating societies in general with nation-state societies, and seeing states and their national ideologies as the cornerstones of social-scientific analysis, methodological nationalism has been the ruling paradigm in Israel/Palestine. This methodological stance is a deep-rooted epistemological position that cuts across the spectrum of both Palestinian and Israeli political viewpoints and operates by fixating social agents as independent oppositional actors (settlers vs. natives, colonizers vs. colonized). Under its spell, urban scholars have conceptualized social relations and cityscapes in mixed towns in dualistic terms, namely, either as historical anomalies or as segregated ghettos (Soffer 2004; Yiftachel and Yacobi 2003; Zureik 1979). The standard narrative of this approach is premised on a functionalist convergence of variables, which results in systemic geopolitical effects. Thus for neoconservative geographer Soffer (2004), Israel's wealth, combined with structural demographic disadvantages vis-à-vis the growing Palestinian population, will eventually result in its annihilation, unless drastic measures are taken to ensure a Jewish majority and "decrease" (read transfer) the Palestinian population between the Jordan River and the Mediterranean Sea. Conversely, the critical theory of ethnocracy (Yiftachel and Yacobi 2003) postulates a systemic effort on behalf of the Israeli state toward ethnic discrimination, domination, and subordination of its Palestinian citizens, which hinges on the territorial segregation between the two populations. Conceptualizing nationalism as a top-down and state-centric process, both theories turn a blind eye to the unresolved tensions among the constitutive elements of the urban sociospatial order (ethnonationalism, capitalist logic, and modern governance), as well as to the quotidian relations between majority and minority groups in Israel.

In mixed towns, the analytic limitations of methodological nationalism can be summed up as follows:

1. It reifies urban configurations as dualistic "structures" and overlooks social practice. Consequently it conceptualizes spaces as disjointed and homogenous ethnic territorialities.

2. It reduces social actors to predetermined ethnonational roles by overstating the power of the state and nationalist ideologies. Downplaying cross-communal coalitions and mixed sociality, it overlooks the tensions among urban capitalism, ethnic regimes, city planning, and local governance.

3. It essentializes cities as metonymic cultural representations of the nation, thus dismissing the internal complexity and potential change of urban imaginaries.

OUTLINE OF A THEORY OF URBAN ETHNIC
MIX IN ISRAEL/PALESTINE

In line with the first principles of relational sociology, the proposed theorization of ethnic-urban mix seeks to de-reify the problem of binational sociality by outlining a tripartite model of spatial relationality.[8] Largely inspired by Henri Lefebvre's *The Production of Space* (1991), considered by many to be the single most influential work on urbanism and everyday life, and accredited with triggering the "spatial turn" in social theory in the 1990s, the following proceeds with a spatialization of binational sociality.[9]

Adapting Lefebvre's triadic theorization of the production of space to the generalized study of sociality and spatiality in mixed towns, the proposed model consists of three propositions of a social theory, which counter the prevailing reification of urban space as ethnically bounded territory (figure 1.1). Ethnically mixed towns are thus characterized as

1. ramified spatial configurations composed of diverging urban logics (*spatial heteronomy*) that dialectically
2. instantiate and reproduce simultaneous patterns of proximity and distance vis-à-vis self and Other (*stranger sociality*), which in turn
3. further perpetuates in the urban imagination a collective pattern of semiotic ambivalence and unsettled contestation over space and identity (*cultural indeterminacy*).

Rather than a linear stream of causation, however, these factors form a cyclical trialectic whose mutual interactions drive the social processes I analyze. Thus, informed by Soja's (1996) conceptualization of three moments of sociospatiality, I propose to view these triadic concepts as, respectively, spatial, social, and symbolic forms, which pattern social relations and concrete interactions between individuals, groups, state institutions, and NGOs in everyday life.

PROPOSITION 1. *Spatial Heteronomy:* Mixed towns are the sociospatial product of unresolved tensions between diverging urban logics, which decouple space from identity.

Ethnically mixed towns emerged out of the hybrid superposition of the old Ottoman sectarian urban regime and the new national, modernizing, and capitalist order (both Palestinian and Zionist). Reconfigured as a new city-form, the mixed town was in actual fact a fragmented amalgam of Ottoman, British, Palestinian, and Israeli urban legacies (AlSayyad 2001; Rabinowitz and Monterescu 2008).[10] In the Ottoman city, urban spaces were predicated on the logic of religious communalism (Braude and Lewis 1982). Residential patterns corresponded by and large to the administrative *millet* system of patronage and classification, which granted significant legal autonomy to Jewish and Christian minorities. Consisting of separate ethnic quarters that housed religiously defined communities regulated by imperial law, it had cultural difference

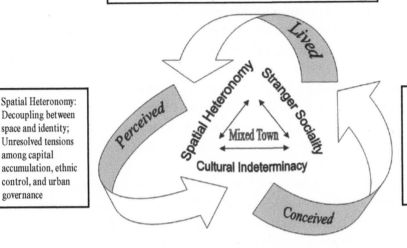

Stranger Sociality: Implicate relations, Forced coexistence, Social fragmentation; Low social capital; Neighborhood contact hypothesis; Ambivalent subject-positions

Spatial Heteronomy: Decoupling between space and identity; Unresolved tensions among capital accumulation, ethnic control, and urban governance

Cultural Indeterminacy: Contesting narratives; Unstable definition of the urban situation; Disrupted national mediation

FIGURE 1.1. Relational Spatiality: The Sociospatial Configuration of Jewish-Arab Mixed Towns.

semiotically marked and socially recognized within the material and symbolic walls of the "old city." The late nineteenth century saw this old *millet*-based social order gradually dissolve, as a new form of public space emerged which was to a great extent informed by a new national—rather than denominational—awareness. Resonating with an ever-growing logic of nationalism, ethnonational competition between Jews and Arabs was clearly feeding an exclusionary demand for spatial segregation. Following the 1917 Balfour Declaration, the violent clashes of 1921 and 1929, and the Arab Revolt of 1936, escalating ethnoterritorial conflict saw explicit and conscious remodeling of urban space as bifurcated nationalized place. The struggle over land and identity reached its climax in the 1948 war with the occupation of these towns and their official designation as "Israeli cities" with a residual Arab minority.

A major port town, Jaffa was Palestine's main gateway through which the Jewish and then Zionist settlers entered the land. In fact, until the "Third Aliyah" (1919–1923), Jaffa was the capital of the Zionist *Yishuv*

(British-ruled settlement). Conversely, as early as the 1930s, Tel-Aviv, which started in 1909 as Jaffa's "Jewish garden suburb," was overshadowing Jaffa, economically and demographically. The power balance capsized in 1948, when Jaffa was conquered by Israeli forces and emptied of most of its Palestinian inhabitants. In 1950 Jaffa was officially incorporated into the municipal jurisdiction of Tel-Aviv—its mother city turned rival—a move which rendered it the chronically dilapidated south side of the "White City," perpetuating an economic and political dependence on Tel-Aviv and cultural otherness from it. This radical urban transformation turned Jaffa from an Arab city with a Jewish minority of 30 percent (35,000 Jews out of a total population of 110,000 in 1947), to, today, a mixed city with a Palestinian minority of 30 percent (15,000 out of 45,000 in 2012). Since 1948, it has been perceived as simultaneously a postcolonial city (by Jews) and a still-colonial city (by Palestinians). Currently Jaffa houses heterogenous populations of diverse backgrounds and class positions: a fifteen-thousand-strong Arab community and a Jewish population of thirty thousand, made up of veteran residents and some two thousand well-to-do gentrifiers, as well as foreign workers and Palestinian collaborators relocated from the West Bank and Gaza.

For the Palestinian residents of Jaffa, the 1948 Nakba remains the key structuring event of the bleak recent history of their town. That war, which truncated the course of normal urbanization of most Palestinian towns, sealed Arab Jaffa's fate as well. With over 90 percent of the Palestinian inhabitants who had lived in Jaffa prior to 1948 in exile, the early years of Israeli statehood saw the final transformation of Jaffa into a predominantly Jewish town (Morris 1987; Mazawi and Khouri-Makhoul 1991). As late as the summer of 1949 Jaffa, like other mixed towns, was subjected to martial law which concentrated the residual Palestinian population in a bounded compound in 'Ajami (a.k.a. the "ghetto").[11] Gradually, however, Jewish squatters, preferring empty Palestinian houses to transit camps established for them elsewhere, were infiltrating areas initially designated for Palestinians only. This penetration, coupled with an increasing willingness on the part of Palestinians to test the spatial limitations they were subjected to by the authorities, subverted spatial segregations designed and administered primarily by the Israeli security services.

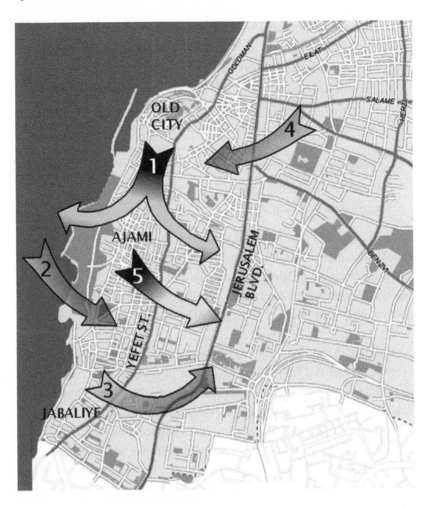

FIGURE 1.2. Population Movements in Jaffa—1948 to Present.

The cultural logic of urban mix in contemporary Jaffa is a product of dramatic demographic dynamics. This spatial history unfolded from postwar loss and chaos on the part of Palestinians through waves of newly arrived Jewish immigrants, three decades of disinvestment, and, since the mid-1980s, a surge of neoliberal urban renewal. These processes are represented in the map in figure 1.2, where population movement includes five chronological phases:

1. The 1948 war and its aftermath: the exodus of 95 percent of Jaffa's Palestinian residents
2. 1948–1960: Jaffa becomes a proletarian immigrant city
3. 1960–1985: Disinvestment and demolition as part of the Urban Renewal Plan and the fabrication of the Old City as an Israeli artists' colony
4. 1985–2000: The municipality's policy change and the promotion of gentrification
5. October 2000 to the present: Al-Aqsa Intifada and the struggle against gentrification

Approximately two-thirds of Jaffa's Palestinian population of fifteen thousand reside in two fairly distinct parts of the town. One is 'Ajami and Jabaliyye—two Palestinian neighborhoods which developed since the late nineteenth century south of the old walled city. The other is an area roughly to the east of Jerusalem Boulevard, the main commercial and transportation thoroughfare.

The spatial and demographic histories of the two areas are quite divergent. 'Ajami and Jabaliyye, which prior to 1948 had been established as middle-class Palestinian residential neighborhoods overlooking the sea, became, in the aftermath of the war, a primary destination for Jewish immigrants. In this period, contrived coexistence went beyond material aspects involved with sharing stairwells, entrance halls, kitchens, and bathrooms in previously Palestinian houses now split between multiple residents, and included cultural and political exchange. The Suez crisis of 1956 and the 1967 Israeli-Arab war provide particularly salient reference points. In 1967, a Palestinian informant recounted, when Israel had not yet begun operating television broadcasts, members of his family were gathered with their Jewish-Iranian neighbors around the only radio in the house to listen to battlefield reports. As he put it, "We waited for the results of the war as if it were a soccer match. When we learned about the results, my father got up in anger, turned the radio off, and said, 'OK, you won ...'"

This surreal condition of intimate neighborliness began to disappear, however, in the 1960s and 1970s, as the systematic neglect and disinvestment in the western neighborhoods of Jaffa triggered an out-migration of Jewish inhabitants, mostly to new housing projects in the eastern out-skirts of Jaffa and neighboring Bat-Yam and Holon. Consequently the population in 'Ajami and Jabaliyye—the areas singled out for gentrification in subsequent decades—decreased from twenty-two thousand in 1961 (mostly Jews) to only four thousand in 1989 (mostly Palestinians).[12] Paradoxically, the unintended consequences of the relocation of the Jewish residents eventually made 'Ajami the kernel of the Palestinian political community, which already in the late 1970s drew on a new generation of university graduates and activists (Mazawi and Khouri-Makhoul 1991).

The decades since the 1980s have seen an intensified process of gentrification, mainly in 'Ajami. Local Palestinian proprietors as well as Israeli and international entrepreneurs build luxurious housing projects, some of which are fully fledged gated communities, marketed primarily to wealthy Israeli and foreign Jewish buyers, as well as to foreign business-men and diplomats. The visual opulence of these projects, taking place in times and spaces in which most Arab residents are desperate for afford-able housing, are transforming 'Ajami into a mixed neighborhood again, only this time it is assuming strikingly different connotations, with a glaring and highly ethnicized class gap between the local Palestinian residents and the Jewish gentrifiers.

In contrast to 'Ajami, the Jerusalem Boulevard area to the east is going through a process of intermixing involving several marginal incoming groups. In the 1950s this area had Jewish immigrant families (of mainly Bulgarian, Romanian, Moroccan, and Turkish origin) occupying small apartments, typically on the second and third floors of buildings that had shops, workshops, and warehouses on the ground floors facing the street. By the 1970s, however, many of these immigrants were leaving for new housing projects outside Jaffa, much like the Jewish residents of 'Ajami and Jabaliyye at the time. Meanwhile, the neglect and disinvestment in 'Ajami and Jabaliyye pushed Palestinian residents to leave that area too, and many of them purchased apartments further east, along Jerusalem Boulevard. Throughout the 1980s, the eastern part of Jaffa thus turned into a mixed lower-class Jewish-Arab neighborhood. In the 1990s this demographic complexity increased further with an influx of hundreds of migrant workers from Asia, Africa, and Eastern Europe, as well as students who found cheap housing in the city.

Two points emerging from the demographic and spatial history of Jaffa are worth noting here. First is that the urban space in Jaffa has always been characterized by constant motion and demographic instability. Second, these dynamics have been dominated by inherent institutional and sociopolitical contradictions, rendering a unified definition of the ethnic and class-based urban situation quite impossible.

Such demographic processes, geographic intermixing, and planning policies—some designed and others unintended—created Jewish spaces within Arab ones and Arab spaces within Jewish ones. As a result, Jaffa's spatial logic is characterized by an absence of clear correspondence between national-ethnic boundaries and spatial ones. Put differently, in mixed towns space and identity are decoupled. This urban regime that I propose to term "heteronomous space" can be defined as a paradoxical terrain whereby constituent parts follow divergent, sometimes mutually contradictory organizing principles.[13] Borrowed from Friedrich Meinecke's work on medieval prenational territoriality, which allowed for simultaneous and overlapping identifications (Meinecke 1970), the concept of spatial heteronomy (cf. Foucault 1986; Ruggie 1993) captures the apparent anomaly of mixed towns in relation to the ostensibly clear-cut ethnonational logic of the nation-state.

The logic of heteronomy describes spatial systems, whereby parts are subject to divergent modes of growth, behavior, and development. In Jaffa, spatial fragmentation is such that within an area not larger than two square miles one finds seven totally different forms of spatial organization: (1) Old Jaffa (a.k.a. the "Artists' Colony"), (2) the housing projects built in the 1960s and '70s for Jews (*shikunim* in Hebrew or *shikunat* in Arabic), (3) the Al-Nuzha/Jerusalem Boulevard mixed lower-income neighborhoods, (4) the Palestinian neighborhoods of 'Ajami and Jabilyye, (5) the new gentrified gated communities of Andromeda Hill and Jaffa Courts, (6) individual gentrifiers' houses in 'Ajami that are quite different from gated communities, and finally (7) enclaves such as Byaarat Dakke and Abu-Seif, where kin-based Palestinian communities have built compounds in what remains of the old orange groves. The high density of heteronomous space is perhaps unique to Jaffa. Its principles, however, are common in other mixed towns as well.

My argument about heteronomy and the spatial logic of the nation-state can be summarized as follows. Methodological nationalism is predicated on the convergence of boundary-making mechanisms, which produce in concert ethnically segregated spaces (Yiftachel and Yacobi 2003). Conversely, spatial heteronomy stems out precisely of the unresolved tensions between three main "engines" of urban order: the logic of capital accumulation (through incomplete gentrification), the evolution of modern governance (through unsuccessful urban planning), and the drive for ethnic and national control (through demographic intermixing). Thus rather than taking at face value the disjointed, essentializing, and exclusionary territorialities fetishized by states and urban governance systems in ethnonational regimes, the notion of spatial heteronomy questions models premised on such dichotomies. The concept, however, suggests not a denationalization of nation-based citizenship (as some writers on globalization were suggesting) but an internal, binational challenge to it which productively employs its "contact zone" (Pratt 1999) to create a "new geography of power" (Sassen 1996). This new geography, far from being overdetermined by national identities and state ideologies, operates through quotidian spaces of interaction and transaction, which enfold nation and class, both within and between ethnic communities.

THE EFFECTS OF HETERONOMY: IDENTITY POLITICS AND PROJECTS OF NATIVIZATION

Urban heteronomy is a product of dialectic relations between society and space, which disrupt the correspondence between social boundaries and spatial divisions. On the one hand, through the years, social processes such as immigration, forced relocation, and demographic interpermeation have recreated unresolved spatial facts on the ground. The entangled and implicate relations (Portugali 1993) between the Palestinian and Jewish national movements played out in these cities as the byproduct of the conflict's unintended consequences. Thus under social conditions of forced coexistence, the mixed town remained a historical binational singularity, which points to the limits of the Judaization plan. The unique demographic makeup of these cities constituted a problematic reality that cannot be analytically exhausted by unidimensional dichotomies, such as Palestinian natives versus Jewish colonizers. Conversely, spatial processes, such as the Urban Renewal Plan and gentrification, reproduced an unprecedented urban complexity that only exacerbates the political implications of the Jewish-Arab encounter.

Far from fostering peaceful harmony or any form of unproblematic coexistence, the main defining characteristic of the heteronomous living space is its systemic instability and incoherence. This feature of mixed towns is characteristic of a larger systemic divisiveness in both Jewish and Palestinian societies in Israel, whose main expression is the fragmentation of the political system. Bereft of the power to impose effective social control and urban order, the state often views these spaces as pockets of anarchy and deviance, whereas for the local residents, the present situation allows no mass mobilization (as organized by the Communist Party until the 1980s), progressive class-alliances, or even nonfactional voluntary organizing within the local communities. In the case of the Arab community, these divisions are even more fraught as it suffers from deep and quasi-anomic fragmentation on the political, organizational, and social levels.

Structurally, therefore, the institutional-cum-spatial force field in mixed towns lacks a clear center of power—an instability that pushes each faction to develop particularistic politics around local issues "dissociated from anything beyond themselves" (Comaroff and Comaroff 2001, 322; Jameson 1991, 47). Thus the Jewish gentrifiers and the municipality emphasize the need for law enforcement without adequately handling the systemic failures, which are the reasons for crime and disorder in the first place. Similarly, the Islamic Council caters to the sectarian interests of the Muslim community without involving the Christian population. This breakup of solidarity networks and mobilization patterns and the subsequent crystallization around particularistic identities, known in social theory as "identity politics" (Calhoun 1994), produce a regime of pragmatic transaction and ad hoc exchange between Palestinian and Jewish (both newcomer and veteran) elements.

In Jaffa we can identify three communal formations and identity groups which follow this pattern: the Palestinian population (which also can be divided into religious and class-based subgroups),[14] the new

Jewish residents (called by many "new Jews" or simply "Northsiders," *Tzfonim*), and the veteran Jewish population (made up of working-class immigrants from the Balkans and North Africa who immigrated in the 1950s). Each group is engaged in a different "project of nativization" that aims at constructing a discourse of rootedness and authentic locality, which in turn serves to legitimate their respective political agenda and identity-based claims for the city (Holston and Appadurai 1999).

THE PALESTINIAN POPULATION: IDENTITY WITHOUT COMMUNITY

The organizing principle of the Palestinian population draws negatively on a deep sense of enduring discrimination and on a positive demand for civil equality coupled with an ideology of historical belonging and "original" (*asliyya*) or "indigenous" locality. Faced with the existential challenge of collective survival and politicocultural distinction (*wujud*), this discourse of rootedness has been successful and encompassing enough to overcome rampant communal divisions that would other-wise undercut any efficient political coalitions—between Muslims and Christians, between religious movements and secular ideologies, be-tween the associations of the Islamic Council and the Association for the Jaffa Arabs (Al-Rabita), and finally between the ex-Communist Hadash/ Jabha party (the Democratic Front for Peace) and the nationalist Balad party (the National Democratic League). More than sixty years after the Nakba, it is clear that the Palestinians in Jaffa have succeeded in defin-ing their local identity in the most stable manner. Thus for Arab migrant laborers from the Galilee or the Triangle who chose in the 1960s to settle down in Jaffa, a presentation of self and an adoption of a "Jaffan" identity became often self-evident. More significant is the total integration and enculturation of the second-generation children of migrant laborers and even of "collaborators" (*'umala'*) from the West Bank and Gaza who come to perceive themselves as "Sons of the City" (*Ibn Yafa*) for every cultural and political purpose. This acceptance is possible because the city offers economic resources and employment opportunities otherwise unavailable in the Arab villages, and because culturally Jaffa is seen by its inhabitants as *Umm al-gharib* (the Mother of the Stranger)—that is, a city with open borders—which allows "strangers" (labor migrants and even collaborators) to enter its gates. The politicogeographic consequence of this project of nativization is that the overwhelming majority of the fifteen thousand Jaffa-born Palestinians express an urgent need to maintain community cohesiveness and rarely choose to reside elsewhere.[15]

This ideology of autochthonous belonging is accompanied by a crisis-laden discourse of nostalgia, which presents Jaffa as a fallen city licking its wounds. This double discourse of urban identity is the only site enabling a unified front of social solidarity. In all other issues pertaining to communal, sectarian, and class-based politics, the Arab population remains split and fragmented, as demonstrated time and again by the struggles over funds and leadership between the Islamic Council on the one hand and the secular Association for the Jaffa Arabs on the other. Tellingly, in both the 2003 and the 2013 municipal elections, the Arab Yafa List lost its seat in the city council due to local disputes between rival political factions. A local intellectual summed up this predicament, saying, "Jaffa is an identity without community. People in Jaffa are stuck—it's a broken society that cannot pull itself together."

A graphic expression of this collective structure of feeling was designed by the members of the "Young Leadership" group of activists who posted graffiti on the "Fraternity Wall" on the main Yeffet Street (figure 1.3). The scene portrays the murder of a drug addict amidst the city going up in flames, a group of women mourning over a grave, a mother holding a baby, and a helpless old man. Under the headline "Violated Rights" (*Huquq mafruma*), the text posted on the same wall voices the general state of mind in Jaffa, vacillating between hope and despair and attesting to the depth of the crisis:

> Saber is a patient boy—he has dreams but has difficulty fulfilling them. He is a part of a whole that wants to move on—stuck on a wooden horse. All his life he has been trying to move on and break the barrier. Now Saber is old and holds a hammer. But he is old and does not have the force any more. He breaks the barrier and dies. And in the graveyard he finds equality—everybody is dead, everybody is together.... The woman and her baby step toward the light and the warmth; she does not forget her past but continues to march on. We too will continue to march, but we have not reached the end yet—we are still stuck.

FIGURE 1.3. "Violated Rights": Graffiti on Yefet Street, entitled "Fraternity Wall" by the Young Leadership group.
Photo by the author, 2006.

THE VETERAN JEWISH COMMUNITY:
NEITHER IDENTITY NOR COMMUNITY

Jewish presence was formed in Jaffa in a period when the city was re-covering from the trauma of the 1948 war. Responding to the Zion-ist myopia regarding the Palestinian history of the place, these Jewish newcomers saw the city as an "empty shell" to be filled with communal content.

Ambivalently viewed by the establishment in the wake of the war as disobedient squatters and as a social burden, but also as the strategic counterbalance to Arab demography, these immigrants—numbering about forty thousand newcomers from the Balkans and North Africa—managed to create *ex nihilo* a lively proletarian community, which came to be known in its heyday in the 1950s and 1960s as "Little Bulgaria" (Haskell 1994). This social world fostered a vivid subculture complete with distinct local patriotism, culinary culture, cinemas, youth movements, a chorus, and above all a mythological football team (*Maccabi Yafo*). That many Jewish old-timers and some Arab Jaffans still express nostalgic longing for the ideal neighborly relations that existed before the 1948 war and during the first decades in its aftermath—when "we really lived together and shared the same houses," as one elderly Jew relates—attests not only to their naiveté and the postwar political repression of the Palestinian tragedy, but also to the denationalizing and depoliticizing power of intimate residential proximity.

Beginning in the 1960s and 1970s, the Jewish inhabitants took advantage of the opportunities for social and spatial mobility, thus perceiving Jaffa as a temporary stopover on the way to better living and housing in Bat-Yam, Holon, or Tel-Aviv. Today, the main rhetoric of this communal discourse invokes a sense of internal disintegration and the loss of control over the city "taken by Russians and Arabs." An aged Bulgarian resident thus expresses her frustration: "Jaffa was once a Bulgarian city but what the Jews took by force, the Arabs now take by money." In contradistinction to the Palestinian residential pattern, the majority of the second and third generations of Jews in Jaffa chose to leave the stigmatized city, whose communal institutions gradually disintegrated. Failing to maintain a strong discourse of rootedness, this aging population positions its withering local identity vis-à-vis the wealthy Jewish gentrifiers and the Arab population alike. With the loss of the communal institutions in Jaffa, and in tandem with the integration of the veteran Jewish population into the larger metropolitan space of greater Tel-Aviv, the "Jaffan" collective identity has been undermined and the distinction between Jaffa and South Tel-Aviv has been blurred. From the stigmatic vantage point which stereotypes Jewish Jaffans as "Southsiders" (*Dromim*), the latter perceive the new gentrifiers as "Northsiders" (*Tzfonim*), that is, as agents of the well-to-do and alienated North Side. Still perceiving Jaffa as a transit city, it seems that the old-time Jewish population remains at the margins of the urban renewal project and is not expected to make substantial profit from gentrification. Thus while they are not excluded from the political hegemonic project, they inhabit an aging social space deserted by most of its founding fathers, with little hope for generational revival.

THE NEW JEWISH GENTRIFIERS:
COMMUNITY IN SEARCH OF IDENTITY

The third group advancing a distinct project of nativization and identity politics is represented by the gentrifiers, who began to purchase real estate in the city in the mid-1980s. Consisting of predominately "bourgeois bohemians" ("Bobos"), this population has been driven by a neoliberal multicultural ideology on the political level, and on the cultural level by a romantic desire to return to "authentic" urban neighborliness in search of "high ceilings and internal space," as one resident put it. The communal organization that represents this population is Jaffa, Belle of the Seas, also known as Jaffans for Jaffa. Composed of members of liberal professions, such as architects, journalists, and schoolteachers, this group shifts uneasily between a clear preference for class distinction and a desire to be an integral part of the local social world.[16] The principles followed by this group, and its civilizing mission to "embellish" Jaffa by turning it into a bourgeois space, emerge from their Hebrew-language monthly magazine (published for a few years beginning in April 2003).

The magazine's marketing strategy sheds light on its public orientation and target audience. While the first issues were titled in Hebrew only "My Jaffa—Association Belle of the Seas—Jaffans for Jaffa," starting in April 2004 the title was complemented by a translation into Arabic (*Yafati*), in addition to the subtitle "distributed in thousands of copies in Jaffa, Tel-Kabir, Neve-Tzedek and Florentine" (the last two being heavily gentrified neighborhoods in South Tel-Aviv). The tension between the new bilingual title and the Hebrew original subtitle reflects the gentrifiers' ambivalent effort to address the Arab audience (which includes recruiting Arab board members) on the one hand, and to secure distribution in the network of regenerated neighborhoods undergoing a similar gentrification process in Tel-Aviv (Neve-Tzedek, Florentine) on the other hand. This ambivalent strategy, which approaches the Jaffa Arabs (in a magazine written entirely in Hebrew) while addressing a Jewish audience in comparably fashionable neighborhoods, reflects this group's dilemma of locality. For this reason, although they recurrently declare that they are true Jaffans and that Jaffa is indeed "theirs," they remain in a

class position apart from most of Jaffa's residents and send their children
to schools in Tel-Aviv rather than to local institutions (one of the association's activists thus humorously referred to the group as "Ashkenazi
fans of Jaffa"). While Jaffa, Belle of the Seas, is a well-organized social
community and an interest group (vis-à-vis the city), it remains in search
of local identity which reconciles a (Tel-Avivan) bourgeois habitus with
the authenticity of (Jaffan) locality.

Faced with the dwindling veteran Jewish community and the rising visibility of the "new Jews," Palestinian collective action is organized around an indigenous discourse of "the right to the city," which
remains at the end of the day deeply divided. Unable to stand up to the
market forces of real estate and to the gentrification plan, its position
is constantly negotiated in relation to the Jewish communities in Jaffa,
producing in the process circumstantial coalitions concerning local issues. Estranging the Palestinian natives and indigenizing the Jewish
immigrants, these respective projects of nativization further disrupt any
unified definition of the city as either Jewish or Palestinian.

PROPOSITION 2. *Stranger Sociality:* Mixed towns simultaneously
produce and problematize the co-presence of ethnic Others,
resulting in circumstantial coalitions between rival communities
and pragmatic transactions between individuals.

Under conditions of spatial heteronomy, communal fragmentation, and
sectarian identity politics, the decentralized urban regime in Jaffa gives
rise to unexpected circumstantial coalitions between Palestinians and
Israelis, private and public agents—all promoting particularistic interests which further disrupt an inclusive definition of the urban situation.
Thus, for instance, in the 2008 municipal elections the Yafa List consisted
of a Jewish-Arab coalition between Palestinian and gentrifier candidates.
Nevertheless, the same left-wing gentrifiers were reluctant to enroll their
children in an experimental bilingual program (at the Weitzman School),
due to the significant proportion of Arab pupils in it. Similarly, the Andromeda Hill exclusive gated community (see chapter 5) was facilitated
through an ad hoc coalition comprising the Greek Orthodox Patriarch
(who owned the land and was eager to sell), a Jewish-Canadian entre-

preneur, Tel-Aviv's municipality, and potential residents—all joining forces at the expense of the weak Palestinian community. At the same time, however, the escalating struggle over gentrification and the "future of the city" triggers new forms of social action and legal activism. Creating yet another coalition of Jewish and Palestinian activists, artists, and NGOs, a new discourse of urban rights calls for an inclusive redefinition of citizenship tailored for the "city of all its citizens."

The intersecting webs of affiliation, mobilization, and identification call into question the principle of common belonging, which organizes the symbolic codes of the urban community and determines who is the "Other" existing outside it and who is the "stranger" located on its boundaries (Simmel [1922] 1955, [1908] 1971). The fragmented composition of ethnic communities in Jaffa, the history of contrived coexistence, and the embedded existence of mixed neighborhoods for over sixty years problematize the politicized distinctions between "us" and "them," "here" and "there," familiarity and otherness. They fundamentally undermine the spatial ordering of the world—the sought-after coordination between moral and topographical closeness—and create, in Zygmunt Bauman's terms, a city of "strangers": "There are friends and enemies. And there are *strangers*. . . . The stranger disturbs the resonance between physical and psychical distance: he is *physically close* while remaining *spiritually remote*. He represents an incongruous and hence resented synthesis of nearness and remoteness" (1993, 60; italics original). Bauman further elaborates on the categorical threat the stranger poses to the entire social system and the very possibility of sociation:

> Apparently, there is a symmetry: there would be no enemies were there no friends, and there would be no friends unless for the yawning abyss of enmity outside. Symmetry, however, is an illusion. . . . Friends are reproduced by the pragmatics of co-operation, enemies by the pragmatics of struggle. . . . With all the opposition between them, or—rather—because of that opposition, both sides of the opposition stand for relationships. Following Simmel, we may say that friendship and enmity, and only they, are forms of sociation; indeed, the archetypal forms of all sociation, the two-pronged matrix of sociation. . . . Against this cosy antagonism, this conflict-torn collusion of friends and enemies, the *stranger* rebels. The threat he carries is more awesome than that which one can fear from the enemy. The stranger threatens the sociation itself—the very *possibility* of sociation. He calls the bluff of the

opposition between friends and enemies as the *compleat mappa mundi,* as
the difference which consumes all differences and hence leaves nothing
outside itself. As that opposition is the foundation on which all social life and
all differences which patch and hold it together rest, the stranger saps social
life itself. And all this because the stranger is neither friend nor enemy; and
because he may be both. And because we do not know, and have no way
of knowing, which is the case. (53–55; italics original)

National minorities and cultural strangers are first and foremost
products of the modern state's exclusionary logic, which is predicated
on the perpetuation of collective alterities (Isin 2002). However, this
is by no means a direct causal corollary of their spatial or structural
position in society, but rather is a culturally mediated product of political interpretation and symbolic action. "Groups," Jeffrey Alexander
reminds us, "are *made* strange by the active intervention of interpreting
subjects" (2004b, 94). For the Palestinian citizens of Israel this logic
corners them as a "trapped minority" between the Israeli state and
the Palestinian nation (Rabinowitz 2001). Complementing Bauman's
line of argument, strangeness can thus be understood as a conceptual
borderland between communities, categories, and cultures, and the
mixed town as a material space that produces and inhabits instances
of strangeness.[17] This notwithstanding, strangeness cannot be reduced
to being a product of a classification principle of the nation-state with
respect to a national minority. Rather, in Jaffa it functions as the basis
for social interaction and transaction. In other words, the relationship
underlying "sociation" in Jaffa is neither one of friendship nor one of enmity, but a complicated synthesis of both (cf. Simmel [1908] 1971). The
designation of Jaffa as a city of strangers enables us to understand daily
phenomena and paradoxes that are otherwise obscured by methodological nationalism (such as mixed marriages, joint ventures like Yafa Café,
counterhegemonic personal narratives, Jewish-Arab criminal networks,
and binational activism).

Mechanisms of strangeness-production include, among others, the
fragmented schooling system which produces hybrid national subjects,
state policies which legitimize the ambivalent status of the Palestinian
minority as the potential "enemy within," the history of uneasy cohabitation and the exigencies of daily life which push actors to interact for

practical purposes, the corruption of community representatives, and structural constraints on collective mobilization. To be sure, the problem of strangeness is perceived by local communities as a crisis of identity, political representation, and pervasive alienation.

The paradox of educational pluralism is as good an example as any to illustrate the institutional production of strangeness. In Jaffa, the schooling system consists of no fewer than four main groups: Hebrew state schools, Arab state schools, Christian private schools, and bilingual experimental schools (Ichilov and Mazawi 1996). Around 10 percent (400) of the Arab pupils study in Hebrew schools and receive no instruction in Arabic language, history, or culture, while 44 percent (1,600) study in Arab schools that prepare their pupils for the Israeli matriculation certificate for Arabs or for low-status occupations such as carpentry, mechanics, and hairdressing. A miniscule group of no more than 3 percent go to new bilingual schools. The rest, 43 percent (1,700), are enrolled in three ethnically mixed church schools awarding French matriculation (Collège des Frères), British matriculation (Tabitha), and Israeli matriculation in Arabic (Terra Sancta).

This decentralized system, which ostensibly allows maximal freedom of choice among alternative educational options, in fact features parallel subsystems that produce hybrid national subjects and allow for little transition between them. The educational system in Jaffa therefore represents a "tower of Babel" of languages and incommensurable curricula (Shaqr 1996). Due to its fragmented diversity, it contributes to the perpetuation of class polarization in the Arab community and hinders the creation of a common national-cultural identity (Ichilov and Mazawi 1996). For individual Palestinian students enrolled in Jewish and Christian private mixed schools (around 50 percent of the Arab students in Jaffa), a state of "confusing identities," as defined by one of my informants, prevails. Arab students are sometimes demanded to sing the Israeli national anthem, "Hatiqva" ("The Hope") or to wear costumes for Purim (the Jewish carnival), and many of them learn from childhood to identify with the rival national heroes, protagonists of their elementary school textbooks (as in the omnipresent image of the brave Jewish soldier who saves his wounded friend from the "hands of the Arab

murderers").[18] The following testimony was given by one of my Palestinian informants who studied in the French school which caters to Arabs,
Jews, and children of diplomats:

> An Arab kid doesn't know who he is. The identity in school gets all mixed up.
> ... My sister loved Theodor Herzl because he had eyes just like my father's.
> And I adored Trumpeldor [a nationalist Zionist hero, whose last words in
> the battle over Tel-Hay were "It is good to die for our country"]. ... I was not
> aware that I was an Arab until the fourth grade. Then I saw my grandfather
> wearing a white *kaffiyeh* [head-cover] in a family event. In the *Miqra'ot Israel*,
> which we studied in school, the Jews were good soldiers and the bad guys
> were Arabs. The Arabs wore the same white *kaffiyeh* that my grandfather was
> now wearing. Until then my grandfather used to wear only a checkered *kaf-
> fiyeh,* so it made sense. Only after this event did I begin to ask questions.[19]

Precisely because the products of strangeness are confusion and ambivalence, the educational system and other sites of unequal encounters between Jews and Arabs cause considerable frustration for iden-
tity-minded community activists. From the vantage point of individual
actors, however, the situational practice of strangeness enables us to
analyze the space of action extending between rival subject positions
and Jewish/Palestinian notions of self and Other. Thus, for instance,
strangers are dual-identity teenagers changing their names ad hoc from
'Ali to *Eli,* from *Mer'i* to *Meir,* from *Mussa* to *Moshe,* when they feel they
have to hide their Arab identity in romantic encounters with Jewish girls
from Bat-Yam or Tel-Aviv. These "identity plays" (Steinberg 2002) are
obvious markers of national subordination and humiliation, but they
can also be read as a momentary liberation from the normative gendered
chains of Arab society and culture. As an analytic concept, situational
strangeness exemplifies the dramaturgic character of social action. It
enables us to rethink the lives of Palestinians and Jews in Jaffa not as a
static instantiation of dichotomous subject positions, but as a constant
motion between contradictory yet overlapping social worlds and alter-
nating identity masks.

   A city of strangers, Jaffa's unique profile is predicated on the mitigating effect of cultural and functional proximity between rival social
types. Under conditions of political ambivalence, communal fragmentation, low social capital, and neighborhood contact, the pragmatics of ex-

change and utilitarian transaction is tied to the paradoxical co-presence of relevant and agentive strangers. From this relational perspective, the mixed urban space can be fruitfully seen as an enabling environment which produces cultural practices, social dispositions, and circumstantial coalitions, otherwise impossible in mononational cities by virtue of ethnic monitoring and spatial segregation.

PROPOSITION 3. *Cultural Indeterminacy:* Mixed towns point to the failure of nationalist mediation in forming a hegemonic narrative sequence of identity and locality. Instead, the indeterminate definition of the urban situation opens up alternative spaces of binational agency.

Despite its convoluted complexity, the contested terrain of the mixed city is not without cultural idiom or sociological sense. The symbolic management of space thus frames the organization of physical space (spatial heteronomy) and provides meaning and signification to the practices of social space (stranger sociality). Under conditions of systemic conflict, the three moments of social action—spatiality-sociality-culture—coexist in a pattern of mutual constitution. While the generative order of nationalism (Portugali 1993) certainly looms large in mixed towns, it is by no means reducible to the dualist causal determination of domination and resistance subscribed to by methodological nationalism. Stating that "JAFFO [sic] IS THE JEWISH CITY TOO," the graffiti described in the introduction illustrates that the debate over the identity of the mixed city is far from being resolved. Indeed, at least since 1948, recurrent attempts to establish a definition of the urban situation that unequivocally positions the city as either Jewish or Arab point to the failure to sustain a viable identity cleansed of ambivalence and ambiguity. With no communal hegemony to speak of, the fringe quality of ethnically mixed urbanism renders the cultural management of space a dialogic and open-ended battleground. More often than not, the role of the mixed city as a scale of sequential mediation among the citizen, the nation, and the state is challenged rather than confirmed.

The Palestinian image of Jaffa emerges in a striking structure of incongruity through collective self-perceptions and mythical language.

The Palestinian discourse of pre-'48 Arab Jaffa gives the city three nick-names that position it within a cultural and geographical field of mean-ing. The first nickname, "The Bride of Palestine" (*'Arus Falastin*), locates Jaffa in the national Arab space. The second name, "The Bride of the Sea" (*'Arus al-bahr*), locates Jaffa in the Mediterranean space as a major port town and as an important trade center. The third and less familiar name, "The Mother of the Stranger" (*Umm al-gharib*), was assigned to Jaffa due to the liberal cosmopolitanism that had characterized it as a flourishing city hosting labor migrants and other foreigners from the region. This triad of names symbolized Jaffa's status in the first part of the twentieth century as a national cultural and commercial center. After 1948 this im-age lost its anchor in reality and was transferred onto the mythical plane.

At present, the Palestinian tropes of Jaffa exist within a different triad of meaning—one which traps the fragmented community between nos-talgia, utopia, and estrangement. While terms like "The Bride of Pales-tine" and "The Bride of the Sea" position Jaffa in a nostalgic, utopian space of national longing awaiting a return to glory, current realities spell marginality, frustration, and dismay. Jaffa, the Mother of the Stranger, which once symbolized cosmopolitan openness and attracted Palestin-ians from surrounding villages and beyond, is now experienced as a refuge for a new type of "strangers"—poor foreign workers and, more recently, Palestinian collaborators (*'umala'*) with the Israeli security forces, transplanted from their homes in Gaza and the West Bank and settled by the Israeli government in Jaffa to protect them from the wrath of Palestinians in their home environments. Failing to make a firm claim on the city, Palestinian discourse frames the problem of strangeness *qua* alienation as an existential crisis (Shaqr 1996). Thus, an aged Palestinian commented on Jaffa's current predicament, "Jaffa is the Mother of the Stranger. It welcomes him [the Jewish stranger] and feeds him, while it neglects its own sons and leaves them to starve" (Minns and Hijab 1990, 156).

The Jewish image of the city, in turn, has been historically rooted in an Orientalist discourse, chronically unable to come to terms with Jaffa's Janus-faced heritage as the indigenous alter ego of Tel-Aviv, "the city that begat a state." Vacillating between romantic historicity and political vio-lence, the image of Jaffa has posed a political and hermeneutic challenge to the territorial project of urban Judaization, which ultimately failed to define the national-cum-cultural identity of this "New-Old" city. As we shall see in the next chapter, this failure results in a persistent pattern of semiotic ambivalence which, from the Jewish-Israeli point of view, positions Jaffa both as a source of identity and longing (in the Biblical distant past) and as a symbol of alterity and enmity (in the recent past)—an object of desire and fear alike. An obvious analysis à la Edward Said of such fractured representation would interpret this exotic/threatening split as a discourse of control and colonial reification. While valid, this is only a partial explanation. The discursive rupture represents rather a deeper sense of cultural indeterminacy within Tel-Aviv's own self-image as modern, ahistorical "white city" faced with the moral dilemma of taking over the historicity of Arab Jaffa while at the same time appropriating Jaffa's biblical connotation and Jewish presence since the eighteenth century. Unable to reconcile this tension, both aspects of this image have fueled a century-long dialectical conflict. Adding to the representational facet is the lived experience of actual residents of Jaffa who are faced with governmental attempts to rewrite the history of the city and celebrate exclusively the Zionist narrative. The following vignette illustrates the clash between the top-down imposition of a Zionist narrative and local resistance to it.

In 1998, commemorating the fiftieth anniversary of his death in the battle over Jaffa, the City of Tel-Aviv-Jaffa named a street after Natan Panz, member of the Jewish militia (the National Military Organization, or Irgun) and football player. The street was located at the core of a predominantly Arab residential neighborhood. Soon after the ceremony, which was attended by the prime minister and the mayor, Islamic Movement activists placed, next to the new street sign, a green metal plate inscribed with a Quranic verse calling believers to seek atonement for their sins: "Do penance with your God, for He is Oft-forgiving." In 2003, on a square planned by the municipality in the midst of the same street, a statue was erected in memory of the same ultra-Zionist combatant.[20] The stormy debate which ensued denounced the municipal authorities not only for dismissing the Arab history of the city, but for hurting the feelings of the residents and thus further alienating them from their lived space.

FIGURE 1.4. Sign posted by the Islamic Movement on Panz Street.
Photo by Hicham Chabaita, 2007.

These struggles are part of an ongoing campaign over the ethnic and cultural identity of urban space in mixed towns. Street naming is a political act of territorial marking, often triggering heated debates (Azaryahu and Kook, 2002). Street names constitute spatial texts that imprint historical events and public figures in the local collective memory (Pinchevski and Torgovnik, 2002). Of late, the issue of street names in Israel's mixed towns made the headlines when the mayor of Ramle (another mixed town) disregarded requests by Arab residents to change some of the street names from Zionist symbols (e.g., national poet Bialik or the Ghetto Fighters) to Arab and Islamic figures (e.g., Sultan Suleiman or Tawfiq Ziyad). The mayor was recorded saying, "If they don't like it, let them go to Jaljulia [an all-Arab village], which is an Arab name. Why would I rename a street because one Jamal or Muhammad wants me to? Let him change his god."[21]

The political history of street names in Jaffa has been turbulent. In the aftermath of the 1948 war, street names (e.g., King Georges, King Faisal, and Al-Hilwa) were dropped and changed to numbers.[22] Then, with the 1950 annexation of Jaffa to Tel-Aviv, they were clustered according to the group system (*shitat ha-kvutzot*) already in effect in Tel-Aviv since 1934. In Jaffa, the group system comprised different categories of street names:

1. righteous gentiles (figures from world history such as Plato, Aristotle, Michelangelo, Leonardo da Vinci, Dante, Racine, and Louis Pasteur, as well as non-Jewish literary figures who have influenced Israeli culture, such as the French poet Lamartine, who in his *Travels in the East* dedicated a eulogy to Jaffa and its Jews);

2. Biblical names (such as Pinhas, Yochanan, Hiram the King of Tyre, Tarshish, Yefet);

3. names from the New Testament (such as Simon the Tanner);

4. names from Greek mythology (e.g., Andromeda);

5. names from Zionist and Jewish history (such as Rabbi Yehouda of Ragouza, the Immigrants of Zion, the Work of Israel, the Tribes of Israel, Isaac's Fear);

6. geographical markers (such as the Port, the Red Sea);

7. plants, zodiac signs, and miscellaneous (such as the Necklace, Pisces, the Dolphin); and finally

8. a handful of Arabic names mainly in small alleys (including Ibn-Sina, Ibn-Rushd, Naguib Mahfouz, Khalil Jubran, 'Abd al-Ra'uf Al-Baytar, George Nassar, and 'Abd al-Karim 'Abd Al-Ghani, of whom the first two were medieval philosophers, the third and fourth writers, the fifth Jaffa's mayor in the 1920s, the sixth a trade union member, and the seventh a Jaffan who died in 1992 while protecting a Jewish girl attacked by a Palestinian armed with a sword).

The relative absence of representative Arab names has been a constant bone of contention. These tensions have politicized what has already been an unresolved spatial order, derived from the persistent noncorrespondence between the layout of unmistakable Jewish street names, such as the Rabbi of Pshista or the Work of Israel, and the Arab population that inhabits them.

These visual representations and the communal struggles underlying them point to the crisis of nationalist mediation. Estranging the Palestinian local population and indigenizing the Jewish immigrants, these struggles produce fragmented "projects of nativization." This space of rupture, while hindering a nationalist definition of the situation, enabled, paradoxically since the October 2000 events, new political claims for equal citizenship, binational cooperation, and Palestinian presence. Led by a general sense of frustration vis-à-vis the political stalemate, new initiatives and actors came to the fore (such as Autobiography of a City and Yafa Café). Thus the very marking of Jaffa as a space of violent contestation and political mobilization further attracted various groups that had already expressed interest in Jewish-Arab cooperation through actual residence in the city, including hippie communes yearning for Mediterranean and multicultural exoticism (which have settled in Jaffa since the 1990s); individual leftists coming for ideological reasons to implement coexistence on the ground; binational youth communes; and Jewish-Arab mixed couples who cannot find their place in Tel-Aviv. Finally, the October 2000 events also attracted political Palestinian-Israeli groups that are directly engaged with conflict-related activism, such as Re'ut-Sadaqa ("Friendship"), Anarchists against the Wall, Ta'ayush ("Jewish-Arab Partnership"), and the Zochrot ("Remembering") Association.

HETERONOMY, TRANSACTION, AND THE DISJOINTED SCALES OF MEDIATION

The concept of heteronomous space reveals intersecting spatial logics at work; socially, it highlights a Simmelian configuration of strangeness as an expression of ambivalent and nondichotomous subject positions; for cultural representation, it looks at the indeterminate image of the city for both Israeli Jews and Palestinians. More generally, an analytical vocabulary which emphasizes relationality can form the basis for a heuristic theoretical model applicable to most ethnically mixed towns.

Focusing on sociospatial relations, my argument has been that an indeterminate dialectical cycle exists which relates social to spatial processes and vice versa. Spatial heteronomy therefore enables stranger relations, and strangeness constitutes heteronomy. One theoretical vector from the social to the spatial begins with the mutually constitutive relations between the Israeli and the Palestinian national movements. The two groups and their identities were constituted in a series of dialectic oppositions and homologies which not only opposed each other but at the same time dialectically created each other, in dynamic but constantly asymmetrical relations of power. As intergroup relations play out on the ground, the mitigating factors associated with demographic intermixing, stranger sociality, and the blurring of ostensibly essential-ist images corrupt any possibility for mononationalist definitions of the urban situation. These processes, compounded by unresolved ethnic relations, economic tensions, and public policies, produce the cultural and political urban regime I call "spatial heteronomy."

At the other end of the dialectic, spatial heteronomy produces a so-ciality of stranger relations. The combination of demographic inter-permeation, unintended consequences of municipal policies, systemic spatial fragmentation, and the failure on the part of national definitions to define the full span of urban situations corrupts the correspondence between spatial boundaries (which would delimit neighborhoods) and social boundaries (of a certain class or ethnicity). Thus, rather than in-habiting segregated social worlds, spatial proximity keeps strangers, aliens, and allies within what Alfred Schutz (1971) terms the "horizon of relevance"—a twilight zone of borderline sociality in which nobody is truly friend or enemy (Simmel [1908] 1971).

Reformulated as a problem of mediation, binational urbanism pres-ents two axes of self-defeating dialectic between the city and the state. One is vertical, mediating local, national, and transnational/diasporic strategies of mobilization and identification. The other, which is horizon-tal, illuminates the reciprocal workings of nationalism and class-based forces.

Looking at the vertical axis first, we see that while the ideal typical model of the European nation-state and the logic of nationalism had evolved in a structure of symbolic amplification (Sahlins 2005) predi-cated on the "nationalizing of the local and the localizing of the national" (Sahlins 1989, 165) and the increasing differentiation of national cul-tures and spaces, cases such as Jaffa, where contradictions between the national and the local are anything but resolved, profoundly challenge this complementarity. Having failed to mobilize support from the Pal-estinian Authority or, for that matter, from others in the Arab world, Palestinians in Jaffa are too deeply implicated with Israel and its in-stitutions to aspire to a meaningful autonomous Palestinian assertion of the collective self. Community organizing, cultural practices, and political behavior remain fragmented, exemplifying a synchronic dialectic of schismogenesis and homology (Bateson 1972).

As for the horizontal axis, the mediation between nation and class is best exemplified in action and reaction surrounding gentrification. From a methodological nationalist perspective, one might have expected a natural coalition between different groups of Jewish residents in Jaffa on account of their shared national identity. In reality, however, a deep (and deepening) social and ideological division is apparent between Jewish residents, which clearly stems from class and intra-Israeli ethnic cleavages. One counterintuitive result of this is that the residents' association representing most Jewish gentrifiers turns to the Palestinian community leaders for cooperation (only to find that there as well, their Ashkenazi and middle-class characteristics set them apart).

In his elaboration of Lefebvre's theory, Neil Brenner (2000) proposes to read urban theory as a "scale question." Nevertheless, while urban social theory has defined the specificity of the city as "a mediation among mediations" (Lefebvre 1996, 101)—containing the near order and contained in the far order—certain types of cities, *pace* Lefebvre, disrupt such mediation and assume their identity by the act of disrupting. In the Israeli-Palestinian contested terrain, when vertical governmental superimposition between city, state, and nation fails, the organizing logic which governs social relations in the mixed town gives rise to a regime of pragmatic transaction and symbolic exchange among entrepreneurs, state officials, and common residents, Jews and Arabs. In everyday life this crisis of representation dissipates a nationalist definition of the urban situation and enables institutional and individual social actors to open the cultural "toolkit" of nationalism and modify its hegemonic repertoire—its scripts, practices, and subjectivities (Alexander 2004a; Swidler 1986). Cultural strangeness thus inhabits the incongruent and heteronomous space between a regime of mediation and a regime of exchange. In mixed towns, where social control over collective identity is relatively weak, mediation works in inverse proportion to transaction.

Jewish-Arab mixed towns are an understudied and distinct phenomenon in Middle Eastern history and urban sociology. Such cities challenge the hegemonic ethnonationalist guiding principles of the Israeli state, which fails to maintain homogeneous, segregated, and ethnically stable spaces. This failure results in the parallel existence of heteronomous spaces in these towns, which operate through multiple and often contradictory logics of space, class, and nation. Analyzed relationally, these spaces produce peculiar forms of quotidian social relations between Palestinians and Israelis, engendering counterhegemonic local identities and social formations that challenge both Palestinian and Jewish nationalisms. Based on the details of this case study, we can draw some of the characteristics of the ethnically mixed city into a tentative theoretical model. This could function as a conceptual scheme to be examined, refined, or challenged in future studies. The proposed model has outlined three key propositions, which may produce further falsifiable hypotheses:

1. Spatial Heteronomy: Mixed towns are the sociospatial product of unresolved tensions between diverging urban logics, which dissociate space from identity. Segregated ethnic enclaves are dissolved from within (outmigration) and from without (gentrification).

2. Stranger Sociality: Mixed towns simultaneously produce and problematize the co-presence of ethnonational Others, resulting in circumstantial coalitions between rival communities and pragmatic transaction between individuals. Subcommunal sectarian identity politics further undermine collective solidarity and communal unity.

3. Cultural Indeterminacy: Mixed towns point to the failure of nationalist mediation in forming a hegemonic narrative sequence of identity and locality. Instead, the indeterminate definition of the urban situation opens up alternative spaces of binational agency. The struggle over the future of the city produces differential discourses of rights.

Such processes of border-crossing have largely gone unnoticed in studies of Israel/Palestine, a field dominated by methodological nationalism and its tendency to equate the nation-state with society and political culture. Perceiving relations between Palestinians and Israelis as a zero-sum game, this paradigm often loses sight of processes of mutual determination continuously at play between Palestinian and Jewish communities, as well as the political cultures and urban spaces they occupy. Acknowledging these interstitial processes and their productive potential by no means ignores the power of the Jewish state and (Palestinian) resistance to it. It does however give voice and visibility to the productive negotiation of cultural identities and social worlds even at the core of one of the region's most violent conflicts.

On a more abstract theoretical plane, I endeavor in the following chapters to rethink the problem of spatial relationality in triadic terms rather than in dyads. In line with the Simmelian sociological mode of analysis that Michel Maffesoli has termed "triplicité" (Freund 1983; Maffesoli 1991), rather than erecting dualities (such as exclusion/inclusion, colonized/colonizer, friend/foe) and then deconstructing them, a triadic approach attempts to analyze Jewish-Arab mixed towns as a nonreifiable relational field which persistently produces third spaces (Soja 1996). As Lefebvre (1980, 143) has poignantly put it,

> Reflexive thought and hence philosophy has for a long time accentuated dyads . . . [including] those that constituted the Western philosophical paradigm: subject-object, continuity-discontinuity, open-closed, etc. Finally, in the modern era there are the binary oppositions between signifier and signified, center and periphery, etc. . . . The dialogue between friendship and hatred, the grapplings of love or combat, offer moments of incomparable intensity, of presence. But the relationship between two entities (duality, opposition, dyad) vanishes as it takes shape, turning into image and reflection, a mirror effect, a rivalry that is derisory to the primacy of either one. Hence the annihilation of one by the other, or sometimes their arrival at the logical compromise of mutual representation. . . . But is there ever a relation only between two terms? One always has Three. There is always the Other.[23]

TWO

The Bridled "Bride of Palestine"

Urban Orientalism and the
Zionist Quest for Place

Above the mosques the moon is rising
Above your house the neon lights are lit
And again the jasmine bush gives its scent
And again we're here by the clock tower

And again a girl without "why" or "how come"
My hands are holding yours
There's something strange and unknown
Something wonderful about this town

The seagulls flew from the dock
The sea has gone silent
This is Jaffa, girl, this is Jaffa
That penetrates the blood like wine.

—YOSSI GAMZU, "This Is Jaffa"

THERE'S SOMETHING STRANGE ABOUT THIS TOWN

The gentrified city is a cultural space of unyielding desire for the quality of life lost in the metropolitan chaos or in the emptiness of suburban sprawl. Imagining a new authentic lifestyle in the erstwhile disinvested yet quaint "inner city" is bound to cause considerable adaptation pains for the individual(ist) newcomer, but these are often overshadowed by the promise of a new enabling environment—a horizon of creative possibilities for the "new middle class." In cities like Jaffa, located at the periphery of the metropolitan center, gentrification bridges the anonymous functionality of the big city and the communal intimacy of the neighborhood. Seen as a convoluted shell of negation and passion, alienation and purpose, the cultural problem of gentrification echoes early formulations of the modern city as a site of "bitter hatred" as well as the seat for urbanites' "most unsatisfied yearnings" (Simmel [1903] 1950, 420).

It is this urban scene of tense fascination that Galit entered when she "finally made the move" and settled in her recently renovated "Arab house" in Jaffa. I asked Galit why she decided to move to Jaffa from her spacious apartment in North Tel-Aviv. "I got hooked," she said. "We found here a place like no other. We were looking for something different. Something you can't find in Tel-Aviv. We had friends here and after a few visits I got hooked. It's like the song, you know— it gets into your blood." Tellingly, however, like many of her fellow gentrifiers, she decided to keep her two children in their original elementary (Jewish) schools in Tel-Aviv, "for lack of good facilities in Jaffa."

What has drawn Galit, an interior designer, and her family to Jaffa is a search for a specific alternative cultural space: "You need crazy, non-normative, multicultural people who are looking for contact with other cultures to settle down here. People come to Jaffa because they look for style. They look for a place in Tel-Aviv that has historical depth and the charm of locality." Galit's search was over once she found what she was looking for—"inner space and high ceilings." Notwithstanding Galit's celebration of multicultural individuality and cultural distinction ("crazy, non-normative . . . people"), in what follows we shall see that her romantic quest for authenticity rests upon a longstanding Orientalist imagination of Jaffa in Zionist discourse.

While this chapter is not about gentrification per se, it traces the genealogy of a specific place-oriented discourse, which constitutes an evocative yet politically contested image of the city (Lynch 1960). This discursive formation reveals a new form of pro-urban, neoliberal agency as much as it conceals an implicit set of colonial tropes and Orientalist interpretative schemata (Fernandez 1991). To understand the cultural grounding and political effects of such imaginaries we must track the historical construction of these categories of urban action—which in turn allow the agents of gentrification to make sense of the city—from the beginning of the Zionist settlement project to the neoliberal present (Tissot 2007).

For more than two generations now, a select set of Hebrew songs about Jaffa, the most famous being Gamzu's "This Is Jaffa" (1960), has attained the exclusive status of a popular canon. These songs are part of the "local knowledge" of almost every Jewish child and adult in Israel: they are memorized, sung, broadcasted, and circulated in youth movements, singsong events, nostalgic radio shows, and the now-popular Hebrew-music TV programs. However, beyond the sociology of reception of such musical cultural forms, Gamzu's specific lyric—as a paradigmatic example of this canon—actively participates in the production of a specific cultural image of the city. The central themes in Gamzu's depiction of Jaffa are its exotic strangeness (*muzar*), denoting in Hebrew a degree of freaky outlandishness ("There's something strange and unknown"), and its addictive idiosyncrasy ("This is Jaffa, girl, this is Jaffa, that penetrates the blood like wine"). Historicizing the symbolic frame of reference which gave rise to such depictions, this chapter interrogates the cultural logic of the Zionist historical imagination that has (re)produced Jaffa as a site of binational and multicultural "strangeness," and, just as importantly, manifests the political effects of such Orientalist representations of the city.

Idioms of Jaffa's "strangeness" are instantiations of the symbolic ambivalence between the romantic historicity of place and the political violence of conflict that has characterized the Zionist collective interpretation of Jewish-Arab relations in Israel/Palestine at large. In Israeli phenomenological anthropology, Gurevitch and Aran (1991; 1994) have fruitfully theorized the Jewish sense of place (*makom*) as conceptually split and historically troubled: "This sense of place is ambivalent, dialectic and paradoxical, moving between poles of place and non-place" (Gurevitch 2007, 8). The authors insist that the cultural ambivalence toward "the Land" (*Ha'aretz*) cannot be reduced to the political economy of diaspora and colonization (cf. Kimmerling 1992). This peculiar notion of placeness, or *mekomiyut*, persistently reenacts the unresolved tension between the longstanding yearning for the "promised land" and the pragmatic reluctance of Jewish settler-colonialists toward actually becoming the place's "natives." This paradox results in a constant play of tropes of place and locality against exile and placelessness, which dominates the Biblical scriptures as well as contemporary literature and popular culture. In their search for place Israelis have ritualized nativity: "They hike and settle the land but hardly ever simply sit in it" (Gurevitch 2007). Israelis are caught between idea and locality poised as two planes of collective orientation: the "big place" of myth and redemption and the "small place" of practical materiality and everyday life. "Living in the 'small place,' in the everyday locality of home, street, neighborhood, landscape," Gurevitch observes, "is constantly encroached upon by a sense of the 'big place'—either by way of positive identification, or by means of disappointment and quarrel."[1] Such phenomenology of place, Gurevitch and Aran conclude, offers a critical outlook on the ideological divisions and foundational controversies in Israeli culture pertaining to themes such as ascent versus descent (*Aliyah* and *Yerida*), territorial politics, and the relationship between Tel-Aviv (the capitalist metropolis) and Jerusalem (the holy capital).

Extending what has been an internal Jewish debate to the binational frontier of the urban mix, I seek to incorporate the Palestinian "Others of the place" as key participants, albeit present absentees, in the cultural process of identity-making in Israel. While most studies have focused on the radicalizing effect of urban mix, as manifested in unequal power relations between Israelis and Palestinians engendered by exclusionary planning policies, economic dependency, martial law, and population transfer (LeVine 2005; Rabinowitz 1997; Rotbard 2005; Slyomovics 1998; Yiftachel and Yacobi 2003), this chapter turns analytic attention rather to the cultural production of ambivalent urban identities.[2]

Positing Jaffa as Tel-Aviv's alter ego, a spatial theorization of *ambivalence* is crucial to tracing the accommodation of categories of representation to changing historical conditions. In social theory, Bauman (1991) locates the counterpart to the order-seeking project of modernity and the nation-state not in Hobbesian chaos or sheer disorder, but in ambivalence, a sphere of social action characterized by cognitive dissonance, strangeness, and contingency. Akin to Derrida's notion of indeterminacy *qua* ubiquitous "resistance to closure" (1996), ambivalence, or "the possibility of assigning an object or event to more than one category" (Bauman 1993, 1), is inherently dialectic —it is simultaneously the stifling "waste of modernity" and the prerequisite for social change (15). In postcolonial theory, Homi Bhabha has encouraged a critical rethinking of nationalism, representation, and performance that above all identifies ambivalence as the locus of resistance to stereotypical fixation and oppressive domination: "The ambivalence of mimicry—almost but not quite—suggests that the fetishized colonial culture is potentially and strategically an insurgent counter-appeal. What I have called its 'identity-effects' are always crucially split." The process by which ambivalence "does not merely 'rupture' the discourse, but becomes transformed into an uncertainty, which fixes the colonial subject as a 'partial' presence" (Bhabha 1994, 91) is acutely articulated in the Jewish-Arab "contact zone" (Pratt 1999). The liminal symbolic space between dominators and dominated, center and periphery, Tel-Aviv and Jaffa, thus becomes a strategic site of action and interpretation in which cultural differences actually produce imagined constructions and narratives of national identity. In Jaffa, the fraught confrontation between rival narratives of heritage results in persistent representational indeterminacy and semiotic ambivalence. The ethnically mixed town thus emerges not as a site of unidirectional zero-sum conflict but rather as an unfolding manifestation of "hybrid urbanism" (AlSayyad 2001)— a contested breeding ground for urban meaning-making, political activism, and resistance to Israeli domination.

Taking the mixed city as a "difference machine" (Isin 2002), which dialectically produces alterities as it molds national identities, the lens of Orientalism is well suited for the purpose of mapping Zionist cultural negotiations with the city's Palestinian past, present, and future (Said 1979).[3] A poetic geography of otherness shapes the internal Jewish strategies of historical representation and collective memory faced with the indelible trace of Palestinian existence in the mixed town. Said's magnum opus, however, poses both a theoretical role model and an analytic challenge. His methodological choice of Foucauldian discourse to encase his argument, his apparent disregard for historical temporality, and his shifting premises have all played a part in stirring controversy. Orientalist discourse, James Clifford (1988, 260) argues, is conceptualized as an oppressive totality that reproduces "discursive consistency" as a trans-historical constant: "Orientalism is 'enormously systematic,' cosmological in scope, incestuously self-referential."[4] Moreover, Said's resort to the Foucauldian framework "underlines the absence in his book of any developed theory of culture as a differentiating and expressive ensemble rather than as simply hegemonic and disciplinary.... Culture as Said conceives it is little more than a massive body of self-congratulating ideas" (263–265). Faced with what Aijaz Ahmad (1994) denounces as "totalizing narrativization," Clifford urges the social analyst to rethink Orientalisms as dialogic and relational configurations: "It is high time that cultural and social totalities are subjected to the kind of radical questioning that textual ensembles have undergone in recent critical practice.... Collectively constituted *difference* is not necessarily static or positionally dichotomous in the manner of Orientalism as Said describes it. There is no need to discard theoretically all conceptions of 'cultural' difference, especially once this is seen as not simply received from tradition, language or environment but also as *made* in the new political-cultural conditions of global relationality" (Clifford 1988, 274).

Responding to this critique, I historicize Orientalist discourses as emerging figurations of indeterminate alterity. Seen in this way, diachronic and synchronic ambivalence becomes more than minor disturbance—rather, it produces scopes of agency, which in turn engage Orientalism's fixations, propose alternative imaginings, and call for its supersession. Starting with the vicissitudes of Jewish cultural engagements with Jaffa, which vacillate between romantic historicity and political violence, the subsequent review describes four major cultural modalities of Orientalism in and of the city, which I term Folkloric Orientalism, Orientalist Realism, Neo-Orientalism, and finally Post-Orientalist/Post-Zionist representations of the city. While the first modality portrays Jaffa as a site of delinquency, Oriental honor, and folkloristic ethnicity, the second reduces it to its social problems and the third reconstructs it as a site of multicultural encounters, liberal utopia, and urban rejuvenation. In the wake of the October 2000 events, the fourth moment marks the emergence of new conditions of possibility for coming to terms with Jaffa's past and present from a post-Orientalist position. Thus, the exotic strangeness which characterized the Orientalist imagination of Jaffa since the founding of Tel-Aviv gave way to new political claims for equal citizenship, binational collaboration, and Palestinian presence. It is important to point out that this classification does not present an exhaustive typology of mutually exclusive cultural formations with discrete cutoff points. Rather it captures analytically the sequential emergence of discursive configurations regarding Jaffa as always-accumulating processes of sedimentation and accretion, which may potentially coexist at any given period.

HISTORICITY AND VIOLENCE: JAFFA JANUS-FACED

A recurrent leitmotif of violence seems to run between David Ben-Gurion's famous statement at the height of the Arab Revolt—"The destruction of Jaffa, the city and the port, will come. And it is good that it will come. . . . If it falls into oblivion, I will not share its sorrow" (*Memoirs,* July 11, 1936)—and expressions such as Etzel member Efrayim Talmi's report of his visit to the city in the aftermath of its occupation in May 1948: "The new immigrant residents who have come down here will no more know the fear and anxiety from the Jaffa rioters. This city, which was a cancerous thorn in the sides of the great *Yishuv*, Tel-Aviv and its daughters, and which according to the Partition Plan was supposed to remain an 'enclave' of sorts, has solved the problem for us. . . . In its malice and malignance it brought destruction upon itself" (Talmi 1957, 256).

Derived from the violent enmity between the Jewish and Palestinian nationalist movements, and epitomized by the menace of Jaffa over Tel-Aviv (inscribed in the Zionist collective memory through the deadly clashes of 1921, 1936, and 1948), this antagonistic view of Jaffa persisted in the Jewish image of the city well after it had begun to be under official Israeli rule. These anxious representations surfaced in times of crisis and were translated into a discourse of "nationalist Jaffa" which loomed large during the First and Second Intifadas.

Thus in 1989, the local *Ha'ir* newspaper published a paranoid article entitled "The PLO Occupied Jaffa without a Single Shot." Similarly, in 2001, soon after the outbreak of the Al-Aqsa Intifada, another of *Ha'ir*'s correspondents, in his weekly column, dubbed Jaffa "Little Tehran" due to the growing numbers of veiled women, thus lumping together Jaffa and Islamist or nationalist extremism.

Particularly pivotal in this context are specific landmarks in the urban space that came to be associated with the history of violence between Jaffa and Tel-Aviv. One such site is the Hassan Beik Mosque, once marking the northern borders of Jaffa and currently—after the razing of the Manshiyye neighborhood—remaining, as if out of place, in the midst of Tel-Aviv's high-rise hotels strip. In Jewish collective memory, the mosque still bears a notorious reputation for the Palestinian snipers who used its tall minaret during the hostilities of the 1930s and 1940s.

More than sixty years after the conquest of Jaffa and the exile of 95 percent of its Palestinian population, the antagonistic ambiance surrounding the Hassan Beik Mosque took a dramatic turn in the wake of the deadly suicide attack known as the "Dolphinarium attack" on June 1, 2001, which occurred in a popular nightclub located just across the street from the Hassan Beik Mosque.[5] The next day, a Friday, several hundred frantic demonstrators stoned the mosque and set fire to the cars in the parking lot that belonged to the few dozen Muslim Jaffans attending Friday prayer. Some of the besieged managed to flee south to Jaffa, while others were trapped in the mosque, absorbing the stones thrown at them by what had become an angry lynch mob. The police force did little to stop the escalating actions of rage, and most of the horseback policemen, unless personally injured by the stones, settled for containing the crowd running amok.

While in the middle of the crowd, I tried to learn from the demonstrators how they interpreted the events. The suicide bomber, I was told by several demonstrators carrying improvised signs calling for "Death to the Arabs" and "No Jobs for Arabs," departed his West Bank village on Wednesday, arrived in Jaffa where he spent the night, and on Thursday prayed the evening prayer at the now-under-attack Hassan Beik Mosque before detonating the belt of explosives he carried on him at the nightclub across the street. "This is why we should never have given the Arabs jobs,"

I was told time and again. "We should never buy at their stores—Jaffa should be embargoed." The demonstrators were thus making the metonymic link between (1) the suicide bomber, (2) the Hassan Beik Mosque, and (3) the entire Jaffa community. This alleged sequence of events formed a narrative triangle that was seen as the ultimate justification for attacking the mosque (complicit by its "hosting" the suicide bomber) in the first instance, and then for boycotting Jaffa's restaurants, bakeries, markets, and stores, all by and large dependent on Jewish buying power.[6]

Violence and extremism have thus long been readily attachable to the image of Jaffa, embodying the Arab "enemy within." However, this facet was often inseparable from a positive and romantic imagery of Jaffa's historical depth, both forming the dual imagination of the city. The most pronounced example of this dialectic pattern is the debate surrounding the renaming of the unified city in 1949–1950 and the identity dilemmas it brought to the surface for victorious Tel-Aviv.

Tel-Aviv Municipality's urban policies were poignantly qualified by Mark LeVine (2005) as a strategy of "erasure and re-inscription." However, notwithstanding its efforts toward ethnicizing and transforming space, the Zionist urban program was not bereft of contradictions and aporias. In the wake of the city's occupation, the main debate on the city's agenda concerned the name of the future unified municipal unit. The naming process was essentially an identity struggle between history and newness, between "distant past" and "recent past," and between the vision of "history-laden Jaffa" and its future as part of Tel-Aviv's modern metropolis. In October 1949, the government first suggested the name "Jaffa-Tel-Aviv," which was met with mixed feelings and public dispute. Alternative names suggested by politicians and journalists included "Tel-Aviv," "Jaffa," "Greater Jaffa," or "Tel-Aviv-Jaffa" (the name that was eventually selected)—each making a different symbolic and historical claim on the relations between the two cities and Jewish attachment to local history and land. This debate dominated the local public sphere until its resolution in August 1950. The reports of the official *Yedi'ot 'iryat Tel-Aviv* newspaper provide a glance into these stormy disputes. Quoting from the national *Ha'aretz* article entitled "Jaffa versus Tel-Aviv," one author remarks,

All the signs point to an upcoming fierce struggle in the state between two ideological blocks. However, the bone of contention will not be the changing cost of living or the freedom of private entrepreneurship, but rather a purely ideational topic—the unified name of Jaffa and Tel-Aviv. On the one hand stands the historical-Romantic school, headed by the prime minister [Ben-Gurion] himself. This school argues for the name Jaffa, one of the oldest names in the country, known in the world as a Biblical city and as the origin of the Jaffa Orange. However, Mayor Rokach is agitated by this idea and vehemently claims the right to the name Tel-Aviv, which the world has learned to relate to the Zionist project, especially lately. *The "historical" school claims that the name "Tel-Aviv" is artificial, an unsuccessful translation of Herzl's "Altneuland," whereas the "Zionist" school is afraid that Jaffa will conquer Tel-Aviv ideationally, after Tel-Aviv has conquered Jaffa militarily.* (*Yedi'ot 'iryat Tel-Aviv*, no. 5–6 [December 1949]: 75; italics added)

Tel-Avivan local patriotism deemed the government's resolution a national sacrilege. Notwithstanding the lead of right-wing Mayor Rokach, local opposition to the hyphened compromise, perceived as giving outrageous precedence to Jaffa, cut across ideological positions and party lines. Thus in an article in the socialist *'Al ha-Mishmar* entitled "Tel-Aviv and Only Tel-Aviv," the author exclaims,

Few are the actions of our government that so severely offended our local patriotism and our self-pride—as the hasty decision to change Tel-Aviv's name to "Jaffa-Tel-Aviv.". . . What is Tel-Aviv to us? Forty years ago, on a sand hill south of the *past-laden city of Jaffa*, a daughter-neighborhood was born, a new branch of an old tree. This branch soon grew and developed into a magnificent fully grown tree, a mother city in Israel [*'ir va-em*], that attracts and caters to a third of the total Jewish population in the country. . . . Attaching the name of Jaffa to the name Tel-Aviv is by no means a "restoration of past glory," for Jaffa has never spread as far as this area in which Tel-Aviv is currently situated. . . . We love our past in this country very much. But this love should not drive us mad [*le-ha'avir 'al da'atenu*] and enslave us to the distant past only, so as to completely blur our recent past and the present. "Tel-Aviv" is a grand Jewish epos. A glorious epos carved by the blood of the first generation to redemption [*ge'ula*]. There is no substitute for Tel-Aviv! (*'Al ha-Mishmar*, October 21, 1949; italics original)

Unlike the local municipality, the central government was clearly in favor of this reconciliation between Jaffa and Tel-Aviv (which was surely also motivated by foreign policy and diplomatic considerations). Once the annexation was completed, the minister of the interior celebrated the symbolic historical act in an article entitled "Jaffa's Annexation: Bond and Bridge between Past and Future":

> The merger of two cities—one 4,000 years old and the other 40 years old—into one big city, one of the greatest in the Mediterranean, is an appropriate fusion of old and new: Jaffa—longstanding in the country and new on the map of Jewish settlements, and Tel Aviv—the youngest city in the country and the oldest city in the new settlement [*Yishuv hadash*]. This is a symbol of the bond between the people and its country, a symbol of the renaissance enterprise, of our war for independence and our victory, and a symbol of the fulfillment of the dream of the ingathering of the exiles. (*Yedi'ot 'iryat Tel-Aviv*, no. 1–3 [1952]: 2)

While these symbolic disputes can be interpreted as resulting from the structural tension between the central government and the local municipality, further testimonies from local journalists and city politicians point to a broader discourse endorsing the recognition of Jaffa's legacy. Some publicists went even further, arguing for "Jaffa" alone as the unified city's official name. This argument was made in a *Ha'aretz* article entitled "The Return to Jaffa":

> The one and united great city should be named Jaffa and only Jaffa. And Tel-Aviv should be one of its suburbs up to the time when some other new city will be swallowed in turn by Greater Jaffa [*Yafo Rabati*] and will inherit Tel-Aviv's place in its newness and beauty. The people of Israel has returned to its old and normal historical path: this is the essence of Zionism's meaning, and this meaning should be symbolized in Zionism's geographical names. We are honored that our Tel-Aviv got not only to conquer Jaffa but also to expand and restore its past glory. (*Ha'aretz*, October 13, 1949)

For the proponents of giving precedence to the name of Jaffa, this was a symbolic means of reconciling the newness of Tel-Aviv with the historicity of Jaffa as part of Zionism's ongoing quest for its roots. The final decision to include Jaffa, but only secondarily, and to baptize the unified municipal entity as "Tel-Aviv-Jaffa," was a loose compromise between the adversarial positions—recognizing the supremacy of Tel-Aviv while extending a gesture to the "historical school" and to the central government. The narrative that eventually got the upper hand was articulated in the polemic section of *Yedi'ot Tel-Aviv*, and revealed the complex array of indecisions and dilemmas. Admitting that "we loved Tel-Aviv and hated Jaffa," this narrative nevertheless sees "Tel-Aviv-Jaffa" as the appropriate name for the new "merged" city:

> There were times that Jaffa was the "metropolis" and Tel-Aviv its suburb.
> Years have passed and Tel-Aviv caught up with Jaffa and even surpassed it. In
> the past twenty years the two cities came to be rivals and strangers to each
> other [zarot], so much so that in our independence war we stood at opposite
> sides of the Jewish-Arab front. Indeed, we loved Tel-Aviv and we hated Jaffa.
> Truly we knew that Jaffa's pedigree is prestigious and important . . . while
> Tel-Aviv was founded only in 1909. No cedars of Lebanon were unloaded in
> its port, but the iron bars, steel rods, and cement sacks were unloaded day
> and night for a generation—our generation—to build the walls of the third
> temple. Thus it is difficult for us to change the name of Tel-Aviv to Jaffa-Tel-
> Aviv. It is hard, as if we were to change the name of our country from "Israel"
> to the ancient historical name—"Canaan." And if we are to give another
> name to the two "merged" [memuzagot] cities, let it be "Tel-Aviv-Jaffa," and
> not vice versa. (*Yedi'ot Tel-Aviv,* no. 5–6 [December 1949]: 76)

In sum, Jaffa's violence which is associated with its *recent* past and
Jaffa's deep historicity which is associated with its *distant* past form the
two valences of the city's ambivalence. Because of this irreconcilable
tension, both aspects of this image have fueled a century-long dialectical conflict. Adding to the representational facet is the lived experience
of actual people who were located in the newly Judaized city. Thus while
Zionist institutions treated the annexation and control of Palestinian
urban space as a sign of historical justice, ordinary Jews who had maintained business and social ties with Palestinians and other Arabs in the
region prior to 1948 were more ambivalent. Some were even perplexed by
the sudden transformation of a familiar town into a space they now felt
alienated from. Reflecting upon the incongruities associated with this
rapid transformation, in 1949 one observer went as far as describing the
"new-old" city as a "sealed book" and as "nothing but the legacy of Arab
Jaffa prior to May 1948."[7]

FOLKLORIC ORIENTALISM: CULTURAL ROMANTICISM, EXOTIC ETHNICITY, AND CLASS STIGMA

Like Gamzu's aforementioned "This is Jaffa," Haim Heffer's "There's No
Place like Jaffa at Night" ("There's no place like Jaffa at night / No other

place like Jaffa in the world / When the chicks pass by / With bloody colored lips") has become a local anthem. Joining these two songs in the Jaffa cultural pantheon are Yigal Mossinzohn's play *Kazablan* (1954) and Menahem Talmi's *Sights and Knights of Jaffa* (1979). The latter two cultural products have played a central role in representing and reproducing the city's post-1948 image, in bringing it to the public's awareness, and in stereotyping it. Dominating the Orientalist gaze of Jaffa from the 1950s to the 1970s, *Kazablan* and *Sights and Knights of Jaffa* encapsulate the depiction of the city as a battlefield of ethnic strife, working-class culture, crime, and immigration. From the 1980s onward, a neo-Orientalist image of Jaffa crystallized—one that merges its exotic and stigmatized vision with a multicultural view of the "New-Old Jaffa."

A Moroccan Gangster in an Immigrant Town: *Kazablan*

> *Kazablan* is without a doubt the most popular musical to become one of the most successful movies in the Israeli cinema. One thousand dancers, actresses and singers take us back to Jaffa in the '60s when all the newcomers from different cultures lived together. Yosef Siman-Tov is better known as "Kazablan." He was born in Morocco and came to Israel as a young child. Now in his twenties he is bitter and desperate. He is the leader of a gang that terrorizes the citizens of Jaffa. Yosef is in love with Rachel, a beautiful and gentle daughter of Polish parents who would never agree to any relationship between their daughter and Yosef. Janosh, the owner of the shoe store, is also in love with Rachel. He decides to frame Yosef for a horrible crime that will ruin his chances with Rachel. How will Kazablan prove his innocence, and will he and Rachel be able to fulfill their love? (Mossinzohn [1954] 1989)

This ad copy for the movie version of *Kazablan* puts forth an antagonistic image of Jaffa, but one that still leaves room for poetic justice and potential synthesis—the harmonic happy ending and intermarriage between the delinquent Moroccan war veteran and the Ashkenazi daughter of a normative middle-class family. However, this multicultural image of Jaffa as an optimistic microcosm of Israeli immigrant society conveyed in the movie is rendered problematic when compared to Mossinzohn's original play. Like its 1973 cinematic adaptation, the original 1954 play features Kazablan, a local hero of the War of Independence who has returned from the front only to find his former brothers in arms already comfortably settled down and avoiding his company. In the play, far more realistically and pessimistically, it is Josh, Kazablan's old military commander, a well-to-do Ashkenazi, who wins Rachel's heart. This dismal scenario was altered and beautified in the movie in order to portray a collective wishful thinking celebrating the stitching together of the social body's ethnic and class wounds. Symbolically, while the movie ends with Kazablan uncovering Yanosh's attempted incrimination and with the neighborhood paying respect to Kazablan (chosen as the hero of the day to be the godfather of a newlywed couple in a marriage scene, suggesting his future union with Rachel),[8] the play ends with the police besieging his house and with his gloomy realization that it is not him that Rachel has chosen but Josh, his well-positioned former commander. In the last scene of the play Kazablan rejects Josh's attempts at appeasement and retires angrily to his room, voicing his deep frustration and despair:

> I can only think how you, you, you suspected me, only me, and played on my nerves until I almost burst like a balloon. . . . I can only think how nice and sweet you were when you put my head under the water time and again, until I almost choked, and then you told me you're saving me from the police. But you don't believe in me at all. That's it. A *swartze-beheime*. A *swartze-moroccan* [Yiddish for "a black beast, a black Moroccan"] . . . why would you believe me? Nice, ah? You spit in my face and you say it's only rain. No, my friend, it's not rain. (Mossinzohn [1954] 1989, 80–81)

On Folklore and Humor in the "Big Territory": Sights and Knights of Jaffa

The second constitutive Orientalist representation of Jaffa is Menahem Talmi's 1979 story series *Sights and Knights of Jaffa*. Like *Kazablan,* this three-volume collection of folk tales is set in Jaffa's "Big Territory" (*Ha-Shetah ha-Gadol*). Previously part of the Palestinian Old City, the Big Territory turned in the 1950s into a quarter of prostitution and crime, which, in the book, is the home for a colorful gang of Moroccan, Greek, Turkish, and Rumanian petty-criminal-yet-friendly characters. Narrated in colloquial Hebrew, and spiced up throughout with Ladino and

Arabic phrases, it is the tale of the adventures and stratagems of "*Jama'at Yafo*"—Hebrew/Arabic Creole for the "Jaffa Gang," or "Buddies." Sitting on Jamily's Kiosk sidewalk, eating to their hearts' delight fried red mullet at 'Abed's restaurant, drinking beer till they pass out at the Greek's café, or alternatively sipping coffee spiced with Kumak at the Turk's place, the Jama'a buddies tell Talmi their stories, which he records during their "interim pauses between court and jail" (Talmi 1979, 7). Focused on the charismatic character of Salomon and his friends (Sasson, Mushon, Sami, Hatuka, and others), these stories are narratives of macho Mediterranean masculinity, full of lionization and boasting, hedonistic Gargantuan gluttony, and constant struggles over honor and status vis-à-vis the police, significant female others, Tel-Avivans, and other competing cities, but mainly within their peer group of the Jaffa men. Although the story is told from the specific perspective of Jaffa's men, Talmi also implicitly conveys the broader image of the city and its local identity.

Embedded in these stories, the image of the city is best illustrated in the tale of the Jama'a's failed attempts to make a pilgrimage to Jerusalem and to the Wailing Wall. The story, entitled "Really, We Must Travel for Once to the Wailing Wall," tells of the group's sincere desire to visit the holy place, a desire matched only by their hedonistic practices and literally crooked ways, which lead them not to Jerusalem but through a merry sequence of feasting, womanizing, festivities, skirmishes, and prison. Metaphorically, this plot can be read as a story of the categorical incompatibility between the "big place" of the holy city—dignified, imposing, and inaccessible—and the "small place" of the Mediterranean city—frivolous, profane, and inviting.[9] The story starts with Salomon's exclamation,

> *Wallah* [*sic*], really it's a shame. We've never been to the Wailing Wall. Every week we say next week, but it never works out. It's only an hour's drive from Jaffa, but you won't believe what could happen to you in an hour! And in the end, when you finally get near the Wailing Wall, bad luck [*nahs*, in Arabic] interferes and blocks the way. Afterward we sit at the Greek's café, drink, smoke, and say, "Really, it's a shame, we must once travel to the Wailing Wall. OK [*tayeb*, in Arabic], on Sunday, come what may, we travel to the Wailing Wall. Agreed? Word of honor!"

On Sunday morning, we get into Joseph's car and we drive. As we approach Beit-Dagan curve, Ben-Shoshan says, "Since we're here, why not pay Shlomo Aqila a visit, say hi and welcome him back after the five years he spent in Frankfurt's prison. How long would it take? Five minutes? Ten at the most." (Talmi 1979, 114)

The Jama'a wind up pleasantly spending many more hours at Aqila's house, exchanging stories, drinking *'arrak,* eating *burekas* (Turkish filled pastry), feasting on barbecued meat, and watching pornographic movies. At one o'clock in the morning, they finally manage to depart and return to Jaffa. Taking a final drink at the Greek's café in the Big Territory in Jaffa, Joseph says, "Wallah, it's been a long time since we last had such a fun day [*yom sababa,* again in Hebrew/Arabic]."

"That's true," replies Prosper, "but really it's a shame that still we haven't gotten to go to the Wailing Wall."

"Really it's a shame," everyone agrees.

"Tomorrow morning we leave," says Prosper.

"One hundred percent," everyone agrees.

"Nine o'clock sharp. Not one minute later," says Prosper.

"One hundred percent," everyone says. "And no messing around on the way, no Aqila and no nothing. Straight to Jerusalem. We're on? We're on!" Indeed, they get up and leave at nine o'clock the next day, but, of course, they go through different amusing adventures and never complete the ostensibly simple task of traversing the short geographical distance (but much wider cultural gap) between Jaffa and Jerusalem. Ten pages later, and after several more attempts to reach Jerusalem, the story finally closes with a vague, indefinite yet sincere collective promise to get to Jerusalem "someday."

Talmi's Orientalism is not merely folkloristic and humoristic; beyond striking a chord in Israeli Orientalist imagination, his naively bemused folk tales and somewhat scornful narrative were closely twinned with a modernistic social worldview that was made public in his enthusiastic and supportive journalistic coverage of the demolition of the very space that provided him with his bestseller. Following the construction of the "Artists' Colony" in the Old City in the 1960s, Menahem Talmi, then a senior figure at a major daily newspaper (*Ma'ariv*), celebrated the "destructive creation" (Harvey 1991) that gave birth to the renovated "Pearl of Jaffa":[10]

> Over Old Jaffa's hill, sensations of antiquity mix with historical light-whispers, and both are saturated in the cool rock paving-stones, chanting the rustle in the southwestern wind that brings the beach odors of Jonah the Prophet. Old Jaffa's landscape of sea and stone once saw the waving flags of Ramses II and Solomon the Temple-Builder. Today artists sell here oil paintings, copper-hammered ornaments, artworks created by tumultuous hearts and quick fingers. Yesterday, this was Jaffa's old, rejected "Big Territory," a pile of ruins and dunghill, the dwelling place of delinquent fringe people and the wrathful site of pork meat merchants [i.e., the Rumanian Jews] and blinding smoke. Today—it is a charming and joyful island, whose anchors are embedded in the depth of authenticity. (*Ma'ariv*, May 5, 1967)

Stemming from his report on the demolition of the Big Territory and its "delinquent fringe people," Talmi's politics—as Orientalist as it is modernist—echoes the municipality's planning ideology, viewing the Big Territory's dwellers and landscape as decadent and obsolete (indeed, "a pile of ruins and dunghill"). In the Jaffa of the 1960s, this was the dominant narrative and only a few observers offered a different vision and interpretation. Apart from local activists, it was not until the 1990s that a more critical scholarly narrative suggested an alternative analysis of the cultural politics in terms of a subculture of resistance: "Some of the residents of former Arab areas endeavored to establish local communities, an initial step toward autonomous urban communities. National and local governments and sectarian institutions suppressed these attempts, which jeopardized their dominance in former Arab areas. Unable to be integrated into Israeli society on their own terms, residents of these neighborhoods turned to strategies of resistance defined officially as illegitimate—violence and crime, and rituals of resistance. These included latent symbolic forms including various styles of dress and patterns of verbal and non-verbal behavior, implying an attitude of resistance to those in power" (Golan 1999, 163).

Jaffan Jews have been stigmatized and kept at arm's length by the Tel-Avivan "North Side" since the establishment of the Jewish settlement in the city. Antinormative behavior, rather than a manifestation of a "delinquent fringe mentality," was usually a nihilistic outcome of alienating state policies and patronizing municipal institutions. Metonymically related to Jaffa, cultural objects such as the Big Territory fed the Israeli Orientalist imagination for thirty years, only to be replaced during Tel-Aviv's current neoliberal phase by two neo-Orientalist trends construct-ing it as "Miserable Jaffa" and "New-Old Jaffa," respectively.

ORIENTALIST REALISM: "MISERABLE JAFFA"

In a recent editorial in a local magazine, *Zman Tel-Aviv*'s special issue on Jaffa entitled "Our Lame Sister" (*Ahotenu ha-Tzola'at*), the author described Jaffa as the underdog antithesis of wealthy and satiated Tel-Aviv. In a typical rendering of what I term "Orientalist realism," this title reflects a longstanding representation of Jaffa as a squalid and straggling city, complemented by a neoliberal moralistic and patronizing attitude. However distinct from previous Jewish depictions of Jaffa as "primitive" and "delinquent" (from the founding of Tel-Aviv through the 1970s), this new approach mixes liberal pity with class condescension and en-genders—good intentions aside—a polarized and external depiction of the city. Thus, in a guide designated for Jewish tourists issued by the "American-Israeli Cooperative Enterprise" and offering a "virtual Israel experience," a long article entitled "Tel Aviv: A Tale of Two Cities" in-vokes a realistic mode to number the differential inequalities between Tel-Aviv and Jaffa. Citing the official *Israel Yearbook & Almanac,* this imagined guided tour mobilizes the language of empirical accuracy to construct Tel-Aviv as a dual city. While the North represents a haven of liberal normalcy, the Jewish South Side ("politically right-wing and traditionally religious") and Arab Jaffa assume the status of a social prob-lem. A space inhabited by unassimilated second-rate citizens, the urban south remains the destitute asylum of Zionism's longstanding Oriental Others:

> Both images of Tel Aviv—its own and that held by the rest of Israel—ignore fully half of the city. By many indices, Tel Aviv really is two cities. The north and center correspond to the myth, while south Tel Aviv is more like a devel-opment town out in the hinterland.
>
> The north is predominantly Ashkenazi, middle class, politically liberal, and secular. . . .

> South Tel Aviv is the demographic antithesis of the north. It is dominated by poor and working class Mizrahim ... politically right-wing and tradition-ally religious....
>
> Beyond the southside, but really in a class by itself within Tel Aviv, is Jaffa. Located along the coast immediately south of Tel Aviv proper, Jaffa has some 60,000 residents, about a third of them Arabs. It is the only place in Tel Aviv where Arabs live, except for a sprinkling here and there. In parts of the area, especially in the Ajami quarter, Arabs and Jews live next to each other, and for this reason Jaffa has gained the reputation as an example of coexistence. But again, reality is somewhat different from the image.[11]

Factual sociological profiling articulated in terms of class and ethnicity is instrumental for establishing the "authority" of this realist mode of representation. Inseparable moreover from this "objective" narrative is a bleeding-heart juxtaposition of two human conditions. Excavating Jaffa, the "report" strategically sensationalizes elite luxury juxtaposed with the wretched predicament of "the single ugliest, most horrific place to live in Israel":

> To foreigners and out-of-towners, Jaffa is the picturesque, exotic, old Middle East with a heavy dash of artiness.... Dank, gray, seedy, irresistible....
>
> Away from the eyes of sightseers, the most beautiful homes in Israel have been and are still being built in Jaffa. The style can be called "Neo-Medi-terranean"—in sandstone, marble, and glass, dominated by arches, these buildings combine ancient and modern, and are a brilliant update of the old Jaffa style. Condominiums start in the range of $1 million and go all the way above $3 million. Sea view included.
>
> No more than a mile away from this luxury, where the southern tip of Jaffa abuts on neighboring Bat Yam, is the single ugliest, most horrific place to live in Israel. This is Pardes Daka, a five-acre former citrus grove owned by the Daka clan and still home to some 350 of its members. The menfolk deal drugs right out in the open. For police it's a no-go zone. Sanitation is abys-mal; the children suffer an unusually high rate of viral diseases.... Trash is everywhere.... Boys ride by on donkeys. Scores of used, undoubtedly stolen, cars are up on blocks, being disassembled for spare parts. Half the children don't go to school.
>
> Such is the harsher side of coexistence in Jaffa.[12]

This condensed narrative encapsulates the elements of "Realist Orientalism." Without understating or beautifying the truly sorry condition of the Daka extended family living long prior to the establishment of the state in its "Daka Orchard" (*Pardes Daka* in Hebrew; *Biyarat Dakke* in Arabic), the narrative outcome of such "realist" discourse is the polarized Othering of Jaffa and the flattening of its complexities. Reducing what is in reality a complex living space of a family dwelling in one of the only two orange groves left in Jaffa, such depiction conveys no humane and graspable dimension to life in underclass Arab Jaffa, nor does it offer any historical perspective on it. Missing from this description is the municipality's longstanding policy of neglecting the Daka Orchard as well as the city's responsibility for supplying basic services to its inhabitants. Equally important is the potential real estate value of the place located in the heart of the metropolis and the municipality's aggressive plan for urban renewal—an option which will undoubtedly result in the displacement of some of the poor families living on the premises. This so-called "realist" portrayal of Jaffa seems *prima facie* fair and balanced; however, it results in a sensational image of the city that obfuscates its human and social complexity. Distancing rather than informing, this discourse reifies a flat figure of ultimate class and cultural otherness. "Realist Orientalism" shares classical Orientalism's tendency to radicalize the subordinate object but does so from a moralistic stance of liberal sympathy.

NEO-ORIENTALIST CONSTRUCTIONS: "JAFFA, BELLE OF THE SEAS"

Neo-Orientalism, or the globalized version of exoticizing Orientalism in high modernity (Chaouachi 2002),[13] is Jaffa's third mode of Orientalist representation. Evolving hand in hand with the city's gentrification in the 1980s, the main neo-Orientalist image of Jaffa revolves around the key figure of "Jaffa, Belle of the Seas (*Yafo Yafat Yamim*), referring back to Nobel Prize laureate S. Y. Agnon's depiction of the city in *Only Yesterday:* "Jaffa, belle of the seas, ancient city Japheth, son of Noah, built it and gave it his name. But of all the beauty of Japheth, what remains is that which human beings couldn't remove from it, and the city changes with the character of its inhabitants. . . . Jaffa, belle of the seas: the waves of the Great Sea kiss her shores, a blue sky is her daily cover, and she brims with every kind of people, Jews and Ishmaelites and

Christians, busy at trade and labor, at shipping and brokering" (Agnon [1945] 2000, 168).

Agnon's secular, poetic view of Jaffa was adopted willingly in the 1980s by the new middle-class liberal gentrifiers who founded the community association Jaffa, Belle of the Seas, also known as Jaffans for Jaffa (see chapter 1). In line with its naturalistic connotation, Agnon's metaphor of a beautiful woman peacefully dwelling on the seashore was in harmony with the gentrifiers' environmentalist pro-urban agenda and civilizing mission aspiring to restore law, order, and cleanliness in the "New-Old Jaffa." During the real estate boom of the 1990s Jaffa was portrayed as "Little Paris":

> Among the alleys and the walls, with an ambiance of port and pirates and a sweet and salty odor, Jaffa entertains a very lively theater scene: How did it happen that Jaffa became Little Paris? What is not provided by ideology is complemented by real estate prices. But the result is impressive at any rate: in the past two years, Jaffa became a remarkable center for theaters. In the past few years different theater groups have *invaded* there: the Gesher theaters, Notzar company, the Klippa theater, the theater club, Mayumana House, the Arab-Jewish theater, and the old Hassimta theater is still alive is well. Thus behind the curtain of T.A. there are things happening on stage, which makes Jaffa a much more vibrant scene than the tiny apple. ("Eikh Hafkha Yafo le-Paris ha-Ktana?" [How did Jaffa become Little Paris?], *Zman Tel-Aviv*, August 31, 2001)

Neo-Orientalist depictions of Jaffa include two other representations, one marketing the city as a multicultural and gastronomical center, and the other constructing it as a site of potential reconciliation. Thus a famous TV cooking show, *Shum pilpel ve-shemen zait* (Garlic, pepper, and olive oil), shot in a gentrified house in 'Ajami overlooking the sea, celebrates the rich and multi-ethnic Israeli cuisine associated with Jaffa's Mediterranean-ness.[14] The second representation is a more contested yet prevalent image of Jaffa as a city of coexistence. Thus, in 2001, Eyal Erlich, an Israeli peace activist and businessman, claimed that his idea of the *Hudna* (truce) with the Palestinians came to him while he was smoking a hookah in Jaffa, in a coffee house on 60th Street he calls the "Peace Hut." Such optimistic images attracted to the city communes of hippies returned from trips to India as well as middle-class and middle-aged liberal leftists, hoping to unite Jews and Arabs for the sake of a better political future. Complementing the bleak and flattening "realist-Orientalist" vision of Jaffa, such a neo-Orientalist mode of representation tends to portray Jaffa with a happy face and invoke the qualities of Mediterranean charm, coexistence, and romantic multiculturalism.

THE UNINTENDED CONSEQUENCES

OF OCTOBER 2000: YAFA CAFÉ

The first decade of the twenty-first century saw several key events in ethnically mixed towns. In tandem with the outbreak of the Al-Aqsa Intifada, the October 2000 events marked an important change in the history of the Palestinian minority in Israel. In Jaffa, Haifa, Ramle, Lydda, and Acre, these outbreaks resulted in no fatal casualties but they made visible the widening gaps between these cities' Jewish and Arab residents and brought to public attention the brutal intervention of state policing agencies (Rabinowitz and Abu-Baker 2005).

These acts of violence and signs of Palestinian national mobilization had two opposing effects, which express the ambivalent and dialectic nature of urban processes in Jaffa. The first and immediate effect was the association in pubic opinion of Jaffa and other ethnically mixed towns with political violence, and thus overnight Jaffa lost its "charm" for many gentrifiers (and potential ones). This upheaval resulted in the immediate (yet temporary) cessation of the previously booming market for real estate. Secondly, however, the very marking of Jaffa as a space of violent contestation and political mobilization further attracted to the city various groups which had already expressed interest in Jewish-Arab cooperation through actual residence in the city. Finally, the tumultuous October 2000 events also attracted to the Jaffa scene political Palestinian-Israeli groups directly engaged with the conflict, such as Re'ut-Sadaqa (Friendship), Ta'ayush (Jewish-Arab Partnership), Anarchists against the Wall, and the Zochrot (Remembering) Association.[15] While these diverse populations followed different developmental paths and organizational itineraries, consequently promoting diverging agendas, they all share a common fascination with the potential for meaning and purpose the contested city has to offer, either through political activism or individual self-searching.

Clearly, the October Events did not bring gentrification in Jaffa to a complete halt, but they did have the paradoxical effect of triggering a political debate and activism, which sought to address Palestinian exclusion and collective memory in a public and direct way. One of the local effects in Jaffa was the joint business venture which resulted in the founding of the Yafa Café.

The Yafa Café is the first bookstore in Jaffa since 1948 to systematically specialize in books in Arabic. Until 2009, the shop was jointly owned by Dina Lee, a Jewish recent newcomer to Jaffa, and Michel al-Raheb, a Palestinian resident of Ramle (due to Dina's untimely death, currently Michel is the sole owner). Heralded by the owners, journalists, and customers as one of the few places of "real coexistence," the café functions as an intellectual meeting place for Jewish/Arab artists and local residents. It hosts readings on Palestinian literature, political discussions, Arabic courses, and musical events. Proposing a real binational alternative to conservative political consensus in Israeli society, the founders symbolically chose the Arabic name of the city (Yafa), rather than the Hebrew name (Yafo) or the more neutral English one (Jaffa).

For the Yafa Café owners, the place has fulfilled a historic role in reurbanizing Jaffa and in restoring the city as an Arab cultural center. In an interview with *Ha'aretz* Dina Lee stressed that the shop is of great importance to the local Jaffa culture: "I can't say that we have opened the McDonald's of Jaffa and now all the Palestinians who were hungry for books are flocking here en masse. But the place is definitely gradually becoming a social center, a center for information about the city, a center of creativity."[16]

In the café the first meeting was held, for example, between political prisoner Tali Fahima (kept under administrative detention by the Israeli Security Service for collaborating with Zakariyah Zbeidi in the Jenin refugee camp) and a group of left-wing activists who coordinated some of her legal battle. Moreover, Yafa Café was the only place in Jaffa to commemorate the fifth anniversary of the Al-Aqsa Intifada and the October Events and is one of the few institutions that consistently mark May 15 as "Nakba Day." Featuring artists such as rapper Tamer Naffar and Fatima Abu-Nil, the Nakba Day event brings together historians and local residents who join to reflect on the history of the city and the land.

Lee, however, notes that she does not like the term "coexistence," and that what is happening in Yafa Café to her delight is not coexistence—in the self-congratulatory sense of the word—but rather a "local experience growing on a street corner."

Among Yafa Café's many activities, three programs stand out as having revisited and challenged the hegemonic Zionist and Orientalist memory and image of Jaffa. One is a group of activists called Yafa Action, or the Jaffa Municipality, which sought to promote social change in the city. Composed of twenty Jewish activists and Palestinian residents, this group studied the history and sociology of the city as it planned its future operational agenda. As one of the main figures in the group explained to me during one of the meetings, "Unlike other groups I've worked with, this one started very quietly. We didn't have grand plans to bring revolution and to overturn the government. But we gradually realized that we can find a shared vision of the city." Based in Yafa Café, the group met weekly to discuss different urban issues or went out to meet various figures and actors in Jaffa such as real estate agents or community leaders.

The second program associated with Yafa Café is entitled "From Yafa to Yafo: Back to 1948." It proposes weekly excursions throughout the city and invites participants to learn about "the rise and fall of Arab Jaffa, and why we know almost nothing about it." Led by a Jewish city planner, Youval Tamari, a Zochrot activist, these tours voice a critical narrative of declining urbanism, disinvestment, and Judaization, which proposes an alternative image of the city as a victim of Zionist expansionism. While Palestinian associations such as the Rabita (the Association for the Jaffa Arabs) have previously organized similar tours in Jaffa, this initiative is unique in that it features a Jewish tour guide who revisits local urban history and proposes a binational future for the city.

The third counterhegemonic site of action is an independent project entitled "Autobiography of a City." Initiated by the Ayyam Association for the purpose of "dialogue and recognition,"[17] the project is led by artists Sami Bukhari and Eyal Danon, who are also active members in the Yafa Action group. Operating through educational work with children, visual arts, and a website which documents the life stories of elderly Palestinians in Jaffa, the project focuses on collective memory as a main site of political action:[18] "The 'Autobiography of a City'. . . is committed to promoting a public multicultural discussion with which to expose, document, and raise awareness of the untold story of different national, ethnic, religious, and gender groups within Israel as part of a future process of reconciliation and healing. The project is an attempt to examine the ways in which urban communal memory and consciousness are being shaped, via the use of artistic and documentary tools and through the direct and wide involvement of community members."

Like the Yafa Café itself as well as other political initiatives in Jaffa, the project started in the wake of the October 2000 events as a reaction to the failed attempts at liberal "coexistence" and the deep sense of alienation and distrust between Jews and Arabs in Israel. By voicing and empowering the Palestinian collective memory of the city the project hopes to challenge the official Zionist narrative: "The complexity of memory and narrative and the way these are constituted are one of the major areas of interest of 'Autobiography of a City.' This led us to start a series of video interviews with Palestinian residents of Jaffa, as a direct reaction to the 'October Events.' The aim of these interviews was to enable Palestinians to tell the story of Palestinian Jaffa, the pre-'48 Jaffa, from their own perspective and memories, thus creating new room for the city's Palestinian history."

The focus on the intricacies of narrative and the politics of heritage explicitly seeks to give pride of place to Palestinian voices. Providing funding and visibility to radical artists, Autobiography of a City has promoted such projects as "Hassan Beck at the Corner of Abu Lughod," by artist Ronen Idelman, which consisted of painting in white calx the imagined layout, blocks, and houses in the now-demolished Palestinian neighborhood that had extended between Jaffa and Tel-Aviv. Restoring fictive Palestinian street names, politically engaged artists proclaimed that "the ghost of Manshiyya awakes," as a means to protest its erasure and imagine its resurrection.

Palestinian artists, however, also use these opportunities to introduce sophisticated ruptures and poetic interventions that undermine not only the Orientalism of the "Zionist story" but also any essentialist nationalist narrative as such. Thus in the project "Bus Tour" (by Jaffan filmmaker Scandar Copti and video artist Yochai Avrahami), Copti led organized excursions which presented the tourists with an alternative history of Jaffa and its landmarks. The fictitious stories Copti improvised bear but a loose connection to the actual historical events of the city. To his surprise, he confessed, the tour's Jewish participants, unequipped with the required knowledge or political authority to refute his "testimony," were inclined, by and large, to "believe" him.[19]

Inside the bus, a video was projected featuring Copti fabricating a doll out of rags found on the local dunghill overlooking the sea. He gives it a name, Sun, takes it on a tour through Jaffa, and addresses it as his son. The video proceeds to show Sun and Copti in a provisional olive orchard of ten trees in 'Ajami (*hursha zmanit* in Hebrew).[20] Planted by the municipality over the ruins of a demolished house in order to prevent "illegal construction," the orchard is located across the street from the imposing Peres Peace House—contested by local Palestinians as one of the symbols of Jewish creeping gentrification.[21] Copti attempts to educate his son and strengthen his attachment to the land. "Come," he tells Sun, "feel the power of the place. Do you smell the wonderful fragrance of olive trees?" The scene becomes an ironic play on the trope of Palestinian autochthony (through its key symbol, the rootedness of the olive tree) mixed with urban debris: "This is very special land here; you have to learn the trade if you are to take my place when I die. You need to take care of the land." Collecting shreds of stones and bricks, residue from the ruins of the old Palestinian house, Copti instructs his son to identify different kinds of materials: "This is called cement. You have to use it as fertilizer and only then the trees can flourish. Come, my son, let's rest under the shadow of the tree. Slowly.... We'll drink some good Arabic coffee from the market." Pointing to the monumental Peres Peace House, he says, "See this building—it's made of the same blessed cement we use as fertilizer. This is the Peres House, and these olive trees symbolize peace, hence the Peres Peace House. Very touching, isn't it? I'm also moved.... When I leave this world you should make peace with Peres, and at night take some of his cement to fertilize our land."[22] Turning to the other side, now facing the neighboring rundown Palestinian housing projects, also known in jargon as the *Safari* for their notorious poverty and crime, he concludes, "One day, Sun, this all will not be yours. When I leave this world you will have nothing, except for the Peres Peace House, the land, and the olives, of course."

Full of bitter irony, this unique video is part of a larger body of work which uses similar strategies of cynical inversion and representational play. Following the success of his 2002 short film "Al-Haqiqa" (The truth), Copti's 2009 Oscar-nominated feature presentation, *Ajami*, introduces seven intersecting Jaffan stories that culminate in a common ending. The protagonist, Copti insists in an interview, "might as well be the bad guy":

> We proceed until the spectators can't tell anymore between good and bad and then they understand that reality is all about perspective. Here we have a story about Jaffa, a spit away from Tel-Aviv yet a world apart, which no one knows, despite it being so close. The story is of different identities at play among Arabs and different perspectives on life in Jaffa. . . . It's a complicated place, hard to understand. I myself cannot figure out all the differences and the alienation between people, although they ostensibly belong to the same thing, the same location. Jaffa is called *Umm al-gharib,* the "Mother of the Stranger," and people are indeed strangers to each other. Almost nothing brings them together.[23]

More than any artist working in Jaffa, Copti has made semiotic indeterminacy and urban ambivalence his creative trademark. Targeting his audience's political confusion and historical ignorance vis-à-vis the image of the city, in "Bus Tour" he juggles nationalist mythologies and reconstructs an imagined world which is truly postnationalist. Ridiculing Jewish Orientalist formulae ("good Arabic coffee from the market"), he also diffuses, from the vantage point of the disillusioned urbanite surrounded by cement, the aura of the Palestinian peasant "as national signifier" (Swedenburg 1990). Finally, he engages the Peres Peace House, which stands imposingly as a gated community, only to conclude with a bitter derisive remark about the unruly Arab "Safari."

Making virtue out of reality, as it were, Copti preaches a rashomon of shifting positions ("reality is all about perspective"). Against the metonymic violent expansion of Zionist ideologies and institutional arrogance, but also contrary to notions of Palestinian local patriotism and communal solidarity, he posits the "perspective" of strangeness and alienation. Contrasting history and fiction, olives and cement, these representations are instantiations of what James Fernandez (1991) calls the "argument of images," namely, the subtle play of metaphor, metonymy, and irony in figurative battles over historical justice and entitlement to place. In this case, the metaphor of the olive and the cement has structured the Palestinian and Israeli discourses of rootedness and modernization, respectively. Such dialogic processes, both within and between adversarial narratives, expose the cultural instability of the image of the city. Copti's intervention and the collective work of Autobiography of a City at large result in the denaturalization of Zionism's key symbols and subversively disrupt respective national mythologies.

BEYOND ORIENTALISM? CULTURAL INDETERMINACY AND THE PARADOXES OF ZIONIST REPRESENTATIONS

Does the current political and cultural moment in Jaffa enable an opening of the Pandora's box of exclusionary Zionist collective memory? Does Yafa Café and its binational agenda represent merely an anomaly in the political landscape of the city, or is it the beginning of a true post-Orientalist phase? As we have seen, the debate over the identity of the mixed city is far from being resolved.

In this chapter I have examined the persistent political problem and representational ambivalence of Jaffa in the Jewish-Israeli imagination, which enable new forms of binational agency and productive hybridity. Manifesting an elusive quality of cultural and political "strangeness," Jaffa's image consists of negative and positive themes that have remained in constant tension since 1948. Confronted with and reproducing Jaffa's double image—as either a nationalist, Islamist, and violent town, and hence a threat to the Zionist political project, or conversely as an authentic, deeply historical, and multicultural site of encounter and political action—different representational strategies have been deployed over the years by different actors who replay these themes without ever being able to reconcile them.

The ongoing debate over the symbolic status of the "annexed," "unified," "mixed," or "shared" city reflects a perception of Jaffa as symbolically indispensable to the definition of Israeli cultural identity in Tel-Aviv and beyond. The decision to name the postwar city "Tel-Aviv-Jaffa," rather than "Jaffa," "Greater Jaffa," "Tel-Aviv," or "Jaffa-Tel-Aviv," represented a compromise that attempted to come to terms with Tel-Aviv's self-image as an ultramodern, history-less "white city." Notwithstanding this symbolic concession, the restraining hyphen that chains Jaffa to Tel Aviv ultimately retains the latter as the master of the mistress (Rotbard 2005). This ambivalence still resonates in recurrent calls from Jaffans, both Jewish and Arab, to separate the city from Tel-Aviv and to institute an autonomous municipal unit which is loyal to its local history and culture.[24]

The analysis thus far suggests that Jaffa poses to the Jewish-Zionist imagination what Zygmunt Bauman (1993) calls a "hermeneutic problem." For Jews, Jaffa is both a source of identity (in the distant past) and a symbol of alterity and enmity (in the recent past), an object of desire and fear alike. Being both a space of identification and a space of negation (LeVine 2005), the image of Jaffa remains split and unstable. An obvious analysis of such bifurcated representation would be a literal interpretation through the lens of Said's *Orientalism* (1979). Such analysis, however, runs the risk of explaining ambivalence away as a trans-historical discourse of cultural domination and colonial reification. Following the lead of postcolonial and postmodern authors (Bhabha 1994; Clifford 1988; Derrida 1996), I have reframed Orientalist discourses as historically situated cultural modalities of urban alterity as well as a critical mode of scholarly analysis. This relational geography of otherness, I have argued, points to a deeper level of *indeterminacy*, stubborn and recurrent, that reflects Zionism's internal contradictions as both a colonial and a nationalist project—driven by a desire for territorial control and historical rootedness alike (Bardenstein 1998). Thus, Zionism's self-image as both autochthonous (in the distant past) and settler (in the recent past) is projected onto Jaffa's image as the site of an unresolved dialectic between historicity and violence.

Beyond Orientalism's initial dichotomies, however, recent developments in Jaffa point to new sites of political and cultural agency. Opening up an unprecedented space for Jewish-Arab collaboration, these "acts of citizenship" (Isin and Nielsen 2008) radically challenge hegemonic Zionist and Orientalist imaginings of the city.[25] Through such initiatives as Autobiography of a City and Yafa Café, joint Palestinian-Israeli projects politicize the persistent and indelible *trace* of Palestinian urban existence and collective memory, thereby enabling a shared vision for a binational future of "dialogue and recognition." While obviously unable to stand up to state-led attempts to Judaize the city, or to the market forces of gentrification, these grassroots initiatives nevertheless produce powerful discourses of resistance and a symbolic re-Palestinization of the city from below.

THREE

The "Mother of the Stranger"

Palestinian Presence and the
Ambivalence of Sumud

Yafa! My tears have dried up.
I weep for you with stricken eye.
Will I ever see you?
Will I live long enough?
How are your sister towns? How are they?
I long for them
As if each were a paradise.
And those we left behind?
Those we left for dead.
I'm weary! I'm weary!
But in my weariness I only complain to God
And to no one else.
Yafa. Yafa!

—MAHMOUD SALIM AL-HOUT, "Yafa," translated
by Reem Kelani and Christopher Somes-Charlton

BONES OF CONTENTION: CITY AND CEMETERY

In the late 1990s, on the crumbling wall of Jaffa's Kazakhane Muslim graveyard overlooking the Mediterranean, faded graffiti comprising a drawing of an orange reads in black and orange colors, "Jaffa, the city of the sad orange that will smile again" (*Yafa madinat al-burtuqala al-hazina allati satabtasim*). A direct reference to Ghassan Kanafani's *The Land of the Sad Orange* (Kanafani 1980), this statement reflects the tragic transformation of the former orchard city known in the Palestinian discourse as "the city of flowers" (*madinat al-zuhur*).[1] The unbridgeable gap between reality and memory is metaphorically represented in the opposition between the "sad orange" and the mythical "Bride of Palestine" (*'Arus Falastin*). "Jaffa came a long way since its golden days before the occupation, the days of the Arabs [*ayyam al-'Arab*]," I was told by my Palestinian walking companion. "Back then, Jaffa was known as 'the Bride of the Sea' [*'Arus al-Bahr*]. Today, *'Arus al-Bahr* is no more than a crappy local newspaper."

Cemeteries are living testimonies that engrave in stone the way the living regard the dead. Often marking the outer limits of the city, urban graveyards signify "the other city" where eternity and permanence meet dissolution and disappearance (Foucault 1986). In cities where postwar destruction was inflicted, cemeteries, like street names, revive traces of previous demographic histories. With one Jewish cemetery, which dates back to the nineteenth century (active from 1840 to 1928), two Muslim graveyards, and three additional Christian ones, these heterotopic spaces bring to the fore the social life of urbicide and the constitution of Jaffa's communities of memory.

In Jaffa, however, cemeteries are not only depositories of the memory of generations past (Nora 1989) but also efficient mobilizing frames, one of the few public causes for which Palestinian residents take to the street in protest—in this case against recurrent attempts by the state and corrupt community officials to sell graveyards to Jewish real estate developers.[2] It is in the Kazakhane graveyard that Jaffa-born Palestinian scholar Ibrahim Abu Lughod was buried in 2001, thus assuming his "right of return in a coffin" (Bukhari 2007, 52). A decade later, the same graveyard has been desecrated by "Price Tag" right-wing extremists who sprayed "Death to the Arab" on the gravestones. Today, bordering on the newly built Peres Peace House, the graveyard symbolizes the Palestinian claim on the city encroached by neoliberal planning policies and radical nationalists.

For Jaffan artist Sami Bukhari, the Kazakhane cemetery is a mirror of Jaffa's fate, past and future. In the photo series *Panorama*, displayed in Jaffa at the Hagar Gallery of Contemporary Palestinian Art, he juxtaposes a distanced view of the landscape of the gentrified neighborhood of 'Ajami with the close layout of the tombstones (figure 3.1). At the back-

FIGURE 3.1. Cities of death: the Kazakhane cemetery and 'Ajami neighborhood. *Courtesy of Sami Bukhari.*

ground of both representations the tranquil omnipresence of the Mediterranean seems both enchanting and treacherous—a quiet testimony to the fact that the cemetery, built on a frail sandstone cliff, is gradually eroded by the sea waves. Looming above is the alarming realization of its slow yet inevitable dissolution into the Mediterranean. "When juxtaposed," the curator writes, "these two panoramic series sketch an analogy between the death prevailing in the cemetery and the post-Nakba Jaffa, with the cultural and social death it brought in its wake" (Ben-Zvi 2006, 15).

In the series *Boar,* Bukhari further expands on the theme of the "dying city." Bukhari depicts a boar immediately after its hunting, a common hobby for Arab men in Jaffa. The wild boar, with eyes wide open, seems at first glance very much alive and vital, until the viewer is faced with its decapitated head served on a platter. The exhibition catalogue reads, "Bukhari created a metaphorical link between the boar image as a representation of sin (in the Muslim and Jewish religions), as something ostracized, and the image of Jaffa in Israeli reality. In this context, the artist perceives post-1948 Jaffa as a reminder of sin. Jaffa remains an outcast, unwanted, an outsider. At the same time, it is the beautiful, made-up, Arab Jaffa that is at the core of the exhibition as a personification, a female figure, in Palestinian culture and literature" (Ben-Zvi 2006, 14).

A political activist and a former schoolmate of mine at the French Collège des Frères in Jaffa, Bukhari voices a collective frustration on behalf of what came to be known as the "stand-tall generation" (Rabinowitz and Abu-Baker 2005). Highly educated (in universities in Israel and abroad), ideologically motivated, and politically engaged, this generation no longer deems liberal "coexistence" the magic cure to the Palestinian-Israeli predicament and calls for political recognition and cultural autonomy based on a national discourse of rights. Both photo series, apparently disconnected, are in Bukhari's eyes instantiations of the same process that has befallen the city since 1948, namely, the agonizing demise of Jaffa in its capacity as a Palestinian city. The recently decapitated boar and the uncared-for gravestones, Bukhari maintains, index a commonplace illusion: Jaffa may appear to be living, but it has in fact long been dead. For Bukhari, another feature of Jaffa's social agony is the structural dependence of Palestinian artists on Jewish galleries. Bukhari formulates this dependence in terms of cultural oppression: "It is much easier for an Israeli Jew to get funding for culture. Jaffa has a well-to-do population, but fear and uncertainty do not allow it to move in a cultural direction. The hardship of everyday life and the need to survive blocked any sensitivity to culture. An oppressed culture would never be able to live at peace with another culture."

How does one live in a zombie city? How do Palestinian citizens survive in a town marked by communal destruction, which is at the same time a bustling center of urban renewal and Jewish gentrification as well as a site of memory of Palestinians in exile? While the lived experience in Jaffa cannot be reduced to deathly tropes haunted by an original sin, memories and traces of calamity do not dissolve under conditions of marginality and exclusion. Such a narrative of decline and despair, while forming the main discursive frame for Palestinian Jaffa, does not exhaust other key aspects of community life and political struggles taking place on a daily basis. These struggles highlight the ambivalence of *Sumud* as a principle of steadfast communal survival, which paradoxically evokes "fortitude in the occupied and frailty in the occupier . . . a tragic sensibility that claims an ethical form of power (and freedom) through powerlessness" (Furani 2012, 3).

The goal of this chapter is twofold. First, it tracks the image of the city as a dynamic of multiple identifications and exclusions. The currency of urban images in particular sites thus reveals how alienation of and from Jaffa is articulated. Second, it narrates the history of its Palestinian community by following the development of its civil society, its main political institutions, and its social movements. This process ranges from the post-1948 devastation of the Arab metropolis to projects of political awareness–raising (*taw'iya*) and social mobilization. Despite these challenges, in contradistinction to the Jewish population, the Palestinians in Jaffa have succeeded in creating a stable sense of place and in establishing local identity. This communal formation, however, is deeply divided along internal lines of political affiliation, religious denomination, and class. The cultural construction of Jaffa as the "Mother of the Stranger" emerges as the relational product of three fields: the Arab local population, the Palestinian Diaspora, and diverse

Jewish actors who seek either to Judaize it or to commemorate its Palestinian heritage. At the intersection of these local histories and the dialectics of their articulation with the encompassing contexts lies the agonistic Palestinian experience in Jaffa.[3]

YAFA IMAGINED: A MINORITY TWICE OVER
BETWEEN DIASPORA AND HOMELAND

For the Palestinian residents of Jaffa, like Sami Bukhari, the 1948 Nakba remains the key structuring event of the bleak recent history of their town. That war, which truncated the course of normal urbanization of most Palestinian towns, sealed Jaffa's fate as well. From the symbol of political modernity and the largest urban center in pre-1948 Palestine, Jaffa was transformed overnight into Tel-Aviv's "backyard." In a critically acute analysis, local intellectuals Mazawi and Khouri-Makhoul (1991, 63) sum up Jaffa's spatial history: "Since 1948 Jaffa was destined to disappear gradually. . . . The city was mostly erased in order to make way for the parade of spatial policy disguised as 'urban planning.' Old Jaffa, the Jaffa Port, the Neighborhood Rehabilitation project, Urban Renewal—all are operations with clear strategic and political goals: to alter the spatial and cultural characteristics of the area. The Arab community in Jaffa is trapped at the crossroads between urban bureaucratic policy and anti-Arab ideology—crucified on the cross of modernization and development."

Struggling since 1948 to sustain a viable collective existence, the Palestinian community makes up a third of Jaffa's total population and 5 percent of the Tel-Aviv-Jaffa metropolitan demographic composition. For the municipality and the state, Arab Jaffa has long presented a political "problem," thus resulting in recurrent strategies of containment, surveillance, and control. Nowadays, Arab community members often describe themselves as a "double minority" excluded twice over: first on the national scale of state institutions, and second on the municipal level vis-à-vis the City of Tel-Aviv-Jaffa. Bereft of the community's traditional elite and lacking coherent leadership or effective institutions, Jaffa Arabs continually struggle with a poor educational system, a high crime rate, and a severe drug problem. With no stable middle class to speak of, Palestinians in Jaffa ache for affordable housing and political recognition. Narrated in terms of an "existential threat," the community struggles for its survival in the present as it laments its bygone glorious past.

As detailed in chapter 1, the Palestinian image of Jaffa is trapped between nostalgia and dystopia, strikingly apparent in a specific metaphoric language. This changing geocultural imagination repositions Jaffa before and after 1948 by means of the three gendered tropes identified in chapter 1: "The Bride of Palestine" (*'Arus Falastin*), "The Bride of the Sea" (*'Arus al-Bahr*), and most tellingly "The Mother of the Stranger" (*Umm al-Gharib*). While the first two personify the city as a center of national prominence and maritime interchange, the latter designation wavers between past cosmopolitanism and present marginality.[4] It remains a painful reminder of Jaffa's shrinking frame of reference from the Arab space of Mediterranean connectivity to the backyard of Tel-Aviv.

As a structure of feeling, estrangement is not restricted to the severance of the abstract glorious past. It is represented also in signifiers of this past living elsewhere, namely, diasporic Jaffans. This leaves the Palestinians currently living in Jaffa trapped between two narratives: that of the national struggle and resistance of the Palestinians in the Occupied Territories, and the discourse of authenticity of Palestinians in the Diaspora (Tamari 2003). Understandably, the latter is sometimes adopted by residual members of the local old bourgeoisie, who are considered the guardians of collective memory. This became apparent in a recent conversation with Dr. Fakhri Jday, an eighty-five-year-old pharmacist and the only surviving member of the pre-Nakba Jaffan elite. Jday insisted on distancing himself from the current Palestinian "populace" (*hamaj*), emphasizing that he has very few social relations. Bemoaning his lost city, he said, "Keeping Arabs in Jaffa after 1948 is the cruelest thing the Jews did to us."

The theme of "paradise lost" invoked by Jaffa-born poet Al-Hout exemplifies the main diasporic Palestinian imagination of Jaffa as mediated through the perpetuity of exilic memory.[5] In narratives on Jaffa, which are part of a larger body of literature of longing and return, the homeland becomes the Palestinian El Dorado or Arab Andalous, which is to be found once again in the indefinite future. This narrative is recurrent in poetry and personal memoirs but also in concrete and symbolic *rites* of return, embodying the political *right* of return (Ben-Ze'ev 2011; 2003). Thus national poet Mahmoud Darwish writes, "I make a pilgrimage to you, oh Yafa / Carrying the wedding joy of an orchard." Not unlike the diasporic Jewish yearning for Jerusalem throughout the generations, the Palestinian city thus becomes an object of longing to which one makes pilgrimage, or where one desires to be buried, but also an inaccessible place where one is unable to share or prohibited from sharing its living space.

This Palestinian imagination of Jaffa reflects the broader problematic position of the Palestinian Diaspora (*al-shatat*), and primarily the predicament of intellectuals dispersed in the Arab world, Europe, and the United States, who publicly debate the concept of return and exile (Sharabi 2001).[6] In an interview with Edward Said, Nouri al-Jarrah (2001) problematizes the very notion of the "diaspora" concept:

> AL-JARRAH: The Jews used the term diaspora to describe a collective nostalgia toward a mythical place. Some Palestinians have adapted this term and used it to describe their expatriation from Palestinian geography. Do you think that Palestinians' use of this term may imply other meanings, especially when the Palestinian exile is from a geographically existent, very real place—real to the extent that they were expelled from homes to which they still keep the door keys? Is there an alternative term to diaspora, which you propose the Palestinian use?

> SAID: In Arabic I use the word *Shatat* (dispersion) despite my continuing caution and criticism of many terms based on myths of imagination. I naturally reject the term "diaspora." But nothing can prevent the term being used. The Jews used it to fulfill their own imagination, but we are talking about a different situation for the Palestinian. The Palestinian situation and the society Palestinians desire is peculiar to that nation.

This difficulty in formulating a case-specific "peculiar" conceptual language of "diaspora" that is not "based on myths of imagination," forewarned against by Said, reflects a systemic ambivalence among the Palestinians in exile regarding their relations with the idea of the homeland. Moving between a nostalgic metanarrative and a realist political recognition, this debate has far-reaching implications for the image of the Palestinian metropolis. In his personal account, Montaigne-style, Raja Shehadeh, born in Ramallah to an exiled Jaffan family, bemoans the mental blockage that has destined the Palestinians to live in a state of permanent exile. Tellingly entitled *Strangers in the House*, Shehadeh's narrative is a counternostalgic critique of the standard discourse of diaspora: "I was always reminded that we were made for a better life—and that this better life had been left behind in Jaffa," he writes. "Jaffa, I was told, was a pearl, a diamond-studded lantern rising from the water, and Ramallah a drab, cold, backward village where nothing ever happened" (Shehadeh 2002, 2). He goes on to observe,

> We had been stunned, bewildered, jettisoned across an imaginary border. We remained on the other side, looking at what we left behind. Because of our loss of the part, we had abandoned the whole. All that remained was a shadow life, a life of dreams and anticipation and memory. We didn't allow the new generation to make a new life for themselves because we continued to impress them with the glory of what was, a magic that could never be replicated. We defined our loss as total, forgetting that we still had something; we had ourselves and a life to live. Why had we allowed others to define for us our privation, our bereavement, and the meaning of our past? With this abandonment we made the same mistakes that had led to defeat in the first place. Learning nothing from our experience, we were doomed like Sisyphus. (65)

The mythical fixation of Jaffa as a "lieu de mémoire"[7] is collectively reproduced through different media ranging from history books, biographies, poems, plays, and films to the online "Jaffa Diaries" (Manthoulis 1998; al-Dajani 1989; Sharabi 1978),[8] which invite the Jaffan diaspora to share their life stories and personal memories. These media collectively reproduce the image of Jaffa and the subjectivity of its exiles. Standing out among these representations is the collection of memories, documents, and photographs edited by Hisham Sharabi and Imtiaz Diab of the Jaffa Research Center, entitled *Jaffa: Scent of a City* (*Yafa: 'Itr madina*) (1991). Compiling interviews with fifty-three former residents of Jaffa now living in exile in Amman, Cairo, and Beirut, this was the first attempt by diasporic Palestinians to reconstruct a collective portrait of the city from the position of exile (Sa'di 2003). In the preface, co-editor Diab explains the rationale of the book:

> When you search for a city and you find it arid, then you would look for someone to inquire about its residents. Alas, you don't find anyone. . . . There is only one way left to seek them out: to remind them of the scent of the city, or to search for its perfume among the boxes of old memories.

> Then the orange-like memories will flow and the mouth will stream with
> fresh words—once upon a time in Jaffa.... This book does not weep over
> the glory of the Arabs or over the loss of Palestine, nor does it claim the
> right to the city. Rather it enables the revival of its people's longing and
> voices their wish to return and smell once again the scent of orange blos-
> som in Jaffa, the "city of the stranger," that has opened its arms to foreigners
> who became part of it, while it, in turn, has become part of their past.
> (Sharabi and Diab 1991, 11)

Written in a romantic and lyrical prose, this preface frames the collected memories as a fairy tale, marked by the stylistic phrase "once upon
a time in Jaffa." Further removing the stories from lived experience and
political reality is the striking fact that although the book is generically
dedicated to the "families" or "people of Jaffa" (*ahaly Yafa*), the editors
have chosen not to include even a single testimony from current-day
residents of Jaffa. This paradigmatic omission is telling, for while celebrating Jaffa's heroic *Sumud* (persistent steadfastness) the book *de facto*
gives no voice to its living and struggling community—the actual *Sami-
din*. As Salim Tamari notes in his article "Bourgeois Nostalgia and the
Abandoned City" (2003), "No vision of the contemporary conditions
of the city is presented to the reader, as if the city died when its original
inhabitants left it in the war of 1948." Along these lines, editor Sharabi, a
prominent spokesman for the Palestinian Diaspora, further elaborates
on the predicament of the Jaffa exiles:

> The Arabic language has no equivalent to the German idiom "Heimat." Our
> language refers to this deep human relation as "homeland" [*mawtin*] or
> "birthplace" [*masqat al-ras*] or "home of the ancestors" [*bayt al-ajdad*]. These
> expressions assume their real meaning only through direct experience,
> such as the one inflicted upon the people of Jaffa.... This place—which in
> time comes to transcend the realm of the concrete—becomes a symbol for
> all that had passed.... One has a homeland only when one has lost it....
> Pre-1948 Jaffa is tantamount to the lost paradise. Nothing compares to its
> perfumed air during the blossom of the orange flowers, or to its white soft
> sand, its clubs and cafés, its unique cultural life. It is the most beautiful city
> of all, the pearl of the Mediterranean. (Sharabi and Diab 1991, 15)

This mythical and emotional memory is revived and ritualized in
organized and individual visits to the city by the first, second, or third
generations of Nakba survivors. In an article published in *Al-Ahram's*

special issue commemorating the fifty-year anniversary of 1948, and posted on the website Palestine Remembered, Salim Tamari, a Jaffa-born historian based in Ramallah, describes his impressions following a visit he made to Jaffa guided by a local resident he corresponded with via an e-mail discussion group. The actual visit to the city pits head-on the memory of the mythical city of the parents' generation against the city of the present. "Jaffa," Tamari (1998) writes, "is really a figment of the imagination. There is no parallel between the city of our parents and this bleached ghost town."

Often seen as the keeper of memory, for his part pharmacist Fakhri Jday summarizes the impact such visits have on the Jaffa exiles: "I show them their houses. They stay for a day and go back with a heavy, heavy heart." The ambivalent relationship of the Diaspora to the city is critically reflected upon by Tamari (1998) as an attitude of myopic longing that both reveals the Jaffa exiles' own emotionally charged memories and conceals the "living features of the people who remained there." Elsewhere, this nostalgic obsession was referred to as "Jaffa-mania":

> Nevertheless, to us, who were expelled from the city in the war, there is little feeling for Arabs who remained there. As if the nature of Palestinians was to leave. Catastrophe became their middle name. Sometimes we go to see the city and always see in it these memories. We don't see the living features of the people who remained there and resisted and were able to rebuild their lives and start a new sense of normality in it. All of this is background to us. . . . but of course Jaffa today is a living city and it's a dynamic city. And it's a city that's fighting for the rights of its original population, for the housing conditions and the struggle against discrimination, and so on. But that's another story, which I think should be retold and told again side by side with the story of the people who left. (Tamari 2003, 184)

The imperative of commemoration among the Jaffa exiles has also been institutionalized by different organizations in different parts of Palestine and Jordan. Preexisting associations such as the Sons of Jaffa (Abna' Yafa) in the West-Bank; the Jaffa Families (Ahaly Yafa) in Gaza; the Welfare Jaffa Association (Jam'iyat Yafa al-khairiya) in Al-Zarqa, Jordan; and the Jaffa Association for Social Development (Jam'iyat Yafa li-ltanmiya al-'ijtima'iya) in Amman were joined in 1995 by the Jaffa Friends Council (Jam'iyat asdiqa Yafa) in Amman, which contributes

about twenty thousand dollars yearly to fund different projects in the
city through the Rabita (the Association for the Jaffa Arabs, Al-Rabita
Li-ri'ayat Shu'un 'Arab Yafa). Through funding, organized visits to Jaffa,
and delegations of Jaffans to Amman, these organizations have helped
institutionalize a commemorative culture based on the image of prewar
Jaffa. Friends of Jaffa, for instance, sees in the city a strategic crossroads
in the relationship between the Palestinians in the *Shatat* (dispersion)
and the Palestinians "inside," thus fulfilling the unwritten contract between the city and its dispersed "children" wherever they are: "We want
Jaffa to stand fast and remain forever an Arab fortress."[9]

Faced with the impossibility of living up to the myth, the incongruence between the diasporic Palestinian imagination of Jaffa and the local
lived experience of everyday life there was brought into sharp relief during the funeral of Dr. Ibrahim Abu-Lughod, the Jaffa-born Palestinian
scholar and famous nationalist. This event, which could have potentially
marked a turning point in the mobilization of Jaffa into the national Palestinian project, was marked instead by a surreal incongruence between
the spatial practice and the symbolic value of the funeral procession.
Winding its way through the streets from the office of the Rabita on
Yefet Street to the Kazakhane graveyard overlooking the sea, the event
was heralded in the local Arabic newspaper *Akhbar Yaffa* as the "first
realization of the Right of Return." This notwithstanding, many of the
residents living on 60th Street in 'Ajami and Jabalyye were ignorant of
Abu-Lughod's place in Palestinian intellectual and political history or
were indifferent to the event, which they regarded as a mere spectacle.

Local observers' comments on the funeral ranged from curious interest in Abu-Lughod's biography to reprimands directed at Palestinian
public figures present at the funeral (some local, like Knesset Member
'Azmi Bishara, and others from outside the country, like Edward Said)
for their regular absence from the daily existential struggle of the local
community. "They come and go," I was told by a Palestinian friend whose
house overlooks the graveyard. At first he had refused to join the funeral
procession, but he eventually consented to tag along out of a mixture of
curiosity and cynicism.

The failure to mobilize Jaffa's masses for this national event marks
Jaffans' alienation from the Palestinian intelligentsia. "It's a class that

flatters itself," my friend concluded at the end of the funeral. "There is no political movement here. These are people from the outside who came for a day to implant in Jaffa the idea of Abu-Lughod's return. They have nothing in common with those of us living here. Most Jaffans do not know who Abu-Lughod is or what he represents—and they don't care." Abu-Lughod's funeral thus emerges as an example of two conflicting cognitive maps of Jaffa: one in which the city is a mythical "lieu de mémoire," and the other in which Jaffa is a living, lived-in place, tragically overlooked and thus excluded by the beautifying diasporic mythical image.

This estrangement and marginality from the Palestinian fold is augmented by the exclusion and marginality of Jaffan Palestinians from the mainstay of Israeli life which takes place all around them. Like Palestinian counterparts in the mixed towns of Ramle, Lydda, Acre, and Haifa, the Palestinian citizens in Jaffa are excluded from real influence in local Jewish-dominated municipal institutions and at the same time lack any representation at the Higher Arab Monitoring Committee, where local representatives of most Palestinian communities in Israel regularly convene as a semiofficial countrywide entity.

For Palestinians in Israel, contemporary Jaffa is notoriously associated with drugs, crime, loose morals, and promiscuous women. Often referred to as the "museum of the Nakba," Jaffa is doubly excluded from the Jewish side as well as from the Palestinian side, a fact illustrated to Jamil, a successful thirty-year-old Jaffa accountant, and his sweetheart Laila, who spent a year attempting to persuade their families to give their blessings to their engagement. Laila's family is from a small town in the Palestinian Triangle northeast of Tel-Aviv. Her father's firm refusal to consider the union was anchored in a variety of arguments, all of which Jamil dismisses as "racist," "patronizing," and even "fascist" excuses. The father used an economic argument, saying that Jamil does not own a house. And while in the village his daughter would be able to get a spacious and well-equipped one, in Jaffa she would have to work hard for many years to pay the mortgage. Then there was the problematic reputation of Jaffa. Jamil, said the father, was born "there" and thus had no choice but to go on living there. His daughter, on the other hand, had plenty of other options.

Successful and well-educated as Jamil may be, his position is further exacerbated by the context that had brought his family to Jaffa in the first place. His father had been born in the village of Hittin in the Galilee, which in 1948 was conquered and demolished by the Israeli occupying forces. The family became "internal refugees" in the Galilee village of 'Aylabun, where their absorption was accompanied by considerable hardship. "To this day," he says, "my family members are still known in the village as the 'refugees'—they are resented by the villagers, who begrudge them their fortune and gloat whenever something in their life goes slightly wrong." This resentment was part of the reason for Jamil's father's decision to move to Jaffa in the 1960s. Having arrived in Jaffa as a young labor-migrant after getting into trouble in the village, he did well, securing a future and a fortune in Jaffa and adjacent Tel-Aviv. For Laila's father, Jamil's background mattered little, and it took numerous attempts at persuasion and some personal meetings with Jamil to break the ice. Eventually Laila's father consented to give his blessing to the union, and the *khutbe* engagement ceremony took place in Laila's village. Currently, the young couple is planning to join in marriage once the apartment Jamil had previously purchased is built. This happy ending notwithstanding, Jamil's story reveals the deep sense of estrangement and internal exclusion of Jaffa and its residents amidst the Arab society in Israel as a whole.

Caught in limbo within Palestinian and Israeli exclusionary discursive frames—portraying Jaffa from without in a Manichean manner—local Jaffans also have to cope with the forces that threaten to tear the community apart from within. Facing social anomie in Jaffa, artists such as Sami Bukhari and youth initiatives such as the Fraternity Wall (see chapter 1, figure 3) interpret and localize their lived reality through the universal themes of life and death, present and future, hope and despair. Jaffa emerges from these representations as a locus which produces multiple and stratified modes of strangeness. But strangeness, as a structure of feeling, has a dimension that is not reducible to alienation of well-defined national subjects. Rather, the urban context can productively blur unidimensional subject positions, creating discourses of entrapment and ambivalent identities. Having surveyed the currency of Jaffa's images in particular sites, which reveal how urban strangeness is articulated, we now turn to the historical reconstruction of Palestinian communal efforts from 1948 to the present.

HISTORIES OF YAFA: THE LOSS OF PALESTINIAN URBANISM AND THE MAKING OF A MIXED CITY

The dystopian narrative of Jaffa is no exception to the rule. Jaffa was part of a network of modern coastal cities, along with other Palestinian cities like Ramle, Acre, and Haifa, that rose to prominence in the first half of the twentieth century only to devolve into poverty after the establishment of the State of Israel (Kimmerling and Migdal 1993; Tamari 2008).[10] Indeed, the loss of Palestinian urbanism is read by most analysts as Palestine's greatest defeat, which precipitated a new hybrid political subject: the Palestinian citizen of Israel. "After 1948," writes 'Azmi Bishara (2000, 73), "the path leading to modernization was blocked to the Palestinian minority because it lost its economic, political, and cultural elites, and most importantly it lost the Palestinian city and remained a rural society that is dependent on labor in the Jewish city, which does not absorb it. In the next stage, it lost the village when it lost agriculture, and thus it remained neither urban nor rural—this, it seems, is the Israeli Arab."

The Posttraumatic Years of Silence

On May 13, 1948, in the wake of the departure of Mayor Haykal as well as most of the city officials, the Emergency Committee led by Ahmad Abu-Laban, Amin Andraus, Salah al-Nazer, and Ahmad 'Abd al-Rahim unconditionally surrendered Jaffa to the Hagana and declared Jaffa an "undefended city" (*madina maftuha*).[11] These representatives, with the exception of Amin Andraus, soon left for Jordan, Lebanon, or Europe. A few more of the leading wealthy families left later in the 1950s, and thus was completed the total deracination of the economic and political elite in Jaffa. Today, in the public landscape of the city, only pharmacist Fakhri Jday remains as the last national and historical relic of the stratum that is no more (see chapter 6). "Under siege," writes Mahmoud Darwish (2002), "time becomes a location solidified eternally / Under siege, place becomes a time abandoned by past and future."

These traumatic events ended a process that started in December 1947, during which time the city was emptied of 95 percent of its Arab population.[12] While prior to the war 85,000 Arab inhabitants lived in the city of Jaffa and the surrounding villages, the first census conducted immediately after the war counted only 3,647 Arab residents in the occupied city, of whom 56 percent were Muslims and 44 percent Christians (*Madrikh Yafo* 1949).[13] This population was composed of inhabitants who remained after its seizure, as well as refugees from neighboring villages (such as Tal al-Rish and Salameh), who were forced to relocate to the western 'Ajami neighborhood in August 1948 for "security reasons" and to facilitate the absorption of thousands of Jewish immigrants.

Due to its pivotal standing in the Palestinian economy, its culture, and its politics, Jaffa was designated by the 1947 UN Partition Plan (Resolution 181) as constituting a Palestinian territorial enclave in Jewish territory.[14] Instead, after the occupation, martial law was imposed in the emptied city for one year, during which time the Arab residents were concentrated in the barbwired neighborhood of 'Ajami (also known in those days as the "Ghetto" by both the authorities and the city residents). The military administration further reduced the segregated living area for the Arabs, aiming to better control the Palestinian population, to prevent the return of its former residents, and to clear more space for new immigrants to be relocated in Jaffa. On June 1, 1949, martial law was terminated and the city was transferred to civil rule. By the orders of the emergency stipulations published in the official municipality newspaper (*Yedi'ot 'iryat Tel-Aviv*, no. 5–6 [December 1949]), the city affairs and welfare services were governed until Jaffa's annexation by the municipality-appointed Minhal Yafo (Jaffa civil administration). In the meantime, Tel-Aviv and Jaffa remained bureaucratically and symbolically separate. This intermediary phase lasted for another year, and eventually, on April 24, 1950, Jaffa was officially annexed to Tel-Aviv's area of jurisdiction.

In the first months after the occupation, under martial rule, the main state institutions in charge of the Arab minority in Jaffa—namely, the military governor, the General Security Service (*Shabak*) and the Ministry of Minorities—debated the future of the Arab population. The options for action were radically different, ranging from concentrating in Jaffa 6,500 more Arabs from Acre, and thus containing "the problem" of Arabs from other mixed towns in the Jaffa ghetto (Golan 2001), or transferring the Jaffa Arabs to the more quiescent and "collaborative" village of Abu-Ghosh, near Jerusalem. Both options were eventually overruled by the government and the Arabs of Jaffa and Acre remained in their respective—now mixed—towns. As a result of family reunifications, the Arab population in Jaffa increased from 3,600 in May 1948 to 5,200 by October 1948. Following the decision to populate Jaffa with Jews in August 1948, part of 'Ajami was designated to include the remaining Arab population in the Jaffa ghetto, which remained in place until the termination of the military rule.[15] Prior to the official dismantlement of the ghetto, however, Jewish residents, driven by their own housing shortage, infiltrated and squatted on the restricted area, thus undermining the governor's plan for ethnic segregation. At the end of the war, the Jaffa Palestinians were given Israeli citizenship and allowed free movement and the right of work under the constant surveillance of the security apparatus.[16]

The first three decades were marked by the remarkable political quiescence of the Palestinian community in Jaffa, and by collective posttraumatic shock in the face of social anomie, destitution, and the disintegration of most previous social institutions (including the Islamic *Waqf* endowment, sports clubs, political parties, and youth movements). All communal and individual property was appropriated by the state, under the authority of the 1950 Absentee Law. During interviews I conducted, elderly Palestinians often preferred to skip this period in their life stories. "It's a period I'd rather forget," said eighty-five-year-old Isma'il Abu Shehade. Conversely, some aged interviewees chose to depoliticize this period by nostalgically invoking it as a time of fraternity between Arabs and Jews who were sharing the same apartments. This nostalgic reconstruction of the past stems from common material hardship that has draped an apolitical cloak over the asymmetrical power relations between the two national groups. The complexities of the transition period are articulated in the narrative of Samia, an elderly Christian living in 'Ajami:

> When I settled back in Yafa, I had Jewish neighbors from Morocco, Iraq and Poland. I was friendly with them. It was the children who used to fight. One time, my son Michel and a Moroccan Jewish boy were playing when the Moroccan boy yelled at Michel: "You dirty Arab." Michel began beating him up. The Jewish boy's mother rushed out to stop him and then called me and began to insult me. . . . I replied quietly: "Neighbor, why don't you come upstairs and we'll have a cup of coffee together. We are sisters and we shouldn't fight together." And then I kissed her. I remember when she was moving out, she said to me: "You are the best neighbor I've had. Forgive me for all the bad things that have happened." (Minns and Hijab 1990, 159)

Old-timers testify that except for one attempt at the end of the 1950s to politically organize through the Nasserist Al-Ard party (outlawed by the Supreme Court in 1964), and less subversive activity under the auspices of the Community Party, most venues of their life were closely observed and policed by the General Security Service, amputating any possibility for assertive political activism. The prevailing sense in Jaffa was that, as with Foucault's Panopticon, there was no escaping the state's disciplinary and policing eye. Bereft of any form of leadership, the "generation of the survivors" (Rabinowitz and Abu-Baker 2005) was preoccupied with personal and social recovery and could not assume the role of an active agent for social change. Not until the 1970s did Jaffa see the rise and maturation of the first post-Nakba generation as a collective, self-empowering, political subject.

Throughout the 1950s and 1960s the small community of around five thousand residents was joined by a couple thousand labor migrants from the Galilee and the Triangle seeking employment opportunities in metropolitan Tel-Aviv. After 1967 further labor migration and marriages to women from the West Bank and Gaza demographically supplemented the Palestinian community. Jaffa offered young and mobile Palestinians an escape from martial rule (until 1966) and from the confinement of their villages. This demographic trend is visible in the current family structure in Jaffa. Most families nowadays include members from different parts of the country, as is apparent in their last names (e.g., Mahamid, Jabarin, Aghbariye, Chabaita). Notwithstanding this demographic influx of Palestinian migrants, for the first two decades the Arab community was largely centered in the 'Ajami neighborhood, where they were outnumbered by a much larger Jewish population (as of 1961 not more than five thousand Palestinian residents were living among seventeen thousand Jews). This situation changed dramatically during the 1960s and 1970s with the advent of the Urban Renewal Plan, as new housing projects were built for the Jewish residents in the eastern parts of Jaffa (Yafo C. and Yafo D.).[17] Gradually the Jewish residents left 'Ajami, leaving behind the Palestinian population, which assumed a dominant presence in the now-Arab-majority neighborhood (by 1972 only six thousand Jews remained). The main consequence of the departure of Jews from 'Ajami was the segregation of the Arab neighborhood, which paradoxically enabled the development of a political community defined by national identity.

National Revival

The year 1979 was a turning point in the communal history of Arab Jaffa. A decade after the 1967 war, which brought about renewed encounters with Palestinians in the West Bank and Gaza, and three years after the 1976 Land Day events, this year saw the political maturation of a new generation of Arab youths witnessing the gradual destruction of their city. Born in Israel, and proficient in Hebrew, Arabic, and often English and French, this generation was well aware of Israel's democratic space of political possibilities as well as its ethnocratic constraints. Throughout the seventies, a small group of university students (in the fields of engineering, sociology, social work, and law), led by the prominent nationalist figure Fakhri Jday, laid the foundations for the first significant grassroots organization in Jaffa since 1948 that would substitute for the co-opted state-appointed committees. On May 26, 1979, they founded the Rabita, which they registered as a nonpartisan, nonprofit civic association.

The anti-sectarian and nationalist ideology of the Rabita espouses a modernistic and liberal representation of local and cultural authenticity. Its central symbols are the language and the place. Thus in an attempt to purge Arabic of its Hebrew influences (*tasfiyat al-lugha*), intellectuals in Jaffa treated Arabic as an icon of cultural authenticity, while combining a national nostalgia for pre-1948 Mandatory Jaffa with a pragmatic sense of integration and cooperation with the Jewish-Israeli hegemonic establishment. Focusing on community organizing and political protest on the municipal level, the Rabita attempted to mobilize the Palestinian inhabitants to form a united national front and a cross-sectarian local identity. As one of the association's brochures reads, "Our members volunteer their time and their skills in order to secure the existence of the Arab community in Jaffa. . . . The Rabita's goal is to confront the social ills and provide the Arab community with a voice in public affairs. It unites a large number of the highly educated and politically conscious volunteers in the community. It builds on a national basis rather than on a religious-factional basis."

Throughout the eighties and nineties, the activities of the Rabita were manifold—from international work camps aimed at cleaning the dirty streets of the city, to renovations of run-down houses for poor families, public lectures in local history, and art exhibitions. Concurrently, it advocated solutions to the housing problem and participated in different events of national significance (such as the commemoration of Housing Day, or *Yawm al-maskan,* devised as the equivalent to the rural Land Day in mixed towns). Indeed, in its first fifteen years of activity the association truly stood up for its promise as a nonsectarian, all-Jaffan, drive of resistance and grassroots mobilization. The Rabita's momentum was further strengthened by the unprecedented achievement in 1987 of its successful appeal to the Supreme Court to stop the "Jaffa Slope" project (a dangerous and unlawful landfill planned by the municipality in order to build a villa neighborhood in the heart of the low-income Arab 'Ajami). The progressive optimism which characterized the movement in the 1980s can be clearly read from the following diagnosis of the prospects of crystallizing a "local identity," by one of the intellectual leading figures in the Rabita: "In the course of a multifaceted dialectic process, new social and cultural patterns are gradually coalescing, and a local identity—of deep historic roots and a face toward the future—is developing. . . . The suffering and despair, along with political developments at the national and international level, all aided the coming-to-be of a local authentic identity with a deep affinity for the city" (Mazawi and Khouri-Makhoul 1991, 76).

The movement, however, was soon to be faced with three factors it failed to take into serious consideration: one was the organization's de-

teriorating public image in Jaffa as it became increasingly institutionalized and rigid; second was the internal organizational shortsighted-
ness in its failing to seek the constant involvement of young activists for
the next generation; and third was its external rivalry with the Islamic
Movement. Over the course of the 1990s such shortcomings eroded the
Rabita's legitimacy and eventually led to the loss of its primacy to the
Islamic Movement.

The Rise and Fall of the Islamic Movement

The Islamic Movement poses a radical challenge to the Israeli state and
the secular Palestinian movements alike. The main principles of its ideology are threefold: to return to the sources of Islam, to turn away from
Western culture, and to fight secular imperialism through pragmatic
activism combined with a strengthening of the Islamic educational infrastructure (Rubin-Peled 2001).[18] Since its inception in early 1980s, the
Islamic Movement in Jaffa attracted increasing numbers of women and
men of all ages, looking at religion for meaning and a cure against crime,
corruption, and nihilism. Represented by its slogan—"Islam Is the Solution" (*Al-Islam Huwa al-Hall*)—it offers a total, yet pragmatic, solution
for the ills of society and a comprehensive, yet concrete, prescription for
every pain.[19]

The program of the Islamic Movement presents an efficient agenda
for the re-formation of the Muslim individual and community, striving for the utopia of the Islamic *Shari'a* society. In Jaffa the escalating
tension between the nationalist-secular discourse of the Rabita and the
Islamic discourse has gradually permeated all social realms, except for
one discursive meeting point: the political struggle against the State
of Israel and its Judaizing policies. Otherwise, on the cultural, organizational, and societal levels, the gap between the two organizations in
Jaffa is unbridgeable and does not allow for institutional cooperation
or conceptual compromises. The sociological correspondence between
cultural "Western" or "modern" principles and the middle-class position
of the Rabita members renders the conflict between the two social actors
even more fraught. In the eyes of the pious Muslims, secular liberals are
blamed for the figurative current return to the *Jahilyya* (the pre-Islamic

era of ignorance). For their part, the supporters of the Rabita accuse the religious Muslims of extremism and of being responsible for the current political state of divisiveness in Jaffa. Rabita supporters complain that the Islamic Movement and its factional (*ta'ifiyya*) and isolationist course of action have been detrimental to the Arab community as a whole. Tellingly, the activities of the Islamic Movement in Jaffa were by and large "tolerated" by the state, unlike the case of the Al-Ard Movement outlawed in the sixties. This relative acceptance conforms with the liberal position of both city and state, which views the Palestinians as consisting of separate confessional communities rather than one national collectivity.

Islamism, like other political movements in Jaffa, was dormant in the first three decades after the establishment of the state. Like the secular-national movement, it emerged in the seventies; however, another decade and a younger audience were needed for it to gain full legitimacy and assume its position as a leading social movement in the city. In the eighties the Islamic Movement launched its activities and first attracted teenagers who were searching for a coherent cultural system and religious meaning. The nineties saw the full-blown development of the movement under the charismatic leadership of sheikhs Bassan Abu-Zeid and Suliman Satel. The movement's rise to power was symbolically recorded in May 1995 in the aftermath of the shooting attack on St. Anthony's Church in Jaffa. Against the Rabita's feeble reaction, the Islamic Movement displayed its mobilizing power by organizing massive demonstrations outside the church, where the movement's green flags stood out among the crowd.

The Islamic turn in Jaffa also manifested itself in the reconfiguration of urban space, with stickers bearing Islamic slogans covering official street-name signposts and acknowledging Muslim presence in Jaffa's neighborhoods. Distributed to individuals in mosques and through the movement's office, these stickers represent a new interpretation of the city—both institutional and private. In one case the resident has painted over the street name and number—69 Pushkin Street—and erected instead a signpost prompting believers to "Be Conscious of God" (*Udhkuru Allah*).[20]

In addition to the traditional institutions affiliated with the Islamic Movement in Israel, such as kindergartens, a religious chorus (Nida' Al-Islam), and religious schools in mosques, the Islamic Council of Jaffa (Al-Hay'a Al-Islamiyya) was founded in 1990 as an explicitly political institution. According to its official platform the council's main goals include "preserving and caring for the Islamic holy places of Jaffa, particularly mosques and cemeteries; changing the status of 'absentee' property under Israeli law in order to allow the Islamic community to use their common and private property for community development and strengthening initiatives; and serving the Arab community of Jaffa in the social and educational fields." As part of this agenda, the council performed activities such as "the beautification and renovation of the Tasso Cemetery in Jaffa; provision of scholarships for Arab students from Jaffa in higher education; and establishment of an educational complex (kindergarten, primary and secondary school, and a community center) in the mosque of 'Ajami, which will serve all the residents of Jaffa."

Jaffa in the 1990s was an ideological and institutional battlefield between nonsectarian nationalists and Islamists, catching up with the rest of the Middle East that saw this process in clear motion especially after 1967. Since its inception, the Islamic Council engaged in constant head-on confrontation with the Rabita over public support and credit for diverse issues ranging from the principled matter of political representation in the City Council to more mundane disputes such as who would manage the funds for the renovation of the Jabaliyye Mosque donated by the Amman-based Asdiqa' Yafa organization. These recurrent confrontations and growing mistrust poisoned relations between the leading organizations in Jaffa and eventually led to the breakdown of any viable cooperation.

The early 2000s marked the escalation of the struggle over housing rights and political representation in the City Council. Refusing to collaborate in one list, the Islamic Council members eventually supported the Jewish mayor rather than the Yafa List, which led to the appointment of Ahmad Balaha as the mayor's counselor for "Arab Affairs." The cooptation of the Islamic Council signaled the waning popularity of the movement and its weakening impact on the public sphere. While it remains an important force to be reckoned with, its political legitimacy and mobilizing power diminished vis-à-vis an increasingly indifferent public and a disillusioned community.

The Rise of the Stand-Tall Generation

Toward the end of the 1990s, as the Islamic Movement gained popularity and legitimacy in Jaffa,[21] the structural tensions between it and the Rabita became impossible to reconcile. While an ad hoc political coalition since 1993 has guaranteed a seat in rotation in the City Council between the Muslim Islamic Council representative and the Christian Rabita representative, this coalition was no longer sustainable in the 2003 local elections. In its place, a new coalition was formed between the Democratic Front (predominantly Rabita members) and activists identified with 'Azmi Bishara's nationalist Balad party. The new Yafa List included Jewish and Arab members alike (although the first three seats were reserved for Arab representatives) and claimed to "promote a shared life based on values of equality and social justice" (2003 Yafa List platform).[22] Bereft of the mobilizing support of the Islamic Movement, however, it gained only 1.97 percent of the votes across Tel-Aviv-Jaffa and failed to cross the electoral threshold necessary to enter the council. Thus, paradoxically, two decades after the revival of civil society which resulted in active and relatively successful participation in the local municipal political scene, the progressive forces in Jaffa were left with no representation in the City Council. Ironically, the only elected Arab representative was Rif'at Turk, the liberal-Zionist left-wing Meretz party member and a former soccer star, who was selected by Meretz as a gesture to the Arab community in Jaffa. Forgivingly disregarded in Jaffa, Turk is commonly seen as a co-opted self-interested appointee without a clear agenda, adequate political skills, or demonstrated achievements (except for funding the sports club he heads).[23] The effects of political factionalism and communal fragmentation rose even more acutely to the surface when the tension between the Rabita and the Islamic Council turned into a legal battle and they exchanged accusations of nepotism and corruption.[24]

In the 2000s, against the backdrop of increasing organizational and sectarian divides, a new actor came to the fore, representing the generational subject that Rabinowitz and Abu-Baker (2005) have aptly termed the "stand-tall generation," which played a prominent role in the October 2000 events. Established as a home for young, politically engaged Palestinians, the National Club (Al-Nadi al-qawmi) comprised some thirty active members in their twenties through mid-thirties. Loosely associated with the self-declared nonsectarian Rabita, in whose offices their meetings were held, National Club (NC) members nevertheless emphasized their autonomy as an ideologically driven, uninstitutionalized group of young adults. Evenly divided between the nationalist Balad party and the leftist Democratic Front, NC members have spoken eloquently and vociferously on the predicament and collective rights of the Palestinian minority in Israel. This assertiveness is evident from the contrast between the name of the previous list and the City Council list's name, "We're All for Jaffa"—emphasizing a shared local identity and common interests both within the Palestinian community and between Arabs and Jews (whose electoral support is indispensable for passing the threshold)—and the current Yafa List, which explicitly foregrounds the Palestinian narrative and invokes (also in the Hebrew platform) the "Bride of Palestine" in the name of historical and social justice. As a political strategy, the radicalization of positions seems to have increased internal political divisiveness in Jaffa and widened the gap with the Jewish population in the city. In addition to the split with the Islamic Council, this was a central factor in the 2003 failure of the Yafa List. Despite these hurdles, in 2008 the Yafa List finally succeeded in securing one seat in the City Council; however, as Omar Siksik, the list representative, admitted, "there was no unity among the Arabs."[25] Paradoxically the success of the predominantly Arab list was made possible by Jewish votes. In the 2013 municipal elections, history repeated itself and the Yafa List lost its seat again due to its inability to mobilize sufficient Arab and Jewish voters.[26] Moreover, for the first time in twenty years, there is not a single Palestinian member in the City Council, including in the Zionist lists.

The absence of a progressive representative in the City Council poses additional obstacles to any attempt to systematically tackle Jaffa's dire social problems (housing shortage, education, employment, and crime).[27] Facing the above internal divisions as well as city plans for privatization and gentrification from without, the Palestinian community at the beginning of the twenty-first century seems doomed to be trapped in a vicious cycle of poverty and powerlessness.

THE "HOUSING INTIFADA"

After decades of urban disinvestment and policies of non-planning, the housing crisis, which became the symbol of Palestinian presence in the city, reached its peak in the 1990s. The vast majority of the Jaffa Arabs do not own the homes in which they live, and thus it should come as no surprise that the housing shortage is seen as the community's most urgent and existential problem.[28] Moreover, 3,125 housing units were torn down in Jaffa in the years 1975–1985, despite the city's population growth. In 'Ajami and Jabaliyye a decrease of 41 percent of the total housing inventory was registered between 1973–1993, compared with a 30 percent increase in the predominantly Jewish neighborhoods in eastern Jaffa. With hundreds of land lots now vacant, the Israel Land Administration launched a wholesale auction of residential property designated for "redevelopment" on the private market.

Faced with creeping gentrification processes and neoliberal municipal planning that seek to privatize real estate and promote the commodification of lived space, a deep sense of unrest triggered the first sign of communal mobilization. In 1995, Local Master Plan 2236, or the Jaffa Slope, was approved, envisaging the doubling of the Jewish population in the predominantly Arab neighborhoods overlooking the Mediterranean (figure 3.2).[29]

The same year, in what came to be known as the "Housing Intifada" (*Intifadat al-sakan*), thirty Palestinian families coordinated to squat in empty houses formally owned by the state, administered by the Amidar governmental housing company, and designated for future private development. In the face of the squatters' consistent refusal to evacuate, a state-sponsored plan for affordable housing put an end to the Housing Intifada and heralded the beginning of a series of negotiations between

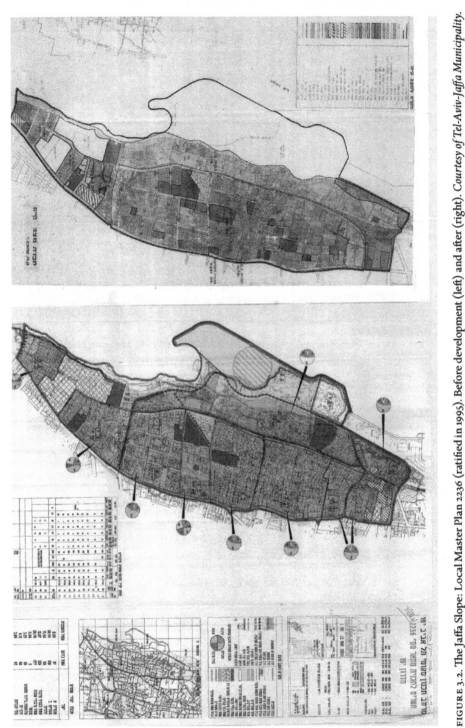

FIGURE 3.2. The Jaffa Slope: Local Master Plan 2236 (ratified in 1995). Before development (left) and after (right). *Courtesy of Tel-Aviv-Jaffa Municipality.*

FIGURE 3.3. The social justice protests in summer 2011: "Jaffa, Housing First."
Courtesy of Yudit Ilany.

FIGURE 3.4. Slogans of resistance, 2012: "Gentrification Is Economic Transfer."
Courtesy of Yudit Ilany.

Palestinian community leaders and municipal authorities. This eventually resulted in the construction of a housing project ("Build Your Apartment") comprising twenty-two apartments out of the ninety-five originally planned in 2002.[30] Over the next decade these concerns steadily increased, leading, among other consequences, to the outbreak of the "Housing Protest" which swept the city in 2011 in response to the "Arab Spring" (figure 3.3).

Such moments of collective action mark a shift from a liberal discourse of "coexistence" (*ta'ayush* [Arabic] or *du-kiyum* [Hebrew]) to an assertive claim to political entitlement and collective "existence" (*wujud* [Arabic] or *kiyum* [Hebrew]). The housing problem thus encapsulates a claim over the historicity of the city as well as the dire need for practical solutions for young couples and low-income families. Increasingly visible since the October 2000 events and the outbreak of the Al-Aqsa Intifada, Palestinian communal mobilization, however, is no match for the market forces which threaten to Judaize the city. Since the 1990s, the emergence of gated communities in Jaffa (like the Andromeda Hill project) has signaled new modes of urban exclusion, which reshape previous forms of spatial distinction. Reviving previous traumas of displacement, gentrification reshuffles communal and spatial boundaries, thus further destabilizing Palestinians' sense of belonging. In 2007, the threat of "urban removal" disguised as "urban renewal" reached a new level when the Israel Land Administration issued 497 evacuation orders to Palestinian families charged with "illegal" construction. That these families all lived in the 'Ajami neighborhood—the hot spot of Jewish gentrification—was no coincidence, and so it was interpreted as yet another attempt to "transfer" the Arab population out of Jaffa (figure 3.4).

The disillusionment from party politics and the gradual delegitimization of longstanding organizations pushed new social forces to the fore which called for a "reversal of the ongoing Nakba" (Abu Shehade and Shbeita 2009). Thus by the time of the 2011 social justice protests, new grassroots initiatives such as Darna—The Popular Committee for Land and Housing Rights (Al-Lujne al-Sha'biyye, founded in 2007), and the Jaffa Youth group (Al-Shabiba al-Yafiyya), as well as professional partnerships such as the Peres Peace House, Shatil (the New Israel Fund Initiative for Social Change), and the Tel-Aviv University Legal Clinic, were replacing the former organizations in the struggle over housing.[31] The crucial role of both Jewish and Arab activists from outside the city

is gradually changing civil society in Jaffa to a binational and translocal space of social action.[32] Despite their original goal of expanding
the framework of struggle to national and class-based concerns, which
extend beyond the local divides between the Rabita and the Islamic
Movement, initiatives such as Darna gradually exhausted themselves
and turned instead into service providers with little mobilizing power.
Paradoxically, the collective effervescence brought about by the 2011
protests on the national scale overshadowed the housing crisis in Jaffa.
Now considered a universal problem cutting across sectors, the call for
a specifically local solution to what remains Jaffa's most existential problem was made redundant. "The housing struggle in Israel at large killed
the local struggle in Jaffa," bitterly concluded one activist. The partnerships that mark civil society in ethnically mixed towns in the twenty-first
century evince an ongoing transition process from popular mobilization
to issue-specific "sub-politics."[33]

PALESTINIAN RECOGNITION IN THE "MIXED TOWN"

In the wake of the October 2000 events and the outbreak of the Al-
Aqsa Intifada, a series of public events addressed the burning problem of Jewish-Arab relations and the so-called coexistence in crisis.
An international conference I attended entitled "Together but Apart:
Ethnically Mixed Cities in a Comparative Approach" (Tel-Aviv University, 2004) opened ceremoniously with a grand *Iftar* dinner at the
closing of the daily Ramadan fast. After the breaking-the-fast meal,
to which select representatives from Jewish-Arab mixed cities in Israel were invited, the mayor of Tel-Aviv-Jaffa, Ron Khuldai, gave the
opening speech. "Tel-Aviv," he stated, "is not a mixed city. Indeed, we
have a small Arab minority of 4 percent but it would be problematic to
consider it as a mixed city. There are minorities—Jews and Muslims
who have their uniqueness—who are involved in a national conflict
and are concentrated in the ancient city of Jaffa, which is itself a mixed
city with an Arab minority of 30 percent. Tel-Aviv however is definitely
not a mixed city."

The infuriated reactions to the mayor's seemingly straightforward
statement encapsulate the identity paradox of the Palestinian minor-

ity in mixed towns. Focusing on Khuldai's assertion that Tel-Aviv is not a mixed city (while overlooking his admission that Jaffa is) and interpreting it as a symptomatic misrecognition of Jaffa's very existence and collective rights, leading Palestinian activists expressed their assertive demand for cultural recognition and proportional budgets from the overwhelmingly Jewish municipality. Interestingly, however, in this oppositional discourse Palestinian cultural difference and communal existence were defined not independently of Tel-Aviv, but rather as the logical corollary of Jaffa's hyphenated affiliation with the first Hebrew city, under whose rule the former could never expect to receive more than limited autonomy. This dialectic process of distinction *through* integration, or Palestinization *through* Israelization, is indicative of the Palestinian minority's increasing difficulty in dissociating itself from the Israeli state and Israeli society. As Raef Zreik (2003, 53) aptly puts it, "One day they are Israelis and the next day they are Palestinians; they are never Palestinian citizens of Israel." Mixed towns, as this book shows, have been central sites where these contradictions have played out.

Such dilemmas, however, are hardly for Palestinians alone to face. Jaffa's ambivalent status—from its 1947 designation by the UN as an Arab enclave in Jewish territory to the present predicament as a contested "mixed city" under Tel-Aviv's jurisdiction—remains a stubborn "bone in the throat of the Zionist project," as one interlocutor observed. Notions of imminent Palestinian return and recurrent nationalist claims over the right to the city (such as the 2011 slogan "The Right of Return to Old Jaffa") are dealt with via the universal rhetoric of citizenship and individual rights. However, this liberal rhetoric seeks to suppress the potential national rescaling of Jaffa and to keep the "1948 file" closed by restricting the city on the local level to being a confessional minority community. After decades of ongoing correspondence between the two narratives of the state and its Palestinian citizens, Jaffa emerges as a mirror image of the way it is viewed by the state. As one acute observer put it, "The tight leash men in Jaffa use to control their dogs is in direct proportion to the leash they themselves are kept on by the state."

Since 1948 the overall challenge facing the Palestinian population in Jaffa has been that of community building and political organizing, both internally and vis-à-vis the city and the state. In the first three decades, in the face of municipal planning policies and the threat of Judaization, the post-Nakba logic of survival dominated the scene. Beginning in the 1980s these preliminary efforts gave rise to the more progressive constitution of a vigorous national revival and a modernization of civil society in the form of various local organizations making assertive demands now framed as collective civil rights. However, while the community's needs were somewhat successfully communicated to the local authorities (through political representation in the City Council) and introduced to the liberal Jewish public in Tel-Aviv (through vocal advocacy), the different grassroots organizations operating in Jaffa fiercely competed with each other over internal resources and legitimacy. Thus, paradoxically, along with the community's political maturation and accumulative experience, social fragmentation and institutional rivalries have been increasingly dividing Arab Jaffa, thus disabling efficient struggle even for the sake of agreed-upon common interests (such as combating gentrification). This in turn has increasingly pushed local politicians toward Jewish voters in the name of the merits of ethnic mix. Therefore, despite his official affiliation with the Palestinian Balad party, which traditionally espouses Arab national autonomy, Sami Abu Shehade of the Yafa List and the representative par excellence of the stand-tall generation, considers the mixed town a "blessing" which challenges the logic of separation. Despite his image among Jews as a Palestinian nationalist, he approached the Jewish gentrifiers as potential "partners":

> For dozens of years we have been the victims of neglect, and now we are the victims of development. Part of it is a result of gentrification. We always talk about the evil side of gentrification but it has also introduced to Jaffa Jews who are politically closer to the Arab population. There are lots of young guys who came to Jaffa precisely because it is mixed and this is what they want. Jaffa is the only sane place where they can survive in this country. These are real partners. . . . The challenge we pose to separation is significant. I say—we live in a mixed reality. And this is a blessing. Let's see how we can develop a model for real shared life.[34]

The co-presence of the political Other who is also a political "partner" exacerbates the Palestinian institutional dependency on the Jewish voter. The political inability to harness effective autonomy is thus reflected in the tortuous attempt to establish Palestinian presence in mixed towns. Encroached on by Jewish gentrification, the chief marker of Palestinian space in the mixed town is its spatial heteronomy—understood here in opposition to political autonomy as well as to the demographic homogeneity of the national "abstract space" (Lefebvre 1991; Eisenzweig 1981).

Trapped between the diasporic image of Jaffa as "paradise lost" and bleak visions of the city as "the museum of the Nakba," the living Palestinian community is struggling to gain recognition both from the Israeli authorities and from the Palestinian discourses of rootedness. Often portrayed from the outside as a story of *Sumud* (steadfastness), local Palestinians instead paint the city in antiheroic colors of estrangement. The tremendous gap between the narrative of nationalist aspirations and the lived realities on the ground expose the open wound still bleeding within the Palestinian city. Jaffa, the Mother of the Stranger, is thus represented through such uncanny idioms of rupture as "an identity without a community," as one observer put it, a zombie city in Bukhari's artwork, or "half reality, neither fully there nor fully gone," as Raja Shehadeh (2002, 62) describes it. The tension between the imperatives of justice and the realities of the balance of power, which Zreik (2003) contends has shaped Palestinian politics since 1948, also bears on the notion of *Sumud* described above by Furani (2012, 3) as a "tragic sensibility that claims an ethical form of power (and freedom) through powerlessness." While the celebration of resistance, defiance, and willpower which were usually associated with the ideology of *Sumud* (with a capital "S") is often dismissed with bitter cynicism in Jaffa, it can be argued that signaling the fact of "estrangement" is a resolutely heroic, subversive, or postsecular practice of *sumud* (with a lowercase "s")—in a state that insists on normalizing the state of exception.[35]

In the Palestinian diasporic discourse itself, the idyllic portrayal of Jaffa as a "city of oranges" has not been without cracks and contestations. As Salim Tamari (2003, 176) shows, the second generation of the Jaffa exiles "was characterized by a critical nostalgia bordering on cynicism." With no firsthand experience of life in pre-'48 Jaffa, this group "had suffered from both the heavy burden of the Nakba experience and from the estrangement of exile. Tackling the memories of their fathers' generation, they directed acute criticism at their patrimony of defeat and defeatism" (179). Insisting on questioning the causes of the exodus and interrogating Jaffa's polarized class structure that made the city vulnerable, the second and third generations criticized the Nakba generation whose "bourgeois nostalgia was seen as a blindness that joined its prewar fragility to its impotent behavior in the war itself" (179).

Not unlike the Jewish inability to make a coherent claim on Jaffa and to construct a political myth of place, these ruptures nevertheless enable creative social action. Thus since 2000 the notion of the "home" (*bayt*), described above by Sharabi, has become the mobilizing frame for a series of initiatives explicitly defined as a binational struggle for housing and justice. The collective sense of crisis and the prevailing state of emergency thus paradoxically yield unprecedented modalities of cooperation. In the heyday of the Arab Spring, during the 2011 Housing Protest, such sensibilities brought together for the first time in Israeli history Palestinian activists from Jaffa and Jewish activists from the working-class neighborhood of Hatikva who marched the streets under the banner "Jaffa, Hatikva—the Same Revolution."

In a similar vein, System Ali, a hip-hop ensemble comprising ten rappers based in Jaffa, calls to "Build the House Anew." Performing in Arabic, Hebrew, English, and Russian, System Ali bemoans the "home that collapsed onto itself" but employs the urban predicament as leverage to expand the horizon of political struggle by means of novel forms of binational action. Mobilizing difference and engaging multilingualism, songs such as "Yafawiye hiye hawiye" (Jaffan is an identity) seek to recover what the band members term "a vernacular Jaffan language." Along with pessimistic refrains such as "Ihna ʿArab—kul ishi indarab" ("We're Arabs—it's all fucked up"), System Ali redefines cultural agency for a new generation: "I sing in Arabic. I face you. You see me. We bring the message from ʿAjami to Hebron. We came to bring the wall down.... My bleeding people, my silent people, my dispossessed people ... like the Suez Canal we are coming through, stirring up a storm, mixing up a new form of your newborn Mediterranean brew. We are Pharaoh if the future is a Nile; we are Mr. Moses for an Israel in denial." Finally, in what seems like an imaginary dialogue with Mahmoud Darwish's poem on the "awkward encounter" between intimate enemies, Muhammad Aghwani and Yonathan Kunda of System Ali published the first Arabic-Hebrew bilingual collection of poems, which they jointly authored. Their "artivist" intervention invokes an affective subjectivity which transcends the narrow confines of territorial nationalism and shares an agonistic view of the mixed city:[36]

Me and you
are fish in the ocean
But whose?
In the city of Andalous
words are
rocks
in our mouth.

PART TWO

Sharing Place or Consuming Space:
The Neoliberal City

FOUR

Inner Space and High Ceilings

Agents and Ideologies of
Ethnogentrification

I moved to a mixed Arab-Jewish building in Jaffa last spring, a refugee from the astronomical rents in Tel Aviv.... Jaffa radicalized me, in a way. I think about politics when I walk through Ajami, the neighbourhood that was, until recently, an Arab ghetto.... I think about politics when I look at the crumbling and neglected Muslim cemetery, right next to the architecturally striking new building that houses the Peres Center for Peace.... Jaffa is an interesting and cool place to live.... I just did not expect to feel like a colonizer for having moved 15 minutes' walk from Tel Aviv. But, I do.

—LISA GOLDMAN, "Jaffa, Habibti, Our Relationship Is Complicated"

ETHNOGENTRIFICATION

In front of a newly built cubist construction on 60th Street in 'Ajami, a large and colorful marketing sign promising "authentic and luxurious housing" read, "Living in Jaffa is a matter of style. Investing in Jaffa is a matter of wisdom." A few days after it had been posted, someone covered the large board with black graffiti exclaiming in Hebrew, "House Thieves" (*Ganavey Batim*). The contractor in turn soon taped over the graffiti a yellow band with additional marketing content. Stemming from a local dispute involving the Palestinian Sawaf family, who originally lived on the lot and claimed to have been cheated out of their house, and Yoseph Shiloah, a famous Jewish-Israeli comedian who bought the land and later sold it to a private developer, this public correspondence of messages captures the political implications embedded in gentrification. Thus aggressive marketing of urban renewal ("luxurious hous-

135

ing"), on the one hand, and local protest against urban removal ("house thieves"), on the other, illustrate the contentious politics of urban space. Claiming to be deceived into signing the contract that positioned them as "illegal squatters," the Sawaf family was promised replacement housing but eventually found themselves without a roof over their heads, living in a tent at the nearby public park.

The case loomed large in Jaffa and received extensive media exposure on a primetime show (*Friday Studio*, Channel 2, February 19, 1999) that presented Shiloah as "a greedy manipulator dispossessing Arabs in Jaffa." Facing these accusations, Yoseph Shiloah appealed to the courts and won both the suit filed against him by the Sawaf family for dispossession and breach of contract and the libel suit he filed against Channel 2's news company. To restore Shiloah's good name, the news company was obliged to compensate him with seventy-five thousand shekels and issue a public apology.[1] Promoted by antigentrification grassroots organizations, this story reverberated in Jaffa as the ultimate symbol of both the predatory nature of gentrification and the weakness and naiveté of the Arab underclass.

In light of the tragedy of the Sawaf family and dozens of similar cases in Jaffa, gentrification appears to be no less than a total urban conflict whereby state, city, and private agents implement a strategic Judaization project, manipulate symbolic and economic capital ("lifestyle" and "wisdom"), and concertedly scheme to displace the underprivileged Palestinian population. Indeed, this critical narrative was espoused by most local grassroots organizations and international scholars (Al-Ja'fari, Lahav, and Adiv 1992; LeVine 2000). Seen up close, however, gentrification breaks down into a much more complex sociopolitical mosaic of myriad vested interests. Without dismissing this narrative and its very real concerns, this chapter aims to uncover in practice the work of gentrification's field agents—real estate agencies and the gentrifiers themselves, all motivated by pro-urban ideologies and potential profit. As the following analysis will show, the field of positions and relations that makes up the phenomenon of gentrification revolves around competing understandings of what I term "spatial capital"—a form of symbolic capital associated with the "quality" of space in Jaffa.

Viewed as a complex and multilayered urban process, gentrification poses a communal and existential dilemma for both the Palestinian and the gentrifier communities in Jaffa. For the Palestinian community, the rejection of gentrification might destine Jaffa to self-ghettoization and institutional disinvestment, while accepting it will result in the demographic and cultural transformation of urban space, the loss of its historical character, and the *de facto* de-Arabization of the last "Arab neighborhood" in metropolitan Tel-Aviv. For the gentrifiers, assuming a local identity and becoming "Jaffan" might fulfill their desire for a new sense of place; however, if successful this "localization" process will require them to accept living in a historically contested and economically underprivileged area—surrounded by poor schools and infested with crime and violence. On the cultural and political plane, living in Jaffa forces gentrifiers to face the "open wound" (as one gentrifier put it) of the history of Palestinian displacement (both in 1948 and as a result of gentrification itself). These dilemmas yield an ambivalent response in the two camps, both failing to mobilize a consistent collective line of action. Among the gentrifiers, who are the focus of this chapter, some take the Palestinian community as their frame of reference and political identification, some avoid the problem by constructing a romanticized notion of gentrification, and still others paradoxically negate the very validity of the concept of locality and belonging.

Addressing these constitutive dilemmas of the actors who make gentrification happen, this chapter identifies five types of social actors: the real estate agent and the architect, who both share the redemptive discourse of gentrification *qua* inevitable and desirable "urban development"; the residents' association of gentrifiers in search of local identity; the radical gentrifiers who perceive their presence in Jaffa in political terms of "making a difference"; and the philosopher-gentrifier who detaches himself from any discourse of autochthony and rootedness. The chapter deconstructs the stereotype of Jewish gentrification in Jaffa as a unidimensional and monolithic process of middle-class "urban settlement" led by ethnocratic motivations. Rather, it is revealed as a profoundly ambivalent field of relations that embodies simultaneous modes of separation and rapprochement. Thus, far from being merely a reflexive response to political economy, for most actors gentrification becomes *ipso facto* a transformative political and cultural experience.

A HISTORY OF GENTRIFICATION

During the first years of Israeli statehood, Jaffa turned from an Arab metropolis into a Jewish immigrant city (Monterescu and Rabinowitz 2007). It lost its autonomous municipal status, and following a short period of military administration was annexed to Tel-Aviv. The Bride of Palestine, which had been a major cultural and economic center under Ottoman and British rule, was transformed overnight into the notorious and dilapidated "Quarter 7." Initially instrumental in the aftermath of the war as an "absorption" site for more than fifty thousand immigrants, Jaffa was soon looked down on as a "slum" inhabited by the Others of the "white city": Mizrahi Jews, poor immigrants, unruly criminals, and above all—Arabs. Echoing Wacquant's (2008, 1) qualification of the spaces of urban marginality, Jaffa was "draped in a sulfurous aura, where social problems gather and fester"—a city positioned at "the very bottom of the hierarchical system of places that compose the metropolis." This stigmatized "aura" associated Tel-Aviv's alter ego with a series of urban tropes that Rotbard (2005) aptly termed the "black city": the Big Territory, the Ghetto, and the South Side. Posing a threat to the categorical order of the city and the state, it was soon destined to be "cleansed" and reborn anew.

Tel-Aviv Municipality's master plan for postwar Jaffa was twofold: a short-term goal of settling the new immigrants in the available housing units expropriated from the Palestinian refugees, and a long-term goal of "modernizing" Jaffa, namely, razing its "slums" and building large co-tenancy housing projects (*Shikunim*) instead. Throughout the late 1950s and the 1960s, the city initiated the relocation of Jaffa's Jewish population to newly built housing projects on the eastern and southern fringes of the metropolis. The Arab population, largely overlooked by these planning policies, remained in Jaffa's western neighborhood of 'Ajami. The very existence of "dilapidated Jaffa" was thus seen by the city as a necessary evil to be done away with as quickly as possible.

Ipso facto, Jaffa retained its urban vitality as a proletarian transit city until the mid-1960s and remained densely populated. The luxurious mansions where the Palestinian upper-class families previously dwelled were now inhabited by poor Jewish and Arab families forced to divide the wide spaces into small and crowded housing units (Golan 2001; Hezi-Ashkenazi 2012). The rapid absorption of more than fifty thousand poor and unruly immigrants arriving from socially disparate backgrounds was replete with organizational difficulties and institutional corruption. In the socialist-led Israel of the 1950s, four public institutions supervised the construction of urban space: Amidar—Israel National Housing LTD (founded in 1949), Halamish—Government and Municipal Company (founded in 1961), the Old Jaffa Development Company (founded in 1960), and most importantly the Custodian of Absentee Property (Ha-Apotropos le-Nikhsey Nifkadim, founded in 1948).[2] Accordingly, Jaffa was commonly known as "the city of the custodian" (*Madrikh Yafo* 1949, 43).

Once the immediate goal of settling immigrants in existing houses was met, the above-named state organizations engaged in rapid construction of housing projects in the new neighborhoods—Jaffa C., Jaffa D., and Tel-Kabir. By then Jaffa was a prime electoral, demographic, and commercial center. (At the time of its annexation in 1950 the population of Jaffa numbered sixty thousand, and in 1953 there were seventy-five thousand inhabitants in the city and its environs, which constituted more than 21 percent of Tel-Aviv's total population [Horowitz 1954].)[3] The long-term process of modernistic "slum-clearing" and urban renewal remained, however, the city's main goal for the next two decades.

From the 1960s to the mid-1980s, Jaffa was systematically disinvested as part of the policy of eviction and demolition euphemized in official planning discourse as "Eviction and Construction" (literally, *Pinuy Binuy*, the Israeli version of urban renewal). The historic neighborhoods overlooking the Mediterranean were conceived at that period to be "slums that should be eliminated and replaced by modern, well-planned, and attractive neighborhoods" (Horowitz 1954). In this process, the coastal Manshiyye neighborhood, where my family used to live in the North Side of Jaffa, was completely erased, creating a no man's land between Tel-Aviv and Jaffa.[4] More than two-thirds of the Old City was demolished, and the neighborhoods of 'Ajami and Jabaliyye were significantly damaged.[5] The ruins and neglect dominating these neighborhoods attracted action film producers who looked for shooting sites in the Middle East but had no access to Lebanon, Iraq, or Iran. In 1985 the director of *Delta Force* commented that he selected Jaffa because "Jaffa looks just like Beirut after the bombing" (Mazawi and Khouri-Makhoul 1991, 67).

In the 1960s and 1970s, the systematic neglect of the western neighborhoods of Jaffa—both physically (infrastructure maintenance) and socially (employment, welfare, and municipal services)—brought about the significant outmigration of Jewish inhabitants who were now eager to relocate to "new" and "clean" subsidized housing in eastern Jaffa and neighboring cities (Holon, Bat-Yam, and Rishon le-Tziyon). Thus in ʿAjami and Jabaliyye (Subquarter 72)—which would become the main attraction sites for gentrification two decades later—the population dwindled from 22,976 in 1961 (most of them Jews) to a mere 4,033 in 1989 (mostly Arabs).[6] While the municipality's initial goals—i.e., demolition and evacuation—were fully achieved in Manshiyye, the neighborhoods of ʿAjami and Jabaliyye saw only partial implementation of this plan due to the Arab population's refusal to leave. As far as the planning authorities were concerned, this represented a systemic failure since "these actions were executed at a rate fast enough to damage the historic structure of the neighborhood, but not efficiently enough to lay the infrastructure for a new modern neighborhood" (Jaffa Planning Team 1997).[7]

The city planners who led the gentrification process in the 1980s have explicitly articulated the institutional narrative of the spatial history of Jaffa during the first three decades. An internal historical report unravels a professional urban discourse which narrates the demise of the lively city dominated by informal construction (Jaffa Planning Team 1997). In the beginning of the 1960s, the British city plans were annulled and the new plans that replaced them (Ordinances 479 and 432) were based on "planning perceptions and ʿmodern European' cultural values formed in the first half of the century in central Europe." Designating historical districts as "Rehabilitation Regions" paradoxically spelled total destruction. Well through the 1980s, in tandem with the gradual deterioration of infrastructure, Jaffa was left to the devices of the housing companies (Halamish and Amidar) that tore down *en masse* hundreds of historic buildings and forced their tenants out of the city. "Within a few years," the report concludes, "the majority of the residents moved out, leaving behind mainly the underprivileged poor population [*ukhlus-siat metzuka*], most of whom were Arabs, who held the area as their communal center."

In want of an efficient systemic operative plan and the financial resources to carry out the official goal of complementary slum-clearance and redevelopment, the municipality and Amidar irreversibly destroyed large portions of Jaffa's landscape but failed to replace them with adequate "modern" infrastructure. This organizational failure was further exacerbated by a dismissive and patronizing anti-Arab attitude that essentialized Jaffa as Tel-Aviv's "backyard" and was blind to its unique historical heritage. This institutionalized approach gradually changed as the city's real estate potential became apparent—which led to the "discovery" of Jaffa.

After decades of disinvestment, the period between 1985 and October 2000 (the outbreak of the Second Intifada) marked a radical change in the municipal planning policy. The newly established "Jaffa Planning Team," set up by the city engineer in 1985, has led a neoliberal planning policy based on a tight coupling of the municipality and the private sector for the sake of "Jaffa's physical and socioeconomic rehabilitation." Privatizing state-owned property, outsourcing services, and luring investors were explicit strategies aimed at regenerating the "decayed" urban fabric and bringing in new affluent and educated (Jewish) inhabitants who in turn would infuse more tax revenues into the municipality's budget. The following is a quote from a Jaffa Planning Team internal report which reflects this planning policy shift under the banner of "With the Face to the South Side" (*'Im ha-Panim la-Darom*): "In the many debates held in the Engineering Department, an understanding gradually crystallized that the 'Urban Renewal' policy had failed miserably and that we should nurture Jaffa's unique traits so that they would attract a new population that would strengthen the existing one" (Jaffa Planning Team 1997, 6).

This final conclusion, which sees Jaffa as a lure for a stronger "new population," is the key euphemism of the powerful redemptive narrative that was planted in the 1980s by the Jaffa Planning Team and bloomed in the 1990s. The municipality's Urban Renewal Project consisted of four steps. First was the preparation of new statutory construction plans. The demolition of Arab buildings, which was widespread in the 1970s and the beginning of the 1980s, slowed down in the second half of the 1980s and eventually stopped altogether. This resulted also in a new architectural language, which came to be known as the "Jaffa Style." Second, in 1987 the municipality applied for government funding and tax benefits as part of the National Rehabilitation Project (Menahem 1998). A third important move was the municipality's signing a contract with the Israel Land Administration, the main owner of land and buildings in the city, in order to institute a "closed economy" apparatus, i.e., to channel some of the profits from land sales into the redevelopment and rehabilitation of public infrastructure in the neighborhood itself. Finally, in the process of raising funds for the project, Jaffa was twinned with Los Angeles through the mediation of the Jewish Agency for Israel. This implementation of urban renewal on the institutional-public level brought about the first buds of private enterprise in the real estate domain—the most prominent of which was the Andromeda Hill Project, which will be analyzed in the next chapter.

Whereas critical geographers usually conceive of gentrification as an unstoppable process and an integral part of the postindustrial city's spatial economy (Smith 2002), the October 2000 events in Jaffa manifested the localized link between nationalist forces and urban dynamics. The violent demonstrations resulted in an immediate (yet temporary) halt to the previously booming real estate market. The events also marked a change in Jaffa's image. The once "charming" and chic neighborhoods of 'Ajami and Jabaliyye were suddenly marked as menacing Arab space, and for many months most Jewish customers and tourists who used to frequent Arab-owned stores and restaurants every Saturday and holiday kept Jaffa at arm's length. As a result of a boycott by Jewish customers, Jaffa became a ghost town for nearly a year, and many merchants and restaurants lost their primary clientele. Notwithstanding this devastating effect on the livelihood of Palestinian businessmen in Jaffa, the 2001 economic recession also brought many luxury projects to the verge of bankruptcy.[8] The Jaffa that was marketed in the 1990s as "Little Paris" and as the "chic cultural quarter of Tel-Aviv" was depicted in the media after October 2000 as a "Little Tehran" that had been taken over by Islamist and nationalist elements.[9]

The ambivalent reaction among the Palestinian residents to the real estate recession is indicative of the inherent dialectics of gentrification. Despite the general frustration toward what was perceived as an anti-Arab embargo, many Palestinians were relieved to see a halt in a process that could have brought about their "economic transfer" and the disintegration of the Arab community in 'Ajami. As one resident put it in a meeting with municipality officials, "I'm not against development [*pituah*], I'm against discrimination [*kipuah*]. I'm for development but against displacing the Arabs from the area. We're talking about a very poor population who mostly don't own their houses and it will bring about transfer. This is our fear. In the October events and the negative image of Jaffa there is something good. It prevents rich Jews from coming. But they come anyway. . . ."

Gentrification in Jaffa evolved in three stages. In the first stage, in the 1960s and 1970s, a group of artists settled in Jaffa, and "bought ruins" which they "rebuilt from scratch."[10] The gentrifiers of the first wave are often described (and describe themselves) as "pioneers" and "cool artists" who came to the city not out of greed, but in search of "inner space and high ceilings." The second stage, in the 1980s, saw the arrival of a group that self-identified as "Bobo" and searched for "a place in Tel-Aviv that has historical depth and the charm of locality." The property values at this stage were considerably higher, and the gentrifiers often had to sell their previous apartments in pursuit of the multicultural blend of "isolation and openness" that Jaffa had to offer.

While most of the second-wave gentrifiers are young professionals of the "new middle class," the third phase of gentrification marks the entry of a new social force into the urban arena: international real estate entrepreneurs and wealthy residents living in gated communities. At this stage, dilapidated buildings in attractive areas were converted into luxury projects, and whole streets were marked as elite and private spaces that most of the city's dwellers—especially Palestinians—avoid entering. In the 1990s real estate prices skyrocketed and reached up to four to five million dollars for a luxury apartment in 'Ajami, which at the same time was ranked as the second-poorest neighborhood in the Tel-Aviv-Jaffa metropolis. These urban actors often purchase chic apartments as a financial investment. By the time this stage began, the presence of the

new gentrifiers was perceived as disturbingly invasive and alienating—
hence the cynical nickname "Northsiders" (*Tzfonim*) invoked by Arab
and Jewish locals alike. This stage swept many developers into the real
estate craze commonly referred to as the "Jaffa bug." At the same time
many of the original residents were tempted to sell their houses and relocate to the cheaper eastern neighborhoods of Jaffa, farther away from
the coastline.

These chronological stages represent three organizing modalities of
the dynamics of gentrification in Jaffa. However, they are not exclusively
linear, as they still continue to coexist concurrently. Other populations,
including hippie communes, individual leftists, Jewish-Arab mixed couples, and students looking for cheap rent, are increasingly attracted to
Jaffa for different reasons. Gentrification in Jaffa, therefore, involves different ideological layers, diverse groups, and social agents—all striving
to maximize what I term "spatial capital."[11]

GENTRIFICATION AND ITS DISCONTENTS

The literature on gentrification is undecided about the social valorization and political effects of "urban renewal." The theoretical inquiry into
the concept of "redevelopment" exposes stark controversies: on the one
hand, partisan neoliberal interpretations view gentrification as a wonder
drug that will cure the ills of the inner city, as the emancipation of the
entrepreneurial individual, and as the dissolution of borders; while on
the other hand, critical accounts regard it as the tyranny of capital, the
imperialism of kitsch, and the defeat of politics (Schlichtman and Patch
2013; Smith and Williams 1986). In Jaffa, some circles view this process
as the embodiment of a utopian "New Middle East," an expression of coexistence, or an economic "upgrade," but others see it as an instantiation of exclusion, Judaization, and economic transfer. Cutting across the
debate is the unresolved problem of boundary-making—the borders
of community and city, in-group/out-group relations, uneven development, and state intervention.

While gentrification is by no means unique to Jaffa, it is deeply
marked by the colors of class and politics of the local urban context and
the gravitational force of Tel-Aviv—Israel's financial capital. Ever since

British sociologist Ruth Glass (1964, xviii) coined the term "gentrification" to describe a new pattern of intra-urban migration in London, it came to express much more than changing housing preferences—it is both a theoretical concept and an ideological token.[12]

Drawing on Neil Smith's (2002) definition of gentrification as a "discrete double-faced process combining the penetration of middle-class and upper-middle-class population to poorer-yet-exotic neighborhoods followed by the displacement of the original residents," we can view the urban process in economic and cultural terms alike (Scott 2000; Zukin 1994). In light of the marked convergence between the spheres of cultural and economic development, I conceptualize the process of gentrification as motion in an urban force field that pits against each other agents competing over different forms of "spatial capital." This approach suggests a combined analysis that integrates supply and demand, class and sign, as well as economic rationality and cultural lifestyles. In Jaffa, marketing slogans for new luxury projects—such as the aforementioned "Living in Jaffa is a matter of style. Investing in Jaffa is a matter of wisdom," or "To Buy or Not to Be"—capture the quintessential logic of gentrification and illustrate the spatial links among economic, cultural, and symbolic capital. Gentrification is thus seen as a relational process of spatial transformation and differentiation anchored in the economy of late capitalism and endowing its new middle-class urban carriers with a distinct sense of identity.

Within the Israeli context, gentrification is taking place in a specific cultural and economic regime dating back to the 1970s and predicated on an individualistic, achievement-orientated, consumerist, and hedonistic identity politics that has challenged the collectivistic, statist, and national frame of reference.[13] This globalist, secular identity is carried by the new Israeli middle class and is characterized by an alliance between liberal ideology and rational professional expertise. To realize the potential of profit and freedom, "this strata strives to release Israeli culture from old (Zionist) nationalism and from new (neo-Zionist) tribalism, and to usher it into modernist, Western, or globalist culture" (Ram 2000, 227). In the local context of Jaffa the Jewish-Arab interface promotes a discourse of a new-old village-like "frontier," delivering the promise of multiculturalism and historical depth to the liberal settlers.[14]

The social world inhabited and crafted by gentrifiers in Jaffa is made up of distinct types of cultural and social actors who eventually chose to settle in the politically contested, formerly disinvested neighborhood. These actors and ideologies fuel the urban process and contribute to what has been described in the literature as gentrification's "complex" and "chaotic" nature (Beauregard 1986). The following discussion identifies five types of social actors that make up the field of gentrification in Jaffa: the architect, the real estate agent, the residents' association, the radical gentrifier, and the philosopher-gentrifier.

The Architect of Gentrification: "A Win-Win Situation"

In the distinguished setting of the French ambassadorial residence in 'Ajami, a group of francophones gather monthly to mingle and listen to popular lectures over French pastries, wine, and cheese under the auspices of the ambassador's wife. The residential compound, built in 1935 by two Jewish architects (Rappaport and Federman) for a wealthy Palestinian Christian businessman, was purchased from the original owner by the French embassy following the 1948 war. Since the establishment of the State of Israel, it has been standing out as a landmark in the poor 'Ajami neighborhood as well as representing a political statement by the French foreign affairs service, which refuses to follow most foreign diplomatic representatives and relocate its ambassador to the prestigious Herzliya Pituah, or Kfar Shmaryahu villa towns.

In the meeting that took place in October 2001, the guest lecturer was Ilan Pivko, a well-known Israeli architect whose name is associated with the aesthetic "discovery" of Jaffa and epitomized in the "Sea Shell House," which he planned and where he lived. A notion of the architect, his vision, and his life's project is conveyed in a documentary broadcast on the France 5 channel entitled *Portraits d'architectes: Ilan Pivko dans le contexte* (Portraits of architects: Ilan Pivko in context), in which Pivko defines himself as a "poet of space and a creator of emotions":

> Israel is built on an idea and therefore an abstraction. I believe that this
> abstraction created in me a need to set out in search of rough and concrete

FIGURE 4.1. The Sea Shell House. Renovation 1990. Architect: Ilan Pivko. *Photo by the author, 2014.*

elements. . . . Here I feel the mixture of time and cultures. For me, living in Jaffa is to live in Tel-Aviv with roots. . . . When I first bought my house it had nothing special. It had to be rebuilt, while preserving the spirit of the district, an Italian spirit. . . . I feel that what has always guided my reflection is a will to create harmony out of concepts that have been too often perceived as opposing: past, present, future, and various cultures. . . . In Tel-Aviv there was a desire to detach oneself from everything that represented the Jews of the Diaspora. Architecture expressed a desire of rebirth, of purification. . . . In Jaffa there were simple things without luxury or beauty. It is perhaps here that I became an architect. . . . Rather than inscribe myself in history, I try to be a poet of space and a creator of emotions.

The lecture that ensued dealt with the topic of "Architecture in 'Ajami." Complimenting the French Embassy for remaining in Jaffa, Pivko began his talk by stating that "France is the only country that understood early on that beauty lies in Jaffa and not in Herzliya Pituah." Well informed in urban theory, Pivko presented a liberal manifesto of the "healthy" relationship between urbanism and economy as embedded in gentrification. Pivko's narrative proceeded to touch on three themes: the history of gentrification, Jaffa's cosmopolitanism, and the reaction of the

Arab population to gentrification. He started with his view of gentrification as a natural process from which everyone eventually benefits:

> All over the world there are old districts in the process of renewal. In Paris or London it's always about architectural problems—here the place is more complicated as the problems are also political. Generally speaking, gentrification starts with the artists, with people with a certain aesthetic sensitivity, and then with people with more money and power. The original population sells their property and they have the possibility to buy another apartment in an area, say, less special, but for them it's usually a step up [*une étape plus haute*]. Therefore, in general everyone is content and this is what one might call a "win-win situation." But little by little a district that had been once very poor becomes very wealthy. And this is gentrification.

For Pivko, the presence of a Palestinian community in Jaffa, however, and especially in 'Ajami, complicates the "natural" course of gentrification, which would normally involve a progressive population exchange and "balance out very well." Although this complexity hinders gentrification, Pivko acknowledged that Arab presence should be protected for the sake of what he calls "fairness":

> In Jaffa, this is not really possible. Precisely because most of the population, half of it, are people who live here not only because they don't have the means to live somewhere else, but also because they don't want to live anywhere else. They live with each other; it's more of a community. So, in Jaffa there's an entire community—there are judges, doctors, there are very rich people, and very poor people. It's not like in other countries where everything balances out [*tout s'égalise*] very well. So, this is why the city and the state try to find the means to allow the Arabs to stay. And this is why all this process doesn't work. It moves but very slowly. Because before there is a solution to improve housing for the Arab population we cannot move forward. And I think it's very fair [*juste*].

Despite the obstacles presented to the warranted project of gentrification by Jaffa's binational demography, Pivko views it as distinctly more heterogeneous, cosmopolitan, or, in short, "charming":

> Myself, I find that all this makes the district much more charming, much more interesting than districts in Europe, where gentrification turns these neighborhoods into very homogenous places. In Jaffa it's more real, deeper, at least for me. Because other places are eventually a bit sterile. The Old City of Jaffa is a good example. It doesn't have the life we find in 'Ajami. Here it's richer in sensation. You have people of all religions and languages:

Christians, Muslims, Jews. You have the church bells, the muezzin, synagogues.... It makes for a very cosmopolitan district.

Unsurprisingly, the French audience protested loudly against this critique of European urbanism, but Pivko continued to explain the difference he saw between a "pristine" tourist town and a livable and "real" neighborhood. "You don't want to live in a touristic town," he insisted. "In Jaffa on the contrary you feel that people live a real life—it's not embellished, pristine [*melukak*]. So I think that somewhere we have to be grateful that these circumstances forced us to create a place of life and genuineness [*vérité*]." His oeuvre as a poet of space and a creator of emotions, Pivko continued, has not only upgraded the state of the art of Jaffa's architecture but has also contributed to educating the local population with aesthetic values and architectural initiatives:

> I think my work has influenced people here. I know that for a fact. I am currently planning two buildings for Arabs in Jaffa who have understood that there are things to preserve. No doubt, the Arabs in Jaffa don't need me to leverage their town. They adore it, but I don't think they have this "scholarly" side [*côté savant*] of the dream of Jaffa's architecture. They love their city because it's their place, because it's their way of life. They love it for the colors, for the light, for the sea. There's definitely sensuality also among people who don't know architecture. But they don't have the knowledge [*connaissance*].

This "knowledge" that Pivko offers Jaffa includes an unorthodox theory of architectural conservation and the built heritage. In this perspective the history of destruction in Jaffa turns out to be a creative advantage and an artistic freedom:

> In my view we shouldn't conserve an idea of what was, but of things that are here. In Jerusalem and in Tel-Aviv a lot of things are here, whereas in Jaffa, unfortunately, perhaps, most of it was destroyed and we conserve an idea. What existed somewhere, phantoms.... When there's nothing you can conserve an idea, a citation. But you can also be more creative and still conserve the spirit of the urban fabric. The architectural language was very European. It wasn't an Arab city. Myself, I have decided not to conserve in this way. I created "with," not "like." I did research on the architectural language and what I found was slang [*argot*]. If there's an architectural language, there's also a language of life.

Although professedly fascinated by the vernacular architecture of the "language of life" in a city he considers "very European," Pivko symp-

tomatically neglected to dwell on the political and economic predicament of the Palestinian population. He addressed the Arab reaction to
gentrification only in response to a direct question from the audience:

> The Arabs' reaction toward the Jewish inhabitants who took control, in a
> way, of their town is very complex. Most of the people find it very flattering
> because for years no one wanted to come here, and suddenly people like us
> arrive and invest a lot of money. There's a lot of this. But of course, there is the
> other side. There are those who say, "We're being invaded. We'll get chased
> out of our hometown." And therefore there's fear. I think that politically there
> was somewhere an attitude of what is called the Judaization of Jaffa [*Yihud
> Yafo*]. But eventually everyone understood that it won't work. It's not the path
> to be taken. At this moment the authorities start to see how it would be pos-
> sible to let the Arabs stay in place [*rester chez eux*]. This starts to tone down
> the reaction. The Arab reactions are very good; they were always good.

On our way back from the ambassador's residence, while we were
walking through the empty lots in 'Ajami, which was half destroyed in
the 1960s and '70s, a French resident of Jaffa who has been living there
since the 1960s told me angrily, "This was a talk of lies and cover-ups. The
political essence was omitted. He talked about real things but the lecture
was not real because he didn't talk about the politics of destruction."
Euphemizing the history of Palestinian displacement, municipal disinvestment, and social inequalities, Pivko put forth an aesthetic discourse
of spontaneous development, professional knowledge, and a civilizing
process, which characterizes the selective liberal imagination of gentrification. Pivko's ideas and the different forms of capital supporting them
are indicative of gentrification's depoliticizing ideologies.

Agents of Gentrification: Real Estate Agencies in Jaffa

The second type of agent—less learned but nonetheless aggressively
market-oriented and effective—is the real estate broker. In Jaffa about
ten agencies work in the area of Jerusalem Boulevard, specializing in
marketing relatively cheap apartments for low-income target populations. Five additional agencies operate in 'Ajami and market luxury housing in gated communities such as the Andromeda Hill project or the Jaffa
Courts (with 270 units each), as well as smaller, "more intimate" housing
projects such as Pivko's Sea Shell (offering 26 housing units).

At the office of Nadlan Yaffo (Jaffa Real Estate, http://www.nadlan
-yaffo.co.il), strategically located in Maronite Hill in the luxurious North
Side of 'Ajami (marketed as "North Jaffa"), I was welcomed by Nimrod
Peri, an experienced real estate agent who has been working in Jaffa for
five years. Declaring at the outset that he "fell in love with Jaffa," Peri
seemed eager to relay his take on gentrification and share his professional
and personal experience:

> I see things in a very particular light. I'm no Jaffan even though I walk
> around here all the time and I talk to people a lot. This is also my process
> of recognition [*hakara*]. Often when I talk to local people [*anashim me-
> komiyim*] I realize that I got it all wrong. I realize that we all live the cover-up
> of after the riots [*pra'ot* (the October 2000 events)]. It overwhelms me not
> from the sociological side but from the humanitarian aspect of it. When
> I see a policeman arresting people whom I know and letting them stand
> two hours in the sun—I can't accept it. It drives me crazy. These things are
> what turn, unfortunately, the situation to what the Rabita association calls
> a situation of an occupier and an occupied. But I also see the other side
> of neighborliness, of the connection between the people.

A self-proclaimed observer of the social dynamics in Jaffa, Peri dis-
cerns a reciprocal transformation among both Palestinians and Jews
due to daily social interactions between them. In his personal case, he
admits, working in Jaffa brought him to a political realization:

> Here my political outlook meets real estate and my everyday life. It's the
> middle of Tel-Aviv here and many Arab youth are completely Tel-Avivan.
> It's not that we take control over them and force them to be part of Tel-Aviv.
> They are much closer to us than anyone else. But we also have to change
> somewhere. I can tell you that in my case the effect was that I became *de
> facto* more leftist. I use this word because there's something in it. It has a
> humanitarian value and coming here did change me. I can tell you that I
> grew up in North Tel-Aviv. When I just got here I was in a terrifying fright.
> What am I doing here? But there's a process of falling in love firstly with the
> ambiance, the freedom and kindness. And then once you start getting to
> know people, you suddenly understand that this is a person to whom I give
> a sea of respect who's being treated in an awful manner and it hurts. When
> you think about it humanely it's appalling. To think that in our state there
> are two levels of people . . .

In spite of his profound attachment to his new workplace, Peri still
chooses to reside in Ramat ha-Sharon, one of the main *Tzfoni* (North-

sider) suburbs and among the wealthiest cities in Israel. Repeatedly in his narrative, Jaffa takes the form of social "connectedness" as opposed to the alienated aloofness of Ramat ha-Sharon:

> It's a disadvantage that I don't live here. I'm positive that had I lived here I would have known many more people. Still I take the car and drive up to pristine Ramat ha-Sharon. But the truth is that I'm much more connected to here. Jaffa has a set of things. It's not the beauty and it's not the squalor. It's not something you can explain with these tools, but Jaffa stems from other places. In Jaffa, I don't know why, people are more connected. Maybe it's their need, because they're dominated, to connect with someone stronger, as it were. I don't know. However, there's here another connection. For example, someone crosses the street the twentieth time—he says hello and I say hello, for two years now. We chat. In other places it doesn't exist.

Deeply rooted in his intersubjective position as a salesman, Peri's views present a fascinating merger of his social role as a real estate agent and his romantic outlook on Jaffa as the only place in Tel-Aviv where convivial South Side neighborliness still exists:

> People live in a neighborhood because it's a neighborhood. In Tel-Aviv an agent is connected like anyone else. One doesn't have any advantage. On the North Side people don't rent through the grocery store. In Jaffa they do. That's one of the nicest things here. There are things that a man needs to be whole within himself and live in an environment, in a district. That's what I try to show people as a salesman. Sometimes it works, sometimes it doesn't. I don't know how to judge if it's my view as a salesman that took over me and that I don't actually see things right, or if these are the real things.

Not surprisingly, in view of the coupling between Peri's professional self and his private self, the issue of gentrification is perceived as a non-problem and as the right thing at the right time for Jaffa:

> I think the entry of Jews in here has its advantages. First, in terms of property value and the upscaling of everybody's level. It improves the level of infrastructure, of schools and education. It's healthy for everyone and it's right for the neighborhood. I once told someone that in my opinion Jews should come here. And I don't say that from the perspective of taking over the place. I say that from the positive side, like the Americans say "Put your money where your mouth is." I want to be here because it's right, because it's important for me as a humanitarian person, because it's important to the area. Because the fact that I'm in here makes a difference. And I can help. So he told me that that's what the settlers also say. . . .

Proposing that the very existence of Jews helps the Jaffa Arabs deal with their predicament, Peri warns against the voluntary "ghettoization" of the Arab residents, i.e., their self-segregation within the confines of a mononational community:

> It's clear that the Jews might eventually get out of here, and this is possible; if they hurt us we'll go. We're not strong enough to be here. There's a small part that comes for ideological reasons and even then ideology has its limits. Most people choose comfort in one way or another. So they'll hurt us and then they'll turn into a ghetto and it'll be terrible. Because they won't make progress. They'll disappear. Yafo will suffocate. If that's how the Arabs think then they're blind to everything that happens in the world. What leads the world now is integration: peace, shared life, common wishes, common goals.

Consistently attempting to reconcile his professional interest in gentrification with his liberal sociopolitical views, Peri contrasts the exclusive and luxury individual apartments he specializes in marketing with the "alienated" gated communities that he "sets apart from Jaffa":

> Our office works with Andromeda and the Jaffa Courts; we also have a project on Louis Pasteur Street, the Sea Shell, and one building on the flea market. However I set apart Andromeda from Jaffa. They are painted in local Jaffa colors, but they are closed compounds. If you put them in North Tel-Aviv it will be the same thing. They don't have life due to their location in Jaffa. They are cut off. Jaffa is not up to these massive projects. Especially since Jaffa is a small place. And there are things that really put me off. For example it kills me that people in Andromeda can call the police and complain about kids [Boy Scouts] playing the drums in church. It's after all the church's land that you got—damn it. It hurts. And that's the most anti-Jaffa thing there is. The big projects are predators. The Sea Shell is completely different. The people who live here are interested in Jaffa. They came out of a choice to live in the area and these are people who are connected to the neighborhood and know the Arabs. And this is something I really like.

Despite his overall euphemistic and romantic narrative, Peri doesn't refrain from criticizing the "pitiable passivity" of the Jaffa Arabs who refuse to "empower" themselves through Jaffa's "urban revival":

> Here's a place with good land, and good people chose to live here. Look at it in a different light. . . . For instance, I live in Ramat ha-Sharon and I'm not rich. But for my girls' sake I prefer living in this area so that our kids will enjoy the good environment, the social services. Here you are in a weak area, strong people get in—get some strength from them. I wish people would

listen to what I say! It's true that they are afraid but the "Judaization" has its merits. Secondly, your house is worth more money. On the one hand they bitch and moan about it, on the other hand they know to ask for much more money for their houses. Instead of complaining let's empower ourselves. It's their pitiable passivity that says, "Shit happens and here I remain." The fact is that some people did advance because of this—either through selling their apartment or through work.

In closing, Peri unfolded his credo of the redemptive role gentrification plays in the salvation of Jaffa. In a quasi-Christian narrative of self-sacrifice, integrity, and wholeness, he completes his conceptualization of Jaffa's spatial capital as a place where one can be in harmony with self and community:

> I'm happy that people come here even if I don't make a profit off them. I see it as an advantage because Jaffa is moving forward. I'm happy that people are coming because you can characterize them by their political views, by their education level, and by their humanitarian qualities. And this is one of my gratifications. I'm interested in the right house for the right person. And I don't deal with brokerage manipulation. I lost hundreds of thousands of shekels in broker's fees but I gained a sense of integrity and completeness. That's also how you gain a broader basis with people. These are the things I work for—for my mental wholeness.

Both the architect and the real estate agent endorse and reproduce the "redemptive" discourse of gentrification. With a vested interest in the future of gentrification and the privatization of land, they make virtue out of reality and profession. Devout individualists, theirs is a "charming" Jaffa of warmth and "humanitarian" values—bereft of collectivities in conflict and structures of inequality. Their naiveté notwithstanding, these neoliberal agents are positioned well enough in the planning and marketing apparatuses to play a significant part in the transformation of Jaffa into a bourgeois space of consumption.

Organized Gentrifiers: "Ashkenazi Fans of Jaffa"

While many associations have risen and disintegrated throughout the years, the gentrifier-led organization Jaffa, Belle of the Seas (Yafo Yafat Yamim) stands out. Manned by skilled and well-networked architects, lawyers, and politicians (one of whom is the wife of the former deputy mayor), the gentrifiers have taken a firm and active hold on Jaffa's civil society space. Demanding what they see as their lawful civil rights, the members of Jaffa, Belle of the Seas (hereafter J B S) increasingly make demands to improve infrastructure and street cleaning, create an adequate educational system, and rid the city of its infestation of drugs and crime. Largely ignored by the lower-class Jewish population and regarded with suspicion by Palestinian activists, gentrifiers in Jaffa pursue nothing less than an urban civilizing mission. Their democratic, modern, and liberal core values, such as order, antisquatting, legal ownership, bureaucratic transparency, and resident participation in policy decisions, threaten to transform the Jaffa space in ways that would significantly improve the "quality of life" of both the Jewish and Arab middle classes but at the expense of the city's current character (with its late-night bakeries, small workshops, loud Narguileh coffeehouses, squatters, and free wandering horses). To cite one extreme example, both the mayor and the Jaffa resident ex–deputy mayor were threatened with murder by the Turq Arab family in Jaffa if further investigations into the legal status of a property the Turq family squatted on proceeded.

In April 2003, J B S began publishing a monthly magazine entitled, significantly, *My Jaffa*. In the editorial of the first issue, Tzur Sheizaf, the association's chair, defines the organization's agenda in class-blind, civic, and liberal terms:

> The Jaffa, Belle of the Seas, association, one of the oldest associations in Jaffa, was founded in the 1980s in order to stop the demolition of 'Ajami, the landfill project, and the destruction of the seashore. The association is an initiative of the Arab and Jewish residents of Jaffa, of all political positions, who wish to endow Jaffa and its residents with an appropriate quality of life. . . . Since 1997 we work in a framework that includes all the arenas of life in Jaffa. The association's goals are to act for the preservation of the values of history, landscape, architecture, and nature in Jaffa and to promote collaboration between the different groups in the city. One has to add, of course, civil security, cleanliness, infrastructure, and all of what the city lacks.

The association takes pride in a long list of communal and civil projects, including closing down the methadone clinic, adding a division in the Weitzman elementary school, halting the privatization of the Jaffa port, and conducting intensive debates and continuous communication with the municipality. "Most of the infrastructure renovation and rehabilitation," Sheizaf boasts, "follows the working papers the association has been preparing since 1998." Indeed, by the late 1990s JBS established itself as the leading Jewish effort in creating a discursive and activist space for civil society in Jaffa. While drawing on the aforementioned discourses and values of urban regeneration and law enforcement, JBS's success should be assessed on both the organizational and the cultural levels.

In one of the association meetings I attended, the board members negotiated their relations with another organization's delegate while revealing in the process some of the association's main ethnic and class-based characteristics. "After all, we are Ashkenazi fans of Jaffa," joked one of the main activists. Opposing her wholesale generalization, Tzur Sheizaf explained,

> We founded the association fifteen years ago, but in its present form it's five years old. We do public activism without funding. We work constantly with the Rabita and we drag them by the hair to all the activities. We have a special connection with the Rabita first, but also with the Orthodox Club and the city local bureau [the Mishlama]. Absurdly, our relations with the Jaffa Arabs are much better than our relations with the Jewish population of Jaffa C. and Jaffa D. Really we don't have any contact with Jaffa D.'s folks. After October [2000] we were shocked by their right-wing racist nationalism and their hatred. We're miles apart. They want other things.

After establishing the disparities with the Jewish residents' associations of the lower-class neighborhoods, Sheizaf detailed the reasons for the limited collaboration with Arab civil associations:

> The most noticeable thing is that we don't have Arab activists in the association. But we've reached an agreement with the Rabita that they do their job and we do ours. And we cooperate on any subject that is important for the good of Jaffa. I once wanted to unite the Jewish and Arab associations, but we couldn't get the Rabita to show up to the meetings. When I set up a personal meeting with 'Abed Satel we sat for two hours. When I told him let's join together as one organization he didn't show up. We learned that we're good at operating by ourselves. We have one hundred and fifty registered members but fifteen active ones. I've known Jaffa for twelve years and it's in the worst state I've ever seen it.

JBS's operative agenda is based on a discourse of Jewish-Arab coexistence bereft of any class analysis. Focusing on specialized activities in the realm of civil society, the association's organizational ideology is marked by an instrumental approach to the advancement of peaceful coexistence. Thus one of the members proposed a snowball solution to the impasse in Jewish-Arab relations:

> What's happening in Jaffa is happening all over the country and if we succeed with Jewish-Arab relations we might still have a chance to live together. We get everything we want from the authorities. Our problem is totally different—our problem is to create trust between Jews and Arabs. Our goal is that one hundred Arabs would get to know one hundred Jews, the same relationship as 'Abed Satel and I have. That's how I feel that we could create a stable kernel in Jaffa. Jaffa is in a bad state and this stems out of a lack of familiarity. Our challenge is to get to a state where there's a level of personal familiarity between most of the Jaffa Jews and most of the Jaffa Arabs so that people from the outside won't be afraid. Now, the most critical and urgent thing is to create cooperation between the Arab and Jewish activists in Jaffa.

A romantic and culturalist view of Jaffa as a site of potential political salvation is reflected in narratives of many individual JBS members. One of the active members, an interior decorator and the wife of the former deputy mayor, captured the cultural essence of the gentrifiers' liberal image of the city:

> I was always interested in culture—I always looked for a cultural soul [*neshama tarbutit*]. In Jaffa there are groups but there's a common denominator among people here—we all look for a lifestyle with aesthetics, culture, and statement. People came to Jaffa because they were looking for high ceilings and inner space. I've been here for eight years and when I came there was such a group already here for fifteen years. Those who were here before Ilan Pivko were more artsy and bohemian; they arrived when Jaffa was in ruins. If I were to define myself—I'm a bourgeois bohemian, "Bobo." I was accepted here even though I had to sell my apartment to buy one here. But the old-time residents kept moaning about the neglect and did nothing about it. I came to the Maronite neighborhood for the tempting price. We came at the last minute, I sold a three-and-a-half-bedroom apartment, and I bought a house for two hundred and fifty thousand dollars. A year later I got an offer for four hundred thousand dollars.

Middle-class gentrifiers differentiate themselves from both the "right wing" tenants of the gated communities and the lower-class Mizrahi "Arab haters" of the Jewish neighborhood. As such, they welcome the entry of a young middle-class population that "improves the area." The interior designer continued,

The Maronite neighborhood differs radically from the Andromeda project that doesn't integrate into the environment. I was there once at their swimming pool and I heard them talk about going to a right-wing demonstration. Also in Lev Yafo [the Heart of Jaffa neighborhood on Jerusalem Boulevard] there are a lot of Arab haters. In contrast, the Noga compound has one-hundred-and-ten-thousand-dollar apartments. This will bring a young middle-class population to Jaffa and this is not an economic transfer anymore. We in the Meretz Party wanted the concept of Jaffa as a "sub-city" [*tat-'ir*]. Michael Ro'e demanded in 1993 that Jaffa be a "closed economic circuit." He claimed that economic transfer should be avoided at all costs so that the Arabs would be able to remain in the area. There was definitely a conceptual and political war on this. That's why people hate Pivko, it's because he's the symbol of the skyrocketing land values. Ro'e changed his mind and finally agreed that as Northsiders [*Tzfonim*] move in they improve the area.

The phenomenology of gentrification in Jaffa is predicated on multiple registers of differentiation: between liberals and "Arab haters," between left-leaners and right-wingers, between integrationists and snobs, and among the nouveau riche, the bourgeois, and millionaires. Despite internal animosities (toward Pivko or working-class nationalist Jews), this differentiation ultimately allows all actors to justify their urban position in moral, cultural, and political terms.

Radical Gentrifiers: "Committed to Multiculturalism"

Gentrification in Jaffa does not consist exclusively of middle-class liberal Jews implicated in the economic "revitalization" of real estate and in the bourgeois "civilizing mission" of its landscape. In what follows, I examine three alterative subtypes that *participate* willy-nilly in the transformation of Jaffa's urban space but *oppose* it on ideological grounds. The first case tells the story of a middle-class couple, the second of a student activist, and the third of a commune of students.

Living in a Mixed Community: "We're Not
Leaving, Unless It's for the South Pacific"

Lisa, an educator with a PhD from an American university, and John, a former civil servant, are a couple of retired English Jews who decided to settle in Jaffa in the early 1990s. They see themselves as local activists. Lisa dedicates much of her time to promoting education in Arab schools and developing extracurricular educational activities, while John is more invested in local party politics and engaged in struggles with the municipality and its administrative extension, the Mishlama. Volunteering in different organizations, Lisa and John are deeply committed social brokers of civil society and community empowerment, holding firm opinions on everything from the functioning of the municipality to the local Arab associations and Jewish-Arab relations.

Replying to my question about her decision to settle down in Jaffa, of all places, Lisa unfolded an itinerary that leads from the UK to Chicago and ends in Jaffa:

> It's interesting you're going to ask the question, because the landlord [*ba'al ha-bayit*] here wants to sell next year, so we're just starting the last year of the contract unless we buy. We can't afford it. And I have friends saying to me, "I know a place [outside of Jaffa]—why don't you move there?" No, no. I want to be here! I always wanted to live in, quote, a mixed community, and when I lived in the Chicago area I wanted to live in Hyde Park. . . . On my first visit here I met this guy who was working with deprived kids in Jaffa. He drove me around here. And I looked at it, and we went to the good areas and the bad areas. And he told me about his institute for the advancement of children in Jaffa. I was interested and excited and I said, we can do something with this. And I said, I want to live here, I love the sea, always wanted that.

In the early nineties, Lisa and John's first dilemma revolved around the question of whether to own a house in Jaffa or to lease a property. This started a process of integration into the Arab community and of increasing identification with its cause:

> JOHN: We almost bought by the mosque, a gorgeous apartment on the top floor of a three-story building. And we were ready to put money on the table when the assessor who was looking at it came with the fact that the apartment was registered in the name of thirteen people. All in the same family, but half of them they didn't even know where they were. The things that are worth buying are expensive. This place would probably sell for seven hundred thousand dollars. If you buy, in the end it costs you just as much as renting.

> LISA: To cut a long story short, we finally rented a house in Jaffa, but although I'm committed to multiculturalism, and was willing to live with a mixed population in Israeli terms, I really didn't know anything about Arabs. We came to live here and as you know now my Hebrew is

better, but I didn't know aleph from bet. Anyway, all my life I had been working with minorities and I assumed I could do something here. By the time I came to live in Jaffa, I realized that nobody was willing to work with minorities in Israel. And they were telling me things like, "We don't have problems like you have in America, it's different."

Gradually their involvement with the community increased along with a realization of the complexities of the local political condition. Living in a mixed community added "another layer of understanding":

> LISA: Meanwhile we got pulled into the community—one of the best things was the Matnas [community center] almost eight years ago, there was a woman called Orna from the 'Irya [municipality] who pulled together a group of Jews and Arabs called "Neighbors Talk" [*Shkhenim Medabrim*], half and half. Many of the Arabs that I know today in Jaffa we met in that group. That was a very helpful entrance into Jaffa; it added to my already multicultural background. This was just another layer of understanding—here's another culture, another way of life. We became more and more part of the community, and I understood what life is like here and what it was like for people.

Lisa and John describe their everyday life experience as the key factor in their integration and increasing political involvement. For them, the demographics of their street represented a multicultural "cross-section of Jaffa":

> LISA: You always make more connections, people on the street. And you know we have Christians on the street, we've got Ashkenazi Jews, we've got Sephardic Jews, and we've got Muslims, plus a Polish diplomat and a drug dealer and a young yuppie couple. A cross-section of Jaffa. You live in a community, you know the people in the street, and you become more and more part of the scenery. John spends a lot of time going around and talking to people. I don't mainly because I can't, couldn't, and women do much less of that anyway around here.

> JOHN: Take for example Omar Siksik [the former chair of the Rabita and a vocal local spokesman]. Our first meeting with him was the election before last to the 'Irya. And I parked the car, there was a vegetable shop on Yefet, that is no longer there, and I come back to the car and it's covered with stickers: "We're All for Jaffa." We didn't live here in Jaffa. So I went into the office of "We're All for Jaffa," and I said, you put it on my car, now get them off. The second time we started to talk and since then it's become a very firm friendship. Actually this whole area is Siksik, there's a family of Siksik over there, his uncle lives down there.

As with many other gentrifiers, the particular appeal of Jaffa for Lisa and John was its liberating makeup and the dynamic engagement of cultural difference in contrast with Tel-Aviv's "monoculture":

> LISA: All the fringe Jewish groups are coming in now. That's interesting, you know, like a Haight-Ashbury in San Francisco of the 1960s, a fringe group that found a haven in an urban area that was going downhill but quite picturesque. But you see, it's so beautiful here and it's free of the social constraints of Tel-Aviv. Because you cannot behave that much differently to your neighbors there. There's a monoculture, there's a common denominator. But in Jaffa whatever you want to do—you do. We have a relationship in this street that we never had when we lived in Ramat ha-Sharon. But we're the Other in that respect, for the majority are the Arabs.

> JOHN: We're in between, we're obviously not Andromeda or the Old City. We're also not from that point of view Yafo D., which is something else again.

> LISA: One of the most amazing places that I've seen for Arabs and Jews being together is the clinic I go to. It's next to the mosque on Sdertot Yerushalayim. The mixture—old, young, religious, not religious, Jews, Arabs—absolutely amazing. The secretary, I asked her the other day—very kind of Bat-Yam type—"What's your name?" She said, "Daisy." I said, "Daisy?" It's like an English name. She said, "My grandmother came from Iraq and it was also her name in Iraq." You never know.

Taking a more realistic position, John, for his part, doesn't take these examples of functional coexistence and intermixing at face value. In his view, Jaffa has yet to become an island of peaceful coexistence:

> JOHN: I would say it's totally isolated. Here [in 'Ajami] there is no interaction between Jews and Arabs, because there are very few Jews, but if you go to Lev Yafo [on Jerusalem Boulevard] the interaction is perfectly normal. There's no friction that you hear about.

> LISA: The old question is, does familiarity breed contempt or the opposite. In the 1950s they created mixed housing. What's so extraordinary I find here is that people live in the same building but their kids go to separate schools. The Greek Orthodox schools began also to have a lot of Muslims who send their kids because there education is better. But as long as you get this segregated style of education—it's not going to go very far. You know, somebody was saying the other day, "Doesn't it get to you to hear the muezzin all the time?" I miss it when I don't hear it.

> JOHN: I would be far more bothered by church bells.

Addressing the topic of gentrification and land privatization in Jaffa, John maintains that the problem still remains a systemic one, stemming from the state's discriminatory policies:

> The problem remains what it has always been: the "dark" presence behind the scenes of the Minhal [the Israel Land Administration], which has a different agenda from the agenda of the municipality. This municipality at the moment is not where Mayor Tchich was, they're not driving Arabs out by any means. The Minhal wants to sell, and obviously, who are they going to sell to? From my point of view, what I suggested to the Rabita and no one took it up, was that they should press the Ministry of Finance and the Minhal: "You took this land from Arabs—now give it for free and reduce the price of the apartments." But nobody took it up. It's too moral! But obviously the Minhal don't want to sell to Arabs; they want to sell to Jews. Quite frankly if I was a member in good standing in the Arab community, I would be talking to the real estate developers in Nazareth, Arabs, who've got money to come in and buy. It comes down to this problem that they don't know how to stand up for their own rights.

Differentiating himself from the organized gentrifiers of JBS, John explains why their ways diverged on grounds of principle and the disparity between physical planning and social planning:

> Tzur Sheizaf [the association's chair] asked me at one point to take on the function of general secretary of the amuta [association]. I went to one meeting and it was enough to put me off for life. Basically, the problem there for the most part is that there should be streetlights, that there should be good garbage collection—all this for the Jews. They don't have any interest whatsoever in the surrounding community. Sheizaf may be different. The others aren't.

Concluding the conversation, both Lisa and John expressed their determination to remain in Jaffa. "We're not leaving Jaffa," exclaimed John jokingly, "unless it's for the South Pacific." Their determination notwithstanding, living at the heart of an Arab neighborhood requires them, as Lisa observes, to deal with such profound questions of historical justice as, "You always live with the possibility of someone knocking on the door saying 'I lived here.'" John puts it in more explicit terms: "One of things we said to ourselves a number of times is that from what we know today, there's no way we would buy a house or rent a house, if we knew that by doing it we were preventing an Arab from getting it."

Politicized Gentrifiers: Engaging the Conflict

A second type of radical gentrifiers is the students and communes moving into Jaffa for explicitly ideological reasons. Predominantly students
and/or grassroots activists in their twenties, with a background in a
youth movement, these idealistic, educated, and mobile actors are bereft of any economic capital and bring to Jaffa only their commitment to
social change. Currently there are several such groups operating in Jaffa:
an anarchist commune, Reu't/Sadaqa (a binational youth movement
whose name means "friendship" in Arabic and Hebrew, respectively),
two hippie/New Age communes, and a Ha-Shomer ha-Tza'ir commune
(a socialist youth movement)—all amounting to no more than a hundred individuals. Note that these communes have settled in Jaffa only
since the mid-nineties as a product of the neoliberal "discovery" of the
city. Shelly, a thirty-year-old activist, decided to move to Jaffa in 2000
as a result of political encounters with Palestinian women from the Occupied Territories:

> At first I wanted to live in a mixed city and I thought about Lydda but it
> wasn't realistic because back then I was working in Tel-Aviv. Eventually I
> ended up in Jaffa. I had just returned from a dialogue project in the U.S.,
> a project called Building Bridges for Peace. It was for girls only, Israeli
> teenagers and Palestinian girls from the Territories. And I came back with
> a sense that it's no big deal to make it in a peace camp. That was my think-
> ing—to reduce segregation and live more together. From what I knew prior
> to that, when I was working at a Meretz office [a leftist Zionist party] in
> Tel-Aviv, Jaffa seemed to me the most reasonable place. Near work, the sea,
> and my friends.

Once she made up her mind, Shelly strolled the streets of Jaffa in
search of a place to live. The reactions surprised her: "It was pretty
amusing, because people were astonished, that I'm Ashkenazi, that I'm
Jewish, that I'm searching." Eventually she found an appropriate apartment owned by a Palestinian couple. "It probably looked suspicious and
strange, but I talked to the woman and she told me she has to wait for
her husband and then she said they want sixteen hundred shekels for a
studio [about four hundred dollars]. It was expensive for me but it was a
renovated apartment with a view of the sea. So eventually I was happy."

Shelly's integration into life in Jaffa was only partially due to her busy schedule outside the city. Her unfamiliarity with the local scene became clear during the October 2000 events: "I have reservations about saying that I had a 'Jaffa experience' because ultimately I didn't get to know many people. I never spent much time at the flat; I arrived late at night and I didn't have the time to talk to people on the street. I remember "Neighbors Talking" and the "Peace Tent" [two Jewish-Arab dialogue initiatives in the aftermath of the October events] and a meeting at the Rabita but mostly I sat and listened and didn't make any particular contacts. At the same time I was very active in things related to Palestinians, but in the Territories."

Her experience of the October events centered on both Jaffa and the Occupied Territories. "In October 2000, when it all started," she says, "I stayed at home glued to the radio and all the time just cried. The Palestinian girls from the peace camp wrote e-mails full of anxiety and anger. It was very tragic for me." Unfamiliar with the Jaffa scene, Shelly took a while to be able to venture outside:

> When the riots started here I didn't understand yet what was going on. Today I would have gone out myself and try to stand between the policemen and the residents, but then I just stayed at home. I closed myself off. Once after the mess [*balagan*] people from Bat-Yam came and I had just returned from work and the landlady called me and was scared. She said she heard people at the mosque calling to 'kill the Jews.' I didn't know what to do. I walked about a bit to Bat-Yam and back and I saw the police separating [Jewish demonstrators from Arab ones]. I think they actually did a good job.

After a period abroad, and along with an experimental binational commune called the International Women's Peace Presence, Shelly eventually returned to Jaffa and learned to appreciate what she calls "the increasing advantages of the city." The proximity of the seashore and the multicultural experience reinforced her sense of satisfaction: "I just enjoyed living here. I truly hope that I will be able to live in a place where everyone is not like me, Jewish and Ashkenazi. I want to live where there are Jews and Arabs, religious and secular. This would be the best thing." As a devout socialist, being a part of the general process of ethnic gentrification does not seem to preoccupy Shelly, as she thinks her lack of means distinguishes her from the wealthy Jews who settle in the city:

What can I say? It's very irritating. It's really not fair. If I want to live here I will want a flat in an apartment building or something of the sort. And when there are people who build huge villas it comes at the expense of apartment buildings. But it's irritating because people here had property and [Jews] found ways to drive them out or seduce them to leave and this is just aggravating. The whole gap between rich and poor. I don't know who to accuse exactly. We might be part of the same phenomenon but what is the option—for me to go and live in a place with only people like me? I don't think it's similar. Because I don't come to dispossess anyone. The life I try to live doesn't require me to have more than the minimum needed. I wish I had a washing machine and if possible a dryer—but apart from that . . . My friends keep asking me "Aren't you afraid?" but I wasn't afraid. In my political activism I meet people who seek to do what they think is right.

Idealist Gentrifiers: Empowering a Community

My third encounter with radical gentrifiers was with a commune of ideologically motivated students who had recently moved to a large apartment on Jerusalem Boulevard in a mixed neighborhood. The group numbered four activists: a couple who are former kibbutz members (Ya'ara and Ya'ir) and two others whom they met at the Ha-Shomer ha-Tza'ir youth movement (Na'ama and No'a). Their motivation was an attempt to build an urban "community" from which they could make a difference in the surrounding neighborhood. As Ya'ara says,

> The idea to look for a shared apartment, a few people together, in itself was a meeting of interests, both to lower the rent and to live in a community of sorts. The emphasis was to find something on the South Side or in Jaffa. The idea was to live in a place where there is a community and to do it from the standpoint of neighbors, and not on behalf of a project parachuted from above. Say that the municipality is renovating the streets, and we've been here for more than six months and we know people and reached a stage of bitterness about how things are done here, so we can come from an equal footing of class.

One of the commune's first actions was to write a letter of complaint to the municipality about the deteriorating infrastructure, which they posted at the entrance to the building. "We try to empower the community from within," explains Na'ama. The loose organizing framework allowed the members to choose their level of involvement, she says: "We're a group of friends. It's a sort of family, a sort of communalism. All of us have a severe kibbutz trauma and a bad commune trauma." During their military service they came to realize that "it would be easier to do things with social and economic communal backup." Their decision to come together "started from a very spontaneous place." Ya'ara recalls, "Na'ama came back from a trek in Argentina very excited by revolutionary and socialist ideas and somehow we all became excited about it. We all had a remote fantasy of living in a squat but it never materialized and this [their current situation] somehow did happen. We have a kitty—everyone gives according to their income. But we don't have joint bank accounts. It's part of the idea not to do something ideologically extreme but to let the pace of things flow with our conscience."

For this commune, choosing Jaffa rather than another "mixed" or "non-mixed" city stemmed both from the members' biographical backgrounds of political activism and from their realization that Jaffa's unique heterogeneous environment allows for a type of political and social engagement that is repressed in other, more segregated towns like Jerusalem or Tel-Aviv. Ya'ara explains,

> We come from a background of Jewish-Arab activism and moving into a mixed place appealed to us. We almost gave up on Jaffa until we saw this apartment. We couldn't find a big-enough house. The thinking was that you get out of the Tel-Avivan white bubble and mainly that you go from theory to practice. Through this we learned to experience what it means to live with poverty and dirt, with anarchy, with the sadness, with the number of marginal people you have here. But also the good side of it, with the mix of languages and people, the character of the place, which is very unique and complex.

Romanticizing the experience of urban marginality and ethnic mix seems an essential part of the commune's sense of purpose. Na'ama observes, "There's something new and deterring but also extremely curious and beautiful in this mix, in the heterogeneity—the human makeup that is very mixed." Resonating with the narrative of the real estate agent, their attraction to the new environment draws on a theory of street-life authenticity: "In Jaffa reality is there, it's on the surface, it's not whitewashed, and it doesn't hide behind a newspaper," she says. "It's here. It can drive you nuts but it's also a kind of liberation. You get to Tel-Aviv and suddenly escapism and purity are irritating and frustrating. There's something hypocritical about Tel-Aviv." The contrast with Tel-Aviv is completed by Ya'ara's description of segregated Jerusalem: "As opposed to Jerusalem, in Jaffa the situation is not necessarily negative. Segregation is not that blatant, at least not from our eyes. This is especially true in the Jerusalem Boulevard area. In 'Ajami there's more luxury ghettos." Their sense of political liberation stems from what No'a calls a recognition of "binational presence" which joins Arabs and Jews in a "common mentality of the deprived":

> Here you can't hide the binational presence behind fences or walls or neighborhoods cut off by private police. Here it's mixed because the housing is mixed and everyone takes the same buses and shops at the same mixed stores. At the end of the day people cope together with the same shit. Jerusalem makes it a much more violent encounter between the groups—something in the air that you wouldn't feel here. To put it bluntly, here you have a common mentality of the deprived. Houses of Arabs are being broken into, the same as houses of Jews. We haven't been broken into yet, but it can happen any time now.

To my provocative question about their living in a "stolen house," they reacted with a romanticized excitement regarding the realization of the Palestinian right of return. Na'ama says, "The Israeli anxiety is that the Arab would come and say, 'This is my house.' With us it's the contrary— we have this parody in our minds that once he comes we will be so moved that we would say, 'We waited for you all this time.'" Acknowledging that wholesale opposition to the right of return is a point of consensus unifying 98 percent of Jewish Israelis, we may evaluate the degree of this commune's radicalism. Na'ama explains with passion,

> I don't think that his arrival means the negation of my existence; on the contrary, the negation of my existence here will last as long as I refuse to recognize him. As if my right to be here is doubtful as long as it is dependent on the repression of someone else. This is a stolen house, but every other place in the country is also stolen. My parents' house in Tel-Aviv is built on a village that was destroyed without a trace. You can't say that it's particular to Jaffa. The principle of recognition is more global. The point is to acknowledge the wrongs of the past and to take responsibility for it, together with the historical fact that exists today, and to find a solution for it together. Theoretically, we think that to build a community on relations of partnership, of dialogue and equality, is the only viable long-term solution. To maintain here a texture of real neighborliness on equal footing is a small step for us and a big step for humankind.

Living as activists in Jaffa helped them establish networks of affinity and collaboration with like-minded alternative communes. Several
such groups now thrive, forming the political backbone of Jewish radical
activism in Jaffa but also a cool, cultural scene of clubbing and political
art. "The radical scene is moving from Jerusalem to Jaffa," another radical
gentrifier informed me. Activists are conscious of the transformations
they bring about, which we can call "creative marginality" (see chapter 7).
Ya'ara observes,

> There's the anarchist squat on Ben-Azarya Street. They live in a dilapidated
> house. They are active with us in all the demonstrations against the Wall.
> In Jaffa they could squat, while in Tel-Aviv it was impossible. There's also
> the commune of the Ha-Shomer ha-Tza'ir in 'Ajami. They snatched the first
> house we saw. And there is the Mahapach commune,[15] which also joins us
> in all the activities. It's first of all an economic phenomenon of people who
> look for cheap rent and to escape Tel-Aviv and antiglobalization and not to
> be part of the industry of marketing. Jaffa allows for an escape from this—
> a feeling that you arrive here and you're not part of it. We discovered the
> imagined boundary between Jaffa and Tel-Aviv—it runs on Salame Street.
> But I think there is some kind of revival—young folks like us who look
> for communal frameworks of expression. But this is a miniscule quantity
> so it's hard to speak of a phenomenon. It's a marginal phenomenon. But it
> seems that there are more faces like us on the street. When we got here we
> were UFOS and now there are more UFOS like us.

The attraction of leftist gentrifiers to Jaffa repositions it as a space
of engagement, identification, and political activism. While the "radical
gentrifiers" seek a "spatial capital" that is, like that of the liberal gentrifiers, founded on the virtues of alterity, heterogeneity, and multiculturalism, the former also profess a project of community-building and social
activism. This political "being in the world" valorizes Jewish presence in
Jaffa not as a liberal form of coexistence but as an agentive empowerment
of both self and Other. Of late, with the emergence of iconic markers
of gentrification and spaces of consumption such as vegan cafés (such
as the Abu Dhabi-Kaymak café on Gaza Street), as well as binational
"gay-friendly" music clubs such as Anna Loulou Bar, resident radical
activists in Jaffa become willy-nilly part and parcel of the gentrification
process which they oppose.

THE GENTRIFIER OF THIN LOCALITY:
"LIVING IN AN OPEN WOUND"

Eitan, an academic specializing in literary criticism, completed in 2003 the construction of a three-story house in the heart of 'Ajami. The house is rectangular and white, and Eitan characterizes it as "modernistic but not imposing." "Passing by," he claims, "one would probably not take notice of its existence." Elaborating upon key topics such as modernism, dwelling, colonialism, and Zionism, Eitan's narrative of gentrification is a surprising manifesto for nonlocality and intentional distancing from "messianic ideologies." His narrative of "dwelling" began with a childhood dream and evolved into a "long saga":

> I invested here because it was cheap. I had very little money but I had dreamt of Jaffa at night. It was overdetermined [*sic*]—many factors were involved. As a boy, I used to walk around here. My grandmother had a small house near the sea in Tel-Aviv where we spent much of my boyhood. A small house with a garden and a tree, magical summers. . . . And then my father died and my sister and I each inherited one hundred thousand dollars. We looked for something Mediterranean, near the beach with a tree. We used to have a Bulgarian nanny from Jaffa—it was the Jaffa of my childhood and the Big Territory [*Ha-Shetah ha-Gadol*]. Then the opportunity came.

The concrete circumstances that brought Eitan to 'Ajami involved a series of entanglements with several business partners. "There was a mixed couple living here," he says, "but then he passed away and she sold it to me. It was a long saga because afterward I didn't have the money to build." Selling half of his share, Eitan partnered with his sister and later managed to purchase back the whole house: "In the middle of the Intifada we bought the share we'd sold and somehow miraculously we found the money to build. Everything was a coincidence. We bought it in the middle of the eighties. Had we sold it in the nineties we could have made some profit, but we weren't looking for financial gain." For Eitan Jaffa was a natural choice: "Where else if not Jaffa? I now understand why I dreamed of Jaffa."

Acclimating to the rough neighborhood was not without challenges, as Eitan's apartment was broken into three times. However, he accepts these inflictions stoically:

There were three attempts to break into my apartment. They succeeded once, but there's nothing to steal, except for the computer, unless you're interested in Tshernikhovski's collected writings. They stole the pillowcases, and put in them a small TV, a computer, and some bottles of wine, which they tried to sell me later. These are kids, thirteen years old. The neighbors told me to let them in and that they'll see that there's nothing to steal and won't come back. . . . I walk around here with the Arab kids. They like playing with my dog. Amazing children. There's a gang of thief kids and there are truly amazing kids.

In Eitan's narrative, the problem of dwelling in a historically poor and politically contested neighborhood is dealt with by positing his house's presence as nonthreatening. He reflects on the changing environment, which he sees as a form of cultural refinement:

I'm new here. We'll have to see. All this is very complex, and there are many sides to this complexity. The population is poor but on the other hand this whole street is starting to be filled with luxury apartments. Some of it is Jewish-Arab construction, some of Arab ownership. The house in front of us is owned by a Hinnawi [a wealthy Christian family]; here a big house is being built by Abu-Ramadan [a wealthy Muslim family]. Up the street is a luxury house built by a group of Jewish and Arab families together. Most of the houses here are owned by local Arabs who made a fortune. This space is changing in front of my eyes; it becomes refined, as it were. One feels it in the atmosphere of life here. I used to walk around here before I moved in, and there was something rough; now it becomes softer. There's a feeling that everyone looks at you all the time. Plenty of eyes. People know when you get in and out. Like a kibbutz—the panopticon of Jaffa.

Living in 'Ajami positions Eitan in the heart of the political conflict and the class divide. With no way out he chooses to engage the "open wound" as a sort of therapy, which allows him to "live in the micro":

In a sense, the house isolates you from the outside. There's something comforting in the way you have to cope with the conflict in the practice of everyday life, with the history of the conflict. I don't live a political life at the moment. In the everyday you handle things. You live in an illusion of handling. Everyone understands this. But the wounds are open. All this region is filled with incurable open wounds. Horrible things could happen and the fact that you have to keep living, you walk into a café, you talk to people—this keeps the dialectics alive, you don't bracket it. It's living in an open wound—not escaping it. But in a way, it allows me to distance myself from political life and live in the micro, where you solve everything therapeutically, not politically.

Eitan's fascinating rendering of gentrification as a political therapy led to a discussion of larger issues regarding the problem of autochthony and nativism in the history of the Palestinian-Israeli conflict. Responding to my question about the danger of Judaization, he replied,

> This [the Arab fear of Judaization] is the wound. But beyond that there's another discourse. There's an unsolved ambivalence. Not that there's any position that is not ambivalent. It's ambivalence through and through and it cannot be untied. And there's the other side: during the Intifada my neighbors came to me and asked me to come and live here [and complete the relocation]. As a response to the boycott [the Jews who stopped shopping in Jaffa] and to the devaluation of land. My neighbor came and told me, "It's not from here. These are people from the outside," in an attempt to talk me into coming and reassure me. Everything is ambivalent—not only between different people but throughout the soul. On the ethical and political level I don't have anything to say on this, but on the therapeutic level I understand how it's possible to live here.

While some Jewish antigentrification advocates (such as leftist architect Sharon Rotbart) refuse in principle to work or live in Jaffa, Eitan rejects this position and differentiates between such ethical considerations and the principled debate about architecture, modernism, and autochthony:

> Living here is a personal decision; it's also a question of affect. If there were here a position of principle I could have argued. What can be debated are questions on the architecture of this house. Questions that would interest me—how can one build a house in Jaffa? I chose something that doesn't stand out [*mitbahen*]. If you look from the outside you'll realize that the house is barely noticeable, but on the other hand it's not an Arab house. It doesn't project might but it's a modernistic house and one should think why. It's implanted modernism but not aggressive modernism. It's not something that grew out of the land here. It's not autochthonous—it's modernistic but not monumental, in comparison with Pivko's houses that are set in a location of dominance. It's not an Arab house and it doesn't attempt to use any Arab element. I'm a stranger here.

In contrast to the dominant trend among gentrifiers attempting to reconstruct a new sense of locality and identity, Eitan militates against the very idea of romantic locality:

> I'm no local. I'm against locality. I don't have any interest in being local. I didn't come here to become local. At the end of the day, even the Arabs here

will not be locals. If you ask me, on the political level this is the big mistake of all of us—ours and theirs. Autochthonous ideologies are the thing I oppose most. For my part, this is precisely the opportunity to overcome such fantasies. It's not simple; they're messianic. This is why this conflict has such serious issues at stake. It's a change of dwelling, of how you live in a place. How can you live in a place without an autochthonous fantasy? With thin locality [*mekomiyut dala*], not mythical locality, but neither modernistic universalism? A weak modernism! There's a "place" here, but a weak place. Without mythical and autochthonous potency.

Endorsing what anthropologist Zali Gurevitch (2007) termed the "small place" of private life, Eitan rejects the notion of the "big place" of myth and redemption. From the situated debate over gentrification and dwelling in Jaffa, Eitan transcends the local urban context and proposes a critique of the whole Zionist project and its most foundational tenets:

> As far as I am concerned, there is no other way. There's a similar interesting thing in Zionism. Zionism's rhetoric always leaned toward the mythical and autochthonic, but the more interesting force in Zionism was actually its antiautochthonous trend. But mythical and messianic Zionism eventually had the upper hand. It's still dominant but there's another force in Zionism. You see this for instance in Tel-Aviv. This is what interested me about this building. I didn't want it to be an imitation of such an autochthonous fantasy as the "Arab House." I don't want to live in a "place," nor do I want to live on the internet—I want to live near the sea. I don't have anything against the mosque, but on the political level it seems to me that what's at stake is finding a way to be freed from this fantasy—the mythical basis of existence, the mythical land. Hope lies in what I'm talking about. Where there's catastrophic threat there's also a chance for a better existence that is more humble and thin in its relation to land.

Eitan concluded his critique of Palestinian and Zionist ideologies of autochthony in response to my question about the sense of guilt common among gentrifiers, who avoid living in Arab houses due to what one gentrifier has described as the "ghosts of the past":

> It's all filled with guilt. And if you don't reside in an Arab house—there is no guilt? It's not an argument, it's a form of experience, it's an emotion. It's autochthony all over again. In this house there were Jews before I came. But if you live in an Arab house and one day someone knocks on your door and says "This is my house," you'll give it to him. What would you say, "No"? You would ask for your money back, the investment, from the state. But this is

an emotional thing. On the level of principle, if you ask me, on the political level this is history. You always take someone else's place. No one is born out of the land. This is why I can't stand the discourse of settlers and natives. No one belongs to the land. This is the big mistake. Indigenousness is a relative matter and it's very easy to remain stuck. I think one of the problems of the Palestinian movement is that it's stuck in autochthonous fantasies—consider refugee camps for instance. Jewish autochthony has the same problem. It's a problem of mythical Zionism—the settlers and even the kibbutzim. I believe one of the problems of the Zionist movement is its agrarian inclination. The redemption of the land. This is the source of all evil.

The narratives of Jaffa's new Jewish residents reveal a field of various class positions and political subjectivities—all traditionally subsumed under the concept of gentrification. These actors are all endowed with relatively high social capital, ideological commitment, or other personal resources; however, while they all participate in the powerful transformation of the Jaffa space into a bourgeois space of consumption, they exhibit a surprisingly diverse spectrum of political and cultural visions for the city—past, present, and future. Understanding gentrification as a political economy, which introduces new social types into the formerly disinvested area, should be read against the zero-sum "urban removal" scenario. As a cultural and existential intervention, however, these social types open up new spaces for alternatives discourses, coalitions, socialities, and imaginaries. The success of business initiatives such as the Yafa Café, co-owned since 2003 by a Jewish gentrifier and her Palestinian partner, attests to the unintended consequences of gentrification. Choosing to "live in the open wound," certain gentrifiers boldly address some the most profound questions of the conflict: recognition, guilt, and autochthony.

SPATIAL CAPITAL AND THE "NEW JEWS"

The Sawaf family tragedy from the late 1990s, which opened this chapter, proved not to be an exceptional case. In 2007, the Israel Land Administration issued 497 evacuation orders to Palestinian families charged with illegal construction. As these families all live in the 'Ajami neighborhood, the hot spot of Jewish gentrification, it was identified as yet another attempt to "transfer" the Arab population out of Jaffa. Soon it became the symbol of the struggle over Palestinian presence and the landmark of the resistance to ethnogentrification led by the Popular Committee for Land and Housing Rights in Jaffa (figure 4.2).

Up to the mid-1980s Jewish-Arab relations in Jaffa consisted of the interplay among the hostile local government, a working-class Jewish population, and a Palestinian underclass. Marking the end of an era, the neoliberal turn in the Israeli economy and society has brought a new actor to the urban scene: middle- to upper-middle-class liberal Jews who have chosen to make Jaffa their home. This systemic intervention reconfigured the power relations between Jewish and Arab individuals and institutions and gave rise to a new discourse addressing the incoming gentrifiers as Jaffa's "New Jews," or, alternatively, and in a more critical mode, as *Tzfonim* ("Northsiders").[16]

The distinction between the diasporic "Old Jew" and the Zionist "New Jew" looms large in Jewish history and contemporary identity politics.[17] Capturing the urge, since the age of nationalism, to acquire a new collective subjectivity that is cleansed of self-stereotypical vices (bodily feebleness, chronic uprootedness, religious traditionalism), the trope of the "New Jew" came to represent a fresh start, a sense of autonomy and emancipation.[18] Notwithstanding this laden genealogy, for the veteran Jewish and Palestinian communities in Jaffa of the 1990s, the "New Jews" (always in plural, note, as opposed to the generic "New Jew") denoted something completely different. For both veteran Jews and Palestinian Arabs these incomers are first identified by their *Jewishness*—thus aligning them with the Jewish society and state and *ipso facto* opposing them to the Arab inhabitants. Secondly, the gentrifiers are marked by their *newness*—hence opposing them to "old" Jewish and Arab Jaffans alike. The gentrifiers' economic capital and tendency to confine themselves in exclusionary spaces are invoked only secondarily. When addressed explicitly, this class distinction is spatially marked through the alternative term *Tzfonim*—thus aligning the newcomers with the Ashkenazi and wealthy North Side of Tel-Aviv.

Rather than simply excluding the new residents from the cognitive map of local typologies, these tropes capture the ambivalence of gentrification in Jaffa. Negatively indexing spatial, ethnic, and class-based distinctions, these typologies allow no room for symbolic collaboration between the gentrifiers and the Arab inhabitants (who are neither new nor

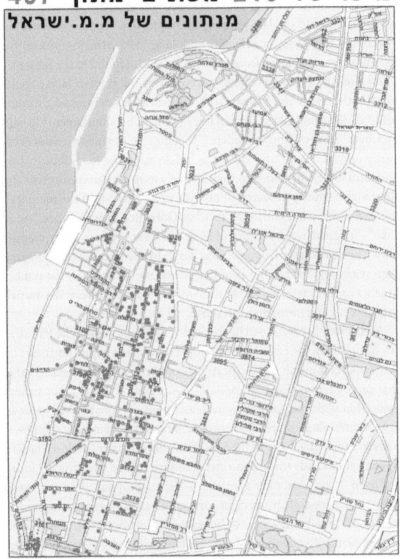

מיפוי של 210 מפונים מתוך 497
מנתונים של מ.מ.ישראל

FIGURE 4.2. A map of the Israel Land Administration plan to evacuate
497 Palestinian families from their houses.

Courtesy of Darna—The Popular Committee for Land and Housing Rights in Jaffa.

Jewish). These categories also challenge, by virtue of the strong emphasis on Jewishness, the existing—albeit weak and nostalgic—Jewish-Arab local patriotism and solidarity among the oppressed. "Today's Jews are not like the old-time Jews," concluded a middle-aged Palestinian commenting on Jaffa's transformation from the days of his childhood to the present.

As a result of this ambivalent reception by the veteran Jaffa population (both Jewish and Palestinian), the gentrifiers developed a liminal sense of time and place that enables them to be simultaneously self-ascribed "insiders" and "outsiders." That most of the interviewees eventually moved out of Jaffa (Pivko to Tel-Aviv, Shelly to a kibbutz, Lisa and John to Berlin) points to their lack of a long-term commitment and their high mobility in search of new life projects. Indeed the temporality of gentrification conforms to what Gurevitch (2007) called "small time"—reigned over by a spirit of Here and Now, urgency, and ephemerality. The gentrifiers all upheld their desire to live near the sea, however, their sea is not the eternal sea of Jewish history or the sea as the symbol of sabra rootlessness, but rather the concrete Mediterranean Sea, its palpable breeze and immediate presence.

Ambivalently positioned in the field of relations among the Palestinian community, the real estate developers, the planning authorities, and the Jewish community, gentrification brought about a new form of value that can be termed "spatial capital"—i.e., a notion of symbolic capital associated with the cultural, social, and political "quality" of space in Jaffa. Combining different modes of attachment—from a quest for local nativization (Jaffa, Belle of the Seas),[19] to political mobilization (the leftist communes and radical gentrifiers), to a principled rejection of "locality" itself (the philosopher-gentrifier)—"spatial capital" produces novel notions of place and city, sociality and politics, history and coexistence. Ranging from a benign view of benevolent gentrification to a profound engagement with questions of recognition, guilt, indigeneity, and Palestinian return, these narratives support the notion of gentrification as an inchoate concept to be analyzed both as politics and as an experiential mode of being. Rather than a determinate reflex of the economic order, gentrification in Jaffa embodies the operative scales of value and alterity implicated in the transformation of urban space from a neglected slum to a space of engagement and self-fulfillment.

FIVE

To Buy or Not to Be

Trespassing the Gated Community

The city is intimidated, the city is breathing its last, the woman on the
rock does not hope for anything anymore! Or perhaps she does? I recall the
beginning of the work in Acropolis. I was hoping for something other than
the architecture of the thick cardboard, the stone mask of death.... Jaffa
—a theater bereft of actors where tourists move about. A thousand years
may pass till the dragon licks this festering sore, and till Andromeda, filled
with shame, steps out of the Hammam, the nightclub, to found the old city
anew. This is an "Old City" resembling an "Ancient City"—says Jouha
with a sad expression on his face.

—ARCHITECT LEON GENEVA, in a publication of the Rabita

"LIVING AN ORIGINAL": ANDROMEDA HILL
AS A NEO-ORIENTALIST SIMULACRUM

Walking with a group of Palestinian and Jewish guests, we silently
crossed the iron gate of the luxurious gated community. Slowly, we tra-
versed the premises toward the western viewpoint overlooking the Jaffa
port. Enjoying the breathtaking sunset we sat on the bench, still thrilled
by the relative ease of our entry. Suddenly, as if reading our minds, a
woman of around sixty approached us and exclaimed in Hebrew, which
she then translated into English, "You can pass but you can't stay!"
Slightly alarmed but somewhat amused by her response, we nevertheless remained seated.

"There's nothing she can do," someone said. "The law is on our side."
The elderly resident, we knew, was voicing her frustration with a court
ruling from August 2007, which concluded a four-year legal battle to al-

low easement and free pedestrian passage through the exclusive project from eight o'clock in the morning until ten o'clock at night. Later she identified herself as Meriam Ben Shachar, a member of the (Jewish) residents' committee of the gated community.[1] A similar encounter was reported later that week in a sensational article entitled "Andromeda Ever Since and Forever" in Israel's biggest national newspaper.[2] Celebrating the symbolic victory of Palestinian legal activism, the article relayed the following exchange between Palestinian advocate Hicham Chabaita, the representative of the claimants, and Ben Shachar:

> BEN SHACHAR: I'm an old woman and I bought an apartment in a closed community so I could live like I would in an old folks' home. There are gated communities all around the country, because of crime. What would you do in my place?
>
> CHABAITA: I would sell.
>
> BEN SHACHAR: No one would buy this.
>
> CHABAITA: I would buy.
>
> BEN SHACHAR: For the price I paid?
>
> CHABAITA: No. You bought a closed compound. Now it's been opened up. The value went down.
>
> BEN SHACHAR: This is really a provocation! In my mind, there is no Arab or Jew. Every person is equally human for me.
>
> CHABAITA: You prefer to keep the Arabs outside this place and out of your sight.
>
> BEN SHACHAR: Why do you say such a thing? I can give you right now the phone number of a person, whose name is incidentally 'Adel, and he's like a son to me. And not just one! A whole family!

This dialogic duel points to the new empowerment of a rising generation of Palestinian citizens of Israel, which Rabinowitz and Abu-Baker (2005) have labeled "the stand-tall generation." More importantly, however, it exposes the powerful mechanisms of urban exclusion and alienation, often hidden under a mask of liberal multiculturalism. These have only recently come under critical public and legal scrutiny, with relatively poor results that do little to change the inherent power asymmetries between Palestinians and Jewish Israelis, or the increasing demand for gated communities in Jaffa and Israel at large.

The emergence since the mid-1980s of a neoliberal regime of spatial governmentality in Palestinian-Israeli mixed towns has radicalized the ongoing restructuring of urban space through gentrification and its political implications—population displacement, a militant discourse of rights, and the production of urban alterities (Isin 2002; Lefebvre 1996; Smith 1996). Addressing such processes, this chapter analyzes the urban paradox embodied in one of Israel's most luxurious housing projects, located at the core of Tel-Aviv's poorest Arab neighborhood. Far from being viewed as a problem, the construction of exclusionary spaces is explicitly mobilized by the project managers, who continue to market Andromeda Hill as a desired enclave. Its elaborate website presents the project as a promise for Jaffa's rebirth in a simulated space that is simultaneously present and absent from the city's actual lived space:

> Andromeda Hill is a virtual "city within a city" surrounded by a wall and secured 24 hours a day. The open spaces and alleys are paved in natural stone, dappled in authentic Israeli vegetation and ornamented with elements of water and authentic, original lighting.... Andromeda Hill has been planned for you to sit at home, view the sea, enjoy the beauty and hear ... only the waves.... Andromeda became a symbol of awakening and renewal, and it is not by chance that the project was named "Andromeda Hill," expressing the rebirth of old Jaffa.[3]

A cultural signifier as much as a spatial fact, Andromeda Hill distinguishes itself from other luxury housing projects by devising a hybrid neo-Orientalist discourse of locality, ultramodern and authentic at the same time. These two motifs combine to form a marketing strategy that invites the potential tenant to "liv[e] an original" in the "New-Old Jaffa" (figure 5.1). The Andromeda Hill project thus functions as a real estate simulacrum and architectural pastiche, aspiring to be both in and out of historical time and political space.[4] It is "a symbol of renewal" and "an original," "abroad" (*hul* in Hebrew),[5] and "Jaffan." This double image, we shall see, represents a paradoxical strategy of coping with the social logic of the real estate project. Presented as a safe and secure gated community ("a city within a city"), it thus remains disconnected from its local milieu and urban texture, while simultaneously constructing itself as the epitome of an imagined Mediterranean mythology (Andromeda on the rock) and local architectural taste (the "Jaffa Style").

ANDROMEDA HILL - THE NEW OLD JAFFA
LIVING AN ORIGINAL

Ilan Gat Engineers Ltd

FIGURE 5.1. "Living an Original": The marketing simulacrum of Andromeda Hill.

The Andromeda Hill project is the largest private housing enterprise promoted by the Tel-Aviv-Jaffa Municipality, which designed it as the flagship of a new planning policy in hitherto disinvested Jaffa. In 1989 Murray Goldman, a Jewish Canadian entrepreneur, signed a "combination deal" with the Greek-Orthodox Patriarchate in Jerusalem, in which both sides agreed to build a luxury housing complex on church-endowed *waqf* land overlooking the Jaffa port. In 1994 the architectural plan for building 270 housing units obtained official approval and work on-site began soon after. Apartment units start at well over three hundred thousand dollars for a fifty-square-meter studio apartment and go up to four million dollars for the most luxurious penthouse. The complex offers a wide array of amenities, including a fitness club, massage services, a big swimming pool, and a vegetarian cafeteria.

Thirty percent of the tenants are foreign residents (mainly businessmen and diplomats) and 70 percent are wealthy Israelis (including a Parliament member, judges, poets, and architects). Andromeda Hill is the product of an institutional and conceptual collaboration between the Canadian entrepreneur, Israeli investors, the Greek-Orthodox Patriarchate, the local government, and Israeli architects. These actors formed a "circumstantial coalition" that used the project as a golden opportunity for real estate profit as well as for the promotion of the gentrification policy, which calls for the "reinforcement" of the local population. The attempt by the Israeli architects to tune in to the conception of the Canadian entrepreneur and his cultural taste, combined with their "local" knowledge and capital, gave birth to the Andromeda Hill project as it stands today. Due to the circumstances of its construction, its unprecedented magnitude, and its urban implications, the project became a mobilizing bone of contention which condensed capital flows, colonial imaginaries, and political struggles over place and identity. In the course of this analysis, Andromeda Hill will evolve from an incidental example of gentrification to a project that radically embodies the ethnoclass contradictions of urban dynamics in Jaffa and beyond.

In the following I interrogate the reconfiguration of class, real estate capital flows, and neo-Orientalist architectural images (foreign residents and investments, aesthetic signs, standards of building, and planning ideologies) in a binational urban relational field. On its broadest level, my argument points to a tight coupling between the practices of global consumerism and the local neoliberal logic of gentrification, energized by the planning authorities and producing a new landscape of distinction. Based on a view of the city as a "difference machine" which engenders urban citizenship as alterity (Isin 2002), the analysis delineates the ways in which gentrification operates to produce and reproduce ethnic differentiation and class distinction through space.

More specifically, I investigate the Andromeda project's *modus operandi* while moving between two intersecting levels of analysis. The first level focuses on the paradoxical discourse of the justification of a "gated community," which functions as a radical maker of ethnogentrification at large. Thus, in order to resolve the contradiction between the exclusionary desire of the project and the impoverished Arab community in which it is embedded, a dual architectural language has been devised— one that makes virtue out of reality and mobilizes its contradictions for marketing purposes. Hence it is precisely the Orientalist reification of the Jaffa space that enabled the project to orient itself outward, beyond Jaffa—to Tel-Aviv, to the Mediterranean mythological space, and to Canada—thereby constituting Andromeda as "the New-Old Jaffa." This level of analysis examines the role of gentrification as a central force that produces Jaffa as a heteronomous space (Kemp 1999). Turning place inside out, it reconfigures opposite and parallel spatial logics of simultaneous inclusion and exclusion. The second level ethnographically examines how gentrification puts neoliberal principles into action. Promoting an urban "renewal" project by outsourcing public services and recruiting foreign capital, it results in the privatization and "enclaving" of lived space. This now-hegemonic logic of action gave rise to a fragile yet effective "circumstantial coalition" between private and public, Israeli and foreign, Jewish and Christian actors, which united forces and interests at the expense of the local Palestinian community.

These two levels of analysis dissect "gentrification in action" not merely as the major consequence of urban neoliberal regimes, but also as a politically driven vector of cultural intentionality oriented toward a fabricated realm of global cosmopolitanism as a means of circumventing the local by recruiting capital, people, and images from outside Jaffa and Israel. The coupling of these two levels of inquiry sharpens the social implications of the Andromeda Hill project and other gated communities. In their present form, they disable sustainable development in Jaffa as they ignore the dire needs of the local Palestinian population, which in turn is rendered a transparent yet necessary element in the neo-Orientalist construction of urban space (LeVine 2005).

CONSUMING SPACE: THE NEOLIBERAL
PRODUCTION OF LOCALITY

The global emergence of gated communities can be theorized as the dialectic product of the political economy of "uneven development" (Smith 1996) and the urban culture of neoliberalism (Comaroff and Comaroff 2001). Anthropologist Setha Low (2001, 46) traces the spread of gated communities back to the economic restructuring of the 1970s and 1980s and the rapid relocation of capital: "This breakdown of the social order polarized relations between haves and have-nots . . . and resulted in people employing new techniques of social control" (see also Harvey 1991; Webster, Glasze, and Frantz 2002). Neil Smith further expands on this trend as part of a process he terms "the generalization of gentrification as a global urban strategy" (Smith 2002, 446). Beginning in the 1990s, he argues, gated communities inherited the abandonment of previously state-regulated urban policy as a "consummate urban expression of an emerging neo-liberalism" (446). As Davis (1992) shows, the addition of guardhouses, walls, and entrance gates to established neighborhoods resulted in the "militarization of the city" as private police forces increasingly monitor the urban space of newly defined "fortress cities" (Low 2001, 46).

In cities, the culture of neoliberalism has reinforced urban self-segregation through the dissolution of the "political," via the fragmentation of the "urban." Radicalizing identity politics, neoliberal regimes propel the atomization of modernist spatiality and communal identity. For Jean and John Comaroff (2001, 322) this results in nothing less than the demise of the social: "Neoliberal capitalism, in its millennial moment, portends the death of politics by hiding its own ideological underpinnings in the dictates of economic efficiencies."

The marketing slogan of the second-largest gated community in Jaffa (the Quarter) encapsulates this social suicidal logic (figure 5.2). "To Buy or Not to Be" thus becomes a civilizing mission programmed to destroy the collective structures capable of resisting the precepts of the "pure market" (Bauman 1999a, 28; Bourdieu 1998). By dissolving the bonds of sociality and reciprocity and submitting them to the laws of the market, neoliberalism gives rise to an intense preoccupation with

FIGURE 5.2. Marketing the gated community: "To Buy or Not to Be."
Photo by the author, 2005.

safety and security and *ipso facto* to an obsession with their emotional
corollaries—risk and fear (Bauman 1999a). Paradoxically, urban risk
society's search for certainty perpetuates a self-defeating cycle, which
reproduces the very alterity it seeks to eliminate (Beck 1992, 49; Isin
2002).

With its hollowing out of sociality, urban neoliberalism reduces lived space to a commodity to be consumed, and thus exposes place and property to theft, transgression, and pollution. In search of a secure form of social organization—protected from the urban chaos lurking outside—gated communities arise as the spatial and cultural nexus around which a new discourse of fear of violence and crime "legitimates and rationalizes class-based exclusion and residential segregation" (Low 2001, 45). While operating chiefly as a mechanism of depoliticization, gated communities lead inevitably to the extreme "enclaving" of social inequalities and hence to the politicized spatialization of privileged "outsiders," thus in turn crystallizing militant local discourses of rights around the politics of their ethnonational identity and class struggle. With the growing scholarly interest in gated communities in the Israeli-Palestinian context (Lehavi and Rosenberg 2010; Rosen and Razin 2009), the following explores the working of neoliberal spatial governmentality as it faces the particular binational realities of ethnically mixed towns. In this contested terrain, gated communities emerged as a new and radical marker of ethnogentrification.

As we have seen, the 1980s saw a radical shift in the municipal planning policy from disinvestment to urban renewal. Neoliberal planning strategies were bent on privatizing state-owned property, on promoting "diversity," and on bringing in new affluent (Jewish) inhabitants who in turn would "reinforce" the existing population and increase municipal revenues.

Planted in the 1980s by the Jaffa Planning Team, the euphemism of a "new population" bloomed in the 1990s into a powerful redemptive narrative of urban regeneration. The municipality's urban renewal project consisted of a series of measures that provided new statutory construction plans and devised a new Orientalist architectural language, now officially registered as the "Jaffa Style." The demolition of historic Arab buildings, which was widespread in the 1970s and the beginning of the 1980s, slowed down in the second half of the 1980s and eventually stopped altogether. Aided by government funding from the National Rehabilitation Project (Menahem 1998), the implementation of urban renewal on the institutional level spurred private enterprise and ushered in a new era of real estate development.

As a global phenomenon, gentrification has proceeded in three stages. In the first stage, a vanguard group of young "risk takers" settles in the neighborhood. This group usually consists of artists or architects equipped with the knowledge, time, and willingness to renovate the dilapidated buildings they have purchased (in Jaffa, this first stage took place in the seventies and eighties). These first-wave gentrifiers express social tolerance toward the original population and try to integrate themselves into neighborhood life. The second stage (which took place in Jaffa at the end of the eighties) is marked by the entry of a different group into the neighborhood, which purchases apartments and buildings at prices much higher than those paid in the first stage. These residents often use their new apartments both as living spaces and as financial investments. Mostly, this population shows less tolerance toward the original occupiers, whose gradual displacement is accompanied by an escalation of social tensions in the neighborhood.

The third stage (which occurred in Jaffa in the nineties) is marked by the entry of international real estate agencies, major contractors, and investors on a much larger scale than before. These agents complete the process and send neighborhood real estate market values skyrocketing to unprecedented levels.[6] In Jaffa the entry of wealthy Jews into the neighborhoods of 'Ajami and Jabaliyye is interpreted by most Palestinian inhabitants as part of the city's Judaization policy and the reproduction of their economic inferiority, whereas in the eyes of the city planners, as well as some Jewish residents and a handful of bourgeois Arabs, the process symbolizes the only path leading to the "leverage" (*minuf*) of the city and the "empowerment" (*hizuk*) of the population. In its heyday, the race for spatial capital swept developers and entrepreneurial residents into the real estate craze commonly referred to as the "Jaffa Bug."

CIRCUMSTANTIAL COALITIONS: MAIN ACTORS IN THE ANDROMEDA PROJECT

The history of urban development in Jaffa since 1948 sets the political-economic scene for the emergence of gated communities in the 1990s. The flagship of these projects, Andromeda Hill, was made possible via a local coalition between the landowner (the Greek-Orthodox Patriarchate of Jerusalem), the private developer (Goldfan Holdings Ltd.), and Tel-Aviv Municipality. In 1989, the entrepreneur Murray Goldman, a Canadian Jew who had served as head of the Tel-Aviv Trust in Canada, signed a contract to lease the land lot known as the "Greek Hill" for ninety-nine years.

Throughout the nineties, the different actors taking part in the project gradually devised a pattern of ad hoc circumstantial coalitions, which regulated their working relations. At times these actors collaborated and at times they confronted each other vehemently. Two such instances are worth noting: the conflict between the developer and the local government (which amounted to tactical disagreements), and the dispute between the patriarchate in Jerusalem and the Arab Orthodox community in Jaffa (which constituted a bitter strategic argument over land and identity). Notwithstanding several internal conflicts, the coalition among the project agents by and large prevailed against the weakened resistance of the Palestinian community. However, despite the common tendency to conflate the interests of the municipality and the real estate agents and to see them as forming one concerted front which conspired against the Palestinian community, a relational analysis of the urban force field in Jaffa reveals its stratified dynamics.

The City vs. the Entrepreneur: Dangerous
Liaisons between Private and Public

To decipher the structural interest partnership between the local authority and the agents of gentrification in Jaffa, without overlooking the situational conflicts among them, it will suffice to follow the planning authorization process of the Andromeda Hill project in the municipality's Engineering Department. In one of the first deliberations, the city engineer asked the head of the Jaffa Team, "Is this the baby we've been waiting for?" To which the latter replied, "We love this baby, but this doesn't mean we have no problems" (minutes of meeting, November 6, 1991). In spite of the declared collaboration between the developer and the public authority, serious disputes surfaced during the planning process and continued well into the construction period. Negotiation first addressed the public implications of the project that was planned as a gated community. Disagreement mainly emerged with regard to the mandatory public tasks required by law for the benefit of the area's residents. The municipality demanded that the plan establish access between the gated community and the surrounding neighborhood by means of public walkways and squares overlooking the port that would be open to the public. In addition, the municipality insisted that the developer erect a public institution (a kindergarten, cultural center, or school) on the premises of the project. Notwithstanding its legal obligation and wishing to monitor the entry of passersby and to minimize expenses, the developer continued to screen pedestrian passage and eventually consented to build a "public" synagogue, which would be of little use to the Arab community or to the project's mostly secular tenants.

Another topic of debate was taxation and construction fees. At the close of a standard negotiation procedure set to determine the asset value, the two sides reached an agreement regarding the payment of betterment fees of two million dollars.[7] But at the same time, the Tel-Aviv-Jaffa Municipality filed an application with the government of Israel requesting that it be permitted to join Jaffa to the National Rehabilitation Project, for the purpose of creating an urban enterprise zone that would exempt small-scale real estate projects in Jaffa from paying betterment fees and construction taxes. Once this was approved and Jaffa was designated a National Rehabilitation Project, the Andromeda developer appealed to the Supreme Court, protesting the government's "discrimination" against the project and demanding eligibility for the benefits derived from the National Rehabilitation Project (government decisions 1481 [June 23, 1991] and 1294 [June 29, 1993]). In a joint claim by the proprietor (the Greek-Orthodox Patriarchate of Jerusalem) and the entrepreneur (Goldfan Holdings Ltd.) against the government of Israel, the minister of housing, and the Municipality of Tel-Aviv (4434/94), the appellants argued that the project was worthy of financial support because it "restore[d] Jaffa's ancient beauty":

> The planning of the property was executed in full coordination with the Municipality of Tel-Aviv in order to renew Jaffa's face and adorn it with new and modern buildings while preserving its special lineament. Throughout the planning period Goldfan Ltd. has argued time and again that it should

pay no betterment fees, not only because it is literally a pioneer who precedes the camp in its investments in Jaffa, but because all these investments were made while taking great financial risk. . . . In addition, of course, the mayor and the city engineer have supported the enterprise enthusiastically all along. . . . While we were handling the public objections to the plan, we realized that all the neighboring areas in Jaffa were exempt from betterment fees. . . . Whatever the reason—the discrimination is clear and visible and a quick glance suffices to realize how great the discrimination is.

Responding to this creative legal fabrication, the city claimed in court that the luxury project was not eligible for state subsidies and benefits originally designed to promote small-scale local enterprise in poor neighborhoods:

The Neighborhood Rehabilitation Project [Shikum Shkhunot] was meant to transform troubled neighborhoods and to endow them with a new urban character, in order to ensure proper community life and to reduce the social and physical gap between different neighborhoods in the city. . . . On June 23, 1991, the government decided to include the 'Ajami neighborhood in Jaffa in the Neighborhood Rehabilitation Project. . . . The rehabilitated area does not include vacant sections of land that will be populated by a strong and stable population. . . . The property is located mostly on an hilltop adjacent to Old Jaffa, which is far from being a poor area; it is isolated from the neighboring buildings by a wide ring road. There is no doubt, therefore, that due to the condition of the land lot under scrutiny, its building potential, and the profile of the population expected to inhabit it, the government was not authorized to include it within the boundary of Neighborhood Rehabilitation, since there is no relevant justification for investing in it the limited resources at the expense of other troubled and poor areas.

Against common sense, the Supreme Court ruled in favor of the appellants—the developer and the patriarchate were exempt from paying the two million dollars in betterment fees. This illustration of legal manipulation reveals the complexity of this field of power and the fragility of circumstantial coalitions. The public and the private sectors join forces for the sake of promoting common goals—but when one of the partners identifies a potential threat to its interests, the coalition breaks down. From the local population's point of view, the case exemplifies the disastrous impact of neoliberal urban regimes on municipal control and legitimacy. The city's original goal was the "upward mobility" and "renewal" of Jaffa by means of privatization, outsourcing, and fundraising from the private market. But it is precisely this reliance on external capital that undermined municipal control over the public goals that initiated it. This case points to the limits of the coalition between capital and governance: the "dangerous liaisons" between agents of planning and agents of finance exacerbated the local discord between private interest and public space. Ultimately, the story demonstrates how efficiently entrepreneurs have learned to manipulate and appropriate the language of development, welfare policy, social equity, and rehabilitation.

The Patriarchate vs. the Arab Community: "What Is Zionism Anyway—If Not Judaism Plus Real Estate?"

Another circumstantial coalition formed through the Andromeda project is the pact between the patriarch and the developers. That the Greek Orthodox Church operates according to organizational and regional considerations that transcend communal-Palestinian concerns is key to analyzing its involvement in the Jaffa real estate market. Drawing his power from the ancient history of the order, the patriarch exerts direct control over dozens of churches and monasteries as well as vast land assets in Israel, Jordan, and Palestine. The crucial importance of his effective control is fully recognized by the patriarchate, and thus administrating this great wealth is one of the patriarch's main occupations.

The previous patriarch, Diodorus, who struck the Andromeda Hill deal, has concisely summarized his view of the relationship between church and real estate: "You know why the Orthodox Patriarchate has survived in Jerusalem for more than 1,500 years? It is only because we stand fast to our real estate. We don't give up one millimeter. . . . What is Zionism anyway—if not Judaism plus real estate?"[8] As part of its strategy, the church has on many occasions leased assets in long-term contracts (ninety-nine years) to Jewish developers around the country, in what seems *prima facie* an irrational paradox considering that its constituency is entirely Arab. However, if one understands that the church's decision-making apparatus is regional and not communal, it becomes clear that such action is by no means inconsistent with its organizational logic. These assets form a central channel for regulating and managing its relationship with the different states within which it operates (Israel, Jordan, and the Palestinian Authority) and, increasingly, its relations with the private and global market.

This coalition between the patriarchate and private entrepreneurs has had a far-reaching impact on the Arab community in Jaffa. In order to secure Greek hegemony, the heads of the Patriarchate in Jerusalem determined, 150 years ago, that only Greek-born clergymen would occupy the senior posts of the church in Jerusalem. This tension is the origin of the recurring accusations made against the Greek clergymen, denouncing their "corrupt" control over gargantuan wealth and their neglect of the local Arab communities. Further allegations claim that the patriarch and his assistants are "collaborators" (*'umala'*) who sell and rent out lands to Jews and the State of Israel, thus profaning the "the sanctity of the place."

Led by the Orthodox Charity Association (Al-Jam'iyya al-Khairiyya al-Ortodoxiyya), which was founded in 1879, the Greek-Orthodox community in Jaffa has repeatedly failed in its demands to "Arabize" the church (*ta'rib al-kanissa*) and to channel its real estate revenues to meet the needs of the local population.[9] One resulting tension is visible in a critical report published in Arabic, entitled *Yafa iza Mukhatat al-Tahwid al-Jadid* (Jaffa facing the new Judaization plan), in which the Andromeda transaction is described in terms of profanation:

> In order to sell the land lot the patriarch has desecrated the sanctity of the place where lie the relics of an ancient cemetery—all with no permission from the residents of Jaffa. The transaction is estimated to have reached a sum of one hundred million dollars, of which the patriarchate has received four million dollars. That, in addition to 34 percent of the project revenues. ... It is only by mere coincidence that the Jaffa Orthodox Association has discovered the existence of this transaction, when the association's chair noticed a warning note registered in the land registry bureau. (Al-Ja'fari, Lahav, and Adiv 1992, 58)

To resist the Andromeda transaction, the Orthodox Association and the Rabita submitted 204 objections in the early stages of planning. These objections dealt mainly with the historical and religious nature of the place and thus were immediately dismissed as "irrelevant," "im-

material," and "political" (Al-Ja'fari, Lahav, and Adiv 1992, 58). The leas-
ing transaction was thus legally flawless from a procedural-bureaucratic
perspective, and the residents' objections and frustrations remained
unanswered. The helplessness of the Arab community only reinforced
the common conception that this was yet another stage in the Judaization policy of the city and that Andromeda Hill had to be fought by any
means possible.

The two types of conflict (the municipality vs. the developer and the
patriarch vs. the Arab community) demonstrate that neoliberal coalitions are not free of contradictions. Indeed, the Andromeda Hill project embodies the bleak outcome of these contradictions: even if the
planning authorities have not formulated an explicit policy aimed at
the full privatization of public space in Jaffa, they have lost control over
the urban definition of situation in favor of the private entrepreneur.
At any rate, the accruing social outcome was that the Arab Orthodox
community in Jaffa fell prey yet again to two circumstantial coalitions
formed beyond its control, forcing it to live under circumstances it could
not legally oppose.

THE NEW-OLD JAFFA: SPATIAL CRITIQUE

The spatial relation of the Andromeda Hill project to its surroundings
is exploitative and arrogant (figure 5.3). This disposition manifests itself in three main domains that constitute the *modus operandi* of the
project in the local urban space: first, the project's integration into the
urban texture; second, the architectural design; and third, the project's
image as tailored by architects and marketing professionals (the Lich-
tenson Company for Marketing Communication). These three aspects
combined demonstrate how real estate greed manipulates a romantic
aesthetic rhetoric that translates a neo-Orientalist discourse into a self-
segregating structure, indifferent to its historical environment and its
surrounding lived space. In these three domains there emerged a double
pattern of inward segregation and outward detachment from local space,
alternatively oriented toward cosmopolitan cultural and economic spaces
and over to an imagined "Mediterranean" sphere.

FIGURE 5.3. Andromeda Hill's monumental presence, bordering on older structures that were later demolished.
Photo by the author, 2003.

Spatial Integration: "A City within a City"

The Andromeda housing complex borders on several quarters of historical significance: the Old City to the north (a.k.a. the Artists' Colony);[10] the Flea Market to the east; the Jaffa Port, planned as a future center for tourism and commerce, to the west; and the 'Ajami neighborhood, populated predominantly by low-income Palestinians and by a wealthy minority of Jewish gentrifiers, to the south. This area used to be an important Palestinian urban center under Ottoman and British colonial rule. It is at this strategic junction that the first European colonial institutions were built toward the end of the nineteenth century in the wake of the city's expansion outside the ancient walls (e.g., the French hospital in 1864, and the Orthodox Church and three Christian schools in the 1880s). Notwithstanding this historical centrality, currently Andromeda Hill is buffered by a road ring, which blocks easy access to the neighboring areas. Moreover, the project lies on top of a hill that stands thirty meters high over the port. This topographic layout emphasizes the compound's segregative profile and further blocks access to its urban surroundings.

Despite these topographic disadvantages, appropriate social planning could have made Andromeda Hill an integral part of the urban texture. The original plan designated a public square on the main Yefet Street as well as a commercial front and open fairways that were supposed to lead to a vista overlooking the port. So far, only residential buildings have been erected, with a private club and a closed swimming pool facing the sea and disconnected from the busy street. The public institution, the commercial front, and the public square are yet to be constructed. Until the August 2007 court ruling, the entrances to the compound were used for ethnic profiling, screening, and deterrence. Private guards patrol the place day and night, parking serves only the residents, and the gate connecting the western viewpoint to the port is closed and shuttered. This is how the Andromeda Hill project stands, secluded and cut off from its urban environment, awkwardly ghettoized, and alienated from the surrounding Jaffa space.

One fascinating contradiction in the functioning of the Andromeda project is the internal tension between the planners' declaration celebrating the "perfect blending in the Jaffa landscape," as a 2003 brochure puts it, and the marketing discourse which promotes Andromeda as "a city within a city," thus erasing the presence of the local Arab population in the process. The concept of a "city within a city" is significant in two respects: first, for the analogy it makes with the early Zionist image of Tel-Aviv as "a state within a state" (LeVine 2005, 158); and secondly, for its representation of a postmodern consumerist concept that endows the project with the qualities of a real estate mall: "The mall offers a new type of space in Israel: a privately owned public space with images of city streets and squares. This space is like a sterilized bubble enabling people to disengage from the space outside—the sweaty, weary, Mediterranean urban space.... The mall offers Israelis the illusion of being 'here,' in the Middle East, yet feeling 'there,' in the opulent West" (Ram 2007, 72).

The poor, crime-ridden Arab neighborhood of 'Ajami is recast as an inviting "suburb" and euphemized as an Orientalist symbol of Mediterranean authenticity. Thus once the existence of the threatening Palestinian neighbors is discursively erased, and the presence of the lower-class Jewish residents is elegantly ignored, the Jaffa space is free, as the brochure makes clear, to be inhabited solely by visiting tourists and wealthy artists living in the "Old-City":

> History was not always kind to Jaffa, but current development and renaissance processes appear to be heralding a new golden era for the city. The first spark of this revival can already be seen in the *Ajami suburb*, with its alleyways and houses that form a history book of architecture. The past decade has seen the houses, abandoned during the War of Independence, being renovated and renewed, restoring Jaffa not only to its historical glory, but also to its realistic financial value, which has been steadily mounting. Andromeda will be the crowning glory of this Jaffa mosaic. The Hill's southern sector borders with the Ajami suburb, populated mainly by artists and galleries, and to the north lies the Greek Orthodox church steeple, breaking the northern skyline.

The seclusion and withdrawal of the Andromeda compound operates in two directions: on the one hand, it excludes the neighboring residents, and on the other hand, it cuts the complex tenants off from their own immediate environment. The three buildings on-site are linked directly through internal underground passages from the parking basement to the health club, thus allowing tenants to access any place in the project without being exposed to the outside. The most common "Jaffan" experience for the project tenants is the view from their apartment window. As the manager of the cafeteria told me, expressing her frustration with the working conditions in the project and its alienated residents: "What do they get here, anyway? A parceling of the sea! Each gets no more than one small window overlooking the sea." The window frames the landscape as a flat object, kept at bay by the monumental height and the distance from the city. It desensitizes dirt, noise, and "unpleasant" odors, only to reify the sensory perception of the city as a whitewashed Orientalist composition. Detachment is central to the project's marketed self-image: "Andromeda Hill has been planned for you to sit at home, view the sea, enjoy the beauty and hear . . . only the waves." The sharpest manifestation of this privatization of public space

is the establishment of a private police force that employs Arab guards
in order to secure the compound day and night. One of them describes
how he sees their role in the project: "All the guards here are Arab. The
project manager is a smart guy—he took us because only we can defend
the place. When it got messy here in October [2000], if not for us, they
[the demonstrators] would have burned the place down. But in the end,
I know that a day will come when they will kick us out of here. It will
surely come. . . . Sometimes, when visitors hear us speak Arabic they
freak out and leave."

A sense of alienation toward the project is recurrent in the narratives
of most of the project employees and the Arab community alike. One
of the employees in the project relates her experience:

> This place has no heart. You don't have anyone to talk to. The tenants don't
> have any sense of belonging to the place. No sense of humor. I feel like a
> servant here. I listen a lot to the residents talk. It symbolizes the ambiance
> here because there's a preoccupation with money above all. These lefty mil-
> lionaires say they brought [former prime minister] Barak to the government
> and now they talk about who they will bring next to power. . . . This place will
> never be a microcosm, by the mere fact that anyone who can afford living
> here is much beyond the average in an area that is much below the average.
> You need a fortune to be here.

For most of the Arabs in Jaffa, Andromeda is marked as off-limits,
both because of the clear antagonism it transmits and because it is perceived as a wealthy Jewish space. Hence the recurrent invocation in the
Jaffan discourse on Andromeda of the tropes "ghetto," "jail," "golden
cage," "settlement," and "fortress." Tropes of detachment are also common among the tenants themselves, who perceive the compound as an
internal enclave of comfortable seclusion. For instance, in one of my
visits to the project I conversed with a married couple who live in the
mega-rich villa town of Savion, and who recently purchased a second
apartment in the project. The wife told me,

> We come on weekends to get away. Andromeda is a marvelous place. With
> his special abilities, the manager has succeeded in bringing together a very
> unique group of very nice people. . . . But Andromeda is not Jaffa—we come
> here to look for relaxation, to rest and get away. It is a "compound" [*mitham*].
> It is not Jaffa. We almost don't do any shopping here. We don't have many
> friends in Jaffa, expect for friends in Andromeda and neighbors from Savion

·who have an apartment in 'Ajami. So we visit them sometimes.... The atmosphere here is like being abroad—you feel as if you're on a Greek island or something. Not like in the country [*lo kmo ba'aretz*].

There are also some Palestinian residents who choose to associate themselves with the place precisely for reasons of class distinction. Salim, a successful restaurant owner and a member of the project's sports club details his outlook, presenting a neoliberal dream of a "new Middle East":

> Israel is a fiesta. Compare it to Syria, Jordan, Lebanon, or Egypt. What's needed here is integration—if they manage to get to a level of integration, it will be heaven on earth. The Arabs are pitiable [*masakin*]—not that that it depends just on them, they're weak. The Andromeda deal was signed in my restaurant.... There's nothing you can do—it's the force of the market. And what's the alternative? What will happen in Jaffa is that there will be integration and then the Jews will come. Probably, the expensive land will remain in Jewish hands, but there will always be Arabs.... It's hard to put populations next to each other when one is worth twenty million dollars and the other barely makes a living of five thousand shekels. It's impossible that someone sees you eating caviar while he is eating *fassulia* [beans]—blow him up with fassulia but put him with people like him. In Jaffa, had there been integration you wouldn't have had the mess of October.

Tellingly, while advocating the pluralistic trope of binational "integration," Salim forcefully invokes the necessity for class hierarchy, and the distinction between "fassulia" and those "eating caviar." He chooses to contrast the *locality* of fassulia, a popular bean-based dish, with the symbolic *internationality* of caviar and its foreign luxury flair. Like Salim, the small Arab group that does manage to associate itself with the image of Andromeda represents the new upper class in Jaffa—a small group of businessmen and professionals. The project and its liberal image advance a circumstantial coalition between the Arab capitalists, who act as "free riders" on the real estate wave, and the project's spatial capital.

Architecture: The "Jaffa Style"

The architectural contest initiated by Murray Goldman dictated no predefined architectural program and allowed the contenders full creative freedom. According to the project's architects, Bar-Lev Architects Ltd. and Alex Cohen, they won because they employed "intuitively the Romantic Jaffa style." Their proposal featured a built front along Yefet Street, public passages, and "romantic" elements (arches, colorful plaster, and a tile roof). In the text attached to the original sketches, the architects have intentionally invoked the romantic "local style" to cover for the "huge building mass": "Romanticism is the main attraction factor that draws new positive population to Jaffa. . . . *The sophisticated use of the Romantic Style conceals the huge building mass and disguises the modern design.* Intimate public spaces of distinct Mediterranean character interlock along clear circulation & view axis, to combine *what seems to be 'Local Style' into modern Urban Design* in order to create a separate 'Quarter' within the layout of old Jaffa" (originally in English; italics added).

The architect explained that the "Romantic Style" was tailored to suit the Canadian entrepreneur's estimated stereotypical taste. This approach also corresponded to the city planners' vision of future construction in Jaffa. And indeed, a few years later, the Jaffa Planning Team made a list of specifications and formulated a new architectural language which define the Jaffa Style.[11] That the architects relied on their professional and aesthetic intuition to discern the Canadian entrepreneur's taste illustrates the "glocal" nature of the project. To win the bid, the Israeli architects imagined the developer's taste and proposed a romantic style designed to fit his Orientalist image. As the text that accompanies the winning proposal shows, the architects designed the project reflexively, as a romantic simulacrum "that conceals the huge building mass and disguises the modern design." The architect has consciously created "what seems to be Local Style," but which is in fact a modern design *par excellence* (see figure 5.3.).

In a later phase of the planning process, and faced with the entrepreneur's demand to pack an extra hundred units into a massive and dense structure, the hostile and alienated relation of the project to its environment took on a more radical tone. Real estate and business calculations gave precedence to the western facade overlooking the port, whereas the eastern front facing Yefet Street was left neglected and still awaits the planned commercial corridor, in clear breach of the Jaffa

Team demands and the approved city plan. The existing buildings are positioned perpendicular to the street and ignore its presence. While in historical local architecture, buildings rise no more than three stories high, Andromeda features buildings up to seven stories high and eighty meters long. In an attempt to break down the built mass and to reduce the visual burden on the delicate Jaffa texture, the planners have created clusters of three and four buildings with independent tile roofs at different heights. To exploit the roof space for more rooms and balconies, the tile roofs themselves were fragmented in a manner that damages their integrity and unity. As a result, the outcome is a bombastic, overblown building with a superficial "romantic" shell and deformed proportions.

Moreover, following the demands of the new developer (Ilan-Gat), the buildings were "upgraded" with stone facing that endows them with what the architects termed a "luxurious Mediterranean appearance." The contrast between the modest old local style (with a plaster finish or local sandstone) and the imported and processed stone buildings emphasizes the latter's aggressive presence and gives the buildings a fortress-like appearance. Seen from the northern and southern neighborhoods, these gigantic structures inevitably remain an intrusive element in the city landscape. Particularly abnormal is the western front overlooking the sea; it sticks out thirty meters above the road and includes two five-story stone blocks (figure 5.4.). The western hill front, which had been for centuries a landmark for pilgrims and visitors arriving from the sea, is exposed in all its hubris as a Herodian castle, displaying Andromeda Hill's distinctive indifference to its Jaffa environment.

Marketing: "One of the World's Four Most Beautiful Projects!"

An examination of the project's marketing discourse reveals a fundamental dialectic between local and global, old and new, original and imitation. The marketing strategy targets two audiences, with different emphases in terms of form and content: to the global audience of foreign customers a continuous spatiocultural discourse is deployed, smoothly connecting the "Israeli experience," the Tel-Aviv business district, Jaffa City, and Andromeda. While the English- and French-language market-

FIGURE 5.4. Western facade overlooking the Jaffa port.
Photo by the author, 2003.

ing discourse creates an effect of spatial compression ("feeling at home,
away from home") and a top-down discursive convergence with a specific location, the Israeli audience is a recipient of a discrete discourse
of "islands" and "bubbles" separating Andromeda from its immediate
threatening environment (i.e., Arab Jaffa) and from the noisy familiarity of Tel-Aviv. Whereas the English advertising campaign stresses
Tel-Aviv's proximity, the Hebrew one undermines the nearness of the
metropolis: "Who remembers that Tel-Aviv is only a few minutes away?"
it asks. These two discursive modalities of parallel convergence and di-
vergence also reflect the inherent dialectics of gentrification in Jaffa:
on the one hand, through Jaffa's unification with Tel-Aviv, Andromeda
markets itself as part of the global trend of urban "upgrading" and local
"regeneration"; on the other hand, it constructs an image of idiosyncrasy,
detachment, and exclusivity.

The semiotic process of the selection of the project's name suggests a parallel dialectic between local and global, between Jaffa and the Mediterranean, and between politics and mythology. The names proposed by the architects, the entrepreneur, and the advertisers for debate were the Diplomats' Hill, the Jaffa Landscape, the Jaffa Observatory, the Jaffa Heights, the Greek Hill (the technical term appearing in the city plan), the Seagull Hill, the Sultan's Hill, the Sea Estate, Above the Port, the Coral Estate, Jaffa in Front of the Port, the Jaffa Towers, the Greek Hill Towers, the Goldman Towers, the Old Jaffa Observatory, the Old Jaffa Hill, the New-Old Jaffa, and of course Andromeda Hill.[12] The selected name—Andromeda Hill—is followed in publications in English and French by the subtitle "The New-Old Jaffa."[13] These image-marketing choices are indicative of a Mediterranean, regional (as opposed to local), and mythological orientation and intentionality.[14] Names that spelled a direct link to the local and contemporary contested space were rejected in favor of mythological Mediterranean folklore, bereft of any political or social reference.

In addition to the implied positionality in the mythical Mediterranean space, the marketing strategy attached a solid global image to the project. Targeting Israeli and non-Israeli audiences alike, the marketing products in English and French (e.g., a professionally designed website in English only) were designated to *internationalize* the project. An additional facet of this globalization effort presents itself in the ads in the Hebrew press, indicating that "Andromeda Hill was selected as one of world's four most beautiful projects!"—a selection made by the American *Stone Magazine,* reportedly "the leading magazine in the world of architecture and building." The advertisement features photographs of the first three winning projects, located in France, Austria, and Switzerland, respectively. Andromeda Hill, touted as "Israel's Most Exclusive Residence," came in fourth in this competition.

The project's logo adds a final idyllic quality to its commodified image (see figure 5.1). Produced in 1958, Nahum Guttmann's naive and picturesque painting—featuring an artist at work against the Old City—mobilizes Israel's national artistic icon in order to convey a message that is dreamlike and past-oriented. The logo and its selection can be interpreted as an analytic metaphor of the project, and arguably of the very problématique of gentrification in Jaffa: it shows a Jewish artist painting himself in the process of painting the Arab, exotic, and Oriental Old City. One of the project's slogans, "Living an Original," poignantly mirrors the campaign's problematic cultural manipulation: it is constructed as the authentic "original" that is at the same time "New" and "Old," mythological and Mediterranean.

GENTRIFICATION AND NORTH-SOUTH RELATIONS: "A BIT OF JAFFA AND A LOT OF TEL-AVIV"

The phenomenology of the Andromeda Hill project is a product of a paradoxical cultural matrix of marketing images, planning ideologies, and architectural style—all mobilized to convey a message of real estate prestige and class distinction while constantly fabricating an imagined local "Jaffanism." To implement the segregative concept of a gated community that functions as a "city within a city" but is also "a symbol of rebirth," the project maintains, vis-à-vis Jaffa, a double relationship of closeness and remoteness, inclusion and exclusion. The erasure of the Jaffa Arabs from the cognitive map of the tenants is achieved by means of a discourse of separation between North and South, a discourse that ties the project to Jaffa, but only to "North Jaffa."

Thus during a guided tour of the project, the sales agent pointed at the predominantly poor and Arab neighborhood of 'Ajami and explained, "This is 'Ajami—most of the apartments there were sold to people from Savion [Israel's Beverly Hills]. Friendly neighbors. This region will be called 'North Jaffa.' It is separated psychologically, bureaucratically, and administratively from South Jaffa. The October riots were mainly in the south side of Jaffa, mainly near the border with Bat-Yam." Responding to my question about the demographic profile of the residents of the project, she answered with a smile: "We have people here who buy their second apartment in the project, they come to do business or to relax, and we have people from abroad. There is only one family with kids. Seventy percent are from Israel, 30 percent are from abroad—all are Jewish. We have no Arab tenants or Arab vacationers. Not that it's not allowed, but they are smart enough to know that it's not appropriate. Naturally, they don't come because people want to be with their own kind."

The boundary discourse demarcating North from South in Jaffa re-produces Tel-Aviv's long-lasting dichotomy between the Ashkenazi well-to-do northern neighborhoods and the poorer, Mizrahi, South Side (Birenboim-Carmeli 2000). This rescaling of ethnoclass boundaries radicalizes spatial fragmentation in Jaffa between its own northern part—the potential site of tourism and capital—and the straggling Arab southern side. Reflected in the narrative of the Palestinian citizens, this boundary discourse constitutes their own labeling of the wealthy newcomers as alienated "Northsiders."

Tellingly, the Palestinian borrowing of this Tel-Avivan spatial metaphor is consistent with the municipality's expansionist strategy for tightening the link between Tel-Aviv and Jaffa. Under the guise of unification, the new discourse of connectivity shrinks Jaffa once again (the first time was the 1948 land expropriation), leaving behind the Arab "South." This plan reflects the city planners' ambivalent attitude: acknowledging the instrumental necessity of marketing the "Jaffan aroma" in the service of redevelopment (*Implementation Plan* 2002, 11), yet keeping Jaffa at arm's length so as to maintain Tel-Aviv's command of the discursive horizon. This ambivalence is reflected in the marketing slogan of another gated community (Jaffa Courts), which sells an experience of dwelling in the border zone: "a bit of Jaffa and a lot of Tel-Aviv."

In sum, the spatial homology of inter- and intra-urban processes implicates two discursive frames at play in Andromeda Hill: an integration discourse of "development," subsuming the new housing complex under the general gentrification process and national tourism; and a compressing "encapsulation" discourse predicated on the valorization of security and exclusivity to be found on the premises of the gated community. Accordingly, two systems of parallel spatial logics shape the space of gentrification in Jaffa—a logic of neoliberal capitalist inclusion and a logic of political and class-based exclusion. Their parallel existence reflects the ambivalent position of the Palestinian minority in Israel, and particularly the status of the Arab population in ethnically mixed towns (Monterescu and Rabinowitz 2007). Mark LeVine (2005, 238–239) has aptly formulated this ambivalence as it manifests itself in the Jaffa architecture: "It is ambivalent in that postmodernist architectural sensitivity to Jaffa's Palestinian Arab heritage has remained 'superficial' and

economic in orientation. The place-oriented postmodern architecture
is used to catch a 'global'—and implicitly, non-Arab—elite, and disal-
low potentially political identification from Jaffa's Arab community. The
double economy of fixing Jaffa for an Orientalist gaze, on the one hand,
and developing it along the line of a changing market economy, on the
other, represents both the economization and depoliticization of the
Arab community."

SPATIAL HETERONOMY AND THE
NEOLIBERAL "MIXED" CITY

The emergence of gated communities in Israel/Palestine signals new
forms of urban distinction, which redefine more established modes of
spatial exclusion. With the advent of gentrification there emerged a hybrid form of neoliberal spatiality—predicated not on a modernistic logic
of unidimensional segregation but on multiple vectors of simultaneous
exclusion and inclusion. Gentrification, Janus-faced, constitutes Andromeda Hill and Jaffa as spatial heteronomy.[15]

A radical marker of ethnogentrification, this gated community seeks
to maximize the symbolic and financial gains to be made from its unique
location on the Mediterranean coast, while remaining a safe residential
enclave. It hence attempts to accomplish the impossible task of positioning itself both in and out of local place and inhabited time. Operating
as a neo-Orientalist simulacrum, it subverts, spatially and semiotically,
the dichotomous logic of urban representation (Rotbard 2005). Here
Oriental otherness is dialectically mobilized, contained, and converted
to symbolic distinction and spatial capital, thereby repositioning the
gated community as the Perseus of the "New-Old Jaffa." Circumventing the local and projected onto a mythological plane of Mediterranean
fantasy, Andromeda Hill can thus become the "princess on the rock," a
place of dreamlike urbanism.

In its neoliberal moment, the decentralized urban regime in Jaffa
gives rise to unexpected coalitions between Christian and Jewish, Israeli and Canadian, private and public agents—all celebrating the commodification of space and eager to take part in the bourgeois civilizing
mission of the city. The neoliberal definition of the urban situation is

best exemplified in the discourses around Tel-Aviv's oedipal discovery of Jaffa. Once the "Bride of Palestine" and hence Tel-Aviv's enemy, and then its disinvested "Arab neighborhood," Jaffa is now embraced by its "daughter-turned-rival" global city (Alfasi and Fenster 2005; LeVine 2005). Heralding this rediscovery in terms of corrective historical justice, Tel Aviv mayor Ron Huldai has recently launched a new policy of "affirmative action," which further depoliticizes Jaffa's gentrification:

> Ever since the Hebraic residents of Jaffa first left the city to build Ahuzat Bait that later became Tel-Aviv, the city begat a state. The dream became a metropolis. Now Tel-Aviv reaches out to Jaffa, and for the first time since the establishment of the state, Tel-Aviv comes to rehabilitate and build Jaffa. Tel-Aviv-Jaffa will be, in this list of priorities and related to this matter, Jaffa-Tel-Aviv. The metropolis will make Jaffa a place to dream of. (Peleg 1999, 5)

Ethnically mixed towns emerged out of the superposition of the old Ottoman sectarian urban regime onto the new national, modernizing, and capitalist order. Reconfigured as a new city-form, the mixed town was in actual fact a fragmented amalgam of Ottoman, British, Palestinian, and Israeli urban legacies (Monterescu and Rabinowitz 2007). A product of these intertwined urban histories, Jaffa saw demographic processes, political transformations, and planning policies constantly create Jewish spaces within Arab ones and Palestinian spaces within Israeli ones. Reviving previous traumas of displacement, gentrification reshuffles communal and spatial boundaries, thus further destabilizing Palestinians' sense of belonging. Beyond a deep sense of alienation, however, it triggers new forms of mobilization and legal activism. Translated into aggressive "acts of citizenship" and identity politics (Isin and Nielsen 2007), ethnogentrification pushes new social actors to the fore. That the 2007 easement claim of the Jaffa Association for Human Rights against the Andromeda Hill project is considered in Israel a legal precedent challenges the city's liberal ideology of proper citizenship. Instead, a new discourse of urban rights calls for the institution of an inclusive redefinition of citizenship tailored for the "indigenous national minority." Increasingly visible NGOs like Shatil's Mixed Cities Project and Adalah are beginning to do precisely that.

Extending well beyond the urban scene, the preceding analysis points to a pressing problem on the larger scale of the nation-state. With the escalation of the Israeli-Palestinian conflict, the gated community and its spatial precedents, notably *Homa U-Migdal* (Tower and Stockade), have been criticized for providing both a model of and a model for Israel's own regional positioning (Yacobi and Cohen 2007). While the gated community is hardly a peculiarly Israeli phenomenon, the language of separation that underlies it resonates with a longstanding discourse among scholars, laypeople, and politicians who frame Israel as a regional "ghetto" which is both "refuge" and "island." In Jaffa, as one Palestinian activist stressed in response to the new municipal policy, this discourse of closure touches the raw nerve of communal survival: "First they take over a place, close it off, and prevent others from entering, then they want to put us in a ghetto. . . . Today, Andromeda is like a settlement, but life is stronger. . . . Soon, Jaffa will vanish, it will be swallowed by Tel-Aviv; it's certain; but just as Jaffa will be swallowed by Tel-Aviv, so Israel will be consumed by the Arab Middle East."

Trapped between national security and subaltern protests, these concerns, as a metaphoric afterthought, propose a view of state practices, criticized for functioning along the principles of a gated community in an alien geopolitical neighborhood. Relentlessly producing a utopian rhetoric of a westernized "New Middle East"—i.e., a capitalist regional space of "free" exchange—Israel consistently shuts itself off from the Arab world, as it erects symbolic and concrete "separation walls" in a doomed-to-fail search for certainty and security. The self-defeating logic of heteronomy, dialectically perpetuating economic inclusion and political exclusion, has been the main paradigm of Israel's "predatory nationalism" (Appadurai 2000). Fulfilling its own gloomy prophecy it perpetrates acts of "enclaving" that tragically demonstrate, as Zygmunt Bauman (1993, 9) has observed, that "modern states . . . need chaos if only to go on creating order." Unprecedentedly obsessed with hermetic territorial closure, ghetto-like existence, and secured borders, Israeli national and urban spaces are constantly threatened by infiltration and contamination. Ironically, however, these anxieties of transgression serve as an ultimate mobilizing pretext for the state to violate the very borders it seeks to protect by means of occasional military raids into Palestine, Lebanon, and Syria (Kemp 1998). The heteronomous management of borders, threat, and security reproduces demarcations as it situationally legitimates their dissolution. It is an autothelic practice of power that justifies its *raison d'être* by any means necessary. To conclude the exchange from early in this chapter, the following voices the frustration of Hicham Chabaita, the Palestinian advocate and the leader of the legal struggle to "open up" the gated community, who finally confronted the Andromeda Project manager: "I was driven out of my house because I'm Arab and to you they give a closed neighborhood." To which the manager replied coldly, "You were driven out of the house not because you're Arab. You were driven out of your house because you have no money!"[16]

PART THREE

Being and Belonging in the Binational City: A Phenomenology of the Urban

SIX

Escaping the Mythscape

Tales of Intimacy and Violence

Peace, doves of two strangers who share
The last cooing at the edge of the abyss.

—MAHMOUD DARWISH, *State of Siege*

Jaffa was once a Jewish city, but what the Jews took
by force the Arabs are now taking by money.

—PAOLINA, an aged Bulgarian Jew in Jaffa

BREAKFAST IN JAFFA C.

Safiyya Dabbah and Hanna Swissa, two elderly neighbors living in the
Jaffa C. (Yafo Gimel) neighborhood, meet daily over breakfast. Safiyya,
a Muslim woman in her nineties, was widowed thirty years ago and
today lives on her own in a dilapidated shanty only a few steps from the
building where Hanna lives. Hanna is a Jewish Moroccan woman in her
seventies who has been a widow for twenty years. Despite the class differences between Safiyya and Hanna, which are metaphorically embodied
in the buildings they inhabit—a ramshackle hut on the one hand and a
tidy apartment building on the other—the two elderly women found a
common ground they use to nourish their symbiotic friendship: both
came from strict patriarchal families (Safiyya's husband used to forbid
her to leave the house, while Hanna's husband was jealous and violent)
and both gained considerable personal freedom after their husbands'
deaths; both speak Arabic and share a common cultural background;
both are going through the experience of aging; and they live in geo-

graphical and functional proximity next to each other. While Hanna, aided by her welfare-funded housekeeper, shows concern for Safiyya, whose means are more limited, by supplying the food for their daily rendezvous, Safiyya keeps Hanna company and makes this pleasant morning routine possible.

The political and social reality that brought Safiyya and Hanna together has constituted in Jaffa a paradoxical "contact zone" (Pratt 1999) —a social medium that both separates and relates the city's Jewish and Arab inhabitants. In this chapter I focus on this encounter between strangers through the analysis of life stories recorded by four of Jaffa's elderly residents—Arab and Jewish, male and female, rich and poor. *Prima facie,* Palestinian and Jewish elderly people in Jaffa inhabit two parallel and incommensurable existential planes: the Jews' national story unfolds from Diaspora to immigration (*Aliyah*), and from Holocaust to nation-building, whereas the Palestinian collective story is one of traumatic passage from the golden "days of the Arabs" (*ayyam al-'Arab*) to the national defeat of the Nakba in 1948. Their ensuing civil exclusion and economic marginalization is represented as resistance (*Muqawama*) and steadfastness (*Sumud*).

Diametrically opposed, these collective narratives tell, on the one hand, a success story of settlement, progress, and return (*Shivat Zion*), and conversely, a story of dispersion (*Shatat*), decline, and struggle. This is the official narrative, which has been produced and reproduced by the social institutions in charge of maintaining the national collective memory. Indeed, on this collective level, the main relationship between the Israeli memory and the Palestinian one is that of negation and mutual exclusion (Gur-Ze'ev and Pappé 2003; Slyomovics 1998). This frame of reference creates a unidimensional paradigm of "liberation" versus "victimhood" that nourishes the biographical narrative, which in itself can either adopt it, reject it, or alter it to suit its own needs.

Notwithstanding collective representations of the body politic, a close examination of personal life stories unravels a whole universe of contradictions: some of Jaffa's Arab residents reject major chunks of the Palestinian national narrative, while some of the Jewish residents do not see their own trajectories as the metonymic celebration of the "predatory" nationalist project (Appadurai 2000). Oftentimes they personally identify with the predicament of the Palestinians. The result is a fascinating set of multilayered personal histories, which differentially reposition citizens vis-à-vis the state and the nation. The following examines the discrepancy between the top-down collective memory and local biographical memories. These tensions give voice to private experiences that have been systematically silenced by the hegemonic national register (Trouillot 1995).

The argument for dismantling the dichotomous totality of nationalist categories is achieved by an analytic scrutiny of three main themes that present themselves in the recorded life stories: nation and community, gender and family, and liminality and old age. Rooted in specific religious, ethnic, and gender- and class-based positions, the interviewees delineate the binational relational field in Jaffa, exposing it as a stratified web of cultural meanings and informal social relations. Revisiting the collective *doxa* of both Palestinian and Jewish essentialisms, these stories invoke the "gray area" surrounding the margins of the collective self as a much wider and muddier quagmire than we may have been led to believe. Constantly in dialogue with the national narration, the ambivalence of these stories illustrates that the Israeli and the Palestinian narratives do not consist of a single nationalist, antinationalist, or postnationalist narrative, but of a mosaic of memories and reminiscences. Thus, rather than act as a monolithic script of self and Other, aligned along imagined communities and myths of redemption, these narratives weave political violence (uprooting, immigration, and imprisonment) together with an experience of social proximity and cultural intimacy. Disabling a flat image of the other, the critical narration of the nation enables residents to redefine coexistence and escape the mythscape (Bell 2003).

FOUR LIFE STORIES

Subhiyye Abu-Ramadan was fourteen years old in 1948. In the course of the war she was forced to marry her cousin because her family feared that the Jewish occupying forces would desecrate the young girl's honor. She was born in Tal al-Rish—a village on the periphery of Greater Jaffa that later became part of the Tel-Giborim neighborhood in the city of Holon—to a family of poor tenant farmers who leased land and sold its produce in the Jaffa market. As the battlefield approached Tal al-Rish, her family sought refuge in the city of Jaffa and settled in the Coptic Monastery compound. Abu-Ramadan got married and was widowed twice, and is the mother of eleven children. After residing for twenty years in Lydda, she returned to Jaffa where she lived by herself in an apartment she owned. In her sixties she became an observant Muslim and went on the Hajj pilgrimage to Mecca. Abu-Ramadan's story offers a gendered insight into the relations between the political upheavals and patriarchal oppression, and reflects on the central presence of the welfare state in her life, given her status as a strong woman struggling for the well-being of her family. The interviews with Abu-Ramadan were conducted in her house in the mixed Jerusalem Boulevard area, while she was surrounded by her grandchildren, who were visiting her following the incarceration of her son. In 2005 she died at the age of seventy-one.[1]

Naziha 'Assis was born in 1920 in Aleppo, Syria, to an indigent Jewish family. After her mother fell sick, she was raised by her grandmother, who could not afford to send her to school. Following a failed first marriage, 'Assis worked as a seamstress and played the violin at local parties and weddings. In 1967 she was arrested by the Syrian Intelligence Agency (the Mukhabarat) and was indicted for assisting in smuggling Jews into Israel. She was under arrest for a period of two years without trial. In 1978 'Assis immigrated to Israel with her family, and since then she has resided with her husband in Jaffa. 'Assis is the mother of seven daughters and one son. Since her immigration, she has been recognized as an *Assirat Zion* (Prisoner of Zion, or *refusenik*—a privileged official status given to people imprisoned for their Zionist activities). During the interviews held in her house, 'Assis unfolded a story of successful immigration and personal autonomy under the auspices of the state, in contrast with her husband, who bemoaned his previous life in Aleppo and his lost patriarchal status. In 2004 she was fatally injured by a horse kick while taking her evening walk on Jerusalem Boulevard. She was eighty-five at the time of her death.

Fakhri Jday (Abu-Yussef) was born in 1926 to a well-to-do Christian family in Jaffa. In 1945 he left for Beirut to study pharmacy at the French University. He returned to Jaffa in 1950 under the family reunion legis-

lation, and had firsthand experience with Jaffa's dramatic transformation from an Arab metropolis to a Jewish mixed town. After sixty years
of Fakhri's managing the pharmacy established by his father at the beginning of the century, the family business is now managed by his son,
who was trained in the United Kingdom. Fakhri was one of the founders
of the Al-Ard nationalist movement in the 1950s as well as Al-Rabita (the
Association for the Jaffa Arabs) in 1979. He is the only surviving member
of the Palestinian urban elite of Mandatory Jaffa. The interviews with
Fakhri Jday took place in the palatial guest room of his 'Ajami house.

Rabbi Avraham Bachar was born in 1914 in Bulgaria, and served for
fifty years as the Bulgarian community rabbi in Jaffa. After pursuing
religious studies and serving as a renowned cantor in Bulgaria, he immigrated (along with most of Bulgaria's Jews) to Israel in 1948, together
with his spouse and their two children. His son has immigrated to the
United States and his daughter passed away from illness. His story relates the rise and fall of the Bulgarian community, for which Jaffa was
known in the 1950s as "Little Bulgaria." The community, which had
numbered forty thousand, gradually shriveled until the only Bulgarian
synagogue, privately owned by Bachar, remained desolate on Jerusalem
Boulevard. For almost a decade until his death in 2005, Bachar lived with
his wife in the Bulgarian home for the aged in Rishon le-Zion, where the
interview was conducted.

METANATIONALISM AND THE BIOGRAPHICAL ILLUSION

Analyzing life stories in Israel/Palestine poses a challenge that is both
theoretical and methodological. The conundrum is best put in negative
terms: how can we analyze personal narratives of Jews and Palestinians, who are steeped in economic and political power relations, without
overlooking the complexity that at times dismantles the same power
relations? The following scrutiny draws on the insight that apolitical
narratives and politicizing tactics are both the product of identity politics, for the hegemonic nationalist discourse and subordinate discourses
alike. Instead of rejecting the validity of these narratives or, conversely,
accepting them at face value, I position them within the Jaffa force field
in order to decipher the tension between the personal and the political.

Reflexively treating these narratives as stories "is not to reduce them to fictions made up out of whole cloth and therefore false" (Stoler 1992, 183). Thus, rather than treating them as a "Rashomon tale, a multi-stranded set of equally plausible claims," I seek to "recoup the inconsistencies of these narratives, to explore how subaltern inflections entered these stories . . . tangled by multiple meanings that could not be easily read" (184). I address these concerns by resorting to an analytical approach that can be characterized as "metanationalist." Like metaphysics (which can be defined as second-order thinking about the phenomenal world), metanationalism is a second-order reflexive deconstruction of national narratives. This inquiry necessitates a systematic mapping of the life stories and their internalized representation of the collective memory. This approach is based on Ulrich Beck's (2003) critique of "methodological nationalism," namely, the seeping of paradigmatic and national categories into sociological analysis (see also Wimmer and Glick-Schiller 2002). Metanationalism is therefore first and foremost a call for ethnographic sensitivity as a method for dealing with this bias.

Conceptualizing for instance aged Palestinians as "strangers" who are members of a "trapped minority" between nation and state (Rabinowitz 2001), my intention is to avoid subordinating their stories to a methodological nationalist account that reduces their positions to mutually exclusive frames of "resistance" or "steadfastness," on the one hand, or naive "coexistence," on the other. Bracketing such dichotomies opens up these narratives to an alternative reading in terms of class and gender.

An additional challenge addresses the tendency of the life-story narrative genre to impose coherence where there is none (Bourdieu 1987; Ewing 1990; Gubrium, Holstein, and Buckholdt 1994). Some researchers have conceptualized the aged person's life story as an evolving internal "myth" whose elements unfold sequentially to create unity and purpose (McAdams 1997).[2] The myth—from the Greek word *mythos,* meaning "word and story"—is arguably a coherent framework constructed by the narrator to supply her- or himself with a *telos*—destination and meaning. However, as a mode of symbolic interaction, one's identity is determined by the story one tells oneself and significant others in the ethnographic present. Often this story is told, especially in a situation of a life-story interview, as an orderly and meaningful chain of events. Bourdieu (1987, 2) terms this tendency "the biographical illusion" and calls it into question as a trajectory within social spaces: "To produce a life history or to consider life as history, that is as a coherent narrative of a significant and directed sequence of events, is to conform to a rhetorical illusion, to the common representation of existence that a whole literary tradition has always and still continues to reinforce."

The discontinuity that defines Palestinian experience and the drama of Jewish immigration renders such "coherent narratives" hard to sustain. Thus, like the difficulty in maintaining a cohesive collective discourse in times of crisis (see chapters 2 and 3), there is difficulty in maintaining the biographical illusion in the generational context of old age. The analytical challenge is therefore to follow the dynamics of narration in a mixed cultural environment and to capture its multiple significations at the crossroads of gender, ethnicity, age, and nationality. If the epistemological status of the life story is that of a nonreferential "text" (Crapanzano 1984), we should read it against the context of its production. The following illustrates how the interviewees navigate between different frames of reference and identity—rewriting in the process the relationships between self and Other.

STRANGERS IN THEIR OWN TOWN: NATION AND COMMUNITY IN THE NARRATIVES OF FAKHRI JDAY AND AVRAHAM BACHAR

Fakhri Jday and Rabbi Bachar are perceived as the official spokesmen of the Palestinian and Jewish communities, respectively. Jday often gives interviews to international newspapers in Arabic, French, and English, and writes a regular personal column in the local magazine *Akhbar al-Madina* on weighty matters in Arab and Palestinian politics. Due to his unique status in the community as a senior representative of pre-'48 Jaffa, several ceremonial events have been organized in his honor (on the occasions of his seventy-fifth birthday and the publication of his book on Mandatory Jaffa).[3] As the head of a notable Jaffan family, which had managed pharmacies in Jaffa from the beginning of the twentieth century, he is perceived as the most articulate and assertive nationalist spokesman of the community. Notwithstanding his public image, in the recorded interview I conducted with him he presented a bitter and bluntly critical narrative that was remarkably incompatible with the polemic nationalist and pan-Arab ideology I expected to hear from him. Fakhri Jday criticized the Israeli state and the Arab bourgeoisie alike, as well as the Arab rulers and the local politicians. Read together, the main theme in narratives of elderly representatives of the community is alienation and loss. While the Palestinian laments the loss of the cosmopolitan city and the thriving bourgeoisie, the Jew mourns the fragmentation of the Jewish community and the replacement of the veteran inhabitants by a young generation which "knew not of Joseph." I have purposely selected the official "representatives" of the communities in order to show the cracks in the personal stories of those who were expected to embody the collective narrative in the most distinct fashion.

Fakhri Jday chooses to begin his life story with the singular memory of Jaffa as it was in its days of glory:

> Before '48, Jaffa was the best city in all of Palestine. In the national sphere, most of the dignitaries who protected the Palestinian cause were from Jaffa. I know them because they were my father's lawyers. My father had a pharmacy on Bustros Street, which he owned in partnership with Dr. Fu'ad al-Dajani. They had a pharmacy near the clock tower, and on February twenty-fourth, 1924, my father opened the pharmacy here, in 'Ajami. I went to school at the Collège de Frères, because before '48 the French school was thought to be the best. In 1945 I traveled to Beirut to study pharmacy. At that time, ninety percent of the youngsters who completed their academic studies did so in Beirut—some went to Germany, and a few to Cairo, Baghdad, and Syria. I studied at the French University and graduated in 1950. I returned to Jaffa on October fifteenth, 1950. I returned when the Family Reunion Law was still in effect. I was the last to return, and then they closed the gates. My father, mother, and brother were here. There was still military rule in Jaffa.

Since Jday was not present in Jaffa during the war, the transition was abrupt, and the gap between the city he remembered and the city he experienced upon his return was radical. The mythical construction of Jaffa as a "lieu de mémoire" (Nora 1989) is the main motif in his life story, against which contemporary Jaffa and its historical time are no more than a poor reflection:

> I knew Jaffa when it was still built up [*'amira*] and full of people. And when I returned, most of the Manshiyye neighborhood was in ruins, and there were only thirty-two hundred people left in Jaffa. I would walk the streets and cry for Jaffa. All of the people were gone, people you knew, the families, the friends. It was very sad. The truth is, there were days when I thought about leaving because the disappointment was so great. Why had I returned? What kind of life was this? When I returned I found my mother ill. They told me, "Where will you go without us, and leave us behind?" Just as a man's family sacrifices for him, so he must sacrifice. My father considered leaving, but my mother and sister wouldn't agree. They told him, "If you want to go, go. We're staying."

Jday then targets the concerted efforts of the state to dispossess the Palestinians of whatever land they owned. While his family lost most of its land, he frames it as a general tragedy shared by other wealthy families:

> The military regime in the Triangle and the Galilee had one goal: to take the land. How would they steal the land? They created a law. You know, Israel is the leading country in the world at creating laws. They're known for stealing land—every day there is a new law. In Jaffa they abolished military rule earlier because they finished the job here; they took all they wanted. We had two thousand three hundred eighty-four dunam, which were confiscated, in Bat-Yam. My father went there in '53 and saw that they were building there. He was told, "It's confiscated." We have the maps and the *kushan* [title deed]. We filed a lawsuit that reached the Supreme Court, which ratified the confiscation. Others in Jaffa also had everything confiscated. Amin Andraus [one of the leaders of the community before '48 and one of the signatories on the resignation document of the city to the Hagana] had his orchard taken, and when he went to court, he got four thousand Israeli lira. He told them, "I don't want them. Put them in the toilet. When Abu Khaled comes, he will give me back my land." A judge from the Supreme Court asked his lawyer, "Who is Abu Khaled?" So the lawyer told him, "Abu Khaled is Jamal Abdul Nasser." This is written in the court protocols.

In spite of his efforts in the first thirty years to reorganize civil society and political activism in Jaffa, the social devastation Jday faced when he returned to Jaffa was never fully rehabilitated, and he suffers from a sense of loss to this day. As the state authorities and the General Security Service (*Shabak*) diligently worked on dividing the community from within and pitting Christians against Muslims, he criticized the middle-class Arabs who were preoccupied with their own self interest. In the face of this social anomie, interpreted by Jday as materialistic egoism, his own response in past years has been one of seclusion, distantness, and disdain:

> Today there are no social classes in Jaffa—an upper class and a middle class existed only before '48. Today the majority is shit, pardon the expression.... There is no basis for improvement. At the time, I formed the Rabita in order to create an intellectual class, and thank God, today there is an academic class. But to our dismay, about ninety to ninety-five percent of them want only money. There is no spirit of giving. "Stay away from me [*Ib'ad 'anni*]—I want to save money and buy a BMW." In our community, if you need to open a school—you must first have a school for the family. Because the family is ninety-nine percent at the zero level or worse. I was head of the Rabita for six years. But when the parties began to put their fingers in the Rabita, especially the Communist Party, I felt that I didn't want to quarrel with them anymore and told them, "Guys, I came in peace and depart in peace." This is the current situation, and because of this I have stayed away from all things. Now—nothing. I come back home from the pharmacy, close the gate at seven. I don't want to hear what's going on in Jaffa because there is nothing that will make my heart glad. Everyone hates each other. Everyone wants to steal from the other. So I've given up.

In addition to his dismay at the dysfunctional class structure and the loss of the middle class, Jday ambivalently engages the nationalist discourse. In contrast with the official narrative that extols the value of steadfastness (*Sumud*)—a national story Jday himself reproduces in his articles and public appearances—in his personal account he raises doubts about the worthiness of personal sacrifice in the face of the departure of his brothers and his remaining the only survivor of the old bourgeoisie in Jaffa:

> Had I known that the situation would reach such a state, I would have left long ago. What am I doing here? I have a friend from Beirut who came to visit, and said, "Fakhri, what are you doing? What is this dump you're sitting in? What are you doing? I live in Chicago and I have four children. I work for six months and I travel the world the rest of the time." Before the Intifada we used to go to Ramallah and to Jerusalem to visit friends, to chat with people. Not like the mules here! Here there's no hope. Hope will come from the people, not from the fancy houses they build. I wish everyone would build stone houses, but who will live in them?

Full of nostalgia and bitter irony, Jday bemoans the lost city and his lost youth. Constantly reminded of his tragedy by his brother, he sees no way out. The specters of the past keep haunting him:

> Sometimes, I start thinking how the families were in those days. I think of this one and that one, about this one's house and that one's house. And where are they today? Even after fifty years it doesn't go away. Sometimes I dream about them at night. Back then, I used to live a certain kind of life, and now, a different kind. Like one who lives his life in the Garden of Eden and the other who lives his life in a garbage dump. My brother came from America; he left Jaffa in 1945 and stayed there and got married. He didn't visit until 1979. When he saw Jaffa like this, and saw house after house, he quarreled with me. He said to me, "What is this? How do you live in this dump?" Just so, he said the word "dump." "What are you doing?" he told me. "Sell the house and come to us." He was supposed to spend a year here—he stayed three months and ran away. . . .
>
> I remember the loveliest part of my life in Beirut. At the time there were Iraqi students who cursed whoever was close to King Faisal. There were students with standards and awareness. That was the best time. After that in the last fifty years, the best time was the time of the Al-Ard Movement when 'Abd Al-Nasser was in power. That was the period of glory. He gave them dignity, and shook all the countries of Europe. Not like today—King Hussein and 'Abdallah ran like children to the airport to welcome [Colin] Powell. All the Arab leaders are dogs!

In spite of the self-evident differences in content, the stories told by Fakhri Jday and Avraham Bachar are similarly narrated from a position of disillusionment. The main theme in their life stories situates both of them as strangers in their own town—Jday was deprived of the class and status that were his family's share, and Rabbi Bachar is lacking the material means that would allow him to age in dignity. Bachar, ninety years of age and one of the notables of the Bulgarian community in Jaffa, expresses similar frustration about the community to which he contributed so much. Compared with Jday, a man of property, Bachar's wealth consists of an apartment and the synagogue for which he cannot find a suitable buyer. From his small room at the Bulgarian home for the aged in Rishon le-Zion, where he is allowed to reside only in exchange for religious services he supplies to the tenants, Rabbi Bachar comments on the impoverishment and fragmentation of the Bulgarian community in Jaffa. Incidentally, despite their clear position on opposite sides of the

national fence, both Jday's and Bachar's sons have studied in the same
school (the French Collège de Frères, on Yefet Street). Like Jday, who
directs his criticism at the Israeli state, the Arab rulers, and the community in Jaffa alike, Avraham Bachar's frustration targets the ungrateful
Bulgarian community and the rabbinical establishment that refuses to
acknowledge him. And like Jday, Rabbi Bachar begins his story with a
description of the golden age of his youth—for him, this was during the
revival of the Bulgarian community. In the beginning, says Bachar, "God
helped us plenty":

> I arrived in '48, on July thirtieth from Bulgaria to Haifa. With the great
> *Aliyah*. Fifty thousand people got up and moved in. I arrived on a ship with
> sixteen hundred people in really bad shape. We arrived to safe harbor in
> Haifa and they took us from there directly to the *ma'abara* [immigration
> transit camp] in Pardes Hanna. A week after, the rain began; seventy days
> we were in a *ma'abara*. Meanwhile Jaffa was liberated, and the Arabs fled,
> and from there they transferred us to Jaffa. They gave us an apartment at
> the port, with rocks and stones inside. But we were happy. We knew we had
> come to a safe haven.
>
> After two to three months, they gave us an apartment in Jaffa on Nuzha
> Street [now Jerusalem Boulevard], and we settled down. I came with a
> daughter, maybe ten years old, and an eight-year-old son. We enrolled the
> son in the French Collège, and we began looking for work. I opened a place
> in the port for smoking fish. In the end I saw that I had no choice and I went
> back to my old ways. With twenty-two thousand lira we bought a shop and
> made a synagogue there. I smuggled three Torah books from Bulgaria. One is
> ancient—four hundred years old. I still have it. We put up chairs and opened
> the synagogue. God helped us plenty. The synagogue was full. We were the
> best. I was an honorary member in any wedding. But this politics has ruined
> me now. Fifty years ago I thought I was the Baron de Rothschild without a
> penny in my pocket. I was an altruist, I was an idealist. This was the biggest
> mistake of my life. Because of this idealism I can't get into an old folks' home
> today. I'm here working as a rabbi, but I don't live here. I live here temporarily
> because my son went to America. And another thing. A tragedy. My daughter
> died three years ago. It ruined our family. But that's not so important, my
> private life. In all the organizations I was number one. Jaffa blossomed . . .

For his economic predicament, Avraham Bachar blames his own naiveté ("I was an idealist"), as well as the community that deserted him
and the Orthodox rabbinical establishment that refused to acknowledge
him as an accredited rabbi:

I'm not recognized by the Rabbinate. Why? Because I'm free. I travel on Shabbat, I go to soccer games on Shabbat, and the rabbis didn't like it and didn't support me. For fifty years I never got a dime from the central Rabbinate, or from the ministry of religions—I was ostracized, even though I was the best cantor and rabbi. In Jaffa and everywhere, they would call me to do a circumcision. Slaughtering, memorials, funerals, weddings, marriage, divorce. I would do everything for no money. That was my big mistake and why today I have no money to go to an old folks' home after productive work of fifty years, fifty-two years! For one day I didn't stop working for the Bulgarian *Aliyah*. And today I don't have a place in an old folks' home. I have my synagogue. If I want to sell it, I'll get forty, fifty thousand dollars—it's worth a hundred and twenty thousand. I don't dare sell. I have a clear conscience. I served the Bulgarian people, I put in all my efforts. Now I'm old, I'm eighty-nine, but I'm disappointed. The Bulgarian *Aliyah* should have taken me under its wings and helped me go to an old folks' home without paying.

The decline of the Bulgarian community is tied in Bachar's narrative to the bleak and uncertain future of the Jews in the city overall. Out of forty thousand who had lived in Jaffa, he says, "barely three thousand Bulgarians remained." For Bachar, the loss of control over urban space in Jaffa, due to the outmigration of Jews, is symbolized by the disappearance of the Hebrew and Bulgarian languages from the cityscape, where Russian and Arabic now dominate the scene:

We were the bosses of Jaffa—the Bulgarians. Jaffa is a Bulgarian city; that's what they used to call her. We love this city, we care about it, we built our houses in it. Families grew, kids, grandchildren, great-grandchildren. That's no joke. Today everyone is leaving. They're leaving because there is no livelihood in Jaffa. I myself, I have my synagogue. I want to sell the synagogue. There's no future in Jaffa. No future for the Bulgarians, for the Jews in Jaffa. Living side by side with the Arabs would only work if there is an Arab state here and we're on good terms with it. In Jaffa we're not a force to reckon with anymore. Barely three thousand Bulgarians remained in Jaffa, tops, out of forty thousand. All the other neighborhoods around Jaffa—that's all an Arab area now. See how you hear more Arabic and Russian than Bulgarian and Hebrew.

Abraham Bachar ends his life story with a commentary on the relations between Arabs and Jews. As in the story of his own journey from glory to decline, these relations have also increasingly deteriorated. However, Bachar is ambivalent about the Arab "Other." On the one

hand, he says, the relations used to be good, and now they have deteriorated because of the Arabs' claim over Jaffa; on the other hand, he
admits, "We are to blame, not the Arabs. We took their land, took everything from them. So they want to come back." He continues,

> Relations between Jews and Arabs in Jaffa were always good. Relations be-
> tween Bulgarians and Christians were very good. I'm telling you, we sent our
> children to the French School, Collège Français, and not to a Jewish school.
> We started Maccabi Yafo [the famous soccer team], and Arabs joined in on
> the team. We lived like brothers. Now, maybe five, six years ago, Arabs started
> coming to Jaffa in droves. And every house sold in Jaffa is bought by Arabs.
> They're doing it on purpose, so that one day they'll say that there are sixty
> thousand Jews in the city and there are two hundred thousand Arabs—"This
> is our city, we want it back." This is politics: Jaffa, Haifa, Lydda, Ramle—they
> are waiting so one day they'll have a country and they'll ask for it all. But only
> we are to blame, not the Arabs. We took their land, took everything from
> them. So they want to come back. In '48 we won the war. Where will they put
> us? We came here and looked for a house; we went into what the government
> gave us. The Arabs ran away, they left the food and ran. And we went into
> their homes, and we found everything ready. After thirty years, forty years,
> they started: "My father was here." That way, slowly, slowly, they come back.
> This doesn't let us believe that it will be good here.

In his narrative, Avraham Bachar voices the apprehension of the veteran Jewish community about losing control over the city space, and
ambivalently echoes the grievances of the Arab community and their
rightful historical claim. Taken together, the oppositional narratives
by Jday and Bachar are examples of negative identification with the local community, its politics, and the state establishment. Jday clearly expresses the nationalist, secular, and pan-Arabist perspective—he is a
proud Palestinian Arab, always was and always will be—however, even
his solidified view is cracked by internal and external criticism of the
agents of nationalism on the regional plane, in neighboring states, and
in his hometown. Bachar, for his part, presents himself as the pillar of
the Jewish community in Jaffa, but this line of argument is always fractured in the face of the community's ingratitude and the Rabbinate's
disavowal. In contradistinction to these bitter and oppositional narratives of the community's ex-leaders, the next section gives voice to two
"ordinary" women, free from the constraints of public status, and supplies a domestic yet critical perspective.

"HERE, THANK GOD, IT'S LIKE I HAVE A MOTHER AND
A FATHER": GENDER AND STATE IN NAZIHA 'ASSIS'S
AND SUBHIYYE ABU-RAMADAN'S STORIES

While Fakhri Jday and Avraham Bachar bemoan Jaffa's changing face,
the women in this sample, from the relative safety of the domestic sphere,
tell the story of their partial deliverance from the shackles of patriarchal rule personified by their husbands and brothers. In contrast with
Bachar's and Jday's life stories, which begin with a nostalgic description
of a productive era of activity and community-building and end with
personal loss and communal atrophy, the stories narrated by Subhiyye
Abu-Ramadan and Naziha 'Assis open with a counternostalgic description of the hardship inflicted by the tyranny of patriarchy and conclude
with their release from the men's yokes and their receipt of material support from state institutions.

Abu-Ramadan starts her life story with a description of her place
of birth in a small village in the Jaffa district. Born in Tal al-Rish, she
belonged to a poor family who leased land from the wealthy Jerusalemite
Khalidi family, selling their share of the produce in Jaffa's market. Her
narrative begins with an account of what happened in April 1948, as the
frontline closed on Tal al-Rish:

> At the end of the English period, when they wanted to give Palestine to the
> Jews, they came to us. I was still little. I was born and raised in Tal al-Rish.
> Also my father and my grandfather and my great-grandfather. The English
> ruled here in Palestine for thirty-three years. They gave the Jews the Balfour
> Declaration, and then they started to give them the country bit by bit. My
> father was a farmer. We would grow vegetables and sell them in Jaffa. But we
> weren't *fallahin*. The difference is that *fallahin* make a living in agriculture in
> a nonurban area. We leased the land from the landlord. In the war, the land-
> owners went to Beirut, all of them. They used to call us *birawiyye*—village
> people. We didn't live in the city. Those who lived in the city, we called "city
> folk" [*medan*]. But we weren't *fallahin* either—that was something else. In the
> '48 war, we were close to Bat-Yam. We stayed and the shells reached up to our
> house. In the lemon grove near the house, a shell would hit a tree and uproot
> it and make a hole in the ground. We were in the house, hiding. Before '48
> there were a lot of battles with Bat-Yam. All the Jews were fortressed in Bat-
> Yam and would shoot at us. There were Arab soldiers who fought, but there
> wasn't an army. All our neighbors left except for us. The Jews took over the
> water towers that the Arabs built, and shot at us. There was a group of Arabs

that started to work with the Jews—they would bring bullets full of powder. You shoot the bullet and it does nothing—less than a stone. This was treason. Now that the Arabs had left, the houses emptied out. We left there and came to the Coptic monastery [*deir al-Aqbat*] in Jaffa. We loaded up the donkeys with what we had and moved here, all of us. No one was left, for fear of the shootings. There was no one to fight—whoever stayed there, died.

In the rest of Subhiyye Abu-Ramadan's story, the aspect of gender saliently emerges. In the wake of the Deir Yassin massacre, on April 9, 1948, word had it among the Palestinians in Jaffa that the Jews would desecrate the women's honor and rape them; in Abu-Ramadan's words, "they corrupted the girls in Deir Yassin." As a result, there was a dramatic increase in forced marriages of young women whose male relatives feared for the family honor:

My husband's sisters, who now live in Khan Yunes, were here but they left in '48. They lived near us, but they had money so they left. What frightened the Arabs? When the Jews came in, they went to Deir Yassin and this is what frightened the Arabs. We were afraid that they would come and slaughter us and corrupt our girls. They corrupted the girls [*kharrabu al-banat*] in Deir Yassin, and slaughtered the young men, killed mothers and fathers. In Tal al-Rish we heard of the massacre in Deir Yassin on the radio. The Jews had not gotten everything yet, and they went in village by village. We heard it on the Jewish and the Arab radio. The Jews filled a truck with unveiled women, and went around 'Ajami. They went around the grove, where we lived, to frighten people, and anyone who had a daughter married her off—even at twelve and fourteen years of age—so that the Jews wouldn't come in and dishonor them. I married at the age of fourteen in the Coptic monastery. We didn't have a wedding. There was a war. Who has a wedding during a war? We were afraid of the Jews, afraid that they would kidnap the girls! They wrote a marriage paper and that was it.

Already in the brief period that Abu-Ramadan spent with her family in the Coptic monastery's courtyard, before moving to 'Ajami after her marriage, she began to realize the far-reaching consequences the political regime change would have on her as a Muslim woman:

When the Jews came, the first thing they did was to take a census of how many people there were in each house. When they came to survey our place, the women covered their faces with black veils. The Haga [Civil Defense] officer turned to my father, and what he said was true. The officer said, "Hassan, hear me out, now they cover themselves?" My father told him, "They're not allowed to go out unveiled." The officer laughed and said to him, "In a few years they'll go out wearing nothing." My father told him, "That's not possible—if one goes out with a bare head, I'll slaughter her." The officer told him, "We'll meet again, Hassan, in a few years—all these will go out bare." My father said, "It cannot be, it won't happen." The officer told him, "We'll see you in a few years. You'll see your wife, your daughter-in-law, and your daughter—they'll all go out with uncovered hair." He spoke in Arabic, and it turns out he was right.

In the course of her life in Tal al-Rish, in her father's household, Abu-Ramadan worked in the field and handled the housework. While her brother was encouraged to learn to read and write at the *kuttab* (elementary school) and then went on to pursue his studies at the Scottish school in Jaffa, her father prevented Abu-Ramadan and her sister from acquiring a formal education. Abu-Ramadan reminisces about this discrimination as a form of harsh patriarchal violence.

> When we were in Tal al-Rish, the boys studied in a kuttab. Today there is no such thing. My brother studied in a kuttab and after the world turned upside down during the war, he went over to the Tabitha school [the Scottish school in Jaffa]. They studied in the kuttab for four to five years. They would lay out a mat on the floor and teach them Arabic and arithmetic. After school my brother would come home and teach me and my sister everything he'd learned. And then he would beat us to death. He taught us the A B C s, then he'd beat us up, even though he was younger than us.
>
> When I was little, I had a dream to study to read and write. It's hard for me when I have to go to the bank and I have to ask someone to write a check for me. It hurts me [*ko'ev li*]. I say to someone, "Excuse me, write me a check." Imagine some stranger coming to you and asking you to write a check for him. So they laugh, and I tell them, "My parents are to blame, I'm not to blame. They wouldn't allow me to go to school."[4] They didn't like it that girls should study. In my time they would say it's better that she shouldn't study so that she won't have a boyfriend. Crazy! Before the coming of the state, they wouldn't send girls to school. When I told my father that I wanted to study, he beat me. But life has taught me. If I had been this way before, neither my father nor my brother would control me. I would go to study despite them, sure! Now, my head is developed—why did you not let me study? What do you care? I want to learn. They'd kill us with beatings. We lived a very hard life.

The language of patriarchy and family mediates matters that are apparently not gender-related. For instance, the family decision to remain in the shaky shanties of the Coptic monastery rather than squat in the comfortable houses left behind by the Palestinians in Jaffa, as did many

Jews and Arabs during the first months and years after the war, was at-
tributed by Abu-Ramadan to her father's cowardice. He "went to live
in a tomb," she says. "In the end he was left with nothing—no land, no
honor" [la 'ard wa-la ard]:

> Once I went to Tal al-Rish to see the place. There are Moroccan Jews living
> there now. They made me coffee. I sat with them and told them, "I was born
> here." They laughed and said, "Welcome." I don't know since when they've
> been living there, but I wanted to see what happened to the house after we
> left. I went to the place my father used to tie the cows. And they called to me:
> "Lady, lady." I started to laugh. They said, "What is this?"
>
> I said, "My father put it here, he would tie the cows here."[5] It hurt me. The
> place where you are born is half of you. I remembered those days when I was
> a little girl in the orange groves, how I worked the land with my sisters, and
> how none of our neighbors are left, how it's all in ruins. It hurts. If they'd
> give me a chance today, I'd renovate the house and live in it. I wish. But
> they didn't give me the chance. If my father had stayed in the house, we'd
> have stayed, but my father was crazy. Too bad, we'd have stayed. The Jews
> wouldn't have made us leave. There was no Amidar [governmental housing
> company], no Apotropos [Custodian of Absentee Property]. You could go
> and settle in whatever house you wanted, even rich people's houses. The Jews
> and the Arabs went in like that. My father is crazy, went to live in a tomb.
>
> In the end, we stayed in the monastery for over twenty years. My family
> left the place not long ago, in '75. We had Jewish neighbors in the grove and
> there were excellent relations with them. Doesn't matter that they're the
> occupiers since the homeowners left the houses and ran away, and we had
> nothing against the Jews who arrived. We had no quarrel with them. When
> we came to Jaffa all the houses were empty. You could walk into the grandest
> palace, open the door, and set in. And the Jews wouldn't chase you out; they
> didn't know whose house it was. They didn't ask for a *kushan*. You'd say,
> "This is my house"! And they registered it all from the beginning. Let's say
> Moussa lived in house number thirty-two, that's it. Too bad, all the houses
> were empty. We stayed in the Coptic monastery paying rent for nothing. All
> because of my coward father. Crazy. In the end he was left with nothing—no
> land, no honor.

Subhiyye Abu-Ramadan's critical and uncompromising position does
not gloss over other facets of the Palestinian existence. Her narrative
presents an a-nationalist position that deconstructs even the Palestinian
consensus over the "right of return," thus shedding light in problematic
ways on the place of the state in the life of an elderly woman in Jaffa. I
suggest reading such narratives not as stories of "betrayal" or "collabora-

tion," but rather in relation to each narrator's personal life history and the class- and gender-based exclusion that was her lot throughout most of her life. This attitude is a result of a series of historical events and a deep-rooted feeling that "the Arabs left us to be humiliated":

> The Palestinians who left Jaffa don't deserve to return here. I'll tell you why. If I had left, God knows where I'd be, Jordan, Syria, Libya . . . But where did I have my children? Let's say I left and deserted my house, and I had six or seven children. I had my children there—how come they should ask to return? Return to where? Do they know where my house is? Even my relatives in Khan Yunes, they should stay there. Why should they come? Didn't they buy houses there and settle? Even in the refugee camps, why should they return? Me, for my part, if they'd put me in the government—no matter if it's a Jewish government or an Arab government—I would say they should not return. Why did they leave? It's their problem—why should they return? And if they return, where will all the people who are here go to? Four million Arab refugees who want to return—that's the number of the people in Israel. Where should they go? Who will build for them? They shouldn't come. Let them stay where they are. The Arabs left us to be humiliated [*l-al-bahdala*] and thank God, we weren't humiliated. How is it that we weren't killed? When Gaza was opened in '67 they started to covet what we have here. Before the Jews came, what were we, we lived like dogs. If I'd left, I'd be dead.

To the astonishment of her nephew who was present for the interview, and to the fury of her daughter, who called and argued with her, Abu-Ramadan kept on dismantling the nationalist discourse as she numbered the merits of the welfare state and cast her arrows of criticism at the Arab "tyrants." A similar identity claim was made by Abu-George, another working-class elderly interviewee who participated in the study (and who died in 2003 at age 103), who contended that one's identity is determined by "whoever governs you" [*illi hakimna*]. Or, as he phrased it, "In the Ottoman days I was Ottoman, in the English days I was English, and now that Israel governs us—I am Israeli." Abu-Ramadan relates her criticism to her personal experience and fears as an unprivileged proletarian woman:

> I'm an Israeli. Where was I born? Here. Israel has ruled over us since before I gave birth to my children, so I'm Israeli and my children are Israelis. I'm not Palestinian. The one whose country you live in, the one who rules you, that's it. Even if the rule changed now, I'd stay with the Jews. I'm pleased with the Jews. I wouldn't go to an Arab rule. Swear to God! The most oppressive

rule in history [*azlam hukm*] is the Arab rule. The Jews massacred in the war—you massacre me, I massacre you, that's how it is in war. They also had people slaughtered. Because of this they guard the land. They were promised this land here! The Jews bought this land. The English promised them this land and the Arabs left it.

If the Arabs here have brains they'll cooperate with the state—and not go crazy and die of hunger like the Arabs there [in the Occupied Territories and the Arab states]. Here the medicine is good, the care is good for the children, there are schools for the children, everything is clean. I get social security. What, I should rely on my children? Today they give social security, and a pension and free hospitalization. And not only me—everyone is taken care of in their old age. It used to be that the old women had to beg in the streets and beg their children. Today, no need for favors. My money is in my pocket. The aged live a very good life here—anyone who says this isn't true, I'll step on his face. Let the Arabs do what they will to me, let them blow me up. Here my son is in prison, and he has six kids—and they get a state allowance and they eat and drink and dress better than when he was working. In the days of the Arabs and the English, when a woman was widowed, she would collect used clothing to dress her children, and receive a little bit of charity—rice, sugar, whatever they would give her out of pity. That's how it was for the widows of that time. Today, old women don't have to work, they don't have to beg. You're not dependent on your son.

Abu-Ramadan's story offers a gendered insight into the relations between the political upheavals and patriarchal oppression, as well as into the impact of the Israeli welfare state on the lives of independent women struggling to keep their families together. Her critique of the unyielding patriarchal order that barred her and poor young women like her from getting an education is sobering. She has not forgiven her father and her brother for forcing her into an unwanted, premature marriage at fourteen, and remains suspicious toward the patronizing middle and upper classes. Her account thus gives voice to a non-hegemonic Palestinian narrative, representing an uneducated underclass which refuses to idealize its pre-'48 condition, insisting on a sense of betrayal by both the Arab states which failed to come to their rescue and the Palestinian families which failed to live in solidarity with each other. Her position reflects strangeness and structural inferiority, deep frustration, and a lack of nostalgia for *ayyam al-'Arab* ("the days of the Arabs" in pre-'48 Palestine), revealing an unfamiliar and often silenced facet of the intra-Palestinian discourse on and within Jaffa.

Some might dismiss Abu-Ramadan's account as a narrative of betrayal and collaboration, or as an unrepresentative story of an old woman
whose age got the better of her. Thus Swedenburg's study of the memories of Palestinian combatants in the Great Revolt (*al-thawra al-kubra*)
of 1936–1939 interprets such narratives as "collaborationist," "accommo-
dationist" rhetoric, which "repeat well-known Zionist ideologemes" and
"cave in to Zionist pressure" (Swedenburg 1995, 139). My concern here,
however, goes beyond these initial dichotomies. Instead anthropological
analysis should seek to uncover the particular conditions of possibility
of the social fields in Jaffa that are producing such counterintuitive and
often paradoxical discourses.

These narratives, I argue, reflect a complex perception of identity in
terms of both the Palestinian "self" and the Jewish immigrant "Other"
(cf. Bishara 1993). As such, they express an ambivalent subject position
(Bhabha 1994): subordinate Palestinian elders who are rights-bearing
citizens of the same state that had occupied their cities and brought
about their collective and personal ruin.

Abu-Ramadan's transformation from a poor woman in a rural patriarchal society to a formal citizen entitled to social security benefits and
an old-age pension, as well as her varied experience in ethnically mixed
social environments for more than fifty years, yield a complex view of the
Jewish Other and of her own position of strangeness. Seen among other
Palestinian personal narratives of resistance, frustration, and nostalgia
documented fifty years after the Nakba (Tamari 2003), her ambivalent
life story emerges as both the existential product of urban mix and an
element of mixed towns' sociological uniqueness. Thus, for instance, in
Abu-Ramadan's description of her relations with her Jewish neighbors,
her memory of that time is typically counterintuitive:

> After the wedding we moved to 'Ajami—we found an empty house and we
> entered. Back then the neighborhood was still built up [before the urban re-
> newal of the 1960s]. There were lots of Jews. Now, why are the Jews leaving?
> They bought better houses than the ones here. They bought in Holon, in Bat-
> Yam, in Rishon. What houses! Fantastic houses in Rishon. Since they left,
> the Arabs who remained are constantly fighting with each other [*bitqatalu*]:
> this one curses the other, the other hits him. . . . Arabs together are no good.
> Arabs and Jews together get along [*mistadrim*]. My son, the mechanic, he has
> more Jewish friends than Arabs and Christians. That's how it is. It suits him.

Once, he was hospitalized. On Saturday, at seven in the morning, I went to the hospital and I found Shlomo there. I said, "What are you doing Shlomo, isn't it Saturday today?" He said to me, "This is my brother." He's crazy about him. How we were happy when they discharged Shlomo from the army! He was drafted and his mother cleans offices and his father has epilepsy. So he said to the army that he's the main breadwinner. So they discharged him. This was before the Intifada. We prayed that by the time he was drafted there wouldn't be wars anymore. When they discharged him I was very glad. They're here for a long time, they grew up here. Moroccans. Good people. I like it when neighbors are human beings. It's good that he was spared from the war. If something had happened to him, I would have gone mad. Those who fight in the army, it's not these Jews, maybe it's Bedouins or Russians. These aren't cruel like them. Seriously, they aren't Jews, them.

In a pacified tone similar to that of Hanna Swissa, Safiyya Dabbah, and Subhiyye Abu-Ramadan, the story of Naziha 'Assis, a Syrian *refusenik* (Prisoner of Zion), conveys a similar transition from life under patriarchal rule and communal isolation in Aleppo to personal autonomy in Jaffa supported by state institutions. 'Assis describes her recruit and activity in the service of the immigration to Israel as an incident that had changed her life:

My life didn't start well. At a young age, around six or seven, my parents divorced, and my grandmother raised me. I had no father and my mother was ill. In short, when I was eight years old, I wanted to study, but we had no money. So my grandmother said to me, "Come, I'll teach you a trade." She took me to a dressmaker; I learned very well.

I grew up and was sixteen. Then they married me off to someone forty-four years old because I had no parents. My husband took me to Beirut. But after a few months, I got divorced and came back. But I have a talent, I have a musical ear. I hear a melody—I go nuts. I hear Umm Kalthum, 'Abd al-Wahab, Farid al-Atrash. Until then I was a dressmaker at home. I left the sewing, said to my grandmother, "I want to buy a violin." The weddings in Syria were separate [between men and women]. I learned to be with the women. There, the Muslims have music bands that are all women.

One day, I was out. Someone came with an umbrella, walking slowly. He asked me, "Are you Naziha?" I said yes. He told me, "Get into the house and don't close the door." He came in after me. He told me, "I'm Abu Mahmoud. Ester told me that you want to leave [for Israel] but that your husband doesn't. Can I see him?" Suddenly my husband came. He asked Abu Mahmoud a few questions, and told him that he's not interested. After two months he came again and asked, "Can you help me? I met a guy in Turkey and he asked me to bring his sister to Israel." This was the beginning. That was in 1964, until they caught a group at the Turkish border. They were interrogated and gave my name. They took me to be interrogated. The place was underground. Thank God I didn't go mad. After two months I told them everything, I had no choice. I told how I got to know the man and what I did. They closed my file and put me in jail. They released me after two years. All this in Aleppo.

How did I get to Israel? When my son had his bar mitzvah, the girls came from Damascus and Lebanon and all the rest. We had lunch. Then the husband of my daughter told my husband, "Don't you know? All the people are leaving." My husband became yellow all over and asked me, "Who said that? Now I'll go to the intelligence [Mukhabarat]." I told him, "Calm down, what do you want? You want to have your daughters be taken by Arabs? Seven daughters should go to Arabs?" Slowly he calmed down. One Friday, we left. A taxi came, and drove us to Ankara in Turkey. They gave us tickets for a plane for Israel. We arrived at the airport. This was '78. And thank God that I am here.

After her immigration to Israel, 'Assis made her home in Jaffa, where she raised and married off all of her children. Her good relations with her Arab neighbors, she notes, were formed due to the common Arabic language and her pleasant ways ("We, thank God, have a sweet mouth"):

We lived in a new-immigrants' lodging for two years until the house in Jaffa was ready. We were the first who came into the house. And what honor we received in the new-immigrants' lodging! They gave us the nicest spot. And the neighbors said, "You have many children and you are a Prisoner of Zion—of course you'll be treated with such respect." They asked us, "Do you want to go to Tel Aviv?" No. "Bat-Yam?" No. "Where do you want to go?" My sister told me, "Don't you want to be in Jaffa? Say yes, because you speak Arabic—you know the language and know the culture."

I worked as a dressmaker from home. My clients were Arabs, Jews, mixed. They said to me, "You'll get a flat and you'll be happy." We rented the house but for a token price, because I'm a Prisoner of Zion. Seventy percent reduction for the rent, and thank God, now I get a salary from Prisoners of Zion from Germany. I also get an allowance. I have no problems. I have three Arab neighbors. I have one Christian, good morning, good morning, sometimes happy holidays. And you greet them with a smile in Arabic. And we, thank God, have a sweet mouth and we understand and know how to speak with them. In Syria we were the only Jews in the whole neighborhood.

Naziha 'Assis casts her life story in terms of family and gender rather than nation. After being raised in Aleppo with no parents and no guaranteed spouses for her seven daughters, she found in Israel a place to which she could belong. Her husband, for his part, missing his friends and privileged social status in Aleppo, failed to adapt to the new environment and constantly disapproves of the gender permissiveness in Israel:

> I feel good in Jaffa. If they told me, "Take two bags of gold and we'll buy you a flat in Syria," I wouldn't agree. When I hear "Syria," I tremble. There, I didn't live a bright day. Because I had seven daughters. There is no today and no tomorrow. Excuse this language, there is no dog that will knock on the door and say, do you have a girl for me? Here, thank God, it's like I have a mother and a father. In Syria, the Jewish girls were afraid that Arab guys would try to pick them up. Here it feels like home. I have someone who comes to clean twice a week. Thank God the Jewish Agency recognizes me. What more do I need? All my daughters are married, I have eight families, may they be in good health. What do I want from my life at eighty-one and a half. But my husband isn't happy here. He wants Aleppo, he want his clients. He always tell how Abu Jamil used to deliver him tea every morning and how they used to love him in the neighborhood. And I say, stone upon stone should descend on Abu Jamil and on Hayat and Fatma and everyone. And although there is social security, except for my salary, I give him a little. It bothers him that he isn't in control and also that he sees women dressed revealingly with their belly showing, and he comes home agitated. What do we care? Man, what do we care? Let them go out naked. We don't care. Why, are my children like this? My children grew up with respect.

OLD AGE AND TIME: LIMINALITY AND SOCIAL CRITIQUE

The third perspective for analyzing these life stories examines the themes of old age and aging (Hazan 1994; Myerhoff 1978). The category of aging is of crucial importance in understanding the mutual constitution of biographic memory, collective memory, and history as mediated by the narrators' interpretations of nationalism and the state. The liminal position of the aged person enables him or her to raise criticisms that do not emerge in earlier stages of the life cycle. In contrast with middle-age adults, the elderly—Jews and Arabs alike—are situated on the margins of society and on the edge of their life-careers, and therefore are less reluctant to reflect outspokenly on the complex facets of their personal and political condition as well as on the "tyranny" of the young majority that excludes them. The two men, formerly community leaders, sense their marginality more intensely than the women, who have always felt subordinate in both the public and the private spheres. Moreover, the intervention of state welfare governmentality and the political and cultural changes that have occurred in Israeli and Palestinian societies throughout the years have altered the division of labor and the structure of the patriarchal family, and consequently have caused the men to lose their status of dominance once again—that is, within the family as well as in the political sphere. The female elderly are the relative beneficiaries of these changes, and are therefore more appeased in relation to their past (Sered 1992). For the female interviewees, the political-national dispossession in the case of the Arabs and the immigration to a new place in the case of the Jews are paradoxically translated into a set of profits with respect to the men as well as within the changing family structure. Thus, for instance, Avraham Bachar and Fakhri Jday, in old age, stress their failure in leading their ungrateful communities, and hence their self-imposed withdrawnness into their private bubble. Rabbi Bachar describes the phase of old age as a period of helplessness and longing:

> It's good that we have old folks' homes. It's very good. An old folks' home is a good income for the bosses of the place. So new ones spring up all over. Here in Rishon le-Zion there are ten to twelve old folks' homes. It's good but it's all for the money. Money will answer for everything [*hakesef ya'ane et-hakol*; "will answer" also literally means "will torture"—in Hebrew both words are derived from the same root]. In Bulgaria, very few would think about an old folks' home. The old people were connected, were respected. They were looked after at home. They were given a good place to sleep, the best place to eat. Old people first. In Bulgaria there was "morale," no joke. In Bulgaria there was happiness. People would eat bread and olives but with respect for the family. They didn't sit down until the head of the family sat down. I am ninety already. What do I matter? I was married at twenty-three and thank God the woman was faithful, good, and bore me two sons and a daughter. One died, of cancer, and since then my family has been ruined. Nothing matters anymore to me. My son didn't succeed in America. They sold his house, sold his car, and he came back empty-handed to his father's house. I used to be very strong. A year ago, I was iron. I could break a building board with a punch. Today I'm not the same. I'm done for. How long shall I live— one year, two, maybe three, who knows? Maybe ten days. My wife deludes herself and thinks she has ten to fifteen years to live. She's fallen in love with the old folks' home, but I miss Jaffa very much.

In contrast, Subhiyye Abu-Ramadan expresses a sense of relief from the normative shackles of patriarchal society and feels free to criticize the Palestinian national narrative, her relatives who departed [*rahalu*] in 1948 and left her behind "to be humiliated," the religious conservatives in Jaffa [*al-mashayikh*], her brother who had hit her, and her father who showed no initiative and did not return to their native Tal al-Rish when it was still possible.[6] Against all these representations of normative Palestinian society, almost spitefully, Abu-Ramadan enumerates the advantages of the welfare state and the favorable demeanor of the Jewish Other:

> In the past no one took interest in the old or treated them well. They weren't respected. My brother beat my mother up because the cow trod on the vegetables; my mother passed away still angry with him. They told her, "Forgive him!" She said, "I cannot." They insisted, "Tell God to forgive him. You're going to Mecca for the Hajj!" She lived in his home and was thrown in a corner. Look at the Jews—they take the old in a car out for drives. Spend money on them. With the Jews, the children spend money on their parents. It's good that they put them in an old folks' home. There they are washed, dressed, their nails are cut, they're fed and cleaned. Today neither the daughter-in-law nor the daughter is willing to bear the burden. Where shall your mother go? The old is left there in his house. If he doesn't want to eat, they complain. My neighbor is paralyzed—her daughters change her once a week and they complain about it. They don't give her anything to drink so that she won't piss, don't feed her so she won't soil herself. They abuse her. There are a lot of old people who would prefer to go to an old folks' home. But not from their heart—who really wants to leave his home? Myself, if I'm not able to go, I'll get someone who will service me. I won't go to an old folks' home; I'll give her money and she'll service me. I don't want to grow old. I think about this a lot at night. Before I fall asleep I think about the days to come. But the future is gone. It's over. What do I want, after all? But death will come. Every Muslim person reminds himself of death every morning when he wakes. We say, "God let me die while I'm strong, and on my feet." One mustn't be afraid of death. The Jews are more afraid of death. But the Arabs are also afraid. Those who don't think of the next world, they are afraid of death. They say "Tomorrow we'll die," and when they get sick they begin to cry.

Naziha 'Assis, as a Jewish woman who earns a decent living from the state pension, adopts a stoic and serene tone that stands out in comparison with her husband's bitter dissatisfaction with Israeli culture and values. On a typical note of acceptance she explains why her "life isn't hard in old age":

I'll tell you something about my nature: I call myself a hero. Something happens to me, I wait, am patient, and if I can solve the problem, I act. With patience I arrive at the solution. I don't care about the time, I don't take much to heart. Because of this my life isn't hard in old age. I've learned with time. Previously I would keep score with my husband; he was very rough. I wouldn't answer, only listened, mustn't answer. He was very nervous. I would get very angry; I would get nervous. And now, I answer him with respect. You wanted a son? I gave you a son. The happiness that is in my heart, if I share it with people, there will be enough for everyone. That's me, that's how I am. My greatest happiness is that I came to Israel and that I'll die here. And people that I sent here, they died here. It's a *mitzvah* that can't be compared. Because of this I'm not afraid of death. God should only give me three days before death so I should be *wa'iya* [Arabic for "aware"], alert, not fuzzy. Like my grandmother. She asked for three days. And indeed, on the fourth day she was gone. What I deserve, God will give me; I've had enough. There in Syria, there is no Jewish Agency, no social security. In Syria, those who don't have—they die. Today, thank God, I have everything, thank God. Today I see an old person in a wheelchair and it breaks my heart. I pray to God that I won't be like that.

As an existential category of being, old age is a lens through which the interviewees relate time and meaning. In *Number Our Days,* an ethnography of a Jewish-American senior citizens' center, Barbara Myerhoff (1978, 272) characterizes the human species as a storyteller (*Homo narrans*). As Victor Turner notes in the book's foreword, "Culture in general—specific cultures, and the fabric of meaning that constitute any single human existence—is the 'story' we tell about ourselves" (xv). "The tale," Myerhoff concludes, "certifies the fact of being and gives sense at the same time" (271). Facing the existential themes of life and death, national pride and defeat, continuity and finality, the life stories of Palestinian and Jewish elderly people in Jaffa tease meaning and identity out of their memories and experiences.

STRANGER RELATIONS, VIOLENCE, AND INTIMACY

In his *After the Last Sky,* Edward Said (1986, 14) addresses the tensions between form and content in search of a language that defines the discontinuity of Palestinian experience: "Most literary critics in Israel and the West focus on what is said . . . who is described, what the plot and contents deliver, their sociological and political meaning. But it is *form*

that should be looked at. . . . Our characteristic mode, then, is not a narrative, in which scenes take place seriatim, but rather broken narratives,
fragmentary compositions, and self-consciously staged testimonials, in
which the narrative voice keeps stumbling over itself, its obligations, its
limitations." Following Said's lead, this chapter has focused on the life
story as the distinct autodiegetic narrative genre of the first generation
of Palestinian survivors and Jewish immigrants. The analysis situates
the dynamics of narration in its own cultural and political context, by
interpreting the multiplicity of meanings at the crossroads of ethnicity,
gender, age, and nation.[7]

The relations between these foundational categories can be characterized in terms of form and content alike. First, with regard to the organization of the narrative and its directionality, one of my findings is that
the categories of gender, class, and age emerge as more significant variables than nationality. The similarity between the life stories of Jewish
and Arab elderly people is shaped by their class positions, generational
experience, and gender histories in a more significant way than by their
national or ethnic identity. Thus, for instance, the stories of Fakhri Jday
and Avraham Bachar move along parallel trajectories from a mythical
past of personal and communal prosperity to a present time of rift and
seclusion, while the stories of Subhiyye Abu-Ramadan and Naziha 'Assis
unfold from patriarchal subordination to a continuous present of relative
autonomy and control. The men's nostalgia is contrasted with a counternostalgic discourse in the women's narratives. Secondly, in terms of content, the interviewees point to the relationship (either correspondence or
tension) between the official national narration and the personal story, as
mediated by the narrating "I." Numerous studies on life stories of elderly
subjects emphasize the coherence of the narrating "I" and the continuity
and consistency of the story told (Ewing 1990; Gubrium, Holstein, and
Buckholdt 1994; McAdams 1996; Schely-Newman 2002). This sweeping
claim, however, should be qualified and instead diagnosed as a function of the specific frame of reference it invokes. This chapter points to
several alternative frames of reference: while Fakhri Jday's life story is
anchored in a nationalist frame of reference, Avraham Bachar focuses
on the communal framework, Naziha 'Assis on the familial one, and
Subhiyye Abu-Ramadan on the class and gender ones. In these stories,

even if the private "I" remains coherent in itself, the situated narrative points to aporias gaping along the seam line connecting the personal to the collective. In old age, these cracks become wider, unavoidably deconstructive, and more reflexive.

The narrated stories indeed frame a meaningful "identity," however, this identity is incoherent and often deviates from dominant nationalist frames. Inspired by Ann Stoler's mode of analysis, I sought to "represent that incoherence rather than write over it with a neater story we wish to tell" (Stoler 1992, 154). The identities of all four interviewees negotiate such inconsistencies: Jday's national identity, frustrated in the face of a fragmented community and failing leadership; Rabbi Bachar witnessing the disintegration of his community that abandoned him; Naziha 'Assis's self-presentation as a mother to seven daughters and a son, and as a former *refusenik*; and Subhiyye Abu-Ramadan's portrait, which focuses on her firsthand experience of the Nakba but also on the merits of the welfare state. The coherence in the perception of self is retained for Fakhri Jday on the declarative, ideological, and most abstract levels (in his words, "I haven't changed with the years. My political goals were and didn't change. My worldview hasn't changed. My understanding of what is the world and who is the foreigner [*al-ajnabi*] hasn't changed"). However, the cracks reveal themselves precisely in relation to the lived space—in his critique of the Arab rulers, the fragmented community, the local leaders, the political parties, his regrets about staying in Jaffa— rather than in reference to the nationalist value of *Sumud*.

Similarly, Avraham Bachar declares himself to have been "a great patriot of the State of Israel"; however, the only time he mentions his patriotism is in the context of the legendary Maccabi Yafo soccer team. He feels betrayed by the rabbinical establishment and by the community he has nurtured. In reference to the Arab residents of Jaffa, he acknowledges the responsibility of the state for their frustrations ("Only we are to blame. . . . We took their land . . . so they want to come back."), but at the same time he expresses his fear of their taking control over the Jaffa space. Naziha 'Assis, a Syrian Jew, is accredited by the state as a "Prisoner of Zion," but the lion's share of her story is framed in terms of family and gender, in a narrative structure bereft of any ideological nationalist organizing principle. And finally, Subhiyye Abu-Ramadan's fragmentary life story launches a razor-sharp critique of the patriarchal order and the Palestinian nationalist *doxa* alike.

Rather than affirm and solidify nationally defined political ideologies, social agendas, and subject positions, these four narratives seem to call them into question. This critique takes the form of what can be called "negative narrativity"[8]—clustered in this case along gender lines. Marked by oppositional and bitter pronouncements of failure and resentment, Jday's and Bachar's narratives are negative insofar as it is the object being criticized—the Israeli state, the Arab rulers, the local corrupted bourgeoisie, the Orthodox Rabbinate, or the ungrateful Bulgarian community—that defines their mode of being and belonging. In contrast, Abu-Ramadan and 'Assis, although by no means short on strong opinions—often highly subversive ones, as we have seen—have managed in their life stories to recoup a sense of positivity, synthesis, and continuity. Taken together, these life stories attest to the multilayered complexity of Jewish-Arab relations and forms of sociality characterizing life in the "borderland" of a mixed town. Within the narrated fragments, in the contradictions between the unequivocal and the ambivalent, lies the all-too-human tragic element underlying both Palestinian and Jewish histories in the twentieth century. However, what makes these stories sociologically significant is that as they unfold, the private and the collective narratives intertwine, the personal interacts with the political, and they reflect the fears and hopes of Palestinian and Israeli societies as a whole.

Throughout these narratives, the shared existential themes of profound injustice (Abu-Ramadan), state violence (Jday), and personal loss and suffering ('Assis and Bachar) are woven together with stories of intimate neighborliness (Abu-Ramadan), cultural affinity ('Assis), and political engagement (Jday). Taken together, these themes emerge as a constitutive mode of relational ambivalence embedded in the fabric of everyday life. While the Palestinian narrators have clearly been the major historical victims, it seems that an intimate engagement with the victimizer was necessary even for the most articulate subject. Thus Fakhri Jday, the spokesman for Palestinian victimization, has developed through the years an almost therapeutic relationship with his Jewish clients, sharing with them at length his critique of both the Israeli state authorities and the Arab regimes (compare this to the narrative of the philosopher-gentrifier in chapter 4). Similarly Abu-Ramadan, who has been a victim of domestic violence, war, and crime (via her imprisoned son) engages in a warm relationship with her Moroccan neighbor (released from military service) and other Jewish friends and employers. Mediated through urban space, this sociality refuses to align itself with ethnonational positions and ideologies of victimization. How are this ambivalent pattern of experience and the narration of everyday life in the mixed city to be conceptualized?

In Jaffa the "implicate relations" (Portugali 1993) between sociality and spatiality—as expressed through the recurrent themes of violence and intimacy, otherness and familiarity, social distance and proximity—produced the dialectic social and interactional form that I have termed "collective strangeness." Stranger relations are therefore the social product of a binational third space whose hybridity is not temporary or individual, but permanent, shared, and embedded in the social structure. The sliding of the "Other" into the domains of the "familiar" is recurrent throughout the daily social interaction.

Adopting strangeness as an analytical tool avoids reducing the social world of men and women in Jaffa to the ethnonational logic of resistance or victimhood, while at the same time taking into systematic account their urban, political, and historical context. The ambivalent narratives analyzed above reflect the "trapped" position of the Palestinian citizens in Israel at large, and particularly the effect of the mixed spatial sociality, which disrupt the sweeping stereotyping of the significant stranger. The fragmented universe of meaning of both Jews and Palestinians in Jaffa compels them to skip alternately between perceptions of familiarity and otherness in ways that denaturalize nationalist mythology. As social forms of urban ambivalence, stranger relations are thus the interactional product of the history of spatial relationality in Jaffa. Along with other cultural forms of interdependence, collective strangeness constitutes Jaffa as an unresolved "hermeneutic problem" (Bauman 1993) that reflects the fragility of Jewish-Arab relations in the contact zone.

A city of strangers, Jaffa is recognized by its residents as the Mother of the Stranger, for good or ill. Its unique profile is predicated on the mitigating effect of cultural and functional proximity between rival social types and disparate trajectories. Under conditions of contrived coexistence, the pragmatics of utilitarian transaction with the state and their neighbors enable ordinary citizens to rewrite their place in the national order of things and to reformulate hegemonic scripts of nationalist subjectivity. From this relational perspective, the mixed urban space can be seen as an enabling environment, which produces social dispositions and cultural imaginaries otherwise impossible in mononational cities by virtue of ethnic monitoring and spatial segregation.

SEVEN

Situational Radicalism and Creative Marginality

The "Arab Spring" and Jaffa's Counterculture

For one evening we will revive old city Jaffa from its constant death to a clear
night, and to a bright imagined future that doesn't give up the connection
with the surrounding Arab World. An Art and Music Movement aware
[of] where it all started from, and... where we are all heading to.

—7ARAKEH FAWREYEH's "Music/Art/Struggle/Rave—Struggle for Home"

"TAHRIR IS HERE": MIMETIC DIFFUSION AND THE SUMMER REVOLT

One of the striking features of the "Arab uprisings" is their cascading
effect on social movements worldwide. The rapid diffusion and mimetic
circulation of their core revolutionary principles to markedly different
political contexts throughout the Middle East, Europe, and the Ameri-
cas pose a conceptual challenge for the social sciences. Another distinguishing feature of the Arab revolts is the central role cities play in both
enabling mobilization and repressing protests. While some revolts have
worked their way from the periphery to the center (notably in Libya
and Syria), in most cases their success has hinged upon the urban co-
presence of others to turn the local revolts into a transformative historic
event (Sewell 2001). Thus size, density, permanence, and heterogeneity—the four classical sociological characteristics of the city identified
by Wirth (1938)—have been strategically mobilized by the masses in
Tunis, Cairo, Madrid, and Tel-Aviv to reclaim political space and redefine citizenship.

The magnitude of the Israeli social justice protests of summer 2011 came as a surprise to observers and participants alike.[1] For a period of three months, hundreds of thousands took to the streets in a rallying cry to redefine national priorities, in the process turning Israel's major metropolises into "rebel cities"—festive spaces of struggle and collective effervescence (Harvey 2013). Heralded as the largest popular protest in Israeli history (equivalent to the "400,000 Protest" staged in the wake of the 1982 Sabra and Shatila massacres),[2] the 2011 movement was yet another instance of what Saskia Sassen (2011) recently called "the global street"—a social space that problematizes the relationship between powerlessness and empowerment. "Powerlessness," Sassen writes, "is not simply an absolute condition that can be flattened into the absence of power. Many of the protest movements we have seen in North Africa and the Middle East are a case in point: these protesters may not have gained power, they are still powerless, but they are making a history and a politics" (2011, 574). In a similar fashion, the official video trailer on the website of the Israeli protest movement streams pictures of revolt from Cairo, Madrid, and Tel-Aviv, and features a narrator wearing a Guy Fawkes vendetta mask and reciting in Hebrew, "They have banks, they have the military, they have the police, they have the apartments, but we have the streets and we take them." Framed as a collective awakening of an otherwise relatively quiescent public, the reflexive realization of the coming of a historic moment became a mobilizing call for action which swept through the Israeli public: "We are the people we've been waiting for. We'll return the state to its citizens."[3]

With hindsight, this chapter interrogates the emergence of a political subjectivity and its embedded urbanity as part of the making of the new public sphere.[4] Rather than taking at face value the Israeli folk ideology exalting the "great summer of the new Israeli hope,"[5] I probe the limits of mobilization, which manifested a radicalizing process without revolutionary results. The discrepancy among its multiple grammars of revolt resulted in a modality of action I term "situational radicalism," which reproduced an ambiguous yet profoundly Zionist notion of the sovereign people posed as a revolutionary subject. Analyzed as an "empty signifier" (Laclau 2007), the collective subject invoked throughout the protest was predicated on the exclusion of political alterities, thus even-

FIGURE 7.1. "Depart [*Irhal* in Arabic]: Egypt Is Here [Hebrew]."
Courtesy of Yudit Ilany.

tually undermining its own radical potential. Fraught with tensions and
internal conflicts, the rise and subsequent dissolution of an Arab-Jewish
movement for "social justice" in the ethnically mixed city of Jaffa pits the
ideal of translocal connectivity between Arab and non-Arab societies
against the fragile ambivalence at the core of the movement.

Notwithstanding the politics of numbers, the truly remarkable feature of these events was not merely the emergence of a collective agency, but the fact that for the first time in Israeli history, bottom-up mass
mobilization grounded itself explicitly *in* and *of* the region. Mediated
through the Spanish 15-M movement, symbolic networks of solidarity
and models of contention spread from the Arab world all the way to
the yuppie epicenter of Tel-Aviv. Banners exclaiming "Egypt is Here,"
"Tahrir Corner of Rothschild," and "Walk Like an Egyptian," and above
all the mantric chant "The People Demand Social Justice" (mimicking
the Egyptian slogan "The People Want the Fall of the Regime"), seemed
to celebrate this unprecedented connectivity as the birth of a new historic generation (see figure 7.1).

In most conservative media and decision-making circles, the spectacle of regional solidarity performed on the streets and in the liberal media was generally met with more apprehension of the anticipated "Arab Winter." A few radical Palestinians, Mizrahi Jews, and leftist voices, however, saw the Arab revolts as a historic opportunity to "strive for a dialog with the Arab world" by framing local struggles for Palestinian liberation and housing rights as a joint regional revolt against colonial oppression and capitalist domination. In a statement titled "Ruh Jedida: A New Spirit for 2011," young Jewish descendants of the Arab and Muslim world living in Israel wrote an open letter to their peers in the Middle East and North Africa, expressing their solidarity with "the major role that the men and women of our generation are playing so courageously in the demonstrations for freedom and change across the Arab world."[6] Uri Shani, a signatory to the letter who dubs himself Abumidian and chose to live in a tent during the protest, concluded, "I don't talk about the 'Arab Spring' from the outside. I speak about the 'Arab Spring' from within, as an integral part of it.... The news portal Bokra.net stated: 'The Arab revolution begat the Arab-Jew.'"[7] With similar interests in mind, a coalition of twenty left-wing political parties and NGOs on both sides of the Green Line, from the Democratic Front for the Liberation of Palestine to the Israeli Communist Party, issued an unusual joint declaration in September 2011, praising the participation of Palestinian citizens of Israel in the Israeli protest movement, and calling for a "joint popular struggle of Israelis and Palestinians" against the occupation.[8]

Notwithstanding such efforts at expressing solidarity, these initiatives remained on the margins of the Israeli public discourse over and above the consensus of the mainstream movement for social justice. They were equally ignored or disavowed by most international protest movements. Thus missives sent from the Spanish *Indignados* in support of the Israeli protest soon turned into a direct critique of its course of action and eventually refused to acknowledge its legitimacy until the continued injustice "in the form of military occupation and segregation" was addressed.[9]

Posted on J14's Facebook page and displayed throughout the protest tent cities, the Spanish response exposes the ambiguity of the Israeli "Housing Protest," which according to some critics was responsible for its ultimate shortcomings. "On Tel Aviv's Rothschild Boulevard," writes one critic, "the middle class demonstrators are attempting to wage an Arab Spring without any Arabs."[10] Based on a longstanding hegemonic Zionist paradigm, another observer remarks, "their claims do not derive their legitimacy from universal democratic or social rights but rather from the contract supposedly signed between the Jewish-Zionist citizen and his state."[11] Circumventing "political issues" such as the occupation of the Palestinian Territories, the protest also neglected to address the grievances of the Palestinian and Mizrahi citizens and remained a predominantly Jewish Ashkenazi phenomenon, hence its being sometimes dubbed "Jew14" and "the middle-class protest." Drawing on an ethnography of the summer protest in Jaffa, the following analyzes the attempt to create a feasible alliance between the Jaffa Arabs, the Jewish neighborhoods of South Tel-Aviv, and the protest movement nationwide. While it ultimately failed to reconcile the multiple grammars of revolt, the Jaffa protest nevertheless exemplifies a rare experiment in radical democracy.

SITUATIONAL RADICALISM AND THE POLITICS OF SMALL THINGS IN TEL-AVIV-JAFFA

The 2011 uprisings in cities throughout the Middle East and North Africa heralded the birth of a new political subject and the rise of a new historic generation (Challand 2011; Khosrokhavar 2012). Notwithstanding the emergence of a revolutionary collective imaginary, predicated on principles of freedom, accountability, and distributive justice, these events threw into relief the foundational question of the coherence and unity of this fledging political subjectivity. In the face of ethnic diversity, class inequalities, and urban fragmentation, the notion of the nation invoked in each of these countries called for collective negotiation between rival factions, often with dire consequences. In Cairo, slogans such as "Christians + Muslims = One Hand" have mobilized a cohesive view of the sovereign people (*al-sha'b*) as a moral community (*watan*) composed of a solidary Muslim majority and a Christian minority. Tragically, however, the aftermath of the regime change in Egypt soon gave way to ethnic violence directed against the very Christian brethren who demonstrated and prayed together with the Muslims in Maidan al-Tahrir. The collective rage (*ghadab*) heretofore directed exclusively against the corrupt authoritarian regime has violently targeted the Coptic minority, perceived as disruptive of a unified image of the Muslim nation (*ummah*). Similarly, in Syria, Muslim protesters were recorded chanting, "The Christians to Beirut, the Alawis to the coffin." Read predominantly as a process of regime transition, the Arab revolts also bring to the fore the dangerous liaisons between ethnic pluralism and political violence, notably in cities marked by a history of ethnic mix.

From its inception in Tunisia in December 2010, political violence soon spread across the Middle East to other Arab states, as well as non-Arab countries such as Israel and Iran. In some of these countries the mass mobilization brought about a regime change (Egypt, Libya, and Yemen) or timid reforms (Jordan and Morocco), while in others it was violently repressed (Bahrain) or led to a bloody civil war (Syria). The regional unrest has not been limited to countries of the Arab world, or even to the Middle East per se. Across the Mediterranean Sea, European cities (notably in Spain and Greece) saw hundreds of thousands of protesters respond to the democratic agenda of the Arab Spring, as well as to local grievances such as austerity measures, national financial crises, and the European sovereign debt crisis. Indeed, protests considered to be drawing inspiration from the Arab Spring have been taking place across the globe, with varying degrees of success and prominence (including in Chile and the United States). While the cascading global impact of the Arab Spring is yet to be determined, it is clear to most observers that it is an epoch-changing event that merits further attention and analysis.

In Tunis and Egypt, the uprisings were a classical case of what Marshall Sahlins (2005) termed "the structure of amplification,"[12] with the deaths of Mohamed Bouazizi and Khaled Said serving as the catalyst for a sequence of events that later brought about the overthrowing of the regimes. In these cases, the tragic local event was soon iconized as martyrdom (*istishhad*), assuming in a matter of weeks the abstract form of a national cause with which millions of citizens could identify.[13] The transformation of microhistorical occurrences into a macrohistorical event had an explicit revolutionary intent, which points to structural parallels between the Egyptian uprising and other revolutions (for instance the attacks on Abu Za'bal Prison in Cairo or on Abu Salim Prison in Tripoli, in comparison with the storming of the Bastille on July 14, 1789).

In Israel, the eventful mobilization was far less dramatic and rather reform-driven, as seen in the symbolic modification of the Egyptian slogan calling for the fall of the regime into a vague call for social justice. Chronologically it can be seen as a direct response to the Spanish protests rather than to the Arab revolts. Moreover, like its Spanish forerunner, the Israeli protest was articulated first and foremost as a rebellion against the neoliberal model of development,[14] and thus favored what was termed in local discourse "social" problems (cost of living and class inequalities) over "political" issues (the occupation and the Palestinian-Israeli conflict) and "cultural" identity politics (the Mizrahi and Arab struggles for recognition). Tellingly, the major endogenous precedent to the Israeli mass mobilization was the successful "Cottage Cheese Protest" in June 2011. Beginning as a protest group on Facebook, it targeted rising food prices and launched an effective consumer boycott, which brought prices down by about 12.5 percent.

Subsequently, it was rather the "politics of small things" (Goldfarb 2006) that continued to mark the upcoming events. On July 14, Daphni Leef, a twenty-five-year-old filmmaker, found herself unable to pay her rent and erected a tent on Rothschild Boulevard, one of Tel-Aviv's most expensive streets, a major tourist attraction, and a UNESCO-designated World Heritage Site. The next day hundreds responded to Leef's call for action on her Facebook page and some fifty tents were pitched on the boulevard, gathering a crowd of 1,500. After initially granting a permit to demonstrate, the police attempted to revoke the permit and dismantle the tents. "In an instant the protest became a struggle," one of the founding members recalled about the moment the denial of freedom of speech amplified the protest. A week later, on July 23, a growing constituency already numbering tens of thousands participated in the movement's first rally, and by the end of July the wave of protest had swept the whole country. With home bases in ninety tent camps across Israel, the main demonstrations (the "March of the Million") took place in the muggy weather of August and early September, bringing together the unprecedented number of one million protesters from Israel's center and periphery.

The three months of intense mobilization were marked by a sense of euphoria and *communitas* shared by the multitude of dwellers in the tent camps and squats that sprouted in most cities. "We called it our ex-territory, a place which is outside space and time, outside our normal behavior in the city and the state," wrote one activist. "We called the outside Babylon but we lived in the real world, a world with enough time to talk, a place where ideological enemies can reach an agreement, a place where the law waits outside for a moment, a place where rules are remade. We felt we were creating a new society. Soon enough it was strange—even scary—to venture out to Babylon."[15] The combination of a spectacle of cross-sector solidarity and a liminal suspension of social order ("a sense that the world is coming to an end," in the words of Stav Shafir, a leading member of the movement) left an enduring mark on the Israeli collective memory.

Adopting the naming strategy of the "Revolution of 25 January" in Egypt and the "May 15 Movement" in Spain, J14 (for "July 14") became the Israeli protest's trademark (http://j14.org.il/), complete with a yellow sigil of a tent and a peculiar sign language. The framing in temporal terms of J14's genesis was particularly felicitous, pointing back to the French Revolution and hinting at the radical potential of the movement. Given this cross-reference, it came as no surprise that one artist (Ariel Kleiner) responded by posting a full-size guillotine in the middle of the boulevard, to the general amusement of the gathering crowds and to the dismay of the conservative media. Some commentators went as far as comparing the artistic display to the political incitement that preceded the assassination of Prime Minister Yitzhak Rabin. Tellingly, Muzi Wertheim, head of Coca-Cola Israel, ex–Mossad agent, and owner of Keshet, Israel's most successful television network, was recorded saying, "When I saw the Rothschild guillotine, my neck started to hurt."[16] In a similar vein, Tel-Aviv mayor Ron Huldai was driven away from the Rothschild encampment and responded by blaming the revolutionary radicals in charge: "I have supported the protest and I still support it. But it won't work this way. I believe in the values the protest talks about, but people say, 'We shall demolish the old world,' and they want to wage a revolution, not a protest."[17]

The hopes for and concerns about the imminent revolution soon proved to be equally unfounded. The guillotine was removed with the apologies of the movement's leaders, and most of the youth in Israel's tent cities were preoccupied with public debates on the prospects of participatory democracy, commonly thrilled by the sense of communitas and creative agency. In August, the ambitious demands of the movement's leadership concerning Israel's budgetary and fiscal policies were answered by the right-wing government with an ad hoc committee endowed with a limited budget and virtually no executive power, and led by Manuel Trajtenberg, a prime minister–appointed economist who also served as the chair of the Higher Education Planning and Budget Committee. By the summer's end the official dismantling of the symbol of the protest movement, the tent encampment on Rothschild Boulevard, on October 3, led to the gradual dissolution of the movement, which eventually posed no real threat to the political stability of the government.

While it clearly had a profound impact on collective consciousness, the summer tent protest instantiated a putatively fluid form of situational radicalism—an autotelic political theater that could not transcend its horizontal definition of the situation. The popular attempt to redefine radical politics, which, as Raymond Williams (1985, 210) notes, "offer[s] a way of avoiding dogmatic and factional associations while reasserting the need for vigorous and fundamental change," was met with significant obstacles on Israel's street. Dependent upon a spontaneous collective mobilization, which remained trapped in its charismatic and preinstitutional stage, it failed to bring about concrete changes beyond the impressive fact of its own existence. Lacking political experience and prone to internal division, some of the leaders of the protest for social justice persisted in the aftermath of summer 2011 as icons of a momentary upheaval, subdued by the traditional hegemonic tactics of demobilization–co-optation, accommodation, and intimidation (the threat of an external enemy).[18] Against the background of the Palestinian attempt to seek a UN-endorsed declaration of statehood, the escalating violence around the Gaza Strip, and above all the publicized negotiation over the freeing of the abducted soldier Gilad Shalit, the government was diligently undermining the claims for social security by means of the politics of national security. By the time of Gilad Shalit's release on October 18, the public was already out of the streets and back to its normal routine, consuming the dramatic TV reports about the security situation and the prospects of an Iranian nuclear attack. At the end of the day, the ambitious goals of the movement were traded for an appeasing national symbol.[19]

RESCALING THE STRUGGLE AND THE LIMITS
OF JEWISH-ARAB COOPERATION

The aforementioned internal conflicts and identity politics that were endemic to the Arab uprisings—between Muslims and Copts, Alawis and Sunnis, secularists and Islamists—were all but absent from the Israeli scene, albeit in a different constellation. During the summer protest, two of the main schisms in Israeli society—those between Jewish and Arab-Palestinian citizens and between the Ashkenazi elites and the Mizrahi underclass—resurfaced in the form of a discourse about the uneven development of center and periphery. While the mainstream leadership was largely imagining itself as waging a color-blind, all-inclusive movement, Russian, Ethiopian, Arab, and Mizrahi activists felt systematically excluded, and organized accordingly under the umbrellas of "Forum Periphery," "Hamaabara—The Transit Camp," and many other like-minded frameworks. Indeed, soon after the meteoric success of the movement in July, voices were heard from the periphery saying that the Rothschild leadership misrepresented the popular movement—voices that went as far as charging the unelected leadership with corruption, favoritism, and nontransparency. In a letter addressed to Manuel Trajtenberg, dated August 15, signatories from different encampments claimed that "the Rothschild team lost its legitimacy in the eyes of many of the tent encampments' dwellers."[20] The Rothschild "team" was thus accused of serving sectarian interests and an elitist political faction. Regardless of the validity of these accusations, the rhetorical trope setting the Mizrahi periphery and the proletarian "neighborhoods" in opposition to the bourgeois "state of Tel-Aviv" points to a serious blind spot that afflicted the protest movement—its inability to stand for the working classes and for the marginalized groups. Speaking from the Hatikva tent camp in South Tel-Aviv to which they returned after a disappointing attempt to join the Rothschild leadership, Dana and Itzik Amsalem rearticulated the power relations between north and south:

They speak of affordable housing while we demand public housing. When we saw we had no say there [in Rothschild] we decided to come back to where we came from and fight for our rights. Despite being second and third generation to hardship [*metzuka*], we had no appropriate representation. We had none of the financial support that Rothschild has.... Actually we were supposed to be the spearhead of the protest even before the Cottage Cheese Protest and suddenly we saw on T v that the protest preceded us. We were surprised but happy that someone else feels like we do. Two days later we arrived at Rothschild with our own tent. We were among the first twenty tents, but already from the outset we felt like outsiders. The leadership was dissociated from us. We felt different.[21]

A similar sense of alienation characterized the Palestinian citizens of Israel who joined the protest belatedly and in relatively low numbers. Reviewing the Arabic media coverage of the topic, sociologist Nabil Khatab divides Palestinian participation into three groups: "Between the demand for social justice and the demand for national justice persists a sense of confusion, which caused a split between three groups: part of the Arab public refrained from playing any role in the protest; another part chose to wage a separate struggle; and a third part chose to join the struggle of the Jews. The latter two yielded opposition to each other and even opposition to the opposition. This might have been the reason that the Arab voice had not been heard until three weeks later."[22]

A patently urban phenomenon, Arab participation in the protest movement was mostly visible in the cities of Haifa and Jaffa, in addition to other minor tent encampments in smaller towns such as Upper Nazareth and Carmiel. While historically both Haifa and Jaffa are ethnically mixed cities with a significant Palestinian minority—10 percent and 30 percent, respectively—they have important differences. Haifa functions as the center of the northern periphery (in the Galilee), whereas Jaffa serves as the periphery of the metropolitan center (Tel-Aviv). In addition to its organic Arab population, for several decades now Haifa's location and liberal image have attracted a dynamic group of middle-class Palestinians (Christians and Muslims alike) who left their rural hometowns and chose to live in mixed neighborhoods. The active involvement of educated Palestinians in Haifa's urban culture and politics made them a visible component of the local movement that some observers have described as a joint "Jewish-Arab protest."[23] After the first demonstration, which included only one Arab speaker from the then-only encampment (Merkaz ha-Carmel), subsequent rallies took place near mixed neighborhoods and featured a proportional representation of Arab speakers (including Palestinian intellectuals and political figures and delegates from the Wadi Nisnas and Hadar encampments).[24] "Each rally was bigger than the previous one," writes Or Shai, "and the more Arab demonstrators teamed up, the more that messages against the high rent were coupled with messages against housing demolition and discrimination."[25]

Reflecting a long-term local tradition of joint binational political action that goes back to the British Mandate period, Haifa represented a relatively successful case of urban solidarity and converging political interests. In diametric opposition to "Red Haifa," Jaffa is home to an impoverished Palestinian community, which is facing daily a concerted plan to gentrify the city and cleanse it of whatever constitutes a disturbance to a bourgeois space of consumption. Led by initiatives such as the Popular Committee for Land and Housing Rights in Jaffa, the struggle over the Palestinian "right to the city" is conducted in the courts, in the media, and through grassroots activism, which culminated with the efforts to create an alliance between Arab Jaffa and Tel-Aviv's marginalized Jewish neighborhoods (notably Hatikva). Claiming a right to the city, as Harvey (2013, 5) notes, "is to claim some kind of shaping power over the process of urbanization, over the ways in which our cities are made and remade and to do so in a fundamental and radical way."

FLAGS OF CONTENTION IN THE JAFFA ENCAMPMENT:
AN ETHNOGRAPHY OF AMBIVALENCE[26]

The Jaffa protest encampment was erected in the last few days of July (figure 7.2). It initially consisted of one larger tent that became home to a local Palestinian family evicted from its house, a makeshift kitchen, and an array of smaller run-of-the-mill camping tents that remained empty most nights. Since it was the Muslim holy month of Ramadan, the encampment was almost completely deserted during the day but came to life in the later hours of the evening, when local Palestinian activists, most of them under the age of thirty-five, showed up after the

FIGURE 7.2. First day of the Jaffa encampment, July 30, 2011.
Courtesy of Yudit Ilany.

breaking of the daily fast and the *Iftar* meal. Joining them were a sizeable group of young Jewish residents of Jaffa (several of them politically active through other organizations like Tarabut and Anarchists against the Wall),[27] as well as Jewish and Palestinian residents from different walks of life. Finally, there were also activists who arrived from elsewhere, many from nearby Tel-Aviv, and who were vocal about their discontent with the apolitical approach at the main Rothschild tent city.

The general atmosphere at the Jaffa encampment was often fraught with tension. Curiously enough, several Jewish activists, whether from Jaffa or elsewhere, appeared to be more militant in tone and tenor than the majority of Palestinians, who were acutely aware of the sensitive nature of Jewish-Arab alliances and thus often opted for a more pragmatic strategy. Thus, for instance, Udi Aloni, a Jewish radical activist, exclaimed that this was a liberation struggle rather than just a movement for "social justice," as the Rothschild mainstream leaders insisted on depicting it. Aloni was joined by young and equally vocal Palestinian activists who asserted that since Jaffa is a Palestinian city (under Israeli occupation) and since the purpose of this encampment was to reclaim their right to it, there should be a Palestinian flag present on the grounds to reflect that.

These more militant voices were resisted by a group of older Palestinian activists and residents, as well as Mizrahi Jewish activists who envisioned a joint struggle that would bring together those sectors within Israeli society that had been suppressed and marginalized by the state and municipality. In an unprecedented move, activists from the working-class Hatikva neighborhood in southeastern Tel-Aviv visited their Jaffa counterparts, held a solidarity and strategy meeting, and discussed joining forces for the upcoming mass rally and marching together under one banner—Palestinians (and leftist Jews) from Jaffa and Mizrahi Jews (and mostly Likud voters) from Hatikva. As that historic meeting was later rehashed, several of the younger and more radical activists wondered out loud whether the planned rally on Saturday could lead to a shared struggle. One speaker exclaimed, "Should we even march shoulder to shoulder with reservists who serve in the West Bank?"

Sami Abu Shehade, a local strongman and a municipal councilman representing the Jaffa Palestinians, attempted to appease her: "We should join despite our reservations and even if our gains will be limited—maybe we will be able to save a few homes from demolition and provide relief to a few families." The younger activists seemed a little skeptical, but agreed to abide by the decision of the majority.

This tension between the desire to form a political alliance with Hatikva (and other working-class Mizrahi Jewish activists and locals) and the need to reassert Palestinianness and thus reclaim the city manifested later that night, as the assembly proceeded to discuss the issue of flags. The younger and more militant activists, together with Udi Aloni, insisted on hoisting the Palestinian flag, to remind Israeli Jews of the presence of Palestinians among them (who now made up roughly 20 percent of the population within Israel proper) and as a response to the abundance of Israeli flags and other nationalist markers during these mass demonstrations. Aloni specifically reminded everyone that these flags reflected a form of unity between the Palestinians who happened to be citizens and those in the West Bank who were completely absent from the social justice discourse disseminated by the main leadership of the movement. Others, however, argued that bringing Palestinian flags would be a mistake and would create a rift between the Jaffa group and the rest of the protesters. "We will end up pariahs, like the settlers," one person warned. The municipal councilman concluded, "We are not trying to solve the problems of Palestinians in general, but give voice to our own issues regarding housing rights here, in our city. The most important thing to remember is that we are trying to stop ongoing processes of displacement and demolitions within our own community." By rescaling the struggle to the local community's specific demands for affordable housing, he strengthened the Jewish-Arab coalition while deferring the contentious cause of Palestinian solidarity.

These unresolved tensions indeed came to a head during the Saturday rally (August 6). Based on agreements reached during a previous meeting with delegates from other tent sites, a joint contingent that included the Jaffa, Hatikva, and Levinsky encampments marched side by side,[28] carrying banners in both Hebrew and Arabic that called for the revitalization of public housing and declared, "Jews and Arabs refuse to be enemies," "Bibi ruh min hon" ("Bibi go away"), and mainly "Jaffa, Hatikva, same revolution." All of a sudden, a group of young Palestinian activists, and especially *muhajabat* (veiled) young women, *kufiyye* wrapped around their heads in lieu of the more traditional *hijab*, insisted on flying a sole Palestinian flag and chanting, "Al-Sha'b yurid tahrir Filastin" ("The people want the liberation of Palestine"), which contradicted previous understandings with the Hatikva delegates. Activists from Hatikva and older Palestinians were incensed and an ugly altercation ensued. This intergenerational confrontation ended with the temporary capitulation of the younger activists. But when a few radical Jewish activists started chanting about the liberation of Palestine ("From the river to the sea—social justice"), no one scolded.

The issue, however, was addressed at the next Jaffa encampment meeting. Hani Zubeida, a Mizrahi Jewish activist and academic from Hatikva, remained optimistic that despite the violations of the agreement, there was still space for cooperation, and he proposed another meeting between delegates from the two sites. Local activists of the older generation used a much more accusatory and angrier tone. They pointed the finger at "outside Jews" who "incited young impressionable women" to create divisions within their community. Udi Aloni understood that the speakers were referring to him, and he apologized but also argued that he did not "incite" anyone and that he urged those who wished to wave the Palestinian flag to move ahead in the march away from the block in order to avoid further confrontations.

The young muhajaba activist, Yasmeen, was incensed. She vocalized her rage, argued that she was not "seduced" by a Jew into waving her flag, and insisted on her own agency and continued to argue loudly with others, even after the meeting was adjourned. Sami Abu Shehade tried to calm everyone down and reminded the assembly that this particular encampment was concerned first and foremost with the problem of housing in that community. He added, "We are not ashamed of the Palestinian flag, but we alone will decide when to wave it, as there is a time and a place for everything," suggesting that the mass rally was the wrong place for a demonstration of nationalist affiliation. Another speaker claimed that she did not identify as a Palestinian but as an Arab, and therefore did not identify with the kind of identity the flag seemed to represent. Others made explicit threats toward future renegades. People were invited to express dissent during meetings but were asked to refrain from violating agreements with other groups.

One activist revealed that, earlier, someone hung the Palestinian flag at the very front of the encampment, right on Yefet Street, and that presumably others took it down and replaced it with photographs of house demolitions. At the same time her interlocutor reported this incident, fights broke out all over the encampment—among younger activists and between Jewish and older Palestinian activists—and while all this commotion was taking place, visitors to the main Rothschild Boulevard encampment stood by and watched the scene with growing discomfort and unease. They were invited for a live performance by the hip-hop ensemble System Ali, but wondered whether they should stay, given the awkward moment of discord they found the site in. Eventually, the event went on as planned, and at least temporarily, everyone's attention seemed to be shifted to the music and spectacle.[29]

Discord continued to set the tone for the next meeting. At the encampment, separate circles of people were sitting around and speaking in hushed voices. They seemed angry that a much smaller group of activists, most of whom were Palestinians, met earlier in the offices of the Rabita and formed a committee of people to oversee and manage the encampment. When the separate circles finally merged into the general assembly, several participants confronted Sami, who apparently had organized the Rabita meeting, and accused him of undemocratic conduct. At first, he even refused to name those who were part of the newly formed committee, but did so eventually under tremendous pressure. Supporters of the committee explained that right then, the encampment was dysfunctional and things were in disarray, and there was an urgent need to assign tasks to people and begin to organize better for the upcoming March of the Million. Some participants refused to let "outsiders" vote to take part in outreach, suggesting that those who physically looked "out of place" (i.e., Ashkenazi Jews) should not be part of the outreach efforts.

Amidst this scene of utter chaos, Itay Engel, a well-known journalist who had been invited to the tent, arrived. He was supposed to screen two of his documentaries for us tonight—one was on the Egyptian revolution, the other on 'Ajami. He seemed genuinely embarrassed. The awkwardness of the moment increased when a few participants confronted others about the issue of programming—one said, "I am not here to watch a film. We should continue our discussions instead." Eventually the screening began and gradually people calmed down and seemed to enjoy themselves. At the same meeting, I encountered a veteran Mizrahi activist I used to work with in the 1980s in the Jaffa and South Tel-Aviv youth movement. Active as she was for three decades in social affairs, her optimism regarding the future of the Jewish-Arab coalition was remarkable considering the rampant atmosphere of dissent.

A few days later, Noa, my research partner, arrived earlier than her usual hour. She sat down with a few older Jewish women activists and listened to them recall the history of housing activism in Jaffa. Then, a few meters away, the committee began its meeting. Yudit Ilani, one of the main Jewish activists and a resident of Jaffa, told Noa that as an "outsider," she should not intervene or even attend that meeting, since "outsiders" were not familiar with the specific problems that plagued the community, and that committee members should not waste their time explaining these issues to those who did not even have the right to vote on them.

Questions of inclusion and tensions between the Jaffa encampment and the so-called "leadership" on Rothschild Boulevard constantly resurfaced. When the Israeli Army bombarded the Gaza Strip on August 18, those leaders decided to cancel a rally in central Tel-Aviv and hold a silent gathering on the beach instead. Many Jewish and Palestinian activists in Jaffa felt that the right response to the escalation of state violence against Palestinians would be a protest in solidarity with Gazans, as several Jaffan families had relatives there. Yet only a few of those activists attended the silent rally, holding banners condemning the Israeli onslaught and, later, chanting. They were chastised by many of the Tel-Avivans, who also tried to silence them.

Then the following week, beginning on August 27, the Jaffa encampment was planning to hold a large demonstration in Jaffa. There was talk about busing people in from the Triangle and other Arab cities and towns. There was also talk of having the other "periphery encampments," such as Hatikva, Levinsky, and Beer Sheva, take center stage. Throughout the initial planning stages, the Rothschild leadership had not announced plans to hold a rally in central Tel-Aviv, and therefore delegates from Jaffa proposed in the weekly encampments assembly that instead of holding on in Tel-Aviv, everyone would attend a mass demonstration in Jaffa, and that messages would be coordinated so that everyone felt included. However, as volunteers were hard at work on the plans for a historic rally in Jaffa, the Rothschild leaders suddenly announced a rally for Saturday night, headed by Noam Shalit, father of captive Israeli soldier Gilad Shalit. The response to this move was shock and a feeling of insult among the Jaffan activists. "They don't even acknowledge our existence," one said.

Adding injury to insult, Qalanswa and Taybeh (two of the main Triangle towns) announced their own rally, which ruled out their participation in our event. Fighting ensued during the evening discussion as to whether there was even a point to holding a separate event, but the general feeling was that Palestinian Jaffans were reluctant to participate in the Tel-Aviv rally given its overtly Zionist tone and tenor. Local activists Abu Ashraf and Natalie even suggested canceling the local rally and instead channeling their energy into something more productive than carrying banners in a rally that "we don't identify with"—something like community work that would stress the joint Arab-Jewish venture of our endeavor. One of the Jewish activists, sitting right outside their earshot, mumbled, "Even though the Jews here are minor rather than equal partners, but that's okay."

The Jaffa encampment proceeded to hold its own march and rally in Jaffa that attracted local activists, both Palestinians and Jews, as well as several anti-Zionist Jews, who chanted antioccupation slogans in Hebrew and Arabic and called for the renewal of public housing projects. The march was widely advertised (on Facebook and via traditional media), but it ultimately drew only a small crowd of hundreds instead of the thousands the organizers had hoped for. Under the (Arabic and Hebrew) banner reading, "Jaffa: The periphery at the center—housing first," the march was attended by several national Palestinian political figures, who marched in closed ranks behind the banner and seemed eager to co-opt an event that was struggling to represent an image of bottom-up mobilization (see chapter 3).

Proceeding from the Bloomfield soccer stadium to the symbolic Gan ha-Shnayim (Garden of the Two), also known in local parlance as the Garden of the Gazans, the site of the Jaffa encampment, the march ended with a series of speeches and music performances that reflected the unsettled attempt to reconcile opposite messages and to create a unified collective definition of the situation. The first performer was Yair Dalal, a Jewish ethno-Oriental musician of Iraqi descent who used to live in the gentrified self-proclaimed "Artists' Colony" in Old Jaffa. Dalal was selected because in the liberal imagination he represents world music fused in a Jewish-Arab Andalusia-like cultural repertoire. Tellingly, he chose to sing in Arabic and Hebrew the lyrical song "Zaman al-Salam" (Time of peace), which struck some Palestinian and Jewish radical activists I spoke with as "an inappropriate song of coexistence."[30]

As if reflecting their discontent, the next performance featured a Palestinian oud player who concluded his show with "Mawtini" (My homeland), the national Palestinian anthem. Some younger members of the crowd made the "V" sign, clearly to the dismay of the Jewish participants from Hatikva and south Tel-Aviv. Following the oud player, two hip-hop singers (one of whom was from System Ali) asked to go on stage, and with an emotionless expression they sang a piece with the pessimistic refrain "Ihna 'Arab—kul ishi indarab" ("We're Arabs—it's all fucked up"). After the organizers' speech, which reiterated the goals of the protest, the last speaker was Wafa, a female member of the only Palestinian family who actually slept in the tent camp after they were evicted from their home. Speaking in Arabic, Wafa pleaded for the protesters to unite and leave their disagreements aside. Pointing to the internal divisions among the Palestinian factions in Jaffa, she concluded her speech with a call to the Islamic Council and its rival the Rabita (the largely secular association) to come together and coordinate their actions for the common good of the community. In a conversation with me after the demonstration, Wafa expressed her belief that the camp would not be dismantled, despite the city's official intentions. Wafa's family remained on-site until their final eviction in late January 2012.

In the next encampment meeting, there were conflicting responses to Saturday's rally. Some spoke in congratulatory tones, describing the rally as empowering, moving, and liberating in a manner that had rarely been seen in disillusioned Jaffa. Others voiced their utter frustration, disappointment, and even "heartbreak" (as one Jewish activist put it) at their outreach failure—even though several activists invested their "heart and soul" in convincing the other "periphery encampments" to join with them. To their dismay, only a few individuals showed up (including Dana Amsalem from Hatikva, who also addressed the rally but refrained from attending the meeting). Others complained about what they identified as the passivity and lack of solidarity on the part of local Jaffans, as most remained in their homes and avoided the rally altogether. Moreover, these activists also bitterly complained about the lack of cooperation with other Palestinian organizations, even though they were explicitly invited in. One Jewish Jaffan woman spoke out about what she perceived as "nationalist" chants and banners during the rally and the prevalence of the Palestinian flag and other nationalist and anticolonial markers. She argued that the rally was less about public housing and became more "political" because of "all the symbols" (*kufiyye*) and certain kinds of chants ("Al-Sha'b yurid isqat al-Sahyuniyya"—"The people want the fall of Zionism") she could not identify with and felt excluded from. These complaints led to an entire discussion about responsibility for the messages conveyed during rallies: who decides on chants, t-shirts, flags, and other markers, and what should be avoided. Sami Abu Shehade and his cousin 'Abed vehemently argued that as long as they were the organizers, people should refrain from carrying flags, including red ones. Another man, a Palestinian, voiced his disappointment at what he called the "politicization" of the rally, since he believed the protest should focus on public housing rather than anticolonialism. Others responded that responsibility for the ongoing house demolitions in the city belonged to the municipality and the state, and that calls for the ouster of the government and mayor were more than appropriate during these events.

Attention then turned to the upcoming March of the Million scheduled for September 3. Some of the participants were concerned about the overt presence of Israeli flags and other markers at the rally and wondered whether they even had a place there. Yossi, an older local Jewish activist, suggested that "we should get over that." Sephi and others involved in social activism in South Tel-Aviv voiced their distrust of the main Rothschild leadership and their dictates. Sami tried to reassure everyone that there was a new leadership that was more attuned to the needs and demands of the "periphery." The temporary resolution was to wait for "Forum Periphery"[31] to decide whether they would like everyone, including Jaffa, to march together as a block, even though several attendees questioned the forum itself and wondered about their position regarding Gilad Shalit, nationalist flags, and the issue of "solidarity with the south" in light of the attack on Gaza.

Sami tried to explain that Forum Periphery did not care about any of that and was focused on public housing. Eventually the resolution was to participate in the march as a block, and the organizers began to brainstorm creative ideas that would get some media attention. The decision was to create a large "golden calf" statue to symbolize the greed of politicians and their capitalist allies, which came at the expense of the impoverished masses, especially those at the socioeconomic peripheries. The participants therefore assembled the night before the rally and prepared the golden calf, as well as a car-borne "flying tent" to sym-

FIGURE 7.3. The golden calf as Jaffa's centerpiece during the March of the Million, September 3, 2011.
Courtesy of Haim Schwarczenberg.

bolize the wretched state of the homeless. Zmira, Haim, and Fatmeh decided, on the fly, to drive the golden calf to the site of the wedding of the daughter of one of Israel's billionaires, Nuhi Dankner, where they met another spontaneous mini-demonstration that immediately surrounded them and simulated the biblical story of the Israelites' worshipping of the calf.

While this impromptu operation was considered a success and received wide media coverage, back at the encampment things looked glum. Fewer people than usual turned up for the meeting, and Hanaa', one of the main activists, seemed reluctant and withdrawn, even defeated: "Would you like to prepare flyers? No? Fine. Don't put my phone number on them, please." Gil, another activist, was quite bitter and wondered aloud where all the activists were who called for more intense activity at the encampment. People were upset because those who were chosen as delegates were not even present to report back. There was a general sense of discontent, exasperation, and fatigue even as we sat to think about appropriate slogans for the rally.

Eventually, though, everyone seemed enthusiastic when the time came to march. For the media's sake, the protestors made the golden calf the centerpiece of their march; there was a sense of elation as we marched, sang, and chanted, and some even jumped up and down and caught the attention of the many photojournalists and TV news stations there to cover the rally (figure 7.3). Even passersby wanted to have a photo op with the calf, and Zmira, who came up with the idea in the first place, was walking around like a proud mother. She would not stop talking about the success of the calf even at the next day's meeting.

Overall, the Jaffa envoy to the historic rally in Tel-Aviv was indeed a moderate success, yet one which could not transcend the troubled Oedipal relationship between the two cities (see chapter 2). One full bus carrying about fifty Jewish and Arab activists represented the modest mobilizing force of the local movement, which was all but unequivocal about joining what was perceived to be an all-Israeli demonstration of solidarity at Kikar ha-Medina (the State Square), the icon of the upper socioeconomic echelon. Notwithstanding the success of the golden calf, the contingent itself remained at the very fringes of the assembly. After a brief but dramatic entrance with slogans such as "Jaffans united against house eviction," "No to gentrification," and "Jaffans demand social justice" (figure 7.4), the group left during the speeches, abandoning the crowded square and making its way back to Jaffa. Participants later testified that they could not hear much of the speeches and that most could not really relate to any of it and felt alienated by the Israeli flags right by the main stage.[32] Featuring no Arab speaker, the March of the Million, like the protest movement as a whole, consistently stressed an all-Jewish spectacle of solidarity, leaving the Palestinian voice on the very fringes that it occupied during the rally.[33]

In the wake of the March of the Million, which marked the climax of the summer revolt (as well as the end of the summer vacation), the Rothschild leadership decided to continue waging the protest by other means. A few days later, most of the encampments were evacuated with

FIGURE 7.4. Palestinian and Jewish demonstrators: "Jaffans united against house eviction" and "Jaffans demand social justice." *By permission of Activestills.org.*

the active involvement of the local municipalities. The Jaffa tent camp was no exception. With the gradual dispersal of the activist core, internal discord arose, which in one case prompted one resident to burn the tent of another. Along with an aggressive evacuation policy, the city paid homeless tent dwellers enough for a few months' rent (ten thousand shekels). Altogether, these policies made for a relatively uneventful dismantling process. The process lasted until early February 2012, when the last tent was evacuated.

Trapped between a class-based welfare agenda and a Palestinian nationalist frame of action, the Jaffa encampment remained ambivalent vis-à-vis its role in the Israeli protest for social justice. Visual evidence of this ambivalence remained on-site until the dismantlement of the tent camp was complete. One of these placards featured Handhala, the iconic Palestinian cartoon figure whose back is turned to the world in a gesture of defiant innocence. Reading, "I await a house!! And so does he," with an arrow pointing to Handhala, the sign conveys the converg-

FIGURE 7.5. "The Right of Return to Old Jaffa."
Courtesy of Yudit Ilany.

ing grievances of the Palestinian community in Jaffa and the general
Palestinian cause in the Occupied Territories and the Diaspora. An additional placard, often waved during the protests (figure 7.5), was found
among the debris of the deserted camp, indexing the subversive union
of national collective rights and social housing rights that failed once
again to materialize: "The Right of Return to Old Jaffa."

SUSHI EATERS AND SHISHA SMOKERS; OR,
THE "PEOPLE" AS AN EMPTY SIGNIFIER

Two weeks after the outbreak of the protest, David 'Amar, a member
of the ruling Likud Party, urged the prime minister not to give in to
public pressure: "There is no protest, Bibi, you're being lied to. Everyone
in Rothschild smokes shisha and eats sushi. There's no available trolleys
at the airport."[34] To the fuming protest leaders, 'Amar's statement encap-
sulated the attempt of the ruling class to dismiss the popular demands
for social justice as a mere maneuver of the "delusional left" and to defuse

its revolutionary claims. Regardless of the validity of this accusation it effectively labeled the Jewish, Ashkenazi, middle-class constituency at the center of the action in Tel-Aviv as decadent members of the leisure class. This shortcoming notwithstanding, the protest did initially convince some of the most radical voices in Israel about the sincerity of its intentions. On August 13, 2011, Asma Agbarieh-Zahalka, a Palestinian activist with the workers' party, the Organization for Democratic Action [Da'am], published her vote of confidence in the leftist magazine *Challenge:* "This was the first time that I, born and bred in Jaffa, felt that the human wave washing over Tel Aviv was also carrying me, was also attentive to my aspirations, that the shouts were mine too, regardless of race, religion or gender—even if only for a day."[35]

Coming from Agbarieh-Zahalka, a political figure who came a long way from Islamism to a binational workers' movement, this statement could not be underestimated. Calling on others to "come out of the Arab closet," she concluded, "It's time to wake up and find an ally in the Israeli protest movement, which reflects similar movements in the Arab world, in Spain and in Greece." A year later, the duplicity behind the recurrent declarations of the movement's leaders that they spoke for "everyone" was acutely brought home to her. As part of the attempt to rekindle the protest, a rally took place in Tel-Aviv on June 2, 2012, under the banner "2011—Protest; 2012—Revolution." Agbarieh-Zahalka received permission to allow a Palestinian agricultural worker to address the social justice movement. At the last moment, however, the organizers decided not to let her speak for technical reasons. Infuriated, Agbarieh-Zahalka said, "There was a historic opportunity here that an Arab woman would go onstage and speak in the name of Arabs, and speak to the Arabs and not just to the Arabs in Israel but to the whole Arab world to take Israel out of its isolation. And this country and these protesters are refusing to step out of their hypocrisy and out of their racism. And if they don't treat the Arabs as equal, and treat the workers as equal, there will never ever be social justice."[36]

How can we make sense of the gap between the movement's inclusionary presentation of self and its actual exclusionary practices? Sociologist Sylvaine Bulle points out that "as with other global movements (the 99%, the Indignados, ows), it can be difficult to distinguish between reformist and radical grammars of dissent."[37] The main difference, however, between the Israeli protest and the other global movements is the persistent hegemony of an ethnonational gravitational force, which traps any critical discourse in the orbit of the social contract ostensibly signed between the Jewish state and its (Jewish) citizens. In this state of affairs, the exclusion of dissenting voices, like the Palestinian agriculture worker's, seems but natural.

By now it has become clear that the notion of the "people" invoked throughout the protest functioned as an empty signifier. It constituted the discursive center, but only at the price of emptying its content could it produce an apparently universal discursive formation. In Laclau's terms the concept of the people was "present as that which is absent. . . . It becomes the signifier of this absence" (Laclau 2007, 44). Entertaining simultaneously republican, ethnonational, social-democratic, and liberal notions of peoplehood, the politics around the protest thus articulated "a struggle to fill the emptiness with a given content—to suture the rift of the discursive centre and to create a universal hegemony" (ibid.). In the process, the outside is antagonistically mobilized to affirm the legitimacy of the center: "The outside is not merely posing a threat to the inside, but is actually required for the definition of the inside. The inside is marked by a constitutive lack that the outside helps to fill" (Torfing 2005, 11). During the summer protest, the exclusion of a truly radical agenda was thus not a mere condition of possibility but a condition of necessity for the ostensible universal import of the movement. Cleansed of political alterities such as Palestinian, Mizrahi, and proletarian, whose access to the visible center was virtually blocked, the movement could present itself to itself, to its audience, and to the ruling class as both pragmatic and populist, representational and revolutionary at the same time.

The display of unity in protest, however, was semiotically and politically unstable, inviting moments of radical intervention (like the guillotine) only to disavow them as moments of transgression, inappropriate for a "responsible" leadership. This fluctuating process, which I term situational radicalism, was the outcome of an indecisive play of boundaries, of presence and absence, inside and outside. The double meaning of the concept of situational radicalism reflects the *modus operandi* of the summer protests, first as a performance of radicalism divorced from a revolutionary constitution, and second as a protest held hostage by the "situation" (*ha-matzav*)—a phenomenological emic term Israelis use to collapse the temporality and spatiality of the politics of permanent conflict onto the lived present (Gurevitch 2007).

In the aftermath of the 2011 events, organizers and observers alike pondered the future of the movement, considering the ongoing support from 80 percent of the Israeli public for resuming the protests.[38] One observer recently remarked,

> Would the social protest turn violent? Would the summer of 2012 bring violent clashes, mass arrests, and indiscriminate shooting of pepper gas as we saw in Greece and in other European countries? One thing is clear: the niceness of summer 2011 would not repeat itself. "500 thousand people took to the streets, sang and shouted but achieved nothing," protest activists and ordinary frustrated citizens angrily say. The obvious conclusion is the following: now it's time to stop playing by the rules and turn the tables. . . . The important thing is that in this round the protest would turn from a protest to an explicit resistance. A civil revolt—nonviolent but not nice either. It will undoubtedly lose most of the 80% who now wish for its return—but it may achieve more significant results.[39]

A recurrent slogan for the renewal of the protest was "Maybe Next Summer," indexing both the fantasy of togetherness expressed in a popular song with the same title and the concrete attempt to plan the next stage of the protest (e.g., the conference "Maybe Next Summer: Change in Movement" was held in May in Jaffa).[40] However, for the movement to shift from a mere protest to a revolutionary resistance, as the organizers professed, a radical redefinition of Israeli peoplehood would be required. While this never happened, there were unprecedented signs of a new political awareness which sought to break through years of an established Israeli policy of divide and rule. In a speech given at the Sapir conference in January 2012, entitled "What Is Social Justice and What Makes a Nation," Viki Vaanunu, a struggling single mother and a public housing activist, gave some room for hope:

> The establishment wants me to believe that my people are the Jewish nation, but if there are Jews who exploit me and others like me, and who do not allow us to live a normative life, then this definition is not satisfactory. My people are all those who are oppressed like me: Jews, Arabs, refugees. All those who are exploited by the establishment. . . . The first stone has yet to be

thrown in our struggle, but if the state continues to ignore us, continues to silence us with the police, our struggle will escalate. We are ready to fight for our future and the future for our children.[41]

In late June 2012 thousands of protesters in Tel-Aviv took to the streets in rage, smashing bank windows and blocking the highways. The violent arrest of Daphni Leef, the symbolic leader of the social justice movement, during her attempt to kick-start the movement at the spot where it began in July 2011, has once again ignited the spirit of revolt in Israel's "white city." Facing police violence, the appearance of hooded protesters with banners such as "The Answer to Privatization?—Revolution!" and "Soldier, Cop—Refuse the Order"—a first for this city—marked an escalation that seemed to satisfy the expectations of the previous summer. The intensifying activities on the urban scale brought about the resignation of the deputy mayor and the artists' boycott of Tel-Aviv's signature summer happening, "White Night," in favor of alternative cultural initiatives based in the southern neighborhoods and provocatively labeled "Black Night." Tellingly, however, this seeming radicalization chiefly addressed police violence and the right to freedom of expression, instead of prompting any substantive redefinition of the protest movement's agenda. Going to the barricades against state violence under the slogan "It's no mistake, it's a policy," Israeli protesters remained persistently oblivious to the link between police aggression in Israel and in the Occupied Territories.[42]

Exactly a year after the launch of the social protest, on the night of July 14, 2012, during a march in the central streets of Tel-Aviv, Moshe Silman, a Haifa-based activist, poured fuel over his body and set himself on fire. In a letter he distributed prior to his self-immolation, Silman explained that he was protesting "all the injustice" done to him and others in his situation by the state, naming and shaming those he perceived as responsible for his misery, from Prime Minister Netanyahu to the staff of the Haifa branch of the National Insurance Institute.[43] The following night, a rally was organized in Tel-Aviv in solidarity with Silman, who was at the time hospitalized in critical condition. Hundreds gathered in front of the governmental office complex, located near a major intersection, reciting Silman's letter. The raging crowd of demonstrators then marched along busy urban routes, intermittently blocking traffic and asking stranded motorists to join the impromptu public display of anger and solidarity. Repeatedly chanting "We are all Moshe Silman," protesters stopped in front of the local branch of the National Insurance Institute, but riot police officers prevented them from approaching the glass doors and windows. Despite this performance of spontaneous rage, tension dissipated after the crowd of protesters moved on, proceeding to block the busy Ayalon Highway.

Another march was called after Silman died the following Friday. On Saturday night (July 21), one thousand of the core public housing and social justice activists marched again along the same route, once again blocking the highway for a short time. In contradistinction with Mohamed Bouazizi's martyrdom in Tunisia, although Silman's performative self-immolation ostensibly radicalized public discourse about the root causes of economic hardships shared by many, and even though personal stories of injustice and institutional neglect circulated widely on Facebook, the protest movement had shrunk considerably and ceased to mobilize the masses of the urban underclasses.

In the course of the following year, contentious politics showed clear signs of co-optation. Several of the leading J14 figures have announced their intention to run as candidates for Israel's larger political parties, while the more self-proclaimed radical wing of the movement has formed an independent movement that competed (unsuccessfully) for seats in the Knesset. Finally, throughout the tumultuous events of the summer, the Palestinian community of Jaffa was largely absent from these spectacles of public outrage, receding once again to deal with the harsh realities of forced evictions and house demolitions.

The effects of mobilization and radicalization, however, did not disappear without a trace. Instead they reemerged in the form of an alternative cultural scene, which rebranded Jaffa as a space of creative marginality. Blending business, leisure, and politics to reclaim Palestinian cultural space, Jaffa saw the budding of cafés and clubs that followed the lead of Yafa Café (see chapter 2). Increasingly popular cultural establishments such as the vegan-friendly Abu Dhabi-Kaymak Café, the hip cosmopolitan Anna Loulou Bar, and the Palestinian Salma Café point to the unintended outcomes of political conflict and profit-oriented gentrification. Recent attempts, such as 7arakeh Fawreyeh (Arabic for "immediate action"), discussed later in this chapter, complicate this nexus even further by channeling cultural and leisurely activities directly into political action.

Reflecting the ongoing radicalization of Jaffa's cityscape, the opposing processes of the commodification of urban space, antigentrification activism, and alternative cultures should not be read as disconnected phenomena; rather, they are part and parcel of the broader resignification of mixed towns as spaces of political action and creative marginality.

THE ALTERNATIVE SCENE IN JAFFA:
ETHNOGRAPHIES OF CREATIVE MARGINALITY

Embedded in the political economy of urban exclusion, creative marginality is the product of the agency of men and women inhabiting the city's edge (Harms 2011). While Palestinian activism in Jaffa has been well established—notably with the ongoing activities of the Rabita, starting in the late 1970s, and the more recent Darna—The Popular Committee for Land and Housing Rights, established in 2007—new Jewish activists have become increasingly visible. Left-leaning Jews have become involved in antigentrification activism and at the same time are part of the city's gentrification. In the process these radical gentrifiers and Palestinian actors are rebranding Jaffa as an alternative cultural space (see chapter 4). Some deliberately choose to "live in the open wound," mobilizing memory and trauma as a therapeutic means for political art. For many, however, the political commitment to Jaffa is fused with the emergence of new spaces of consumption. The counterintuitive realities of the alternative cultural scene in the binational border zone illustrate the dialectic between dismal political exclusion and creative urban agency. The following is an ethnographic account of the alternative cultural scene in Jaffa and three of its main sites of action: Anna Loulou Bar, Yafa Café, and Salma Café.

Anna Loulou: Hip Cosmopolitanism, Celebrating Alterity

On a side street in Jaffa's Old City, a number of young Palestinians and Jews are sitting on the pavement, opposite the entrance to a bar, chatting, smoking, and drinking.[44] We nod to the bouncer at the door and we enter. Inside is a dark smoky room, where loud Dabke music resonates from the speakers. At the end of the room is a shining neon sign with the name of the place, "Loulou," written in Arabic. At the center, opposite the DJ stand, some twenty people are dancing, probably half of them Palestinian. Our two companions are thrilled. While one of them immediately joins the ranks of the dancers, the other exclaims, almost disbelievingly, "There are Arab girls here! There are female Arab students here! What is this place?!"

The success story of Anna Loulou coincided with the popular uprisings in Tunisia and Egypt and thus with a renewed Israeli interest in the neighboring Arab countries. The owners of the bar, a Jewish couple, sensitive to the implications of opening a bar in the Old City, were actively engaged in pushing an alternative cultural agenda which would also appeal to trendy Palestinian citizens of Israel. The self-conscious use of Orientalist imagery in interior design, as well as on the bar's flyers, is an explicit pastiche simultaneously mimicking and ridiculing the mainstream Israeli take on Jaffa as an exotic place. This carefully crafted image, combined with the launching of a series of events with contemporary popular Middle Eastern music, headed primarily by a current Palestinian resident of Jaffa, DJ Muhammad Jabali, soon attracted a diverse crowd of people, many of whom, due to a complex interplay of political, ethnic, and sexual identities, feel excluded from their home communities or the more mainstream scenes.

At the height of Anna Loulou's success, *Mako*, a leading Israeli online magazine, branded the bar a "main hangout of the Arab gay scene" and described its owners' decision to open such a place in Jaffa as a "brave, if not scary move."[45] Addressing the possible security concerns of potential customers, the article emphasized the fact that the bar has a security guard, thus reproducing Jaffa's image as a conservative, read homophobic, place, one which remains inherently alien to modern, liberal Tel-Aviv, recently celebrated as the "world's number one gay tourist destination."[46] Niv, one of the owners, confesses that there was never an underlying political agenda to the bar project and that its success, as well as its increasing association with radical culture and politics, took him by surprise. The influx of Palestinian students and Jewish radical gentrifiers, who provided the bar's first clientele, added considerably to the "cool" branding of the place. In the beginning, Niv feared there would be tension between his interests as an entrepreneur and the political expectations of his radical clients, but as it turned out, living up to the image of a culturally and politically exterritorial place was also good for business. By now Anna Loulou has garnered such a reputation that it is not uncommon there to meet tourists from Jordan and Egypt, and even sometimes young Palestinians from West Bank cities, who with or without a permit cross into Israel to pay the bar a visit. Thus a Palestinian activist and regular at the bar wrote on his Facebook page, "Only in Ana Loulou at 03:00 PM will you find a conference between Palestinians, Arabs from Egypt and Jordan, and Arab-Jews [Jews who define themselves as Arab-Jewish and not Israeli]. . . . Power to the eastern people."

The fact that our companion from the above vignette immediately noted the presence of Arab women is telling. While a small part of the Palestinian clientele of Anna Loulou does come from Jaffa, the great majority were born and raised in the predominantly Arab Galilee and Triangle regions and only recently moved to Jaffa to pursue their studies or employment opportunities. Distinguished from the Jaffan community by their relatively better economic and educational background, these Palestinian newcomers can afford the rising rent prices in the city and thus consume the "fruits of gentrification." At the same time, however, their very presence marks Anna Loulou as a site of authentic alterity, in the process increasing its appeal to radical Jewish gentrifiers. Finally there is what Niv refers to as the occasional Jewish-Israeli "tourist" who comes to "see Arabs," but due to a lack of Orientalist signifiers (such as a distinct clothing style), oftentimes fails to single them out in the crowd. The binational spectacle thus works both ways, as Jewish Israelis explore a bar frequented by "Arabs" and Palestinians come to experience a liberating, cool, alternative scene. The conscious re-Orientalizing of internal design, music, and ambiance serves as the place's mark of authenticity.

The sight of a largely Jewish crowd "belly dancing" to the tackiest Arab pop songs does occasionally prompt a segment of the Arab audience to smirk. Similarly, the fact that most of the Israeli customers do not understand the lyrics, and at times unknowingly move their bodies to music that references a future Palestinian victory over the Jewish colonizer, seems quite comical to some Palestinian observers. Notwithstanding the peaceful multinational atmosphere of Anna Loulou, some Palestinian resentment persists there, as illustrated on the bathroom walls, where a small graffiti in Arabic makes clear that despite a Jewish presence, Jaffa remains a Palestinian city.

On other nights, headed by Eyal Bizawe, an Israeli Jew of Egyptian descent and a scholar and DJ, contemporary Mizrahi pop is blended with Turkish psychedelia from the sixties and Greek rebetiko classics, while an Egyptian film from the seventies is projected on a wall. The musical mix clearly celebrates Israel's subaltern identities, while at the same time reinserting the hyphen between the categories of Arab and Jew, otherwise a well-established oxymoron in the hegemonic Zionist discourse (Shenhav 2006).

Transcending the politics of borders and checkpoints, the situational voluntary sociality of Jews and Arabs creates surreal moments of utopian translocal connectivity. Listening and dancing to a recent version of "Wen 3a Ramallah" (Where are you going? To Ramallah), a popular Palestinian song of longing and return, enables a shared affective experience of a cosmopolitan Jaffa, forming an integral part of the Arab Middle East. Thus a liminoid sense of communitas (Turner 1975) instills nostalgia for a place that no one in the crowd has ever experienced, an imaginary place that stands in diametric opposition to the current political climate, where residents of Ramallah and Jaffa, Israelis and Palestinians, are legally restricted from visiting each other. But through the upsurge in new forms of social media, which connect like-minded people in Beirut, Damascus, Cairo, and Tel-Aviv, contemporary Arabic music becomes accessible, and the utopian open Middle East becomes more tangible, at least for a moment.

Notwithstanding wishful thinking, some activists do hope that there will be an additional effect to this affective experience, namely, the slow emergence of a progressive community which will speak out against the separation regime. Such is the belief, and one of the main goals, of 7arakeh Fawreyeh (Arabic for "immediate action"), a benefit held by a group of Jewish-Israeli and Palestinian artists and activists, most of whom first met at Anna Loulou. A manifesto composed by the founding members and published in 2012 reads,

> The movement was established in order to create an alternative reality to the Israeli separation regime: an art community that works together to oppose the unjust actions and exploitation of the regime, through the creation of beauty, inspiration, and meaning. No more resistance for the sake of resistance—we ourselves are here to create the future that we believe we are worthy and capable of! . . . The creation of intimate and natural closeness between the activist community, the artists, and the participants of the event, through the recognition that we are all in the same space, listening to the same music, observing the same art, and part of the same struggle—that's how we imagine and create a new community that we believe can generate a deep political change.

In addition to organizing "music, art, and cultural events," the movement seeks to formulate a new political language and new modes of political action in order to challenge state policies. According to Eyal, one of the founding members of 7arakeh Fawreyeh, the traditional left reiterates and reproduces the language of separation, which constitutes resistance as an end in itself ("No more resistance for the sake of resistance"). Through art activism, 7arakeh Fawreyeh tries to reach and involve the mainstream. "We are like a Trojan Horse," Eyal explains. "We organize events that are hip and sexy, and at the same time we inform the audience about political issues."

By rebranding Palestinian urban culture, 7arakeh Fawreyeh contributes to a growing alternative transurban subculture that is putting places like Jaffa back on the map of Palestinian cities. Viewed from within this network, Jaffa is no longer a spatially bounded and economically defined ghetto. "Jaffa is not a hood anymore," Anna Loulou resident DJ Muhammad Jabali (originally from Taybeh) says. "You cannot look at it without looking at the same time at places like Haifa and Nazareth." The influx of Palestinian gentrifiers, young professionals, students, and artists, though not always welcome by the more conservative strata of Palestinian society, clearly contributes to the cultural and economic diversification of the Palestinian community in Jaffa. Palestinian students, many of whom moved to the city from the north of the country, considerably strengthened the circles of young Jaffan activists. By organizing vigils and protests around issues such as prisoner hunger strikes, the Jaffan Youth Movement (Al-Shabiba al-Yafiyya) thus managed to become one of the most vocal and visible political forces within the community.

At the same time, due to the renewed interest in Jaffa, Muhammad observes that "Jaffa is moving back north." Centered since 1948 in the 'Ajami neighborhood, Palestinian-owned businesses, such as the restaurant Haj Kheil or the Hinnawi chain, started opening branches in the north of Jaffa, in spaces that were until recently seen as lost to the Palestinian community. And yet, one of the main factors distinguishing Jaffa from cities such as Haifa remains the relative lack of Palestinian ownership and investment in culture. The question of who is running a place is essential to the definition of space, Muhammad concludes.

While still focusing on their work of promoting the "acknowledgment of the ongoing Nakba" among Jewish Israelis, the organization Zochrot (Remembering) also increasingly addresses themes relating to the return of the refugees. Similarly, Jaffa 2030 Visitor Center, an initiative organized by Autobiography of a City in 2012, declared its intention to "try and flame the imagination of the city as part of a vivid Arab World surrounding, illustrating how reconciling the urban space is not only a way to deal with the past, but more, a major tool for planning the future," and invited its audience to "visit a city we don't live in still, but we should ask ourselves how we might." It further announced that Jaffa 2030 "will try to actively imagine Jaffa's near future as a cosmopolitan city that gives answer to Israeli populations that are constantly excluded from the cultural hegemony, that can confront the historical-autobiographical fraction line that took place in the urban space in 1948, and that holds daily connections to other regional cities through a Mediterranean transportation network between Beirut, Cairo, Damascus, Amman, Tunise, Barcelona, Marseilles and the ports of Italy, Greece and Turkey."[47]

Located at the Arab-Hebrew Saraya Theater in Jaffa, the event featured a gallery displaying the works of mainly Palestinian artists; an information stand providing instructional maps, postcards, and guided tours of the city; an open-air cinema; and music shows; and concluded with a party organized by 7arakeh Fawreyeh. While the event brought together a broad audience, mostly Israeli Jews but also Palestinians from Jaffa and beyond, it was also criticized by some activists, who denounced it for being funded by the Tel-Aviv-Jaffa Municipality, and thus for whitewashing the image of a state institution implicated in discriminatory policies against the Jaffa community.

From Yafa Café to Salma Café: A Palestinian Hangout

In 2009, the owners of Yafa Café, described in chapter 2, split up. Michel kept the place and in 2010 Dina proceeded to open another space—Dina Café—on Yehuda Hayamit Street, one of Jaffa's central avenues leading to the port. Dina held onto the café, labeled "the café of utmost coexistence" by the Israeli *Time Out* magazine, and tried to maintain its spirit by organizing cultural events, Arabic courses, and political lectures, until she succumbed to cancer in 2012.[48] Yafa Café's popularity, in turn, decreased considerably with the emergence of other cultural venues. It is still a place where older members of the Jaffan community have their coffee and a chat, yet its appeal to the younger activists has waned. The emergence of hipper alternative places, as an unintended consequence of Jaffa's gentrification, has undoubtedly contributed to the decline of Yafa Café's popularity.

After Dina Lee's passing in 2012, two Palestinians from Jaffa bought her place and gave it a new name and identity: Salma Café. Given the potential of its location on Yehuda Hayamit Street, lined with beautiful old buildings—the ground floors of some were already turned into coffeehouses—and opposite a vegan-friendly bakery, an organic store, and a pizza place, Salma Café was from the outset thought of as a real estate investment. Not much care was given to the interior design, or to the creation of a comfortable atmosphere, both of which had characterized Dina Café, yet the place was soon branded a Palestinian hangout, and due to the presence of known local activists its popularity and real estate value rose steadily.

A mere two months after it opened, the new owners sold the place again for a much higher price, this time to a Palestinian entrepreneur from the Triangle region, who regifted it to his then fiancé. Under this new manager—Ibrahim, known to his friends as Buddha, a young Palestinian from the Galilee who is very involved in both the Tel-Aviv and the Jaffa cultural and party scenes—the place slowly changed. Iconic political art was put up on the walls, and the Ikea-type furniture was replaced by a conglomerate of different retro furniture, reminiscent of a hip café in Berlin. The place appealed not only to the binational activist community, who would come there to hold meetings as well as to spend their leisure time, but also to the emergent group of apolitical Jewish hipsters. In a way, Salma managed to become what Yafa Café could never be: a Palestinian-owned popular activist hangout for both Palestinians and Jewish Israelis, and a location for cultural events such as live Arabic music performances. Curiously, at the peak of its success, the owner apparently broke up with his fiancé and was no longer interested in keeping the place, and it was sold yet again. While still keeping its old name, Salma effectively disappeared.

SITUATIONAL RADICALISM AND THE LIMITS OF UNRULY POLITICS

In a series of articles entitled "Jaffa as Is: People among the Ruins," published in the aftermath of the 1948 War, a section titled "Arab Jaffa 'Occupied'" describes the pre-1948 consumer practices between the two rival cities:

> Twice a year was Jaffa "occupied" by the residents of Tel-Aviv, who would "sail" southbound. This would happen during the holidays. During Passover Jaffa would bustle with Jewish holiday shoppers in search of bread, and on Yom Kippur with people looking for a hearty meal. Then, on Yom Kippur, Jaffa's cafés would be filled with Jewish customers, who would chew on kebab and shishlik with a post-fasting appetite. It was a day of great profit for the Jaffa residents, who would eagerly await this annual Jewish prosperity day. Today when you make your way to Jaffa, you feel no real difference between the two cities, which became one.[49]

Despite the author's relegation of the "occupation" of Jewish customers to the pre-1948 past, more then sixty years after the annexation of Jaffa to Tel-Aviv and the exile of the Palestinian population, Jaffa continues to fill the function of Tel-Aviv's shabbes goy. Every Saturday, on the Jewish Sabbath, thousands of secular Jews flock to Jaffa to consume its commodified alterity. In public discourse, this pattern of economic interdependence is framed in cultural terms. Jaffa is seen as an Oriental space of gastronomic and lifestyle authenticity—a notion nurtured by Palestinian merchants and rejected by political activists. The Orientalized foodscape in Jaffa includes Narguileh cafés, street food vendors, restaurants specializing in Arab and Mediterranean cuisine, pastry shops, gelaterias, and most notably bakeries and hummus joints (Hirsch 2011). However, this phenomenon is not limited to economic reciprocity and conspicuous consumption. Rather, it has been a part of a larger system of interactions which have included "violent pastimes" (Carter 2004). In the landscape of my childhood, Palestinian Jaffans were participating in Jewish holidays such as Yom Kippur and Lag BaOmer, but mainly in a negative sense of subverting social order and normative temporality. Carnivalesque rituals of destruction included youngsters cutting down electricity poles to block roads, throwing stones at vehicles passing by, and lighting extended bonfires in public spaces. These rites of combustion, however, were not only "acts of resistance" against the dominant structure of power, but also a form of interaction and ludic participation (Simmel [1908] 1971). Rather than instantiating a nonrelation between sworn enemies, these behaviors displayed an ambivalent relation vis-à-vis the Jewish majority and the imagination of the state.

Since the advent of neoliberal urbanism and gentrification in the 1980s, this pattern has been gradually politicized and increasingly contested. To be sure, local entrepreneurs and Jewish customers alike continue to view Jaffa as a space of Oriental authenticity, mainly in the fields of culinary culture and real estate. Thus the Andromeda Hill gated community still invites wealthy Jews and foreign investors to "liv[e] an original" in "the New-Old Jaffa." Likewise, the *Hummus Blog* states, "Jaffa, an ancient town with a glorious history, turned into a unique culinary gem. Packed with gourmet restaurants and boutique eateries, yet many flock to Jaffa for one reason: Abu Hassan's hummus."[50] Of late, the Oriental commodification of Jaffa as a benign space of folklore and gastronomic consumption has been disavowed by younger Palestinian generations. Resisting the "hummus invasion," antigentrification activists urge, "Visit Huldai's backyard. For Jaffa is more than just Hummus."[51] This critique was only amplified in the aftermath of the 2011 protests.

Emerging from the same post-Intifada field of radical activism described above, the hip-hop ensemble System Ali seeks to formulate a "vernacular Jaffan language." Conceptualized as a "sound box," the mixed city thus emerges as a space of cultural resonance fused with pain: "The fragments of innumerable tunes and songs, stories and legends, tongues and dialects reverberate in its belly, seep into its life and generate its creations.

And the heavy hand of the past continues to strum the chords of Jaffa's present, with fingers that are well acquainted with the scale along which the city's painful refrain slowly ascends . . . a thin seam that runs among the patchwork neighborhoods, languages and historical narratives that make up contemporary Jaffa" (Granowsky, Kunda, and Weter 2009, 9).

Jaffa's transition from the center of the Palestinian national project to the margins of the Jewish metropolis exacerbates the difficulty its residents have in articulating the city's language, namely, the symbolic code that mediates one's experience of place. Reflecting this predicament, initiatives like System Ali, Anna Loulou, Yafa Café, Autobiography of a City, and Salma Café are all grappling with questions of language, recognition, and historical justice. Notwithstanding their revolutionary intentions and postnational frames of reference, Palestinian and Israeli members of Generation Y are disillusioned with party politics and failed mass mobilization. Searching for new modes of political action, they displace their creative energies onto the sphere of art and political activism (a.k.a. "artivism")—which bespeaks radical politics but is distinguished from it. How can we qualify these modalities of political action? Can the alternative scene in Jaffa propose a revisionist radical agenda?

The last two serious attempts at mass politics—the 2007 campaign against house evictions and the 2011 social justice protests launched in the aftermath of the Arab Spring—eventually failed to bring about the desired social change in the power structure. In both cases radicalism remained situational in scope and limited in effect—a far cry from the historic events they sought to become. This failure rested on a persistent inability to formulate an efficacious definition of politics, peoplehood, and power. The two facets of politics stressed on the one hand by Rancière (2001), who argued that "politics is a specific rupture in the logic of power (arche)," and on the other hand by Badiou (2011, 73), who posited that "politics is of the masses," illustrate the conundrum of alternative culture in Jaffa. Trapped between two notions of politics—as symbolic rupture and alternatively as collective action—artivism is an exciting form of "unruly politics" (Khanna 2012; Shankland et al. 2011),[52] yet one whose long-lasting potential for change remains unfulfilled. Proposing "to create an alternative reality to the Israeli separation regime," artivists situate their action in the "creation of beauty, inspiration and meaning."[53] Chained to the field of consumption and the logic of the market, these initiatives eventually conform to the neoliberal order by replacing struggle with utopia. Creative marginality thus springs from the double edge of the nationalist and capitalist order and its history of creative destruction (Harvey 1991).

Whether the alternative scene can redefine political subjectivity and facilitate what Badiou terms the "rupture with oneself," i.e., the unveiling of the workings of power and privilege, remains an open question. By celebrating alterity and projecting binational utopias, these initiatives run the risk of being co-opted by the discourse of *coexistence,* which normalizes the status quo, rather than bringing about *coresistance.* Jaffa's oppositional groups, be they Jewish or Arab, are thus situationally "empowered to organize in place, but disempowered when it comes to organizing over space" (Harvey 1991, 303). Their predicament reflects the larger powerlessness of counterhegemonic movements in Israel/Palestine, yet under current conditions the very act of imagining a different (postnational) world is already a significant achievement.

The City of the Forking Paths

Imagining the Futures of
Binational Urbanism

This land is a traitor
and can't be trusted.
This land doesn't remember love.
This land is a whore
holding out a hand to the years,
as it manages a ballroom
on the barber pier....
It laughs in every language
and bit by bit, with its hip,
feeds all who come to it.

—TAHA MUHAMMAD ALI, "Ambergris"

A land that devours its inhabitants
And flows with milk and honey and blue skies
Sometimes itself stoops to plunder
The sheep of the poor.

—NATAN YONATHAN, "A Song to the Land"

A LAND THAT DEVOURS ITS INHABITANTS

In the agonistic landscape of Israel/Palestine, no place has been more continuously inflected by the tension between intimate proximity and visceral violence than ethnically "mixed" towns. The immanent ambivalence of the binational encounter bespeaks the paradox of the copresence of political Others who are also immediate neighbors. This book

has proposed a historical ethnography of binational urbanism by scru-
tinizing sites of daily interaction and ongoing conflict in contested urban spaces since 1948. Recapturing the *longue durée* of ethnic mix in the
Mediterranean, the Ottoman legacy of confessional sectarianism, and
the enduring effect of British colonial rule, I have conceptualized the
intricate relations between ethnicity, capital, and binational sociality in
these cities and beyond.

The poet Taha Muhammad Ali (1931–2011), an internal refugee who
was never allowed back to his native village, posits the core concept
of territorial nationalism not as an object of yearning but as treacherous
trickster. Echoing the biblical verse "a land that devours its inhabitants"
(Numbers 13:32), this poetic intervention stands in diametric opposition
to dominant Palestinian and Israeli popular cultures which only rarely
address the theme of the "corrupt land" (*ha-adama mequlqelet*).[1] The
nationalist discourse that had constructed the land as a hallowed site
of redemption has made the city into a metonymy of the nation and the
state (Tel-Aviv, "the city that begat a state"; and Jaffa, the Bride of Palestine). However, harnessing the fortunes of the national project to the fate
of the city constitutes a risk, because the latter might not comply with the
dictates of the nation-state. As Simmel ([1908] 1971) and Bauman (1999b)
have shown, the ambivalence toward the loci of modernity is inherent to
urban spaces due to their destructive order and creative chaos. In ethnically "mixed" towns, this tension is both a marker of national tragedy
and constitutive of a subversive urban subculture. In such a potentially
explosive context, cities play a pivotal role in both escalating political
violence and enabling historical reconciliation.

A friction point between the "big place" of territorial mythology and
the "small place" of thin locality (Gurevitch and Aran 1994), between *Sumud* (with a capital "S") and *sumud* (with a lowercase "s"), and between
the time of the state and the rhythm of the city, Jaffa challenges the dichotomies which reproduce the Palestinian-Israeli conflict as a zero-
sum game: indigenous versus immigrants, colonizers versus colonized,
perpetrators versus victims. On the fringes of the hegemonic settlement
project and on the margins of social order, the mixed city brings about
alternative notions of urban agency, which comply not with the precepts
of ethnonational mythology but with the pragmatic necessities of com-

munal survival, social exchange, and spatial cohabitation. By facilitating life on the edge, the tension between nationalist binaries is paradoxically socially productive. As Harms (2011, 223) notes, "Binary categories enable people to craft spaces of the meaningful social action within which they can carve out opportunities in their lives. . . . People on the edge are surprisingly active in the production of the risk-taking social edginess. Edginess often puts these same residents on the cutting edge of opportunity as well. They are not wholly disenfranchised but often find meaningful potential in the spaces that lie between official categories. Life outside the gaze of state power can be refreshingly liberating." The counterintuitive realities of everyday life in the binational border zone illustrate the dialectic between dismal political exclusion and creative urban agency. The violence of pluralism on the metropolitan edge fuels a habitual state of exception.

I have argued for viewing the dangerous liaisons of urban cohabitation between Jews and Palestinians in a relational framework. From this inquiry, mixed towns emerge as a challenge to the hegemonic ethnonationalist guiding principles of the Israeli state, which attempts but fails to maintain homogeneous, segregated, and ethnically stable spaces. This failure results in the parallel existence of heteronomous spaces in these towns, which operate through multiple and often contradictory logics of space, class, and nation. Analyzed relationally, these spaces produce peculiar forms of quotidian social relations between Palestinians and Israelis, enacting in the process circumstantial coalitions and local identities that reconfigure both Palestinian and Jewish nationalisms. Engaging the politics of gentrification, formations of violence, and collective memory, these dynamics unmask the multiple facets of "contrived coexistence."

A critical ethnography of the binational urban encounter requires a recalibration of categories of social analysis in order to "represent incoherence rather than write over it with a neater story we wish to tell" (Stoler 1992, 154). Viewed from the vantage point of urban alterity, Jaffa's history replays a series of hegemonic and counterhegemonic projects that attempt to instantiate in different ways a linear logic of reification, be it Judaization or Palestinianization. Against this superimposed logic, the chronicle of Jaffa manifests the gradual collapse of these projects of purification and their historical casting. Seen up-close as a "scale question" (Brenner 2000), the mixed city is "a mediation among mediations" (Lefebvre 1996, 101), but one that disrupts the sequential mediation between the urban and the national scale, and assumes its identity by the act of disrupting. Against the ethnocratic rationality of the state (its *raison d'état*) rebels an alternative relational rationality of the urban scale. From this ongoing struggle—played out in the interaction between scales of action and rule—emerges Jaffa *sui generis*, shared and shattered. This book has sought to foreground these constitutive contradictions, and to provide the analytic vocabulary needed to theorize the process by which a historical anomaly becomes probable, and the social improbability reasonable.

The emblematic relations between mixed cities and the state point to the radical challenge that mixed cities pose to the national order of things by their very existence. Everyday binationality is far more ominous than any abstract theoretical experiment or political musing might be. Thus in a call to "settle Jaffa, Acre, Lod and Ramle," one prominent right-wing journalist has bemoaned that "Israel, as the state of the Jewish people, is losing its grip on these cities."[2] Ironically, the author seems to be correct in his analysis and has good reasons to worry about the viability of his nationalist dreams and demographic nightmares. The recent arson attack on a bilingual Jewish-Arab school, which left behind the haunting graffiti "No coexistence with cancer," serves as another reminder of the potentially explosive implications of ethnic mix. For the agents of predatory nationalism this amounts to no less than a terminal anomaly ("cancer").[3] Finally, the intermarriage between Mahmoud and Moral from Jaffa at the height of Israel's latest war on Gaza assumed an iconic status in public discourse, provoking heated debates and violent demonstrations and counterdemonstrations over the future of the Jewish state, religious purity, assimilation, and coexistence.[4] That Moral's father vocally opposed the union and refused to attend the ceremony, and that Mahmoud was arrested two months after the wedding for drug trafficking and assaulting a police officer, encapsulates the tragic enigma that is Jaffa.

The critique of ideologically motivated scholarship and "methodological nationalism" de-reifies sociological concepts such as "ethnic communities" and normative concepts such as "coexistence" by tracing the ways they have been used across different geopolitical epochs and politicoeconomic regimes. Similarly, neoliberalism and its implications for urban restructuring and class segregation illuminate the relation between historical continuity and rupture. By zooming in on the practicalities of daily life, local debates on questions of affordable housing, sustainable development, and the politics of affect are turned into matters of public concern.

Since 1948, Jaffa has witnessed the rise and fall of different communal and state-initiated projects. Instead of establishing coherence and continuity, these projects have paradoxically motivated an unruly array of actors to try to make sense of the city and recreate it in their own image. They include the Islamic Movement, radical gentrifiers, and utopian artivists. In the face of longstanding political stalemate, they exhibit new ways of thinking about urban conflicts, indigenousness, and the future of binationalism.

A relational historical approach to Jewish and Arab communal histories, proposes Lockman in *Comrades and Enemies* (1996, 9), "does not focus exclusively on either the Arab or the Jewish community or treat them as if they were entirely self-contained and isolated entities. Instead it explores their mutually formative interactions, how they shaped one another in complex ways and at many levels." Relational analysis also seeks to explore "how each was shaped by the larger processes by which both were affected" (8). While it refers to the understanding of labor history in Mandatory Palestine, this approach is even more urgent in the study of the triadic relations between the Palestinian citizens of Israel, its Jewish majority, and the Israeli state. It problematizes the vertical mediation among ethnic communities, nation, and state by calling attention to the horizontal networks of exchange, reciprocity, and dependency cutting across communities and institutions. The attempt by Palestinian politicians to solicit the support of voting gentrifiers for the Yafa List, the coalition between the Jaffa Palestinians and Hatikva activists, and the history of the Andromeda Hill gated community are notable examples of how a relational analysis might provide a richer understanding of this loaded landscape than top-down narratives of the implementation of linear projects might.

Jaffa is a meeting point between institutional and communal vectors constituting three distinct collective agents: the lower-class Jews, the gentrifiers, and the Palestinian population (which is subdivided along class and religious lines but follows a stronger communal ethnic logic).[5] About the size of an average neighborhood in Chicago, Jaffa localizes forces that are linked to macro structures of powers, national ideologies, and state institutions. While the state functions as the "far order," the municipality mediates the urban "near order" (Lefebvre 1996), thus operating as the local institutional frame of reference. Competing over access to government resources, the three groups are collectively and historically defined by their relation to the municipality.

As we have seen, the municipality has changed from a modernistic ethnocratic regime (1948–1985) to a neoliberal one. Accordingly, the different communal logics and courses of action have also changed. While the Jewish community started in the 1950s as a rising and energetic working-class immigrant settlement, it soon dissolved and is now faced with an aging and underprivileged population. Denied the dividends of "urban development," its main efforts center on the preservation of Jewish presence in the now mixed eastern Heart of Jaffa neighborhood, where Palestinians have been increasingly visible. For their part, the gentrifiers, a recent and much smaller group, have shown a superior ability to utilize their professional and social capital to promote the transformation of Jaffa into a bourgeois living space. Finally, the Palestinians, emerging devastated from the Nakba, have focused their efforts on building a viable community and on developing an active civil society. Increasingly divided from within, they struggle to meet the needs of the community in terms of education, employment, and housing. Consequently, each communal logic has constituted a different kind of relation with the city and the state: local collaboration mixed with resentment in the case of the veteran Jewish community; strategic and principled coalition in the case of the gentrifiers; and control, co-optation, and resistance between the municipality and the Arab population and its representatives. The co-optation of the Islamic Council by the mayor and the divisive yet persistent attempts by the Palestinian representatives to organize as a political community fuel ongoing debates over the future of Israelization, autonomy, and recognition.[6]

Within the communities themselves, these logics trigger circumstantial coalitions as well as struggles over resources. Such interactions are rendered visible in local cross-communal protests, such as the Jaffa Slope petition to the Supreme Court in the 1980s and the struggle for housing in 2011. Thus the candidacy of the Yafa List for the City Council—and its failure—cannot be understood without taking into consideration the coalitions and involvement with Jewish groups and individuals. Notwithstanding their economic disadvantages and educational predicament, the Jaffa Palestinians are not confined to a communal "ghetto"; rather, they actively interact with the Jewish local educational systems, urban economy, and grassroots activism. As we have seen in the description of the population movements in Jaffa, residential patterns also exhibit a clear trend of demographic interpermeation and ethnic mix both in 'Ajami and mainly in the Jerusalem Boulevard area (the Heart of Jaffa). Jaffa therefore should be understood as a dynamic relational field of institutional, communal, and individual interactions and networks creating both situational dissent and consent. Instead of generating segregated communities, these processes produce *ipso facto* Arab spaces within Jewish ones and Palestinian spaces within Israeli ones. Such a view does not overlook the socioeconomic reproduction of Palestinian disenfranchisement; rather, it refines our ability to understand potential change and explain the inherent paradoxes of the urban system.

Scrutinized relationally rather than separately, territorial ideologies loom large in the cultural imagination of the city. In the process of their implementation, however, a denaturalizing effect has accrued over time and generations. As shown in the encounter between the diasporic Palestinian image of Jaffa and the actual residents of the city, the denaturalization of ideologies vex the coherent and stable image of the city. This narrative incoherence by no means erases the structural inequality between Jews and Palestinians in Jaffa, nor does it alleviate Palestinian suffering or discrimination. Rather, it calls our attention to their sense of entrapment. Defined as a measure of historical entropy and cultural incompleteness of national narratives, that systemic indeterminacy in both Palestinian and Israeli visions of Jaffa destabilizes monologic constructions of the mixed city. For both the Jewish Orientalist imagining of Jaffa (oscillating between historicity and violence) and the Palestinian construction of the city (trapped between nostalgia and critical counternostalgia) Jaffa

poses a yet-unresolved hermeneutic problem. Making virtue of necessity, actors who disavow the national reification project, such as System
Ali, filmmaker Scandar Copti, members of the alternative scene at large,
and not least ordinary citizens, articulate the heteroglossia of the mixed
city by containing incoherence without seeking to conceal, wash over,
or resolve its contradictions. From this perspective, the urban can be
reassembled out of the relations between the residues of reified subjects.
The collapse of projects of purification gives rise to Jaffa as we know it—
an emblem of contrived coexistence and a living tragedy, the "museum
of the Nakba" and the future of the region at one and the same time.

BEYOND JAFFA: DISMANTLING URBAN ARCHETYPES

Identifying ethnonational mixed towns as a category for social scientific
scrutiny points to urban sites that challenge the premises of methodological nationalism.[7] Thus rather than circumscribed localities, which
project the logic of the modern state on the urban scale, mixed towns can
be characterized as historically situated sociospatial configurations that
evolved from *millet*-based ethnoconfessional communities to modern
nation-based spaces (Rabinowitz and Monterescu 2008). Under Ottoman, British, and Israeli rule, they gradually emerged as a distinct city
form which simultaneously symbolizes and reproduces dialectic urban
encounters and conflicts.

Extending beyond the specificities of Jaffa, the relational reframing
of Jewish-Arab mixed towns revisits three substantialist images of the
Middle Eastern city prevalent in urban studies: the colonial city, the
divided city, and the dual city. These tropes are not merely popular and
politically efficacious metaphors of racial segregation, ethnic violence,
nationalist struggle, and class division—they also serve as sociological ideal types and geographical models underwriting urban analysis.[8]
Despite their widespread currency in urban theory, each model eventually falls into the trap of reifying relations of ethnic domination, spatial
demarcation, or class divisions.

The classical model of the colonial city has been a major gatekeeping
concept in such analyses. Following Fanon's foundational work on Algiers, urban colonialism has since been viewed through the Manichean

divide between citizens and subjects, Europeans and natives, colonizers and colonized.[9] Colonial demarcations between the (Arab) native town and the (European) *ville nouvelle* signified the superiority of Western modernity and, concomitantly, the absence—perhaps even improbability—of non-European modernities. The colonial city was thus only nominally one city, while in fact it constituted two radically different life worlds and social temporalities.

The violent climate surrounding Arab-Jewish urban relations since the advent of Zionism may induce observer and participant alike to subscribe to a classical colonial paradigm à la Fanon. While this may be an appropriate description of the relation between Jewish settlements and Palestinian towns in the West Bank and Gaza, the configurations of citizenship in mixed towns inside Israel, and in particular the presence of Palestinian citizens within them, complicate this political and theoretical perspective.Urban mix in Jaffa, Haifa, Acre, Lydda, and Ramle presents a historical and sociological context which no longer corresponds to Fanon's "world cut in two" (1963, 29). By posing a theoretical challenge to this idealized polarized dichotomy whereby divisions and frontiers are "shown by barracks and police stations" (ibid.), ethnically mixed towns call for refinements of these analytical tools.

To be sure, the history of ethnically mixed towns in Israel/Palestine since the sixteenth century is an obvious manifestation of the power of urban colonialism and its vicissitudes in the Levant. In the wake of Ottoman rule and throughout the twentieth century, the powerful intervention of European planning ideologies and Zionist projects of territorial expansion resulted in an urban regime that geographers Yiftachel and Yacobi have termed "urban ethnocracy" (2003). In their analysis of Lydda/Lod, they argue that this regime of governmental power and ethnic control is notably predicated on the radical division of urban space between the affluent and politically dominant Jewish settlers and the weakened Palestinian community, which is systematically barred from access to land reserves, economic resources, and circles of policymaking.

While I propose a relational reading of ethnically mixed towns in Israel, such a reading is by no means meant to overwrite Palestine's colonial history. In fact it proposes precisely the opposite: while drawing on urban colonialism as its point of departure, it reveals "the fissures and contradictions" of such projects (Ouzgane and Coleman 1998). Mixed towns are exemplary sites where colonial regimes played their most radical role. Nevertheless, it is also there that they (fortunately) failed in their attempt to instigate and to sustain a stable regime of complete ethnic separation. While such attempts at ethnic dichotomization were effective in terms of residential segregation in some cities, when it came to other aspects of urban synergy, they were often subverted by external resistance and internal failures. Taking these as the objects of elaboration for anthropological and historical scrutiny, my intervention problematizes such linear and functionalist geographical trajectories.

A major case in point is historian Mark LeVine's (2005) characterization of Tel-Aviv as a colonial city which appropriated and dispossessed Arab Jaffa of its land, culture, and history. While this was certainly the case for the first half of the twentieth century, the classic colonial city model subsequently ceased to provide a nuanced analytical framework. The victory of the Zionist forces and the ensuing Palestinian tragedy of the Nakba in 1948 rocked the foundations of the social and political system in Palestine and gave rise to a new political subject—the Palestinian citizens of Israel. Henceforth, despite state-funded projects of Judaization, unbreakable glass ceilings, and limited mobility, Palestinians in mixed towns nevertheless chose to participate in the politics of citizenship. Thus, while Palestinian towns in the Occupied Territories, such as Ramallah, Nablus, or Hebron, remain sharply colonized and cordoned-off by powerful external forces, Palestinian residents of mixed towns within Israel find themselves in a different predicament vis-à-vis the state.

Palestinian citizens of Israel tend to channel their resistance into party politics, civil society, and local-level (municipal) spheres, rather than into the politics of decolonization. While many of them do invoke narratives and images of colonization (Zureik 1979), these are better seen as the Mayday calls of disenfranchised citizens rather than as the collectively organized calls of a national liberation movement. A case in point is the eruption in 2000 of the second Palestinian uprising in Jerusalem, the Galilee, and the Occupied Territories. Triggering pan-Palestinian solidarity and frustration, it bred a momentary surge of heated demonstrations on the part of Palestinian residents in mixed towns and amplified those voices there that call for redefining Israeli citizenship to include Palestinian citizens more fully. Even these events, however, failed to mobilize urban Palestinians within Israel as long-term active participants in the national struggle (Rabinowitz and Abu-Baker 2005). In terms of patterns of political awareness and mobilization, then, mixed towns once again emerge as markedly distinct from colonial cities.[10] This contradiction was best described by sociologist Baruch Kimmerling (2001, 8) in the aftermath of the October Events: "The blunt, violent way that the Arabs claim their civil rights only attest to the growing integration in the state, rather than their wish to secede from it."

Urban colonialism in mixed towns has worked in different ways from Ottoman rule through British administration and ending with the Israeli state. Except for moments of radical confrontation (e.g., in 1936 or 1948), these cities, by virtue of economic exchange, commercial collaboration, and demographic interpermeation, persistently resisted the logic of colonial segregation. Even so, ethnographic sensibilities and historical inquiry should make us wary of treating mixed towns as one monolithic unit. In the case of contemporary Israel, for example, spatial segregation, ethnocratic control, capital accumulation, and political alliances vary considerably between Lydda/Lod, where indexes of segregation and poverty are the highest, and Jaffa and Haifa, which display more varied sociospatial patterns, with Haifa especially offering pockets of more equitable distribution of wealth and access to property, amenities, and political influence.[11] For cities like Haifa (where joint Jewish-Arab mayorship and administration persisted until 1948) and Jaffa (whose relations with Tel-Aviv, as LeVine shows, were nothing if not intertwined), the history of colonialism points also to its own political and conceptual limitations.

The divided city is the second powerful trope and urban archetype, one which conjures up slightly different images of separation walls, barbed wire, and police patrols (Low 1996). They evoke barriers of race, religion, and nationality, encoded in dualistic metaphors of East and West, uptown and downtown, North Side and South Side. Represented by archetypes such as Jerusalem, Nicosia, Berlin, and Belfast, these towns predominantly reproduce formal discrimination through differential entitlement to citizenship and planning rights. The status of East Jerusalem is perhaps the strongest case for distinguishing the divided city from the ethnically mixed town. In addition to the explicit project of Judaization, which is more implicit in mixed towns, post-1967 Jerusalemites are not Israeli citizens but merely permanent residents (Sorkin 2002).[12] The unabashed state violence that Palestinians encounter on a daily basis dissuades even the most optimistic activists and analysts from wishful thinking of equal footing and interaction.

This model, which had been readily available for urban theorists (from the Chicago School to contemporary urban studies), draws on what can be called the "segregation/integration" paradigm (Boal 1999; Bollens 2000; Harloe, Gordon, and Fainstein 1992; Low 2001; Marcuse 1993). Notwithstanding the often-illuminating data provided by these studies, they invariably rely, like the colonial city model, on two problematic epistemological and analytical assumptions: conceptual dualism and linearity. Based *a priori* on a dichotomous conceptual framework (inclusion/exclusion, integration/segregation, center/margins, order/disorder), this modernistic mode of theorizing (in both the conservative and radical camps) often leads to pre-given conclusions, typically reproducing the logic of its conceptual terminology.

A leading figure of the divided cities school, Fred Boal (1999) devised a classification system for the study of cities marked by ethnic differentiation which he designated the "Scenarios Approach," where a scenario is defined as an imagined set of ethnic circumstances in a particular city. It was argued that these cities display different modalities of the "urban ethnic spectrum," from assimilation through pluralism, segmentation, and polarization, all the way to cleansing. A quick indicative categorization would subsume U.S. cities of the early twentieth century under the label of assimilation; late twentieth-century Toronto under pluralism; the contemporary U.S. Black ghetto under segmentation; places like Jerusalem and Belfast under polarization; and Sarajevo in the early 1990s under cleansing. Within this simplified classification, Palestinian-Israeli mixed towns would probably straddle polarization (Lydda, Ramle), segmentation (Jaffa, Acre), and pluralism (Haifa).

Notwithstanding their importance, these models fail to address urban complexity, for they reproduce a linear conceptual framework, which describes ramified spaces by means of unidimensional concepts. While somewhat useful for a preliminary classification of cities, described in these models as unitary essences, this paradigm is of little value for in-depth historical analyses of specific cities or for an ethnographic under-standing of the fabric of social relations within urban spaces. Drawing on extreme cases of social exclusion, this substantialist conceptual lexi-con obscures triadic structures, circumstantial coalitions, and dialogic urban dynamics. To address this diachronic and synchronic variability, relational concepts such as spatial heteronomy and stranger relations pave the way for a multidimensional revision of sociospatial relations. The narratives of Jaffa's elderly as well as the initiatives that sprung up in the aftermath of the October 2000 events (such as Autobiography of a City and Yafa Café) illustrate these intricacies.

The third urban archetype I write against is the dual-city model. While the metaphor of duality has been applied to colonial cities and divided cities alike, it became associated within urban studies with economic restructuring and the vicissitudes of late capitalism. In an age of globalization and increasing disparities between global North and South, the notion of "duality," which theorizes the contemporary city as a site of unequal production of space, successfully captures the uneven nature of social and urban change (Bodnár 2007; Smith 1984). However, even in the context of advanced capitalism, where this concept emerged (Engels [1845] 1958; Marcuse 1989), Mollenkopf and Castells—editors of *Dual City* (1992)—conclude that the dual-city idiom is flawed. As Bodnár (2007, 5) aptly argues, "While there are powerful polarizing tendencies, dichotomies will not suffice: the intersections of class, race and gender inequalities are more complex."

The concept of urban duality is predicated on the primacy of capital-based dynamics and class structure, often at the expense of ethnic dy-namics, cultural exchange, and communal relations. Thus the dual-city paradigm often reduces multivaried urban differentiation to the duality of formal and informal labor, increased professionalization, and capital flows. This analytic weakness notwithstanding, in treating the period of decolonization in the Middle East, the dual-city approach has greatly contributed to the understanding of the agonistic transition from co-lonial occupation to postcolonial self-governance. In her *Rabat: Urban*

Apartheid in Morocco, Abu-Lughod (1980, 220) argues that the "caste cleavages" of social and spatial segregation the French had instituted in 1912 were progressively transformed by the late 1940s into a "complex but rigid system of class stratification along ethnic lines." This, however, was replaced in turn by systemic class-based residential separation, which emerged in the 1970s.[13]

In the context of ethnically mixed towns in Palestine/Israel, the tenacity of ethnonational conflict does not allow class to overwhelm or supersede ethnicity. In recent decades, the creeping neoliberalization of the Israeli economy in general, and real estate in particular, along with the emergence of a new Palestinian middle class and of growing numbers of young Palestinian professionals choosing to live in mixed towns, have introduced class into an already complicated urban matrix, which has consequently become more fragmented and diversified rather than simply dual. Thus, while gentrification in Jaffa clearly breeds class-based duality, it nevertheless creates circumstantial coalitions between Jewish gentrifiers and Palestinian capitalist agents and middle-class residents, which in turn undermine the scope of ethnic duality. It seems that the model of the dual city, as well as of the divided city or the colonial city, does little to provide an adequate framework for explaining and interpreting residential choices, urban planning dynamics, electoral coalitions, and urban violence in these towns.

"THE RIGHT OF RETURN TO OLD JAFFA"

While theoretically significant for revealing the dynamics of urban space and interethnic relations, studies of mixed towns can have political significance as well. More than half a century after the Nakba, the future of the Palestinian community in Israel remains an open wound and a sociopolitical enigma. Embodying both the impasse and the hope of minority-majority relations in Israel, mixed towns are likely to remain pivotal for the region's future. Highly sensitive to whatever course the conflict takes, but relatively independent of the uncertain state of Palestine (in the Occupied Territories), mixed towns will always be "sites of memory" (Nora 1989) of past glory and collective loss. In addition to bearing indelible traces and sediments of the conflict's history, they are also a pressing social problem in the present, to be settled within the confines of whatever "Israeli" society will come to be.

Genuinely trapped between state and nation (Rabinowitz 2001), between identification and alterity, and between past trauma and future normalization, mixed towns are in dire need of a workable framework of equal citizenship. To begin to resolve these problems and secure their future, Israelis and Palestinians alike will have to come to terms with their mutual interdependency and relationality. This is perhaps what Anton Shammas, the Palestinian writer who chose to write in Hebrew, meant in the sobering epilogue of an essay tellingly titled "The Morning After": "There is no political solution to the problem of the Palestinian citizens of Israel. There is only a cultural solution. Their political path to the warm embrace of the Palestinian people was blocked, way back, because they came in contact with one of the greatest blessings of this accursed century—the ability to see the Other from close up, the advantage of bifocal sight, the privileges of bilingualism, the pleasure of trespassing the boundary between two cultures. And a very personal recommendation—the future belongs to mixed marriages" (Shammas 1995, 31).

The extent to which this message subverts nationalism's canons of probability (Sternberg 1993) was made clear in the mobilization of the extreme right against Mahmoud and Moral's wedding, as well as the quick fate of the graffiti "Fuad Love OSNAT" posted on the walls of the Jabaliyye mosque and quickly removed. However, the same optimism regarding the possibility of border crossing and "bifocal sight" may also initiate a multiscalar conversation between the mixed city and its broad surroundings—the Levant, the Mediterranean, and the Arab world at large. This audacious challenge was in fact taken up by Jaffa's Anna Loulou artivists—the city's most utopian but also most daring imagining subjects.[14] The jinn released from the broken bottle of the political project also enabled one (Jewish) activist to coin what became the most powerful Palestinian call for justice. Bridging the national and the urban scale in one phrase repeated during the 2011 protests, the slogan called for "the Right of Return to Old Jaffa."

While this book has been organized according to a tripartite model linking the three moments of urban mix (spatial heteronomy, stranger sociality, and image indeterminacy), it can also be read as a story of meaningful dissolution of reification projects and the rise of relational rationality. When actors step out of the national exclusionary frames of reference, Jaffa stops being an "anomaly" (a cancer, the backyard of Tel-Aviv, the Palestinian slum, or paradise lost). It becomes instead an emblem of a potentially enabling environment—cosmopolitan and post-Orientalist for many, and radically postnational for some. For most actors, relationality is a fact of life. For others it is a vocation. Rather than an exception to the Levantine *longue durée* of segmentary similarity through reciprocal difference, it actually resonates with Lefebvre's (1996, 233) insight that the state "always remains brutal and powerless, violent but weak, unifying but always undermined, under threat. . . . Every form of hegemony and homogeneity are refused in the Mediterranean." Reified by the state, the polysemic city operates between prenational, national, and postnational frames by alternately invoking cosmopolitan connectivity and political fragmentation. Like its immediate and regional "neighborhood," the mixed city is nothing but a relational system of reciprocal oppositions.[15]

Even if the immediate future of Israeli-Palestinian relations is premised on a logic of purification, the very survival and enduring vitality of mixed towns persistently reminds us that nationalistic attempts at effacing diversity and rewriting history in an effort to create a cityscape which is ethnically cleansed are bound to fail. Against all odds, mixed spaces and boundary-crossing sociality never succumb to homogenization. Consequently they signify alternative political imaginings of binationality, coexistence, and mutual recognition.[16] Scaling up cosmopolitan connectivity, artivists lead the expansion of the relational project—in both time and space. The transnational abstraction of Jaffa from a tragic residual exception to an emblem of an alternative possible future allows us to turn the standard scholarly model of the Palestinian-Israeli colonial encounter on its head, and suggests that to understand the conflict we need to start with the subaltern microscale where the local and national are most dramatically implicated. Provincializing state rationality, as it were, the futures of Israel/Palestine lie not in the extension of the settler colonial logic of separation and its political center (Jerusalem), but rather in the hybrid relationality of mixed spaces on the margins of the national project. In this respect we may conclude that

Israel/Palestine's alternative (yet potentially real) rationality is already embedded in Jaffa's relationality.

By way of a conclusion, a utopian literary analogy. In his famous story "The Garden of Forking Paths," Jorge Luis Borges develops a temporal epistemology in which the future is open-ended and the trajectories of time alternately converge and diverge. The protagonist wonders over a sentence he reads in a novel written by one of his ancestors: "I leave to several futures (not to all) my garden of forking paths." Just before being slain by the protagonist, the figure who devoted his life to the study of the novel, knowing what is about to happen and aware of his imminent death, suggests an interpretation of the sentence:

> The phrase "several futures (not all)" suggested to me the image of a forking in *time,* rather than in space. . . . Each time a man meets diverse alternatives, he chooses one and eliminates the others. . . . He *creates,* thereby, "several futures," several *times,* which themselves proliferate and fork. . . . *All* the outcomes in fact occur; each is the starting point for further bifurcations. Once in a while, the paths of the labyrinth converge: for example, you come to this house, but in one of the possible pasts you are my enemy, in another my friend. (Borges 1998, 125)

In Jaffa's historical labyrinth, the space of "possible pasts" collapsed to the specific trajectory in which the Jews and the Palestinians were indeed constituted as respective enemies. However, as we have seen, the city's inhabitants do not consider one another faceless enemies but rather pawns of larger historical powers who are contrived to live next to each other—agents of violent political forces, but not metonymic embodiments of dichotomies of oppressors and oppressed. The Jew for the Arab and the Palestinian for the Jew appear not as flat figures, as ultimate Others bereft of content and deprived of personal complexity, but rather as ambivalent "strangers." The view in "The Garden of Forking Paths" of an open-ended future is suggestive of a political epistemology which may bring hope and recognition to the future of relations between Jews and Palestinians in Jaffa and beyond. In the invisible future, their narratives may converge and create a shared future (and thus also a reconstructed past). This future may include a common memory and a story that neither overlooks the collective memory of the subaltern nor subjugates one story to the hegemony of the dominant narrative.

Anthropological research that challenges the reification of nationalist categories by tracking the dissolution of urban stereotypes can shed light on the workings of nationalism, class, and sociality in ways that make visible not only the symbolic and concrete walls of separation between Israeli and Palestinian citizens, but also a potential space of encounter. In the spirit of Edward Said's insightful quote that opened this book, a relational approach can turn the "sublime grandeur of a series of tragedies" into a program of action and a call for reconciliation. This path unfolds from Palestinian-Israeli poet Raja Natour's sober intervention (read during "an evening on poetry and Nakba"),[17] which frames the conflict as a looking glass of self and Other, where the possibility of direct speech and recognition is bound to the similarity between rivals:

> Talk to us
> Speak up
> When we shall look at you
> On a clear day and when the eyes will meet
> Pain will have a fresh edge
> How did we resemble ourselves when we left!!
> How did we resemble you when we did not return!!!
> How do we resemble all that remains!

NOTES

INTRODUCTION

1. Edward Said, "My Right of Return," *Ha'aretz*, August 18, 2000. See also Said (2007, 447).

2. In Jaffa, for instance, the Palestinian population of fifteen thousand constitutes about a third of the city's total population of forty-five thousand and altogether 5 percent of the Tel-Aviv-Jaffa metropolitan demographic composition (Tel-Aviv-Jaffa Municipality 2012). For a more detailed classification of different types of mixed towns, including "newly mixed towns" such as Natzerat Illit, Carmiel, Ma'alot-Tarshiha, Beer-sheba, and Hazor ha-Glilit, see Falah (1996) and Rabinowitz and Monterescu (2008, 212).

3. Addressing a similar problem in a different context, Ann Stoler analyzes conflicting reports by colonial officials. For Stoler, such an endeavor must address the following question: "How do we represent the incoherence rather than write over it with a neater story we wish to tell?" (Stoler 1992, 154).

4. The status of East Jerusalem is perhaps the strongest case for distinguishing the divided city from the ethnically mixed town. In addition to the explicit project of Judaization, which is more implicit in mixed towns, post-1967 Jerusalemites are not Israeli citizens but merely permanent residents. The unabashed state violence Palestinians encounter on a daily basis dissuades even the most optimistic activists and analysts from any wishful thinking about equal footing and interaction.

5. According to Golan (1999), Tel-Aviv grew into a small-sized town of fifteen thousand in 1921 and forty-six thousand in 1931. Urban growth accelerated in the 1930s with the growing numbers of Jews who fled Europe. In 1934 Tel-Aviv, at that point the largest city in Palestine, became formally independent from Jaffa, and in 1939 its population numbered about 130,000, rising to 166,000 in 1944. In parallel, Jaffa developed at a rapid but relatively slower pace. Its population, which numbered fifty thousand (including ten thousand Jews) in 1913, decreased by almost half during World War I and numbered thirty-two thousand (including five thousand Jews) in 1922. In the next decade, Jaffa's population nearly doubled, from fifty-one thousand (including seven thousand Jews) in 1931 to ninety-four thousand (including twenty-eight thousand Jews) in 1944. The significant increase in the number of Jews in Jaffa after the 1921 violent events resulted from the development of separate new neighborhoods (Florentin and Shapira) bordering Tel-Aviv's South Side.

6. The notion of Tel-Aviv as Jaffa's modern "daughter" is central to the Zionist discourse on the city. In his preface to Aricha's book on Jaffa, Mayor Haim Levanon refers to the conquest of Jaffa as the forced normalization of a mother-child relationship (Aricha 1957, 7). Quoting from the Bible, he writes, "Against its will, Jaffa exemplifies the verse 'He will turn the heart of the fathers to the children and the heart of the children to their fathers' (Malachi 3:24); the heart of the mother Jaffa—Ancient-new Hebrew Jaffa—turned to its daughter Tel-Aviv. And they became one, the city of Tel-Aviv-Jaffa, subject to one municipal authority." See also the discussion on the same topic in "Tel-Aviv and Only Tel-Aviv," *'Al ha-Mishmar,* October 21, 1949, 14.

7. Daniel Ben-Tal, "Old Jaffa Becoming the Darling of Real Estate Investors," *J., the Jewish News Weekly of Northern California,* May 26, 2006, http://www.jweekly.com /article/full/29413/old-jaffa-becoming-the-darling-of-real-estate-investors/. See also Mairav Zonszein, "Arabs and Jews Come Together to Oppose Gentrification in Jaffa," *+972 Magazine,* November 11, 2012, http://972mag.com/arabs-and-jews-come-together -to-oppose-gentrification-in-jaffa/59532/.

8. In addition to national organizations, the main local actors involved in this process are the Popular Committee for Land and Housing Rights, the Association for the Jaffa Arabs (Al-Rabita), and the Islamic Committee, as well as Palestinian youth groups (such as Al-Shabiba al-yafiyya), binational youth movements (e.g., Sadaqa/Reut—Arab-Jewish Partnership), and cultural initiatives such as Autobiography of a City and Yafa Café.

9. Palestinian citizens of Israel, most often referred to in Jewish-Israeli parlance as "Israeli Arabs" and "Arabs in Israel," are labeled by themselves and by other Arabs as the "Arabs of 1948" or "Arabs of the inside." For a comprehensive discussion of the politics of labeling this group, see Rabinowitz (1993).

10. An earlier definition using a three-pronged framework appeared in Monterescu (2005, 367–372).

11. *Madrikh Yafo* [The Jaffa guide] (Jaffa: Kanaf Press, 1949), 41.

12. What is commonly known in Israeli public discourse as the "October Events" or the "October Ignition" (*Habbat October* in Palestinian discourse) refers to the Palestinian mobilization in Israel in response to the breakout of the Al-Aqsa Intifada in the Palestinian Occupied Territories. The violent reaction of the police in the Galilee left thirteen Palestinians dead. In mixed towns, however, for different reasons, these events resulted in no fatalities.

13. Examples of such projects include Shatil's "Mixed Cities Project—Equal Access to Housing Rights," and various initiatives by the Arab Center for Alternative Planning.

14. Ori Nir and Lily Galili, "Mahanot ha-Plitim shel ha-'Arim ha-Yisraeliyot" [The refugee camps of Israeli towns], *Ha'aretz,* December 12, 2000.

15. This term was used a number of times by Palestinian speakers in public meetings and academic conferences I attended during fieldwork. The alternation between "targeted city" and "shared city" is often strategic. For example, during a meeting with potential donors from the Arab world, the term "targeted" will be employed, to underline that the Israeli majority and the state are a shared enemy of those seeking assistance and the potential donor. In contexts in which cooperation with Jews and Israeli institutions is the goal, "shared town" will be more likely to be used. For the notion of the shared city, see NGO New Horizon's project in Jaffa and Shatil's project on Haifa (Rosen 2012).

16. Lily Galili and Ori Nir, "One Fine Day Upper Nazareth Mayor Menachem Ariav Woke Up to Find That He Was the Mayor of a Mixed City," *Ha'aretz*, December 23, 2001, http://www.haaretz.com/print-edition/features/one-fine-day-1.78039.

17. See for instance Rosen (2012).

18. The term "implicate" denotes "enfolded inward" (Portugali 1993, xii), suggesting the enfoldment or imploding into each other of neighboring societies and the territories they inhabit. This notion suggests that the histories of Israelis and Palestinians, as societies and individuals, are not definable and cannot be understood independently of each other (39).

19. This section, which contains ideas first developed in Monterescu (2005), is largely based on Rabinowitz and Monterescu (2008, 195–196).

20. One example was a coproduction of Anna Loulou Bar and the Jaffa Project—Autobiography of a City, under the slogan "Music/Art/Struggle/Rave—Struggle for Home," organized by 7arakeh Fawreyeh (Arabic for "immediate action"). It took place in September 2012 at the Arab-Hebrew Saraya Theater (a.k.a. the Jaffa 2030 Visitor Center). The event advertised, "For one evening we will revive old city Jaffa from its constant death to a clear night, and to a bright imagined future that doesn't give up the connection with the surrounding Arab World. An Art and Music Movement aware [of] where it all started from, and . . . where we are all heading to." Its revenues were donated to cover the legal expenses of the Popular Committee for Land and Housing Rights in Jaffa. See the advertisement at https://www.facebook.com/events/443623622347895 /?ref=ts (accessed January 3, 2015).

1. SPATIAL RELATIONALITY

1. For a comparison with the ways in which working-class youth in Ireland engage in communal violence as a means of rejecting their spatial and social marginalization, see Carter (2004).

2. For instance, on the front page of *Yedi'ot aharonot* in early October 2000, the headline read, "Jaffa Is on Fire."

3. For an account of these events see Rabinowitz and Abu-Baker (2005, 102–104) and Orr, Shamir, and Khatib (2003).

4. In this vein, Foucault famously asserts that "relations of power are not in a position of exteriority with respect to other types of relationships, but are immanent in the latter; they are the immediate effects of the divisions, inequalities, and disequilibriums which occur in the latter, and conversely they are the internal conditions of these differentiations" (Foucault 1990, 94).

5. To further test this hypothesis I asked my barber in Ajami, himself a Moroccan second-generation Jaffa-born Jew, "Why did they break Ochayon's store?" His immediate answer was "They didn't do it on purpose," and he went on to describe how on the first day of the demonstrations, two people from the Islamic Movement politely asked him to close the store for the day.

6. The history of post-1948 Jewish-Arab relations in Jaffa has rarely been violent, but still Jaffa is a very violent city—although violence is mainly intracommunal and criminal in nature.

7. Drawing on Herminio Martins (1974, 276), Wimmer and Glick-Schiller (2002, 301–327) define methodological nationalism as "the assumption that the nation/state/

society is the natural social and political form of the modern world" that establishes "national societies as the natural unit of analysis." Beck (2003, 453–454) further points to the captivating power of this misleading assumption, which allows national categories to seep into sociological analysis: "Much of social science assumes the coincidence of social boundaries with state boundaries, believing that social action occurs primarily within *and* only secondarily across these divisions. . . . Methodological nationalism assumes this normative claim as a socio-ontological given. . . . To some extent, much of social-science is a prisoner of the nation-state."

8. Identifying the five principles of relational sociology (trans-action, primacy of process, dereification, relational perspective, and emergency), Depélteau (2008, 52) admits that relational scholars do not make up a doctrinal "school" (as many were relational *avant la lettre*), "however they have all tried in one way or another to move beyond co-deterministic distinctions between agency and structure, micro and macro-levels, and individuals and society by giving more weight to social relations as the engine of production of social phenomena."

9. Henri Lefebvre's spatial relationalism appears unmistakably in one of his many ontological statements. "Social space," he writes, "is not a thing but rather a set of relations between objects and products" (1991, 83). Seeking to unravel the reification of urban life, Lefebvre formulated a conceptual triad corresponding to three distinct spatial "moments"—perceived space, lived space, and conceived space—held together by dialectic relationships (33). For Lefebvre, "applying this triadic distinction means looking at history in a new light, studying not only the history of space as spatial practice, but the history of representations of space, their interrelations and relations with practices and ideologies" (Peet 1998, 104).

10. This paragraph summarizes a fuller historical description first published in Monterescu (2005, 34) and developed further in Rabinowitz and Monterescu (2008, 218).

11. Martial law was lifted from mixed towns in June 1949. The rest of Israel's Palestinian community, however, remained under military governorate until 1966.

12. In the 1970s, under Shlomo Lahat's mayorship, the Manshiya neighborhood on the north side of Jaffa and bordering Tel-Aviv was completely erased, creating a no man's land between Tel-Aviv and Jaffa. Seventy percent of the old city was demolished and the 'Ajami and Jabaliyye neighborhoods were significantly damaged (3,125 housing units were destroyed between 1975 and 1985).

13. Etymologically, "heteronomy" goes back to the Greek words for "other" and "law." Focusing on the problem of social and spatial order, I maintain that heteronomy is distinguished theoretically from Michel Foucault's (1986, 22) ambiguous concept of heterotopia, or "effectively realized utopia . . . a sort of place that lies outside all places and yet is actually localizable." This section and the concept of heteronomy draw on John Ruggie's (1993) genealogy of state borders and space in modernity. For the postcolonial manifestation of heteronomy, see Mbembé (2003, 30).

14. The Palestinian population in Jaffa comprises about 80 percent Muslims and 20 percent Christians (Greek Orthodox, Armenian, Protestant, and Catholic—Greek, Roman, and Maronite).

15. An additional reason for the low rate of Arab out-migration is the prevailing sense of exclusion on the part of the Jewish majority in Tel-Aviv and neighboring towns.

16. Jaffa's new Jewish residents do not share a common ideology, nor do they belong to the same social class. This segment comprises several subgroups: architects and those engaged in real estate who have financial interests; idealistic youngsters living in left-wing communes who make political plans for social change (such as Re'ut Sadaqa); groups of hippies and new-agers; students in search of cheap housing; upper-middle-class couples who live in gated communities such as Andromeda Hill; and middle-class families who purchased apartments throughout the city. My discussion focuses on the group of bourgeois bohemians that is leading the new Jewish settlement of Jaffa. (For a detailed analysis of the agents of gentrification and the social types that promote it, see chapter 4.)

17. The term "strangeness" (or "strangerhood," as it is sometimes referred to in the literature) draws on a rich sociological and philosophical tradition. Beginning with Simmel's famous short essay "Der Fremde" (1908), where it is conceptualized to describe an individual "social type" which exhibits a "distinctive blend of closeness and remoteness, inside and outside" (Simmel [1908] 1971, 149), through Schutz's phenomenological elaboration (1964), it was further developed by Zygmunt Bauman (1993) and Ulrich Beck (1996), who generalized the concept to theorize a collective cultural condition that is symptomatic of "high" modernity. In American sociology it preoccupied some of the major figures in the field, notably Coser (1965), Levine (1985), and most recently Alexander (2004b). The latter is most relevant to our analysis as it reframes strangeness from a truly relational and cultural perspective which has significant implications for the sociology of urban nationalism and colonial encounters.

18. The constitutive text, in this respect, is the Hebrew textbook *Miqra'ot Israel* (The reader of Israel)—a collection of novels, poems, and testimonies voicing the Zionist narrative in chapters entitled, for instance, "Shoah and Heroism" and "The Wars of Israel."

19. "Because of this confusion," my informant continued, "I joined the Islamic Movement when I was fourteen. I went there for racist anti-Jewish reasons, because it represented for me the place where you talk about Arab pride and the stolen lands." This narrative is an example of an essentializing strategy of coping with strangeness by searching for "authentic" identity while pushing the "Jew" to the pole of ultimate "otherness."

20. See Asher Goldberg's article "Suddenly, in the Middle of Jaffa, a Statue of a Jewish Combatant Who Fell in the Battle with the British," *Ha'aretz*, September 2, 2003. The street sign reads, "Natan Panz (1917–1948): an exemplar athlete, fell in service of the Irgun in the battle over the liberation of Jaffa in 1948."

21. See Yoav Schtern's article "The Mayor of Ramle Apologized for What He Said against the Arabs," *Ha'aretz*, November 30, 2006.

22. At present, ninety streets still bear numbers rather than names.

23. For a partial translation see also Soja (1996, 53), and for a full yet different version see Lefebvre (2006, 50).

2. THE BRIDLED "BRIDE OF PALESTINE"

1. This quote is taken from Gurevitch's synthesis of his own work (http://sociology .huji.ac.il/gurevitch%20research.html, accessed September 13, 2008; site discontinued). The terminological coupling of "the big place" and "the small place" denotes opposing symbolic planes. "The 'big place' is more than a specific site and even more than all sites—it is the idea itself" (Gurevitch and Aran 1991). A "big place" is a mythscape, a

plane of high values, aspirations, and images; a "small place" is a physical, daily, earthy locality. Jerusalem, for example, is a superimposition of "big" and "small" places: it bears myth and eschatology combined with messy realities and daily activities. For a political and sociological critique, see Kimmerling (1992).

2. This leading group of revisionary scholars have articulated a powerful critique of the Israeli "dark side of modernism" (Yiftachel 1994). Notwithstanding the undeniable reflexive and political value of this critique, it is predominantly set in a linear conceptual framework, namely, as a permanent institutional system of convergence and discursive consistency that posits Jewish/Arab spatial configurations and social actors as mutually exclusive. Thus in Tel-Aviv, LeVine (2005) and Rotbard (2005) point to the discursive "erasure" of the Palestinian past superimposed by the "inscription" of Zionist space in the making of the "White City." Similarly, Rabinowitz (2007) masterfully exposes the effects of Palestinian "exclusion" in Natzerat Illit (1997) and the complete removal of Palestinian *Haifawiyye* from the memory of Jewish-Israeli *Haifo'im*. In Jaffa, Tamari (2003) narrates the "bourgeois nostalgia" of Palestinian exiles who transform the "abandoned city" into a mythical and hence inaccessible and virtual "lieu de mémoire." In Ein Houd/Hod, Slyomovics (1998) poetically dissects the neocolonial "conversion" of a Palestinian village to a Jewish artists' colony. Finally, in the case of Lydda, Yiftachel and Yacobi (2003) conceptualize "ethnocracy" as the hegemonic land regime which perpetuates Jewish ethnic domination over Palestinian spaces.

3. Throughout this chapter, "Orientalism" is defined as the dialectic cultural projection of alterity and identity onto geographical space. By the term "Orientalism" Said refers to three related aspects: an academic discourse (fed by an academic representation and reproduction of the Orient); a literary-ideational discourse (a mode of thought based on the epistemological distinction, disguised as ontological, between "East" and "West"); and a Foucauldian discourse (a Western regime of control, manipulation, and authority over the East that has developed since the end of the eighteenth century). The relation between these kinds of discourse, Said argues, is institutionally regulated and coordinated (Said 1979, 2). For previous attempts to apply Said's insights in the Israeli context, see Rabinowitz (1993), Piterberg (1996), and Khazzoom (2003).

4. From an explicit Marxian perspective, Said's denunciation of trans-historical Orientalist discourse has been criticized by Aijaz Ahmad as a bourgeois metropolitan reproduction of a longstanding tradition—"irrationalist, extreme and uncompromising." From Said's anti-Marxian standpoint, he notes, "nothing at all exists outside epistemic Power [and] Orientalist discourse—no classes, no gender, not even history; no sites of resistance ... —and Orientalism always remains the same, only more so with the linear accumulation of time" (Ahmad 1994, 195).

5. The Palestinian suicide bomber detonated a powerful explosive device at the entrance to a popular nightclub, leaving twenty youngsters who crowded in line dead and dozens of others injured. Among Tel-Avivans, this event is remembered as one of the deadliest attacks that have disrupted their Thursday-night-leisure routine. A commemorative monument was erected at the site in remembrance of the deceased, many of whom were teenage newcomers from the former USSR.

6. The worshipers trapped inside the mosque at the time of the attack have recently been acknowledged as "hostility victims" by the Defense Ministry's committee for com-

pensation on nationalist grounds (*Tel-Aviv*, November 7, 2003). This is one of the rare instances in which Arab citizens have been compensated for hatred assault by nationalistically motivated Jews.

7. *Madrikh Yafo* [The Jaffa guide] (Jaffa: Kanaf Press, 1949), 41.

8. Respect and honor (*kavod*) are central Orientalist themes in the film. In the movie soundtrack's best-known song, Kazablan repeats the refrain, "Everyone knows who has more honor."

9. In terms of Gurevitch and Aran's (1991) concepts, for the local merry Jews in Talmi's representations, Jaffa is the "small place" *par excellence*, opposing the mythscape of Jerusalem in every respect.

10. Harvey (1991, 16) interprets Nietzsche's image of "creative destruction" as a key metaphor for the modernist project. Reflecting this dialectic, urban renewal is defined in the *Encyclopedia Britannica* as "governmental programs of encouraging the renovation of deteriorating neighborhoods through the renovation or destruction of old building and the construction of new ones."

11. "Tel Aviv: A Tale of Two Cities," Jewish Virtual Library, accessed October 13, 2014, https://www.jewishvirtuallibrary.org/jsource/Society_&_Culture/geo/tatale.html.

12. Ibid.

13. In Chaouachi's fascinating research on the "world of the narguile," neo-Orientalism manifests itself in the increasing propagation of "Orientalized" and commodifed coffee shops, which reimagine a "dream" to be consumed by tourists and locals alike.

14. This successful show features Haim Cohen, a chef of Syrian, Kurdish, and Turkish origins who used to own the gourmet restaurant Keren, in Jaffa.

15. Zochrot is a group of Israeli citizens working to raise awareness of the Nakba and to promote the Palestinian right of return. See http://www.nakbainhebrew.org. Ta'ayush's website reads, "We—Arab and Jewish citizens of Israel—live surrounded by walls and barbed wire: the walls of segregation, racism, and discrimination. . . . In the fall of 2000 we joined together to form 'Ta'ayush' (Arabic for "life in common"), a grassroots movement of Arabs and Jews working to break down the walls of racism and segregation by constructing a true Arab-Jewish partnership." See http://www.taayush.org. Sadaqa-Re'ut is a binational political youth movement based in Jaffa, to which it relocated in 2003 from Haifa. It brings together Jewish and Arab youth ages fourteen to eighteen in mixed educational groups. In one of its programs, the young activists live together in a shared apartment with programs such as "Leaders for Change," "Toward a Common Future" and "Toward a Culture of Peace." The organization works for social and political change through the promotion of a binational, multicultural, and egalitarian society based on social justice and solidarity. See http://www.reutsadaka.org.

16. Orna Coussin, "Waging War against 'the McDonald's of Books,'" *Ha'aretz*, April 9, 2005.

17. "Dialogue and Recognition" is the slogan of the Autobiography of a City project.

18. The following quotes are taken from the (now-discontinued) Autobiography of a City project website, accessed September 13, 2013, http://www.thejaffaproject.org.

19. Copti's alternative narrative included a play on words on the etymology of 'Ajami's 60th Street, or *Share' Sittin* in Arabic—he claimed it was a code number devised by the Israeli postwar administration to map the streets as part of the new urban grid. Mr. Sittin,

Copti told the gullible participants, was a Bulgarian Zionist figure; however, he added, the Palestinian residents of the neighborhood maintained that the number actually referred to the sixty martyrs who fell under the Jewish shelling of the city in 1948. They expressed their gratitude to the Tel-Aviv municipality for acknowledging Palestinian sacrifice by naming a street after the martyrs, and requested the addition of a public sign with their names. Once the municipality realized the source of the mistake, Copti concluded, it renamed the street "Kedem" ("antiquity" in Hebrew).

20. *Hursha zmanit,* or temporary thicket, is a term used by the Israeli planning authorities for a land plot designated for development, which in the meantime is planted with trees to prevent squatting and provide "green spaces." The term is often cynically received by residents acutely aware of the municipality's real intentions.

21. For the Peres Peace House in Jaffa, see http://www.peres-center.org/ThePeres PeaceHouse.html. The monumental building, constructed mere meters away from the beach and bordering on a Muslim graveyard, is contested because it dominates the landscape and embodies power's disregard not only for planning norms, but for local perceptions of place as well.

22. Yochai Avrahami, "The Jaffa Bus Tour: Yochai Avrahami & Scandar Copti— Part 04," YouTube video, 4:48, July 30, 2010, https://www.youtube.com/watch?v=C30 B47naSZY.

23. See Giora Urian's interview with Scandar Copti, August 25, 2006, http://zvuv .wordpress.com/2006/08/25/ימי/.

24. This call to establish a "mini-municipality" in Jaffa featured prominently in the platform of the Arab-Jewish Yafa List—the main local political coalition in the 2008 municipal elections.

25. The phrase "acts of citizenship" elegantly conceptualizes the performance, enactment, and making of citizens and strangers. Concrete acts of citizenship are those constitutive moments when political rights are claimed, responsibilities asserted, and obligations imposed.

3. THE "MOTHER OF THE STRANGER"

1. This is a reference to the intoxicating blossom of the citrus fruit's flowers in season. See Hisham Sharabi's reference to his childhood memories (Sharabi and Diab 1991).

2. Organized mainly by the Islamic Council, this struggle mobilized most of the Arabs in Jaffa against the dispossession attempts of the state. One of the council's main goals was to reappropriate the two-hundred-year-old Tasso Cemetery's Waqf lands, sold in part in the seventies to a private developer by the corrupt state-appointed Board of Trustees (Va'ad ha-Ne'emanim, or Lajnet al-'Umana'). The corrupt co-optation of the Islamic Board of Trustees enraged the community and eventually led to the murder of its chairperson, Al-Fanjari (Dumper 1994).

3. On the concept of the dialectic of articulation, John Comaroff (1982, 146) writes, "Because the constitution of any community depends in part upon both its (lateral) relations with other communities and its (vertical) linkages with emergent centres, it becomes necessary to explain the processes of interaction involved in what may be termed the *dialectic of articulation* between a local system and its encompassing context. Indeed,

the very manner in which these systems are defined and bounded—and, therefore, the line of demarcation between the 'internal' and the 'external' itself—is entailed in this dialectic."

4. On the demographic transformation of Palestine and the migration to Jaffa and Haifa see Abu-Lughod (1987).

5. The term "paradise lost" (*al-fardus al-mafqud*) is recurrently used by Sharabi to describe the main diasporic representation of pre-'48 Jaffa (Sharabi and Diab 1991, 16). This section mainly draws on the life stories of elderly Palestinians residing in Jaffa and on Palestinian publications: Sharabi's *Memories of an Arab Intellectual* (1978); Sharabi and Diab's *Jaffa: Scent of a City* (1991); al-Jarrah's "House between the River and the Sea: Dialogues regarding the Palestinians and Return" (2001); al-Dajani's "Our City Jaffa and the 1936 Revolt" (1989); Ghariba's "The Story of the City of Jaffa" (1980); and Tamari's "Bourgeois Nostalgia and the Abandoned City" (2003).

6. The debate over the political and social role of the Palestinian exile community has revolved around the issue of its representation in the political negotiations with Israel, its relations with the PLO and with the "Palestinians of the inside" (i.e., the Palestinian citizens of Israel), and its general sense of exclusion from the Palestinian national project, as well as its search for an adequate political discourse that can represent its peculiar position and potential contribution. Under Georgetown University professor Hisham Sharabi's lead, the "Conference of Return" (*Mu'tamar al-'Awda*), held in Boston on April 8, 2002, was an attempt to organize a representation of the "rainbow" (*qaws quzah*) of the 4.5 million Palestinians in the diaspora (Sharabi 2001, 39).

7. Pierre Nora (1989) defines "sites of memory" as the cultural objects which under certain radical circumstances detach from the flow of historical time and gain a life of their own on the plane of collective memory.

8. This electronic forum was organized by Jaffan intellectuals Andre Mazawi and Haytham Sawalhy in the 1990s. It offered a virtual space that introduced the lived reality in Jaffa but it also allowed the reproduction of its mythical diasporic image, through the life stories of its former Palestinian residents and their descendants. Another active website is http://www.palestineremembered.com.

9. Al-Rabita (2002, 11).

10. While Acre was beginning its calculated descent under the British, who favored Haifa, and parts of Jaffa were still recovering from the British assault and demolition of 1936–1939 (mainly in the Old City and 'Ajami), the dramatic watershed in the decline of Palestinian urbanism was the uneven distribution of resources after 1948. See Rabinowitz and Monterescu (2008).

11. The Hagana was the Jewish paramilitary organization in 1920–1948 which later became the core of the IDF. The one-page document, formulated in English as a simple legal contract, acknowledges the Hagana's total control over Jaffa. Striking in its bureaucratic instrumentality, it reads,

An agreement between the commander of the Hagana, Tel-Aviv district (which includes Bat-Yam, Holon, and Mikve-Israel); and the Arab population of the area enclosed by Tel-Aviv, Mikve-Isarel, Holon, and Bat-Yam. Signed on the 13th of May 1948, at the Hagana Headquarters, Tel-Aviv district. Whereas the undersigned: Ahmad Effendi Abu-Laban, Amin Effendi Andraus, Salah Effendi al-Nazer, and

Ahmad Effendi 'Abd al-Rahim—are the Emergency Committee of Jaffa; and whereas they are in Jaffa in order to direct the affairs of the Arabs in the area above defined, following their declaration that Jaffa is an undefended area; and in order to preserve and maintain the peace and welfare of the Arabs in the area above defined, they therefore hereby solemnly declare and affirm that all Arabs in the area are represented by them and that they will carry out all instructions given and to be given by the Hagana commander, today and at any further date.... It is understood that the Hagana always does respect and will respect the Geneva Convention and all international laws and usages of war.

(The original document is kept at the IDF archives). On May 14, the British lowered their flag above their base in Jaffa and left the city for good. Izhak Csizik and later lawyer Meir Lenyado were appointed military governors. The Emergency Committee constituted the official leadership of the Arab community until its demission in August 1948, after which the Heads of the Churches continued to fill the position, joined by the state-appointed Muslim Committees (1950–1965) and the corrupt Board of Trustees (1967–1975). For a detailed historical description, see Hezi-Ashkenazi (2012).

12. The war on the Jaffa-Tel-Aviv border had started on December 1, 1947, and ended with Jaffa's capitulation to the Hagana on May 13, 1948. Toward mid-April, only half of Jaffa's population remained, and by the middle of May less than four thousand remained of its seventy-thousand-strong population. An American journalist who visited the emptied city described it this way: "Never did the contrast between the two neighboring cities—Tel-Aviv and Jaffa—stand out as sharply as today. Jaffa is a city deserted by its inhabitants, police forces, and governing authorities. For anyone coming from Tel-Aviv, a visit to Jaffa is an experience likened to a visit to Israel in the eyes of an arriver from New York. For the residents of Tel-Aviv, Jaffa is now a ghost town" (quoted in Litai 1957, 251).

13. On the eve of the 1948 war the Arab population in Jaffa numbered 73,000; the Salameh village east of Jaffa had a population of 7,600; and 4,200 lived in the villages of Sheikh-Muanis, Jamusin, and Sumayl on the northeastern outskirts of Tel-Aviv. Altogether the Arab population in Greater Jaffa (*Qada' Yafa*) numbered 85,000. In the same area, including Tel-Aviv, Schunat ha-Tikva, Bat-Yam, and Holon, lived 245,000 Jews (Golan 2001, 75; Hadawi 1988, 271; Hezi-Askenazi 2012).

14. The UN resolution was officially rejected by Ben-Gurion on June 16, 1948, when during a government meeting he declared Jaffa "a Jewish city" and subsequently ordered the settling of Jewish immigrants throughout the city in order to create facts on the ground and secure territorial continuity. In his memoirs he insists, "We didn't make war. They declared war on us. Jaffa went to war against us. I don't want those who escaped to return. We need to prevent their return. Because after the war everything depends on the outcomes of the war." See the minutes of the provisional government meeting of June 16, 1948 (Israel State Archives), 34–36; and Hezi-Ashkenazi (2012, 52).

15. Several officials were opposed to the overall hostile treatment of the Palestinian population, including the first military governor, Itzhak Csizik, who resigned on these grounds in July 1948. The most vocal opponent of the relocation of the Palestinians to a

segregated ghetto (Plan Nine) was Moshe Erem, director general of the Ministry of Minority Affairs, who wrote in August 1948 to the minister,

'Ajami will be from now on surrounded by Jewish housing on all sides. We can assume that there is no threat to security in the city. But for some reason this was not enough and now they are about to circle the neighborhood with a barbed wire that will separate the Arab neighborhood and the Jewish housing projects. This arrangement will immediately give 'Ajami the form of a ghetto, closed and segregated. It is hard to come to terms with such a notion, which invokes associations of horror. Is it really necessary? Why do we need to make things worse and deepen in the hearts of the Jaffa residents a sense of bitterness and perpetual hate? A barbed wire is not a temporary project; it will always be remembered as a source of malicious poison. (IDF Archives, August 11, 1948, 1860/1950-1)

16. Martial law was terminated only in the mixed towns of Jaffa, Ramle, Lydda, Haifa, and Acre. Throughout the country—the Galilee in the north and the Negev in the south —martial law was in effect until 1966 (Jiryis 1966). The termination of martial law in mixed towns was due primarily to the practical inability to maintain segregation between Jews and Arabs following the arrival of the new Jewish immigrants who settled and squatted in these new mixed towns, and secondly to the weakness and size of the scant Palestinian communities. As Fakhri Jday, the Jaffa pharmacist, puts it, "They terminated martial law in Jaffa because they finished the job and took everything they wanted to take. Whoever owned land lost it and they confiscated it."

17. Adopted by the municipality in the mid-sixties, the Urban Renewal Plan was predicated on the principle of slum clearing, which resulted in the brutal demolition of Palestinian neighborhoods. Two master plans devised by architect Aron Horowitz in 1954 and engineer Zion Hashimshoni in 1968 were associated with the "Jaffa Slope" Plan (2236), which was ratified only thirty years later in 1995 but was partly implemented already in the sixties.

18. The contemporary Islamic Movement began to operate in Israel in the 1970s under the leadership of Sheikh 'Abd-Allah Nimr Darwish (Abu-Ahmad) from Kafr Qassem. Inspired by Hassan al-Banna, the founder of the Muslim Brotherhood (Al-Ikhwan Al-Muslimun), Darwish combined popular preaching with the distribution of manifestos, religious statements (*risala*), and political publications. The Islamic Movement's intensive activity is mainly focused on the local social domain, but since the elections of 1996, also on the national level and in the Knesset. This decision to normalize the movement's relations with the state brought about the movement's split into two factions: the more extreme "northern faction" led by Sheikh Ra'id Salah, and the more moderate "southern faction" founded by Nimr Darwish, and currently led by Sheikh Ibrahim Sarsur. Following the Second Intifada, Seikh Salah was put in detention after being accused of money laundering and funding the Islamic organizations in the occupied territories. In Jaffa, during the 1990s the northern faction often attacked the southern faction, raising accusations of collaboration and corruption against its members (e.g., City Council member Ahmad Balaha).

19. Bassam Abu Zeid, "Al-Da'wa Al-Islamiyya fi Yafa fi Sutur" [A brief history of the Islamic missionary work], *Yafa 'Arus al-Bahr*, 2003, 5.

20. The metal signposts are signed by the Islamic Movement's Lajnat al-du'a, or Supplication Committee.

21. The Islamic Movement's popularity was such that in the 1990s about a quarter of Jaffa's Muslim population was practicing a religious way of life and/or was associated with the Islamic Movement.

22. At the head of the Yafa List were Amir Badran—a Muslim lawyer and the Rabita's spokesman sponsored by the Democratic Front—and Yussef Dik, a Christian tax consultant, the chair of the Christian-Orthodox Association, and a Balad party activist.

23. The mayor's plan to give Turk the "Jaffa file" and put him in charge of Jaffa affairs was met with furious opposition from the Islamic Council, which had joined the mayor's coalition but won no seats. The Islamic Council's chairman, Said Satel, announced that "Turk does not represent the inhabitants of Jaffa. This is an irrational move" (*Tel-Aviv*, November 14, 2003).

24. Yfaat Confino, "Lo 'Arevim Ze-la-ze" [Not responsible for one another], *Ma'ariv*, January 2, 2004.

25. "Omar Siksik in a Personal Interview," *Portal Jaffa*, January 31, 2010, http://www.yaffo.co.il/article_y.asp?id=717.

26. Due to the fragmentation of the Arab political system in Jaffa and the recurrent disagreements among key community leaders divided across four political lists, the Yafa List lost its seat in the City Council in the 2013 municipal elections although the first three places in the list were reserved for a Palestinian-Muslim (Sami Abu-Shehade), a Palestinian-Christian (Mary Cobti), and a Jew (Zmira Ron). After receiving 3,717 votes in the 2008 elections, it secured only 2,195 votes in 2013.

27. According to the socioeconomic index issued by the Tel-Aviv-Jaffa Municipality's research center, the neighborhoods of 'Ajami and Jabaliyye occupy the second-lowest place out of the sixty neighborhoods in the Tel-Aviv-Jaffa metropolis. In the "Heart of Jaffa" neighborhood (the Jerusalem Boulevard area), for instance, over 35 percent of the residents are on welfare (the national average is 14.7 percent). According to the municipality's Center for Socioeconomic Research, 63.8 percent of the Muslim population in Jaffa is in the lowest quarter of the city's income distribution (Peleg 1999).

28. In 'Ajami and Jabaliyye only 31 percent of the residents own their houses, compared with 49 percent in the Heart of Jaffa, and 58 percent on average in the whole of Tel-Aviv-Jaffa.

29. During most of the seventies and the early eighties, the municipality set up a landfill, known as the Jaffa Slope project (*Midron Yafo*), whereby a large section of the coastline became a huge garbage dump (*tamam* in Arabic), with attendant effects on the health of the residents of western Jaffa. The Jaffa Slope was designed to create land on which a luxury neighborhood could be built for affluent Jews. In the late 1980s, a joint coalition including the Rabita and Jewish activists instigated a public campaign—including media, reports, festivals, and the creation of a Jewish-Arab committee—which began an annual "work camp" to clean up the area. Eventually, following a successful appeal to the Supreme Court, the landfill was declared illegal and the destruction of buildings was stopped. Despite these efforts, Master Plan 2236 was eventually approved in 1995. From 2005 to 2010 the landfill and waste disposal area was converted into an ecological recycling project and seashore park currently known as the Jaffa Slope Park.

Commonly frequented by Palestinian and Jewish families alike, it is hard to forget that it stands on the rubble of hundreds of demolished houses and is an uncanny testimony to the history of creative destruction in Jaffa. As a symbolic gesture toward this history, landscape architects Braudo-Maoz used floor tiles of demolished Palestinian houses to pave a walking path in the park.

30. This attempt has largely failed due to the population's inability to meet the relatively cheap but still high prices, which ranged between $80,000 and $130,000 per apartment. The project's relative failure points unequivocally to the lack of a stable Arab middle class able to bear high mortgage payments.

31. See for instance, http://www.peres-center.org/currentcommunity_projects and http://en-law.tau.ac.il/clinics/Housing_Community_Law. The TAU Clinic's website reads, "The Housing, Community and Law Clinic promotes the right to adequate and affordable housing by initiating Urban Renewal projects in Jaffa. By means of community-work and the provision of legal counseling, the clinic strengthens marginalized Jewish and Arab residents and assists in improving their housing situation."

32. In addition to the aforementioned partnerships these new actors included Palestinian students and activists from the Galilee and the Triangle (such as Fadi Shbeita and Hana' 'Amouri, who led the Popular Committee) as well as Jewish activists from the radical and anarchist left including what I term "radical gentrifiers."

33. Against the traditional form of top-down politics Shamir and Ziv (2001, 291) identify a novel form of politics "based on various forms of 'private' initiatives and on the activities of issue-specific professional organizations. The latter are often funded by international foundations and rely on a limited number of employed activists and expert advisers."

34. Yossi Loss, "Metzi'ut me'orevet zo brakha" [A mixed reality is a blessing], October 15, 2013, http://www.haokets.org/2013/10/15/מצמאיאות-תברועמ-ח-הכרב-ופי-כעיר/.

35. In Jaffa, one activist explained, "Sumud is our attempt to keep a strong community with political consciousness. Sumud is surviving, keeping the language, the mosques, the *adhan* [call to ritual prayer]. If Israel wants a place with one national movement and many populations, our struggle is to have two national movements. We wave the Palestinian flag because we say we are a strong national movement, we are not communities—we are one. We don't want freedom of religion—we want recognition of a national movement." Another example of the manifold expressions of sumud is Existence Is Resistance (*Al-Wujud Muqawama*), "an internationalist organization determined to promote non-violent resistance through cultural arts," which draws inspiration from Albert Camus's famous dictum, "The only way to deal with an unfree world is to become so absolutely free that your very existence is an act of rebellion." See http://www.existenceisresistance.org.

36. Aghwani and Kunda (2012). System Ali members frame their collective work in direct relation to the Jaffa housing crisis: "In 2006, around the time of a wave of expulsion and demolition orders for homes in Jaffa, we decided that it was the time to perform together as a group. We had our first performance on the roof of the shelter, as part of the popular struggle for housing. Since then we have been together, and are continuing with our musical endeavors as well as with our educational work with youth in Jaffa, Bat Yam, Lod and south Tel Aviv. . . . During this time we also established the 'System Ali House'

in Bat Yam, which is a rehearsal/recording studio which houses us, and is used as the center for all our educational projects for youth." Hagar Shezaf, "Arab-Jewish Hip-Hop Group Challenges Israeli 'Melting Pot,'" +972 *Magazine*, August 22, 2013, http://972mag .com/every-song-is-a-fight-for-existence/77720/.

4. INNER SPACE AND HIGH CEILINGS

1. Assaf Bergerfreund, "Actor Gets NIS 75,000 in Libel Damages," *Ha'aretz*, July 16, 2001, http://www.haaretz.com/print-edition/news/actor-gets-nis-75-000-in-libel -damages-1.63659.

2. In July 1948, a custodian was appointed to manage the "deserted property" (*rekhush natush*, i.e., real estate previously owned by Palestinians) as a subordinate of the minister of finance. In March 1950, the Knesset ratified the Absentee Property Law, which allowed the custodian to sell real estate only to the Development Authority (officially founded in July 1950). Upon ratification of the Real Estate Acquisition Law, the Development Authority gradually started to transfer the custodian's properties to different state institutions (mainly to the Jewish National Fund) and to designated individuals. In 1953 the custodian transferred the real estate in the cities to Amidar, which acted as the custodian's agent. Later in 1953, the custodian transferred all of its real estate to the Development Authority (Jiryis 1966, 76–77). During the first decade, efforts were channeled into settling the masses of immigrants in the already existing housing units in Jaffa. Only in the late 1950s and the 1960s were the new neighborhoods of Jaffa C. and Jaffa D. built.

3. The Preliminary Master Plan for Tel-Aviv-Jaffa, also known as the Skeleton Plan, was prepared by a committee headed by American architect Aharon Horowitz. It determined that the future of 'Ajami and Jabaliyye, which were building themselves as the center of the Arab community, should face the same fate as the Old City and Manshiyye. See Hashimshoni 1968; Hezi-Ahskenazi 2012.

4. Prior to 1948, Manshiyye was a predominantly Muslim coastal neighborhood of lower-class Palestinians. Despite being severely damaged in the combats, it was densely populated for more than a decade by Jewish immigrant families. Nevertheless, for the authorities it always represented the "slum" *par excellence,* destined for demolition and "development." In the 1960s it was evacuated and systematically razed. While city officials and planners came out with proud declarations about the forthcoming new Central Business District to be built in Manshiyye (Horowitz 1954), this grandiose plan never materialized, and the desert-like area stands empty to this day. A park marks the presence of absence of the Palestinian neighborhood. For an artistic and documentary engagement with this history, see the project Echoing Yafa, by sound artist Miriam Schickler, at http://www.echoingyafa.org. "Echoing Yafa tells the stories of some of the former Palestinian residents of Manshiyyah and thereby re-enacts what has been destroyed and irreversibly changed throughout the events leading to, and during the war of 1947/1948, and by current processes of displacement and dispossession of the Palestinian community in today's Jaffa." See also SocialTV, "Echoing Yafa," YouTube video, 2:16, March 10, 2014, https://www.youtube.com/watch?v=ms-q6JQxjiI.

5. In 1973 there were 3,176 housing units in the neighborhoods of 'Ajami and Jabaliyye (Subquarter 72), while in the beginning of the 1990s only 1,608 units remained.

A further illustration of the magnitude of neglect and demolition is the data on the age of the buildings in these neighborhoods (statistical areas 722–725): 65 percent of the buildings were constructed before 1939, 9.7 percent were constructed in the 1940s, 1.5 percent during the 1950s and the 1960s, 9.8 percent during the 1970s, and only 14 percent of the buildings in these neighborhoods were built during the period between 1980 and 1998.

6. The statistical data clearly attests to the consequences of the disinvestment policy introduced in the city before the 1980s. Nowadays, the population in 'Ajami and Jabaliyye numbers 5,761, of whom 80 percent are Arabs (Tel-Aviv-Jaffa Municipality 2012).

7. The Arab population in 'Ajami and Jabaliyye grew steadily in this period. In 1961 there were 4,209 Arab residents in the neighborhood, and their number grew gradually until 1995, when it reached a total of 4,752 residents. Gentrification and the real estate price hike in 1995–1999 brought about a demographic turn, and the number of Arab residents decreased to 4,374 (Tel-Aviv-Jaffa Municipality 2012). Residents who sold their houses in 'Ajami moved eastward, to the cheaper and more ethnically mixed Jerusalem Boulevard area.

8. The Mordot Hayam Company that runs the Andromeda Hill project reported a loss of twenty-two million shekels in 2002. Due to the lack of sales since the beginning of the Intifada, the project entrepreneurs have decided to discontinue the construction of the site. In phase one of the project, 132 units were built (of which 30 were for the Patriarchate); only 80 units were sold. An additional building, built in phase two, has 23 units, of which only 10 have so far been sold. In total, to date, 155 units have been built out of 270 planned units, and the project has a stock of 35 unsold apartments (Shai Shalev, "Ilan Gat Gets Going Concern Warning," *Globes,* September 9, 2002).

9. See the magazines *Zman Tel Aviv* and *Ha'ir,* August 2001.

10. The following quotes draw on interviews with past and current gentrifiers in Jaffa.

11. I use the term "spatial capital" to denote a distinct form of symbolic capital associated with the "quality" of space in Jaffa, which is essential to the sociology of gentrification.

12. Glass (1964, xviii) famously portrayed gentrification as a process of "invasion":

One by one, many of the working-class quarters of London have been invaded by the middle classes—upper and lower. Shabby, modest mews and cottages—two rooms up and two down—have been taken over, when their leases have expired, and have become elegant, expensive residences. Larger Victorian houses, downgraded in an earlier or recent period—which were used as lodging houses or were otherwise in multiple occupation—have been upgraded once again. . . . Once this process of "gentrification" starts in a district it goes on rapidly until all or most of the original working-class occupiers are displaced and the whole social character of the district is changed.

13. Sociologist Uri Ram (2007) divides the history of Israeli society into two periods: the "modernization" period, which reached completion by the 1970s and was organized around the root metaphor of "development," and the "globalization" period since the 1970s, and more intensely since the 1980s, which is organized around the principle of "growth." The transition from an organized capitalistic regime to a post-Fordist

economy marks the rise of new market forces that challenge the political-economic old regime and undermine the basis of the statist-centralist hegemony.

14. Gentrification has always been coated with a thick ideological layer of frontier-expansion discourse and the celebration of the new urban pioneering (Smith and Williams 1986, 17). The images attached to the gentrification process are simultaneously cosmopolitan and provincial, urban and rural, general and specific. Attesting to that amalgam are the names of new projects in Jaffa, such as "Jaffa Village" and "Little Jaffa," as well as marketing slogans such as "Living in a Painting" and "New-Old Jaffa." For the real estate agents, Smith argues, gentrification is a moneymaking frontier, whereas for the original population to-be-displaced it represents a transgression and coercion of political and social boundaries.

15. Mahapach-Taghir, "About Us," accessed December 21, 2014, http://mahapach -taghir.org/about.

16. This trope emerges occasionally in different contexts. An indicative example was a series of town meetings I organized in June 2002 under the auspices of the Jerusalem Van Leer Institute which brought together residents, artists, planners, historians, and architects living in Jaffa, or interested in it professionally, to discuss their concerns and opinions. The term *Tzfonim* was freely used by both Jews and Arabs.

17. See for instance one example among many articles: Michelle Goldberg, "The New Jew Is Who?," *AlterNet*, February 10, 2002, http://www.alternet.org/story/12386.

18. The most famous of these new nationalist tropes was Max Landau's concept of a "muscle Jewry," in his call at the 1898 Second Zionist Congress in Basel for a new type of Jew—"corporeally strong, sexually potent and morally fit" (Presner 2003).

19. For a discussion of "projects of nativization," see chapter 1.

5. TO BUY OR NOT TO BE

1. The encounter described above took place during a tour I led for the participants of the international art project Liminal Spaces, organized by the Israeli Center for Digital Lab in October 2007.

2. Tzahi Cohen, "Andromeda Me'az ve-le-Tamid" [Andromeda ever since and forever], *Yedi'ot Aharonot*, November 1, 2007. The article's title playfully paraphrases a famous ultranationalist slogan: "Hebron—Ever Since and Forever."

3. Andromeda Hill website, last accessed August 29, 2008, http://www.andromeda .co.il.

4. For Baudrillard (1988), the simulacrum reflects a negation of realist relations of representation: "It is no more a question of imitation or duplication, not even of parody. It is a sign system that replaces the real itself" (167). In the Andromeda Hill project I identify a similar semiotic *modus operandi* in the guise of an architectural and marketing trickery that attempts to create an "authentic" environment by fictive means. This Janus-faced project creates a postmodern pastiche between authentic and modern. The concept of the simulacrum—like the concept of heteronomy to be developed later—illustrates how the neoliberal logic of gentrification constructs the experience of space in the gated community.

5. "Abroad" is a key trope in Israeli popular culture, defining, by negation of "the country" (*Ha'aretz*), an imagined space of unlimited opportunities.

6. In 1980 in New York City's East Village, some properties were sold for thirty thousand dollars; a year later the same properties were sold for seventy thousand (Smith and Williams 1986). In Jaffa an increase of 500 percent and higher was registered in less than a decade, from the eighties to the nineties. In the third stage of the gentrification process in Jaffa, three projects of about three hundred units each were erected: Andromeda Hill, Jaffa Courts, and the Quarter (previously known as Old Jaffa Front). This chapter focuses on one clearly defined pattern of gentrification, one that is based on the creation of gated communities. This pattern, which crystallized in the nineties, is an extreme but integral manifestation of the general process of the penetration of the well-to-do Jewish population into Jaffa.

7. The municipality requested at first eight million dollars, but eventually settled for a payment of two million.

8. Danny Rubinstein, "Hayinu Kan Lifney Kulam" [We were here before anyone else], *Ha'aretz*, October 8, 2001.

9. The Greek-Orthodox community is the largest Christian community in Jaffa. It numbers four thousand people, who make up 70 percent of the Christian population in town. Other congregations include the Greek-Catholic ("Rum Catholic" in Arabic), the Coptic, the Armenian, the Maronite, and the Protestant communities.

10. In the wake of the Palestinian exodus from Jaffa and later the evacuation of the Jewish immigrants who settled in the Old City after the 1948 war, the Old City was delivered to a group of artists led by Marcel Janco, the famous Dada artist who eventually settled in another artists' colony—Ein Hod (cf. Slyomovics 1998).

11. This "architectural language" is specified and elaborated in a pamphlet published by the Jaffa Team in the municipal Engineering Department, entitled *A Gaze into 'Ajami: An Architectural Portrait* (1995). This publication became the founding text for a new stylistic configuration of power/knowledge. Currently, every new construction in Jaffa is required to follow several key requirements that fit the Jaffa Style, such as arches, pillars, columns, banisters, and terraces.

12. Alex Cohen, interview with the author, Ramat ha-Sharon, June 1, 2002.

13. The similarity between "The New-Old Jaffa" concept and Herzl's utopian *Altneuland* was not deliberate, according to the developer and architects. However, it sheds light on widespread colonial and postmodern analogies.

14. The project website specifies the reason for selecting the name Andromeda Hill: "The hill overlooking the sea from the best place in Jaffa is named after Andromeda, the beautiful daughter of Cepheus, King of Jaffa. Greek mythology tells the story of how Andromeda was rescued by Perseus, who saved her by beheading the monster, and married her in a splendid wedding. Andromeda became a symbol of awakening and renewal, and it is not by chance that the project was named 'Andromeda Hill,' expressing the rebirth of old Jaffa."

15. Drawing on Ruggie's (1993) genealogy of state borders and space in modernity, I use the term "heteronomy" to denote spatial systems which operate through diverging yet parallel organizing principles. For the postcolonial manifestation of heteronomy, see Mbembé (2003, 30).

16. The entire exchange was reported in Cohen, "Andromeda Ever Since and Forever."

6. ESCAPING THE MYTHSCAPE

1. I thank Moussa Abu-Ramadan for facilitating and attending the interviews with his aunt (Subhiyye) and with Fakhri Jday.

2. For McAdams (1997, 11) a personal myth is an "act of imagination that is a patterned integration of our remembered past, perceived present and anticipated future."

3. Fakhri Jday, *Yafa 'Arus al-Bahr* (Jerusalem: Franciscan Press, 2003).

4. Abu-Ramadan's statements "Excuse me, write me a check" and "My parents are to blame, I'm not to blame. They wouldn't allow me to go to school" were said in Hebrew.

5. Abu-Ramadan's exchange with the Jewish residents of her childhood home was said in Hebrew.

6. Tal al-Rish, now Tel ha-Giborim, still has a small number of Palestinian families who chose to remain or were allowed to return after the end of the battles.

7. Ethnography, as Comaroff and Comaroff (1992, 9–10) so eloquently put it, "is not a vain attempt at literal translation, in which we take over the mantle of an-other's being, conceived of as somehow commensurate with our own. It is a historically situated mode of understanding historically situated contexts, each with its own, perhaps radically different, kinds of subjects and subjectivities, objects and objectives."

8. I adapt here to the field of life story analysis Gramsci's concept of "negative class consciousness," which he called "subversivism" (Gramsci 1971, 272–273). Swedenburg uses Gramsci's concept to describe Palestinian combatants' memories of the 1936–1939 revolt. He notes that "this kind of class consciousness was 'negative' insofar as it was the class being criticized (the elite) that defined the notion of class, rather than the subalterns directly articulating their own class interests. Negative consciousness involved the reversal of dominant views, not the articulation of a positive lower-class program" (Swedenburg 1995, 114).

7. SITUATIONAL RADICALISM AND CREATIVE MARGINALITY

1. In local discourse, the protest is also known as the tents protest, the housing protest, the cost-of-living protest, the real estate protest, or the middle-class protest. As it began on July 14, it is also commonly labeled among activists as J14.

2. During the 2011 protests, more than 400,000 people, or 5.5 percent of the Israeli population of 7.75 million, were involved in the largest demonstration (the "March of the Million," held on September 6, 2011)—the equivalent of 3 million people in Britain or more than 18 million in the United States.

3. J14, "Yesh lanu et ha-Ko'akh le-Shanot et ha-Metzi'ut" [We have the power to change reality], last modified March 13, 2012, http://j14.org.il/articles/23912.

4. This chapter draws on two collaborative projects. The first, with Noa Shaindlinger, focused on the Jaffa encampment and was published in *Constellations*, and the second, with Miriam Schickler, focused on the alternative cultural scene and is forthcoming in *Ethnologie française*. I am grateful to both Noa and Miriam for their perceptive insights and fruitful cooperation.

5. Boaz Volinitz and Nir Yahav, "Daphni Leef: Ha-Kayitz shel ha-Tikva ha-Yisra'elit" [Daphni Leef: Summer 2011, the summer of Israeli hope], *Walla News*, September 4, 2011, http://news.walla.co.il/?w=/90/1856625.

6. The letter was signed by a group of Mizrahi intellectuals and activists, was published in Hebrew, Arabic, and English, and has been circulated widely since April 2011 as well as printed in major Arabic newspapers such as *Al-Hayat* and *Al-Sharq al-Awsat.* See "Young Mizrahi Israelis' Open Letter to Arab Peers," April 24, 2011, https://arabjews .wordpress.com/2011/04/24/young-mizrahi-israelis'-open-letter-to-arab-peers/.

7. Uri Shani, "Zehut Mizrahit ve-'Aravit le- or ha-Aviv ha-'Aravi" [Mizrahi and Arab identity in Israel in light of the Arab Spring], January 19, 2012, http://abumidian .wordpress.com/hebrew/maamarim/arab-identity/.

8. See Haggai Matar, "Joint Palestinian-Israeli Statement Supporting J14, End to Occupation," +*972 Magazine,* September 6, 2011, http://972mag.com/joint-palestinian -israeli-statement-supporting-j14-end-to-occupation/22410/.

9. J14, "Shidur Yashir mi-Madrid" [Live from Madrid], last modified August 16, 2011, http://j14.org.il/articles/2164; Equality Tent, "Letter from Barcelona Indignados to J14," last modified September 13, 2011, http://www.facebook.com/note.php?note_id =219340194785985.

10. Greg Burris, "In Tel Aviv, an Arab Spring That Ignores the Arabs," *Electronic Intifada,* September 14, 2011, http://electronicintifada.net/content/tel-aviv-arab-spring -ignores-arabs/10374.

11. Gerardo Leibner, "An Israeli Spring? Critical Reflections on the Israeli Mass Protests," Tarabut-Hithabrut, January 6, 2012, http://www.tarabut.info/en/articles/article /summer-of-protest-2011/.

12. Sahlins defines structural amplification as the symbolic process by which minor differences are projected to turn small-scale or factional disputes into large-scale struggles between collective totalities—thus making macrohistories out of microhistories and vice versa.

13. Tellingly, the website of the group We Are All Khaled Said is http://www .elshaheeed.co.uk/ [*sic*]. ("Shahid" signifies "martyr" in Arabic.)

14. Cf. Joel Beinin, "The Israeli-Palestinian Conflict and the Arab Awakening," Middle East Research and Information Project, August 1, 2011, http://www.merip.org/mero /mero080111.

15. Assaf Mahalal, "Ex-Territory and Babylon," J14, June 18, 2012, http://j14.org.il /articles/27276.

16. Roy Arad, "The Rothschild Guillotine," *LRB Blog,* October 27, 2011, http://www .lrb.co.uk/blog/2011/10/27/roy-arad/the-rothschild-guillotine/.

17. Yuval Goren, "Shotrey Yassam Hevrihu et Huldai leahar she-Pe'iley Meha'a Hekifu oto" [Riot police smuggled Huldai after being surrounded by protest activists], NRG, September 10, 2011, http://www.nrg.co.il/online/1/ART2/282/957.html. The phrase "We shall demolish the old world" is a reference to the "Internationale" anthem. Unlike the French original ("Le monde va changer de base") and the equally moderate English and American versions, the Israeli-Hebrew translation (by poet Abraham Shlonsky in 1922) is largely inspired by the Russian rendering, which introduces violence to the radical transformation.

18. Anat Cohen, "Yesh le-Ra'anen et Hanhagat ha-Meha'a" [The protest needs to be refreshed], *Globes,* May 29, 2012, http://www.globes.co.il/news/article.aspx?did =1000752138.

19. The historical circularity of the limits of social movements in Israel in the face of existential threats and political manipulation is noteworthy in this context. This was the case with the Black Panther movement, which gained much momentum until the 1973 war knocked it out of consciousness, and with the antiwar movement following the first Lebanon war.

20. "Manuel Trajtenberg, Anahnu ha-Netzigim ha-Amitiyim shel ha-Ma'ahalim" [Manuel Trajtenberg, we are the true representatives of the tent encampments], *Black Labor*, August 15, 2011, http://www.blacklabor.org/?p=36380.

21. Tal Ariel Amir, "Kolot shel Tikva: Ba-Ma'ahal be-Shkhunat ha-Tikva lo Mitkavnim Levater" [Voices of hope: In Hatikva encampment there is no intention of giving up], *NRG*, August 29, 2011, http://www.nrg.co.il/online/54/ART2/276/699.html.

22. Nabil Khatab, "Skirat Tiksoret: Hishtatfut ha-'Aravim ba-Meha'a ha-Hevratit" [Media review: Arab participation in the social protest], November 22, 2011, http://www.idi.org.il/BreakingNews/Pages/484.aspx.

23. Or Shai, "Tzedek Hevrati: Mi Doresh et ze u-mi Zarikh et ze" [Social justice: Who is claiming it and who needs it], Communist Party of Israel, September 26, 2011, http://www.maki.org.il/he/workers/122-articles/12347-2011-09-26-18-30-02.

24. Wadi Nisnas is the only historical residential center of the Palestinian population in Haifa that remained a predominantly Arab neighborhood even after 1948. Conversely, Hadar is currently an extremely heterogeneous and dense neighborhood with an immigrant community of approximately 35 percent and a Palestinian population of 25 percent.

25. Or Shai, "Tishkehu me-'Am ha-Netzah" [Forget the eternal people], *Haokets*, November 5, 2011, http://www.haokets.org/2011/10/05/חצנה-סעמ-וחכשת/."

26. Ethnographic fieldwork was conducted throughout the summer of 2011 by Noa Shaindlinger and myself at the Jaffa encampment and related sites of action.

27. Tarabut-Hithabrut ("come together" or "associate" in Arabic and Hebrew) is a joint Arab-Jewish social movement seeking to address the most burning issue: the division in Israeli oppositional politics between struggles against the occupation and struggles against inequality and for social justice within Israel itself (http://www.tarabut .info/en/articles/article/about/). Anarchists against the Wall (AATW) is a direct action group that was established in 2003 in response to the construction of the wall Israel is building on Palestinian land in the occupied West Bank. The group works in cooperation with Palestinians in a joint popular struggle against the occupation (http://www .awalls.org/about_aatw). Both organizations mark the radical limits of binational social action in Israeli discourse.

28. While Hatikva represented an exclusively Jewish neighborhood, the Levinsky encampment, erected near Tel-Aviv's central bus terminal, also catered to homeless people and labor migrants (predominantly of African descent), who used it as a temporary residential shelter. Both encampments were evacuated in early October 2011.

29. In her perceptive analysis of the same event, ethnomusicologist Nili Belkind (2013, 345) describes the crucial role played by the band: "System Ali's presentation did not conceal, wash over or reconcile the paradoxes that constitute Jaffa's multiplex identities. Rather, it fleshed them out within an affective, cohesive musical envelope that both voiced and contained its divergent subjectivities and contingent ruptures. While

further discussions on appropriate representations would continue to take place among both the group members and the tent city residents, in this cathartic moment, nothing further was called for."

30. The historical trajectory of the song "Zaman al-Salam" is telling. It was first performed, in Hebrew, Arabic, and English, at Peres and Arafat's signing of the Gaza-Jericho peace accords in Oslo in 1994, by a Palestinian choir, a Jewish-Israeli choir, a Norwegian choir, and Yair Dalal, with Zubin Mehta conducting. In this context, the song provided a textual and aesthetic symbolic frame for the supposed dawn of a new era. The song has subsequently come to signify a kind of peace anthem for left-leaning Jewish-Israelis and a representation of coexistence for the few Palestinians who know it. However, to Palestinians who are more politicized and wary of cultural histories of so-called coexistence, in the post-Oslo era the song's links to institutionalized visions of coexistence have rendered it yet another version of the hegemonic politics of the Peres Center for Peace. I thank Nili Belkind for bringing this history to my attention.

31. Forum Periphery is an umbrella initiative which sought to represent the encampments from the social and geographical periphery. The forum worked in part by lobbying parliament members for better public housing legislation.

32. The rally featured a long list of Jewish speakers representing the Ashkenazi-Mizrahi spectrum: Dafni Leef (representing the organizers), Eshkol Nevo and Rivka Michaeli (representing writers and actors), Yossi Yona (representing the Mizrahi periphery, and a member of the alternative committee to the Trajtenberg Committee appointed by the prime minister), as well as popular culture icons such as singer Eyal Golan and the hip-hop band Hadag Nahash.

33. As mentioned above, one exception to the exclusion of the Arab voice in the protest movement was the Haifa rally, which consistently represented the concerns of the Palestinian population in Arabic and Hebrew.

34. Attila Somfalvi, "Se'ara ba-Likud: Ein Meha'a, Kulam 'im Nargilot ve-Sushi" [Scandal in the Likud: There is no protest, they are all with shisha and sushi], *Ynet*, August 1, 2011, http://www.ynet.co.il/articles/0,7340,L-4103048,00.html.

35. Asma Agbarieh-Zahalka, "Arab Youth and Social Protest in Israel," trans. Yonatan Preminger, *Challenge*, August 13, 2011, http://www.challenge-mag.com/en/article___300 /arab_youth_and_social_protest_in_israel.

36. TheRealNews, "Israel's J14 Movement and the Occupation," YouTube video, 13:06, June 20, 2012, https://www.youtube.com/watch?v=VWjIBYE4QnA.

37. Sylvaine Bulle, "J14 and the Social Justice Movement in Israel," *Open Democracy*, April 7, 2012, http://www.opendemocracy.net/sylvaine-bulle/j14-and-movement-for -social-justice-in-israel.

38. These numbers draw on a survey conducted by the College of Management in March 2012. See Anat Georgi, "Seker Markerweek Megale: 80% me-ha-Tzibur ba'ad Hidush ha-Meha'a; Rak 30% Merutzim me-ha-Pitronot shel Tajtenberg" [Markerweek poll reveals: 80% of the public supports the renewal of the protest; Only 30% are content with Trajtenberg's solutions], *The Marker*, March 29, 2012, http://www.themarker.com /markerweek/1.1674729. As of June 26, 2012, 69 percent of Israelis remained in favor of resuming the protests.

39. Asher Shechter, "Brukhim ha-Ba'im le-Mered ha-Aviv ha-Yisra'eli" [Welcome to the Israeli spring uprising], *The Marker,* April 1, 2012, http://www.themarker.com/news /protest/1.1676538.

40. The first lines of the song are, "Maybe next summer, we'll meet again, we'll all be moved. That's wonderful . . ."

41. Viki Vaanunu, "What Is Social Justice and What Makes a Nation," trans. Inbal Arnon and Arik Moran, Tarabut-Hithabrut, January 2012, http://www.tarabut.info/en /articles/article/what-is-social-justice-and-what-makes-a-nation/.

42. Noa Shaindlinger, "The 'Wrong' Protest: Why J14 Propagates the Political Status Quo," *+972 Blog,* last modified July 2, 2012, http://972mag.com/the-wrong-protest-why -j14-propagates-political-status-quo/49964/.

43. "Man Sets Himself on Fire at the End of Tel Aviv March (UPDATED)," *+972 Blog,* last modified July 14, 2012, http://972mag.com/breaking-man-sets-himself-on-fire -at-the-end-of-tel-aviv-march/50970/.

44. The following description draws on a collaborative research project conducted with activist and sound artist Miriam Schickler in 2013.

45. Khader, "Ha-Pnina she Yafo: Ha-Bar Gay Friendly she-Kavash et ha-Kehila" [The pearl of Jaffa: The gay-friendly bar that conquered the community], *Mako,* December 6, 2011, http://www.mako.co.il/pride-culture/gay-scene/Article-6934fd404890431006 .htm&sCh=3d385dd2dd5d4110&pId=1018193925.

46. In 2011 Tel-Aviv was named "City of the Year" by GayCities.com. See "Tel Aviv Declared World's Best Gay Travel Destination by GayCities.com," January 12, 2012, http://www.haaretz.com/print-edition/news/tel-aviv-declared-world-s-best-gay-travel -destination-by-gaycities-com-1.406825.

47. Jaffa 2030 website, accessed August 18, 2014, http://thejaffaproject.com. The English translations here are the website's own.

48. Dina Café was advertised in binational terms as "a venue for culture and contacts with whomever and whatever happens here and there—in the Occupied Territories and along the Mediterranean coast to which this nice street leads." See https://www.facebook .com/DinaCafe/info.

49. Israel Goldschmidt-Paz, "Yafo kmot shehi: Anashim ben ha-Horavot" [Jaffa as is: People among the ruins], *Al-Hamishmar,* January 2, 1953, 3.

50. "Abu Hassan, the Glorious Jaffa's Hummus," *Hummus Blog,* February 13, 2007, http://humus101.com/EN/2007/02/13/abu-hassan-the-glorious-jaffas-hummus/.

51. Sheikh Jarrah Solidarity Movement, "Student Excursion in Jaffa," April 30, 2012, http://www.justjlm.org/1875. Ron Huldai has been mayor of Tel-Aviv since 1998.

52. Shankland et al. (2011) define unruly politics as "political action by people who have been denied voice by the rules of the political game, and by the social rules that underpin this game. It draws its power from transgressing these rules—while at the same time upholding others, which may not be legally sanctioned but which have legitimacy, deeply rooted in people's own understandings of what is right and just. This preoccupation with social justice distinguishes these forms of political action from the banditry or gang violence with which threatened autocrats willfully try to associate them." Along these lines, Khanna (2012, 165) argues that events such as Tahrir Square and the Occupy movements "demand a new mode of political enquiry that spills outside of traditional

notions of politics, and in which the relevance of acts and events is not reduced to the effect they have on formal structures of the political establishment."

53. See the manifesto of 7arakeh Fawreyeh, composed by the founding members in 2012.

CONCLUSION

1. "The Corrupt Land" is the title of a 1988 song by the rock band Nos'ey Hamigba'at. The work of Jowan Safadi, now based in Haifa, is another prominent example of Palestinian critical artistic engagement with the *doxa* of territorial nationalism.

2. Nadav Shragai, "Settling Jaffa, Acre, Lod and Ramle," *Ha'aretz*, May 17, 2009, http://www.haaretz.com/print-edition/opinion/settling-jaffa-acre-lod-and-ramle -1.276163. For a response, see Buthayna Dhabit, "Long Live the Mixed Cities," *Ha'aretz*, May 22, 2009, http://www.haaretz.co.il/opinions/letters/1.1261995.

3. Nir Hasson, "Gag Order Lifted: Police Arrest Suspects in Jewish-Arab School Arson," *Ha'aretz*, December 7, 2014, http://www.haaretz.com/news/national/1.630456; Jessica Steinberg, "Thousands March for Coexistence after Jewish-Arab School Arson," *Times of Israel*, December 5, 2014, http://www.timesofisrael.com/hundreds-march-for -coexistence-after-jewish-arab-school-arson/.

4. Orlando Crowcroft, "Israeli Court Allows Protesters to Picket Palestinian-Jewish Wedding," *Guardian*, August 17, 2014, http://www.theguardian.com/world/2014/aug /17/israeli-court-protesters-picket-palestinian-jewish-wedding; Ido Ben-Porat and Ari Yashar, "'Coexistence'? Arab Who Married Jew Arrested Assaulting Cops," *Arutz 7*, October 27, 2014, http://www.israelnationalnews.com/News/News.aspx/186636# .VioieovscTM.

5. While it is still premature to assess their impact on the sociospatial process, urban settlers are likely to constitute a fourth key actor in the future of the mixed city. In the wake of the 2005 withdrawal from Gaza, the settler movement set out on a *Reconquista* operation in mixed towns. With generous support from the government and private associations such as Jewish Head, urban settler communities mushroomed in Ramle (Amihai), Lydda (Elyashiv), Acre (Ometz), and Jaffa (Shirat Moshe). Since its inception in 2007, the national-religious settlement in Jaffa has grown to include fifty-one families occupying mostly Jewish and some mixed neighborhoods. The settlement operates a Yeshiva, a kindergarten, and some synagogues under the banner of a "re-Jew-venated Torani community." The Yeshiva strategically manipulates what it labels "the agenda of Tel-Aviv as a heterogeneous city" as blended with territorial expansionism occurring at the expense of the Palestinian population. Tellingly, in a recent tour with Mayor Huldai, the head of the Yeshiva in 'Ajami, Rabbi Mali (previously of Beit El settlement), was recorded saying, "Every man is entitled to fair treatment except those who are the enemies of the People of Israel."

Featuring the figure of Rabbi Kook, one of the founders of religious Zionism and the Rabbi of Jaffa in 1904–1916, the movement calls for ridding the mixed towns of their Arab legacy and restoring Jewish dominance. In May 2009, the Be'emuna ("in faith") Company won an ILA (Israel Land Authority) bid for a residential project in 'Ajami. Following two years of legal struggle, both the ILA and the Supreme Court rejected the belated appeal of twenty-eight Jaffa residents, Bimkom, and the Association for

Civil Rights in Israel, considering the matter a "fait accompli." The project, which is already under construction, is expected to be completed by 2016, offering some twenty apartments marketed exclusively to religious Jews. See Baruch Gordon, "New Yeshiva to Strengthen Jewish Presence in Yafo," *Arutz 7*, February 12, 2008, http://www.israel nationalnews.com/News/News.aspx/125230#.VIUpZovscTM; Tehiya Barak, "Project ha-Gar'in" [The Torani community project], 7 *Yamim*, December 23, 2011, 24–28; Yoni Kempinsky, "Ha-Hityashvut ha-Yehudit be-Yafo Mahzira 'Atara le-Yoshna" [The Jewish settlement returns Jaffa to its past glory], *Arutz 7*, January 6, 2011, http://www.inn.co.il /News/News.aspx/213792.

6. Compare to Ian Lustick's (1980) groundbreaking work on the Palestinian minority's political and economic dependency. Unlike Israel in his analysis in the 1970s, the increasingly politicized Palestinian community in Jaffa has learned to use legitimate legal channels and advocacy to further its interests. This has led to increasingly assertive and empowered demands in the name of civil rights and more recently of national minority rights. The results of these efforts, however, have been highly unstable, as the recent failure to secure a Palestinian representative in the City Council demonstrates.

7. This section reiterates and expands concepts first developed in Monterescu (2005) and revisited in Rabinowitz and Monterescu (2008).

8. I follow here Bodnár's excellent analysis of the theoretical relations between these key metaphors (Bodnár 2007; cf. Low 1996).

9. This is best exemplified in Fanon's own words (1963, 30): "The settlers' town is strongly built, all made of stone and steel.... The town belonging to the colonized people is a place of ill-fame.... It is a world without spaciousness.... The native town is a crouching village, a town on its knees, a town wallowing in the mire. It is a town of niggers and dirty Arabs."

10. This notion is supported by Bayat's work on the limits on the politicization of urban subalterity in the global South. Bayat (2000, 553) suggests what he calls "quiet encroachment" as the prevailing strategy that enables marginalized groups "to survive and better their lot."

11. The main case study in Yiftachel and Yacobi's analysis, Lydda/Lod indeed displays relatively high segregation rates and a radically disempowered Palestinian community subject to concerted attempts at Judaization. In Jaffa, however, only one-third of the twenty-thousand-strong Arab population live in a predominantly Palestinian quarter ('Ajami), while another third lives in the mixed area of Jerusalem Boulevard. The rest are scattered in the eastern part of the city (Tel-Aviv-Jaffa Municipality 2012). Finally, Haifa, which entertains a predominantly well-off Christian population, became the home for an emerging urban middle class of liberal Palestinians who settle in previously Jewish-dominated neighborhoods and thus display a third residential pattern (see Falah, Hoy, and Sarker 2000).

12. See human rights organization B'Tselem's definition of permanent residency versus citizenship:

> Permanent residency differs substantially from citizenship. The primary right granted to permanent residents is to live and work in Israel without the necessity of special permits. Permanent residents are also entitled to social benefits provided by the National Insurance Institute and to health insurance. Permanent residents

have the right to vote in local elections, but not in elections to Knesset [Parliament]. Unlike citizenship, permanent residency is only passed on to the holder's children where the holder meets certain conditions. A permanent resident with a non-resident spouse must submit, on behalf of the spouse, a request for family unification. Only citizens are granted the right to return to Israel at any time. ("Legal Status of East Jerusalem and Its Residents," B'Tselem, May 9, 2010, http://www .btselem.org/English/Jerusalem/Legal_Status.asp)

13. In his critical review of *Rabat*, Dale Eickelman (1983, 395) points out that Abu-Lughod is making the all-too-easy assumption that French colonial urban policies in Morocco do not differ essentially from racist colonial policies elsewhere, in particular South Africa and the antebellum United States. Abu-Lughod thus ignores these specificities of the local context and "blinds the historian to the fact that French policy from the outset was based upon a close collaboration with elements of the urban and rural Moroccan elite, hardly the policy and practice of South Africa." Such problematic generalizations, I argue, stem from the powerful, yet often flawed, suggestive effect of the metaphor of urban duality.

14. See for instance Eyal Sagui Bizawe's regular column in *Ha'aretz* entitled "Re-Levant," which seeks to reconnect Israelis with their Arab cultural environment. The first article in the series is tellingly entitled, "Relevant: Fantasy on a Cultural Visit in Beirut" (March 17, 2014). Other titles include "For Jews from Arab Lands, Nostalgia Is a Two-Way Street" (April 17, 2014) and "Beirut, the Tel-Aviv of the Arab World?" (September 12, 2014).

For a critical discussion of the notions of coexistence versus shared space and mixed existence, see also Itamar Taharlev, "Sofa she ha-Hitma'arvut hi Hit'arbevut" [The end of Westernization is mixing], *Erev Rav*, December 6, 2013, 6–9 (published in Hebrew and Arabic). Taharlev writes,

The concept "coexistence" offers two types of separate and different lives which allow for only minimal overlap. Coexistence perpetuates separation, as opposed to the notion of "mixing." We can explain the inflational use of the terms of coexistence by the fact that Israelis just don't want to change. For this reason we cannot want peace; peace will force us to change our identity. The term "shared space" as well prescribes separate identities that share the same space while remaining different. "Mixed existence" conversely points to the desire to rid oneself of previous identities, by the very understanding that identity can and wishes to change and mix up. . . . A mixed space is chaotic in its richness, exciting and creative. It's a space that triggers cultural fluidity, or if you wish, cultural queerness. (6)

Taharlev continues, "When mixing operates, there are no sides and no need for sides: the memory of sides as such vanishes and becomes irrelevant. Mixing creates an identity revolution not via erasure or fusion, but by the creation and addition of another memory, newer and broader. . . . Purification and separation, taking place as part of modernity, create the conditions of possibility for mixing and hybridization" (7–8).

15. "To tell the truth," writes Bromberger (2007, 299), "what gives coherence to this world, is not so much the evident similarities but the differences that form a system. And it is doubtless these *complementary differences*, inscribed in a reciprocal field, which al-

low us to speak of a *Mediterranean system*. Every one is defined, here perhaps more than elsewhere, in a game of mirrors (customs, behaviours, affiliations) with his neighbour. This neighbour is a close relation who shares Abrahamic origins and his behaviour only makes sense in this relational game" (italics original).

16. Thus in a public debate published in 2000 in *Ru'ya* (a magazine sponsored by the Palestinian National Information Center [PNIC]), sociologist Khalil Shkaki proposed a scenario of resolution in a future peace agreement whereby "large settlements will turn into mixed towns." See "The Settlements: A Bitter War against the Palestinian People," workshop with the participation of Khalil Shkaki, Ali al-Safariny, and Khalil al-Takatji, moderated by Palestinian parliament member Na'if Jarrad, *Ru'ya*, August 2000. Similarly, "Dialogue and Recognition" is the slogan of the Autobiography of a City project.

17. Raja Natour, "Jerusalem" (read during "These Empty Villages: An Evening on Poetry and Nakba," Zochrot Learning Center, Tel-Aviv, August 28, 2008, https://almog behar.wordpress.com/2008/08/24/ברע-לע-הריש-הבכנו-סוי-ישימח-28-טסוגואב-2008-ש/).

REFERENCES

Abrams, Philip. (1977) 1988. "Notes on the Difficulty of Studying the State." *Journal of Historical Sociology* 1 (1): 58–89.

Abu Shehade, Sami, and Fadi Shbeita. 2009. "Jaffa: From Eminence to Ethnic Cleansing." *Electronic Intifada*, February 26. http://electronicintifada.net/content/jaffa-eminence -ethnic-cleansing/8088.

Abu-Lughod, Ibrahim, ed. 1987. *The Transformation of Palestine: Essays on the Origin and Development of the Arab-Israeli Conflict*. Evanston, IL: Northwestern University Press.

Abu-Lughod, Janet L. 1980. *Rabat: Urban Apartheid in Morocco*. Princeton, NJ: Princeton University Press.

———. 1987. "The Islamic City—Historic Myth, Islamic Essence, and Contemporary Relevance." *International Journal of Middle East Studies* 19: 155–176.

Abu-Lughod, Janet L., and Richard Hay. 1977. *Third World Urbanization*. Chicago: Maaroufa.

Aghwani, Muhammad, and Yonathan Kunda. 2012. *Shurut Musbaqa/Tna'im Mukdamim* [Preconditions]. Jaffa: Mit'an.

Agnon, S. Y. (1945) 2000. *Only Yesterday*. Princeton, NJ: Princeton University Press.

Ahmad, Aijaz. 1994. *In Theory: Classes, Nations, Literatures*. London: Verso.

Alexander, Jeffrey. 2004a. "Cultural Pragmatics: Social Performance between Ritual and Strategy." *Sociological Theory* 22 (4): 527–573.

———. 2004b. "Rethinking Strangeness: From Structures in Space to Discourses in Civil Society." *Thesis Eleven* 79 (1): 87–104.

Alfasi, Nurit, and Tovi Fenster. 2005. "A Tale of Two Cities: Jerusalem and Tel Aviv in an Age of Globalization." *Cities* 22: 351–363.

AlSayyad, Nezar. 2001. *Hybrid Urbanism: On the Identity Discourse and the Built Environment*. Westport, CT: Praeger.

Appadurai, Arjun. 2000. "The Grounds of the Nation-State: Identity, Violence and Territory." In *Nationalism and Internationalism in the Post-Cold War Era*, edited by Kjell Goldmann, Ulf Hannerz, and Charles Westin, 129–143. London: Routledge.

Aricha, Yosef. 1957. *Yafo: Miqra'a Historit-Sifrutit* [Jaffa: A historical-literary reader]. Tel-Aviv: Tel-Aviv Municipality Press.

Azaryahu, Maoz, and Rebecca Kook. 2002. "Mapping the Nation: Street Names and Arab-Palestinian Identity; Three Case Studies." *Nations and Nationalism* 8 (2): 195–213.

Badiou, Alain. 2011. *Metapolitics*. Translated by Jason Barker. London: Verso.

Bardenstein, Carol. 1998. "Threads of Memory and Discourses of Rootedness: Of Trees, Oranges and Prickly-Pear Cactus in Israel/Palestine." *Edebiyat* 8 (1): 1–36.

Bashir, Nabih. 1996. *Ha-Toshavim ha-Falastinim ba-'Arim ha-Me'oravot* [The Palestinian residents in mixed cities]. Jerusalem: Center for Alternative Culture.

Bateson, Gregory. 1972. *Steps to an Ecology of Mind: Collected Essays in Anthropology, Psychiatry, Evolution, and Epistemology*. San Francisco: Chandler.

Baudrillard, Jean. 1988. "On Simulacrum and Simulation." In *Jean Baudrillard: Selected Writings*, edited by Mark Poster, translated by Sheila Faria Glaser, 166–184. Stanford, CA: Stanford University Press.

Bauman, Zygmunt. 1993. *Modernity and Ambivalence*. Oxford: Polity.

———. 1999a. *In Search of Politics*. Stanford, CA: Stanford University Press.

———. 1999b. "Urban Space Wars: On Destructive Order and Creative Chaos." *Citizenship Studies* 3 (2): 173–185.

Bayat, Asef. 2000. "From 'Dangerous Classes' to 'Quiet Rebels': Politics of the Urban Subaltern in the Global South." *International Sociology* 15 (4): 533–538.

Beauregard, Robert. 1986. "The Chaos and Complexity of Gentrification." In *Gentrification of the City*, edited by Neil Smith and Peter Williams, 35–55. Boston: Allen & Unwin.

Beck, Ulrich. 1992. *Risk Society: Towards a New Modernity*. London: Sage.

———. 1996. "How Neighbors Become Jews: The Political Construction of the Stranger in an Age of Reflexive Modernity." *Constellations* 2 (3): 378–396.

———. 2003. "Toward a New Critical Theory with a Cosmopolitan Intent." *Constellations* 10 (4): 453–468.

Belkind, Nili. 2013. "Israel's J14 Social Protest Movement and Its Imaginings of 'Home': On Music, Politics and Social Justice." *Middle East Journal of Culture and Communication* 6 (3): 329–353.

Bell, Duncan. 2003. "Mythscapes: Memory, Mythology, and National Identity." *British Journal of Sociology* 54 (1): 63–81.

Ben-Ze'ev, Efrat. 2003. "Al-Nakha wa-al-Ra'iha fi Tuqus al-'Awda al-Falastiniya" [Taste and smell in Palestinian rites of return]. *Al-Karmel* 76–77 (Summer): 107–122.

———. 2011. *Remembering Palestine in 1948: Beyond National Narratives*. Cambridge: Cambridge University Press.

Ben-Zvi, Tal, ed. 2006. *Hagar: Contemporary Palestinian Art*. Jaffa: Hagar Association.

Bhabha, Homi. 1994. *The Location of Culture*. London: Routledge.

Birenboim-Carmeli, Dafna. 2000. *Tzfonim: 'Al Ma'amad Benoni be-Yisra'el* [Northsiders: On the middle class in Israel]. Jerusalem: Magnes.

Bishara, 'Azmi. 1993. "'Al ha-Mi'ut ha-Falastini be-Yisra'el" [On the Palestinian minority in Israel]. *Theory and Criticism* 3: 20–35.

———. 2000. "Ha-'Aravi-Yisra'eli: 'Iyunim be-Siah Politi Shasu'a" [The Arab-Israeli: Inquiries into a split political discourse]. In *Ha-Shesa' ha-Yehudi 'Aravi be-Yisra'el* [The

Jewish-Arab rift: A reader], edited by Ruth Gavison and Dafna Hacker, 35–70. Jerusalem: Israeli Institute for Democracy.

Boal, Fred. 1999. "From Undivided Cities to Undivided Cities: Assimilation to Ethnic Cleansing." *Housing Studies* 14 (5): 585–600.

Bodnár, Judit. 2007. "Dual Cities, Globalization and Uneven Development." Paper presented at the annual meeting of the American Sociological Association, New York, August.

Bollens, Scott A. 2000. *On Narrow Ground : Urban Policy and Ethnic Conflict in Jerusalem and Belfast*. SUNY Series on Urban Public Policy. Albany: SUNY Press.

Borges, Jorge Luis. 1998. "The Garden of Forking Paths." In *Collected Fictions*, 68–128. Translated by Andrew Hurley. New York: Penguin.

Bourdieu, Pierre. 1987. "The Biographical Illusion." Translated by Yves Winkin and Wendy Leeds-Hurwitz. Working Papers and Proceedings of the Center for Psychosocial Studies, no. 14, Center for Psychosocial Studies, Chicago.

———. 1998. "L'Essence du néolibéralisme" [The essence of neoliberalism]. *Le monde diplomatique*, March, 3.

Braude, Benjamin, and Bernard Lewis, eds. 1982. *Christians and Jews in the Ottoman Empire: The Functioning of a Plural Society*. New York: Holmes & Meier.

Brenner, Neil. 2000. "The Urban Question as a Scale Question: Reflections on Henri Lefebvre, Urban Theory and the Politics of Scale." *International Journal of Urban and Regional Research* 24 (2): 361–378.

Bromberger, Christian. 2007. "Wall, Mirror: Coexistence and Confrontations in the Mediterranean World." *History and Anthropology* 18 (3): 291–307.

Brubaker, Rogers. 1996. *Nationalism Reframed: Nationhood and the National Question in the New Europe*. Cambridge: Cambridge University Press.

Brubaker, Rogers, Margit Feischmidt, Jon Fox, and Liana Grancea. 2006. *Nationalist Politics and Everyday Ethnicity in a Transylvanian Town*. Princeton, NJ: Princeton University Press.

Bukhari, Sami. 2007. "Ha-Mafte'ah ha-Muzhav" [The golden key]. In *Dhakirat Hay al-'Ajami fi Yafa* [Remembering Jaffa's al-Ajami neighborhood], edited by Omar Aghbariyye, 52–54. Jerusalem: Zochrot, in association with Matba'at al-Risala.

Calhoun, Craig J. 1994. *Social Theory and the Politics of Identity*. Oxford: Blackwell.

Carter, Thomas. 2004. "Violent Pastime(s): On the Commendation and Condemnation of Violence in Belfast." *City & Society* 15 (2): 255–281.

Çelik, Zeynep. 1997. *Urban Forms and Colonial Confrontations: Algiers under French Rule*. Berkeley: University of California Press.

Challand, Benoit. 2011. "The Counter-Power of Civil Society and the Emergence of a New Political Imaginary in the Arab World." *Constellations* 18 (3): 271–283.

Chaouachi, Kamel. 2002. *Le monde du narguilé* [The world of the hookah]. Paris: Maisonneuve et Larose.

Clifford, James. 1988. *The Predicament of Culture: Twentieth-Century Ethnography, Literature, and Art*. Cambridge, MA: Harvard University Press.

Comaroff, Jean, and John L. Comaroff, eds. 2001. *Millenial Capitalism and the Culture of Neoliberalism*. Durham, NC: Duke University Press.

Comaroff, John L. 1982. "Dialectical Systems, History and Anthropology: Units of Study and Questions of Theory." *Journal of Southern African Studies* 8 (2): 143–172.

Comaroff, John L., and Jean Comaroff. 1992. *Ethnography and the Historical Imagination.* Boulder, CO: Westview.

———. 1997. *Of Revelation and Revolution.* Vol. 2, *The Dialectics of Modernity on a South African Frontier.* Chicago: University of Chicago Press.

Coser, Lewis A. 1965. *Georg Simmel.* Englewood Cliffs, NJ: Prentice-Hall.

Crapanzano, Vincent. 1984. "Life Histories." *American Anthropologist* 86: 953–960.

al-Dajani, Ahmad Zaki. 1989. *Madinatuna Yafa wa-Thawrat 1936* [Our city Jaffa and the 1936 revolt]. Cairo: A. Z. al-Dajani.

———. 2005. *Madinat Yafa fi al-Dhakira wa-l-Ta'rikh* [The city of Jaffa in memory and history]. Cairo: A. Z. al-Dajani.

Darwish, Mahmoud. 2001. "Al-Bait Ajmal min al-Tariq ila al-Bait" [Home is more lovely than the way home]. In al-Jarrah, *Bait baina al-Nahr wa-l-Bahr,* 85–106.

———. 2002. *Halat Hissar* [State of siege]. Beirut: Riyad al-Rayyis li-l-Kutub wa-l-Nashr.

Davis, Mike. 1992. *City of Quartz: Excavating the Future in Los Angeles.* New York: Vintage Books.

Dépelteau, François. 2008. "Relational Thinking: A Critique of Co-Deterministic Theories of Structure and Agency." *Sociological Theory* 26 (1): 51–73.

Derrida, Jacques. 1996. "As If I Were Dead." In *Applying: to Derrida,* edited by John Brannigan, Ruth Robbins, and Julian Wolfreys, 212–216. New York: St. Martin's.

Dumper, Michael. 1994. *Islam and Israel: Muslim Religious Endowments and the Jewish State.* Washington, DC: Institute for Palestine Studies.

Eickelman, Dale. 1983. Review of *Rabat: Urban Apartheid in Morocco,* by Janet L. Abu-Lughod. *International Journal of Middle East Studies* 15: 395–396.

Eisenzweig, Uri. 1981. "An Imaginary Territory: The Problematic of Space in Zionist Discourse." Translated by Debra Bendel. *Dialectical Anthropology* 5 (4): 261–286.

Elias, Norbert. 1978. *What Is Sociology? European Perspectives.* New York: Columbia University Press.

Emirbayer, Mustafa. 1997. "Manifesto for a Relational Sociology." *American Journal of Sociology* 103 (2): 281–317.

Engels, Friedrich. (1845) 1958. *The Condition of the Working Class in England.* Oxford: Basil Blackwell.

Ewing, Katherine P. 1990. "The Illusion of Wholeness: Culture, Self and the Experience of Inconsistency." *Ethos* 18 (3): 251–278.

Falah, Ghazi. 1996. "Living Together Apart: Residential Segregation in Mixed Arab-Jewish Cities in Israel." *Urban Studies* 33 (6): 823–857.

Falah, Ghazi, Michael Hoy, and Rakhal Sarker. 2000. "Co-existence in Selected Mixed Arab-Jewish Cities in Israel: By Choice or by Default?" *Urban Studies* 37: 775–796.

Fanon, Frantz. 1963. *The Wretched of the Earth.* Translated by Constance Farrington. London: Grove.

Fernandez, James W. 1991. *Beyond Metaphor: The Theory of Tropes in Anthropology.* Stanford, CA: Stanford University Press.

Foucault, Michel. 1986. "Of Other Spaces." *Diacritics* 16: 22–27.

————. 1990. *The History of Sexuality: An Introduction*. Translated by Robert Hurley. London: Penguin.

Freund, Julien. 1983. *Sociologie du conflit* [Sociology of conflict]. Paris: PUF.

Furani, Khaled. 2012. *Silencing the Sea: Secular Rhythms in Palestinian Poetry*. Stanford, CA: Stanford University Press.

Ghariba, 'Izz al-Din. 1980. *Qissat Madinat Yafa* [The story of the city of Jaffa]. Da'irat al-I'lam wa-al-Thaqafah bi-Munazzamat al-Tahrir al-Filastiniyah.

Glass, Ruth. 1964. *London: Aspects of Change*. London: Centre for Urban Studies and MacGibbon & Kee.

Golan, Arnon. 1999. "Zionism, Urbanism, and the 1948 Wartime Transformation of the Arab Urban System in Palestine." *Historical Geography* 27: 152–166.

————. 2001. *Shinui Merhavi: Totza'at Milhama* [Spatial change: The outcome of war]. Be'er Sheva: University of Ben-Gurion Press.

Goldfarb, Jeffrey C. 2006. *The Politics of Small Things: The Power of the Powerless in Dark Times*. Chicago: University of Chicago Press.

Gottreich, Emily. 2003. "On the Origins of the Mellah of Marrakesh." *International Journal of Middle East Studies* 35 (2): 287–305.

Gramsci, Antonio. 1971. *Selections from the Prison Notebooks*. Edited by Quintin Hoare and Geoffrey Nowell Smith. New York: International Publishers.

Granowski, Yossi, Yonathan Kunda, and Roman Weter, eds. 2009. *Sfat Yafo: Mit'an Yetzira Yafo'it* [The language of Jaffa: A bag of Jaffan creation]. Jerusalem: Carmel.

Gubrium, Jaber F., James A. Holstein, and David R. Buckholdt. 1994. *Constructing the Life Course*. Dix Hills, NY: General Hall.

Gurevitch, Zali. 2007. *'Al ha-Makom* [On Israeli and Jewish place]. Tel-Aviv: Am Oved.

Gurevitch, Zali, and Gideon Aran. 1991. "*'Al ha-Makom: Antropologia Yisra'elit*" [On the place: Israeli anthropology]. *Alpayim* 4: 9–44.

————. 1994. "The Land of Israel: Myth and Phenomenon." In *Reshaping the Past: Jewish History and the Historians*, Studies in Contemporary Jewry 10, edited by Jonathan Frankel, 195–210. New York: Oxford University Press.

Gur-Ze'ev, Ilan, and Ilan Pappé. 2003. "Beyond the Destruction of the Other's Collective Memory: Blueprints for a Palestinian/Israeli Dialogue." *Theory, Culture and Society* 20 (February): 93–108.

Hadawi, Sami. 1988. *Palestinian Rights and Losses in 1948: A Comprehensive Study*. London: Saqi Books.

Harloe, Michael, Ian Gordon, and Susan S. Fainstein. 1992. *Divided Cities : New York and London in the Contemporary World*. Studies in Urban and Social Change. Oxford: Blackwell.

Harms, Erik. 2011. *Saigon's Edge: On the Margins of Ho Chi Minh City*. Minneapolis: University of Minnesota Press.

Hartman, Tod. 2007. "On the Ikeaization of France." *Public Culture* 19 (3): 483–498.

Harvey, David. 1991. *The Condition of Postmodernity: An Enquiry into the Origins of Cultural Change*. Oxford: Blackwell.

————. 1997. "Contested Cities: Social Process and Spatial Form." In *Transforming Cities: New Spatial Divisions and Social Transformation*, edited by Nick Jewison and Susanne MacGregor, 19–27. London: Routledge.

———. 2013. *Rebel Cities: From the Right to the City to the Urban Revolution.* London: Verso.

Hashimshoni, Zion, ed. 1968. *Master Plan for Tel-Aviv-Yafo: Facts and Numbers.* Tel-Aviv: Tel-Aviv-Jaffa Municipality.

Haskell, Guy H. 1994. *From Sofia to Jaffa: The Jews of Bulgaria and Israel.* Detroit, MI: Wayne State University Press.

Hazan, Haim. 1994. *Old Age: Constructions and Deconstructions.* Cambridge : Cambridge University Press.

Herzfeld, Michael. 2005. "Practical Mediterraneanism: Excuses for Everything, from Epistemology to Eating." In *Rethinking the Mediterranean,* edited by W. V. Harris, 45–63. New York: Oxford University Press.

Hezi-Ashkenazi, Ariela. 2012. "Ha-Ukhlusiya ha-'Aravit be-Yafo 1948–1979" [The Arab population in Jaffa 1948–1979]. PhD diss., Bar-Ilan University.

Hirsch, Dafna. 2011. "'Hummus Is Best When It Is Fresh and Made by Arabs': The Gourmetization of Hummus in Israel and the Return of the Repressed Arab." *American Ethnologist* 38 (4): 617–630.

Holston, James, and Arjun Appadurai. 1999. "Introduction: Cities and Citizenship." In *Cities and Citizenship,* edited by James Holston, 1–18. Durham, NC: Duke University Press.

Horowitz, Aharon, ed. 1954. *Preliminary Master Plan for Tel-Aviv-Yafo.* Tel-Aviv: Tel-Aviv-Jaffa Municipality.

Hourani, Albert Habib. 1970. "The Islamic City in the Light of Recent Research." In *The Islamic City: A Colloquium,* edited by Albert Habib Hourani and Samuel Miklos Stern, 9–24. Oxford: Bruno Cassirer; Philadelphia: University of Pennsylvania Press.

Ichilov, Orit, and André Elias Mazawi. 1996. *Between State and Church: Life-History of a French-Catholic School in Jaffa.* Frankfurt am Main: Peter Lang.

Implementation Plan of Tourism Development in Jaffa for 2001–2006. 2002. Tel-Aviv: Tel-Aviv-Jaffa Municipality, Ministry of Tourism, and Israel Government Tourist Corporation.

Isin, Engin F. 2002. *Being Political: Genealogies of Citizenship.* Minneapolis: University of Minnesota Press.

Isin, Engin F., and Greg M. Nielsen, eds. 2008. *Acts of Citizenship.* London: Zed Books.

Jacobs, Jane M. 1996. *Edge of Empire: Postcolonialism and the City.* London: Routledge.

Al-Ja'fari, Kamal, Hadas Lahav, and Asaf Adiv. 1992. *Yafa iza Mukhatat al-Tahwid al-Jadid* [Jaffa facing the new Judaization plan]. Jerusalem: Dar al-Sharara.

Jaffa Planning Team. 1997. *Shikum ve-Hithadshut be-Yafo: Gibush ha-Mediniyut ve-ha-Emtza'im le-Yissuma* [Renewal and rehabilitation in Jaffa: Policymaking and its means of implementation]. Internal report, Engineering Administration. Tel-Aviv: Tel-Aviv-Jaffa Municipality.

Jaffa Team and the City Engineering Department. 1995. *Mabat le-'Ajami: Diokan Adrikhali* [A gaze into 'Ajami: An architectural portrait]. Tel-Aviv: Tel-Aviv Municipality.

Jameson, Fredric. 1991. *Postmodernism, or, the Cultural Logic of Late Capitalism.* Durham, NC: Duke University Press.

al-Jarrah, Nouri. 2001. *Bait baina al-Nahr wa-l-Bahr: Muhawarat haula al-Falastiniyin wa-l-'Awda* [House between the river and the sea: Dialogues regarding the Palestinians and return]. Beirut: Al-Mu'assasa al-'Arabiya li-l-Dirassat wa-l-Nashr.

Jiryis, Sabri. 1966. *Ha-'Aravim be-Yisra'el: 1948–1966* [The Arabs in Israel: 1948–1966]. Haifa: Al-Ittihad.

Kanafani, Ghassan. 1980. *Ard al-Burtaqal al-Hazin* [The land of the sad orange]. Bayrut: Mu'assasat al-Abhath al-'Arabiyah.

Kemp, Adriana. 1998. "From Politics of Location to Politics of Signification: The Construction of Political Territory in Israel's First Years." *Journal of Area Studies* 6 (12): 74–101.

———. 1999. *Sfat ha-Mar'ot shel ha-Gvul: Gvulot Territorialiyim ve-Kinuno shel Mi'ut Le'umi* [The border Janus-Faced: Territorial borders and the constitution of a national minority in Israel]. *Israeli Sociology* 2: 319–349.

Khalidi, Rashid. 1997. *Palestinian Identity: The Construction of Modern National Consciousness*. New York: Columbia University Press.

———. 2007. *The Iron Cage: The Story of the Palestinian Struggle for Statehood*. Boston: Beacon Press.

Khanna, Akshay. 2012. "Seeing Citizen Action through an 'Unruly' Lens." *Development* 55 (2): 162–172.

Khazzoom, Aziza. 2003. "The Great Chain of Orientalism: Jewish Identity, Stigma Management, and Ethnic Exclusion in Israel." *American Sociological Review* 68: 481–510.

Khosrokhavar, Farhad. 2012. *The New Arab Revolutions That Shook the World*. Boulder, CO: Paradigm.

Kimmerling, Baruch. 1992. "'Al Da'at ha-Makom" [On the knowledge of the place]. *Al-payim* 6: 57–68.

———. 2001. *Ketz Shilton ha-Ahusalim* [The end of Ashkenazi hegemony]. Jerusalem: Keter.

Kimmerling, Baruch, and Joel S. Migdal. 1993. *Palestinians: The Making of a People*. New York: Free Press.

King, Anthony D. 1990. *Urbanism, Colonialism, and the World-Economy: Cultural and Spatial Foundations of the World Urban System*. London: Routledge.

———. 2003. "Actually Existing Postcolonialism: Colonial Urbanism and Architecture after the Postcolonial Turn." In *Postcolonial Urbanism*, edited by Ryan Bishop, John Phillips, and Yeo Wei Wei, 167–183. New York: Routledge.

Laclau, Ernesto. 2007. *Emancipation(s)*. London: Verso.

Lefebvre, Henri. 1980. *La présence et l'absence: Contribution à la théorie des représentations* [Presence and absence: Toward a theory of representations]. Paris: Casterman.

———. 1991. *The Production of Space*. Translated by Donald Nicholson-Smith. Oxford: Blackwell.

———. 1996. *Writings on Cities*. Translated and edited by Eleonore Kofman and Elizabeth Lebas. Cambridge, MA: Blackwell.

———. 2006. *Key Writings*. Edited by Stuart Elden, Elizabeth Lebas, and Eleonore Kofman. New York: Continuum.

Lehavi, Amnon, and Rotem Rosenberg, eds. 2010. *Gated Communities*. Tel-Aviv: Buchmann Faculty of Law, Tel-Aviv University.

Levine, Donald N. 1985. *The Flight from Ambiguity: Essays in Social and Cultural Theory.* Chicago: University of Chicago Press.

LeVine, Mark. 2000. "The 'New-Old Jaffa': Tourism, Gentrification, and the Battle for Tel-Aviv's 'Arab Neighborhood.'" In *Global Norms/Urban Forms: On the Manufacture and Consumption of Traditions in the Built Environment,* edited by Nezar AlSayyad, 240–272. New York: Routledge.

———. 2005. *Overthrowing Geography: Jaffa, Tel Aviv, and the Struggle for Palestine, 1880–1948.* Berkeley: University of California Press.

Litai, Haim. 1957. "Ha-Krav 'al Kibush Yafo" [The battle for the conquest of Jaffa]. In Aricha, *Yafo: Miqra'a Historit-Sifrutit,* 241–254.

Lockman, Zachary. 1996. *Comrades and Enemies: Arab and Jewish Workers in Palestine, 1906–1948.* Berkeley: University of California Press.

Low, Setha M. 1996. "The Anthropology of Cities: Imagining and Theorizing the City." *Annual Review of Anthropology* 25: 383–409.

———. 2001. "The Edge and the Center: Gated Communities and the Discourse of Urban Fear." *American Anthropologist* 103 (1): 45–58.

Lustick, Ian. 1980. *Arabs in the Jewish State: Israel's Control of a National Minority.* Austin: University of Texas Press.

Lynch, Kevin. 1960. *The Image of the City.* Cambridge, MA: Technology Press.

Maffesoli, Michel. 1991. "Reliance et triplicité" [Reliance and triplicity]. *Religiologique* 3 (Spring): 22–43.

Manthoulis, Robert. 1998. *Jaffa la Mienne* [*My Jaffa*]. New York: Filmakers Library. Videocassette (VHS), 53 min.

Marcuse, Peter. 1989. "Dual City: A Muddy Metaphor for a Quartered City." *International Journal of Urban and Regional Research* 13 (4): 697–708.

———. 1993. "What's So New about Divided Cities." *International Journal of Urban and Regional Research* 17 (3): 355–365.

Martins, Herminio. 1974. "Time and Theory in Sociology." In *Approaches to Sociology,* edited by John Rex, 246–294. London: Routledge & Kegan Paul.

Massad, Joseph. 2005. "The Persistence of the Palestinian Question." *Cultural Critique* 59 (Winter): 1–23.

Mazawi, André, and Makram Khouri-Makhoul. 1991. "Mediniyut Merhavit be-Yafo: 1948–1990" [Spatial policy in Jaffa: 1948–1990]. In *'Ir ve-Utopia* [City and utopia], edited by Haim Lusky, 62–74. Tel-Aviv: Israel Publishing Company.

Mbembé, Achile. 2003. "Necropolitics." *Public Culture* 15 (Winter): 11–40.

McAdams, Dan. 1997. *The Stories We Live By: Personal Myths and the Making of the Self.* New York: Guilford.

Meinecke, Friedrich. 1970. *Cosmopolitanism and the National State.* Princeton, NJ: Princeton University Press.

Memmi, Albert. 1985. *Portrait du colonisé, précédé de portrait du colonisateur* [The colonizer and the colonized]. Paris: Gallimard.

Menahem, Gila. 1998. "Arab Citizens in an Israeli City: Action and Discourse in Public Programmes." *Ethnic and Racial Studies* 21: 545–558.

Minns, Amina, and Nadia Hijab. 1990. *Citizens Apart: A Portrait of the Palestinians in Israel.* London: I. B. Tauris.

Mitchell, Timothy. 1988. *Colonising Egypt*. Berkeley: University of California Press.

Mollenkopf, John H., and Manuel Castells. 1992. *Dual City: Restructuring New York*. New York: Russell Sage Foundation.

Monk, Daniel Bertrand. 2002. *An Aesthetic Occupation: The Immediacy of Architecture and the Palestine Conflict*. Durham, NC: Duke University Press.

Monterescu, Daniel. 2005. "Spatial Relationality: Ethnic Relations, Urban Space and the State in Jewish-Arab Mixed Towns, 1948–2004." PhD diss., University of Chicago.

Monterescu, Daniel, and Dan Rabinowitz, eds. 2007. *Mixed Towns, Trapped Communities: Historical Narratives, Spatial Dynamics, Gender Relations and Cultural Encounters in Palestinian-Israeli Towns*. Aldershot, UK: Ashgate.

Monterescu, Daniel, and Noa Shaindlinger. 2013. "Situational Radicalism: The Israeli 'Arab Spring' and the (Un)Making of the Rebel City." *Constellations* 20 (2): 40–65.

Morris, Benny. 1987. *The Birth of the Palestinian Refugee Problem, 1947–1949*. Cambridge: Cambridge University Press.

Mossinzohn, Yigal. (1954) 1989. *Kazablan*. Tel-Aviv: Or-'Am.

Myerhoff, Barbara. 1978. *Number Our Days: A Triumph of Continuity and Culture among Jewish Old People in an Urban Ghetto*. New York: Touchstone.

Nora, Pierre. 1989. "Beyond Memory and History: Les Lieux de Mémoire." *Representations* 26: 7–24.

Orr, Theodor, Shimon Shamir, and Hashim Khatib. 2003. *National Commission of Inquiry into the Events in the Arab Sector in October 2000*. Jerusalem: Ministry of Justice.

Ouzgane, Lahoucine, and Daniel Coleman. 1998. "Introduction." *Jouvert: Journal of Postcolonial Studies* 1 (2): 1–10.

Peet, Richard. 1998. *Modern Geographic Thought*. Oxford: Blackwell.

Peleg, Israel. 1999. *Ha-Mishlama le-Yafo* [The Mishlama of Jaffa]. Tel-Aviv: Tel-Aviv-Jaffa Municipality.

Pinchevski, Amit, and Efraim Torgovnik. 2002. "Signifying Passages: The Signs of Change in Israeli Street Names." *Media, Culture & Society* 24 (3): 365–388.

Piterberg, Gabriel. 1996. "Domestic Orientalism: The Representation of 'Oriental' Jews in Zionist/Israeli Historiography." *British Journal of Middle Eastern Studies* 23 (2): 125–145.

Portugali, Juval. 1993. *Implicate Relations: Society and Space in the Israeli-Palestinian Conflict*. Dordrecht: Kluwer Academic.

Pratt, Mary Louise. 1991. "Arts of the Contact Zone." *Profession* 91: 33–40.

Presner, Todd Samuel. 2003. "'Clear Heads, Solid Stomachs, and Hard Muscles': Max Nordau and the Aesthetics of Jewish Regeneration." *Modernism/Modernity* 10 (2): 269–296.

Rabinowitz, Dan. 1993. "Nostalgia Mizrahit: Eikh Hafkhu ha-Falastinim le-'Arviyey Yisra'el" [Oriental nostalgia: How the Palestinians became "Israel's Arabs"]. *Theory and Criticism* 4: 141–152.

———. 1997. *Overlooking Nazareth: The Ethnography of Exclusion in Galilee*. Cambridge: Cambridge University Press.

———. 2001. "The Palestinian Citizens of Israel, the Concept of Trapped Minority and the Discourse of Transnationalism in Anthropology." *Ethnic and Racial Studies* 24 (1): 64–85.

————. 2007. "'They Just Left': Israeli Haifo'im Grapple with the Memory of Palestinian Haifawiyye." In Monterescu and Rabinowitz, *Mixed Towns, Trapped Communities,* 51–64.

Rabinowitz, Dan, and Khawla Abu-Baker. 2005. *Coffins on Our Shoulders: The Experience of the Palestinian Citizens of Israel.* Berkeley: University of California Press.

Rabinowitz, Dan, and Daniel Monterescu. 2008. "Reconfiguring the 'Mixed Town': Urban Transformations of Ethno-National Relations in Palestine/Israel." *International Journal of Middle East Studies* 40 (2): 195–226.

Al-Rabita. 2002. *Annual Activity Report.* Jaffa: Al-Rabita.

Ram, Uri. 2000. "'The Promised Land of Business Opportunities': Liberal Post-Zionism in the Glocal Age." In *The New Israel,* edited by Gershon Shafir and Yoav Peled, 217–240. Boulder, CO: Westview.

————. 2007. *The Globalization of Israel: McWorld in Tel Aviv, Jihad in Jerusalem.* New York: Routledge.

Rancière, Jacques. 2001. "Ten Theses on Politics." Translated by Davide Panagia and Rachel Bowlby. *Theory & Event* 5 (3). http://muse.jhu.edu/login?auth=0&type =summary&url=/journals/theory_and_event/v005/5.3ranciere.html.

Rosen, Gillad, and Eran Razin. 2009. "The Rise of Gated Communities in Israel: Reflections on Changing Urban Governance in a Neo-Liberal Era." *Urban Studies* 46 (8): 1702–1722.

Rosen, Roli, ed. 2012. *Haifa bein Metzi'ut le-Hazon Shel 'Ir Meshutefet* [Haifa between reality and vision of a shared city]. Haifa: Shatil.

Rotbard, Sharon. 2005. *'Ir Levana, 'Ir Shehora* [White city, black city]. Tel-Aviv: Bavel Books.

Rubin-Peled, Alisa. 2001. "Towards Autonomy? The Islamist Movement's Quest for Control of Islamic Institutions in Israel." *Middle East Journal* 3: 378–398.

Ruggie, John. 1993. "Territoriality and Beyond: Problematizing Modernity in International Relations." *International Organization* 47 (1): 139–174.

Sa'ar, Amalia. 2006. "Cooperation and Conflict in the Zone of Civil Society: Arab-Jewish Activism in Jaffa." *Urban Anthropology and Studies of Cultural Systems and World Economic Development* 35 (1): 105–139.

Sa'di, Ahmad. 2003. "Al-Dhakira wa-l-Hawiyya" [Memory and identity]. *Al-Karmel* 74–75 (Winter): 7–26.

Sahlins, Marshall. 2005. "Structural Work: How Microhistories Become Macrohistories and Vice Versa." *Anthropological Theory* 5 (1): 5–30.

Sahlins, Peter. 1989. *Boundaries: The Making of France and Spain in the Pyrenees.* Berkeley: University of California Press.

Said, Edward. 1979. *Orientalism.* New York: Routledge.

————. 1986. *After the Last Sky: Palestinian Lives.* New York: Pantheon.

————. 2007. *Power, Politics, and Culture.* New York: Random House.

Sassen, Saskia. 1996. *Losing Control? Sovereignty in an Age of Globalization.* New York: Columbia University Press.

————. 2011. "The Global Street: Making the Political." *Globalizations* 8 (5): 573–579.

Schely-Newman, Esther. 2002. *Our Lives Are but Stories: Narratives of Tunisian-Israeli Women.* Detroit: Wayne State University Press.

Schlichtman, John Joe, and Jason Patch. 2013. "Gentrifier? Who, Me? Interrogating the Gentrifier in the Mirror." *International Journal of Urban and Regional Research* 38 (4): 1491–1508.

Schutz, Alfred. 1944. "The Stranger: An Essay in Social Psychology." *American Journal of Sociology* 49 (6): 499–507.

———. 1971. *Reflections on the Problem of Relevance.* Edited by Richard M. Zaner. New Haven, CT: Yale University Press.

Scott, Allen John. 2000. *The Cultural Economy of Cities.* London: Sage.

Sered, Susan Starr. 1992. *Women as Ritual Experts: The Religious Lives of Elderly Jewish Women in Jerusalem.* New York: Oxford University Press.

Sewell, William H., Jr. 2001. "Space in Contentious Politics." In *Silence and Voice in the Study of Contentious Politics,* by Ronald R. Aminzade, Jack A. Goldstone, Doug McAdam, Elizabeth J. Perry, William H. Sewell Jr., Sidney Tarrow, and Charles Tilley, 51–89. Cambridge: Cambridge University Press.

Shammas, Anton. 1995. "The Morning After: Palestinians, Israelis and Other Musings." In *Arab Politics in Israel at the Crossroads,* edited by Elie Rekhess and Tamar Yagnes, 19–31. Tel-Aviv: University of Tel-Aviv Press, Dayan Center.

Shankland, Alex, Danny Burns, Naomi Hossain, Akshay Khanna, Patta Scott-Villiers, and Mariz Tadros. 2011. "Unruly Politics: A Manifesto." Photocopy, Institute of Development Studies, Brighton.

Shaqr, Nassim. 1996. *Ha-Kehila ha-'Arabit be-Yafo 'al Parashat Drakhim Kiyumit* [The Arab community in Jaffa at an existential crossroad]. Jaffa: printed by author.

Sharabi, Hisham. 1978. *Al-Jamr wa-al-ramad: Dhikrayat Muthaqqaf 'Arabi* [Ember and ash: Memories of an Arab intellectual]. Beirut: Dar al-Tali'ah li-l-Tiba'ah wa-l-Nashr.

———. 2001. "Mu'tamar al-'Awda" [The conference of return]. In al-Jarrah, *Bait baina al-Nahr wa-l-Bahr,* 35–46.

Sharabi, Hisham, and Imtiaz Diab, eds. 1991. *Yafa: 'Itr Madina* [Jaffa: Scent of a city]. Beirut: Markaz Yafa li-l-Abhath and Dar al-Fata al-'Arabi.

Shehadeh, Raja. 2002. *Strangers in the House: Coming of Age in Occupied Palestine.* South Royalton, VT: Steerforth.

Shenhav, Yehouda. 2006. *The Arab Jews: A Postcolonial Reading of Nationalism, Religion, and Ethnicity.* Stanford, CA: Stanford University Press.

Simmel, Georg. (1903) 1950. "The Metropolis and Mental Life." In *The Sociology of Georg Simmel,* edited by Kurt Wolff, 409–424. Glencoe, IL: Free Press.

———. (1908) 1971. "The Stranger." In *George Simmel on Individuality and Social Forms: Selected Writings,* edited by Donald Levine, 143–150. Chicago: University of Chicago Press.

———. (1922) 1955. *Conflict and The Web of Group-Affiliations.* Translated by Kurt H. Wolff and Reinhard Bendix. Glencoe, IL: Free Press.

Slyomovics, Susan. 1998. *The Object of Memory: Arab and Jew Narrate the Palestinian Village.* Philadelphia: University of Pennsylvania Press.

———, ed. 2001. *The Walled Arab City in Literature, Architecture and History: The Living Medina in the Maghrib.* London: Frank Cass.

Smith, Neil. 1984. *Uneven Development: Nature, Capital and the Production of Space.* Oxford: Basil Blackwell.

————. 1996. *The New Urban Frontier: Gentrification and the Revanchist City*. London: Routledge.

————. 2002. "New Globalism, New Urbanism: Gentrification as Global Urban Strategy." *Antipode* 34 (3): 434–457.

Smith, Neil, and Peter Williams, eds. 1986. *Gentrification of the City*. Boston: Allen & Unwin.

Soffer, Arnon. 2004. *Demography in Israel in Light of the Disengagement Process: 2004–2020*. Haifa: Chaikin Geostrategy Institute, Haifa University.

Soja, Edward W. 1996. *Thirdspace: Journeys to Los Angeles and Other Real-and-Imagined Places*. Oxford: Blackwell.

Sorkin, Michael. 2002. *The Next Jerusalem: Sharing the Divided City*. New York: Monacelli.

Stein, Rebecca, and Ted Swedenburg. 2004. "Popular Culture, Relational History, and the Question of Power in Palestine and Israel." *Journal of Palestine Studies* 33: 5–20.

Steinberg, Pnina. 2002. "Contact-Zones En-Route: Nationalism and Ethnicity on a Voyage to Israel." PhD diss., Tel-Aviv University.

Sternberg, Meir. 1993. *Expositional Modes and Temporal Ordering in Fiction*. Bloomington: Indiana University Press.

Stoler, Ann. 1992. "In Cold Blood: Hierarchies of Credibilities and the Politics of Colonial Narratives." *Representations* 37: 151–185.

Strathern, Marylin. 1988. *Gender of the Gift*. Berkeley: University of California Press.

Swedenburg, Ted. 1990. "The Palestinian Peasant as National Signifier." *Anthropological Quarterly* 63 (1): 18–30.

————. 1995. *Memories of Revolt: The 1936–1939 Rebellion and the Palestinian National Past*. Minneapolis: University of Minnesota Press.

Swidler, Ann. 1986. "Culture in Action: Symbols and Strategies." *American Sociological Review* 51 (2): 273–286.

Talmi, Efrayim. 1957. "Be-Yafo ha-Kvusha" [In occupied Jaffa]. In Aricha, *Yafo: Miqra'a Historit-Sifrutit*, 256–258.

Talmi, Menahem. 1979. *Tmunot Yafo'iyot* [Sights and knights of Jaffa]. Tel-Aviv: Ma'ariv Press.

Tamari, Salim. 1998. "Treacherous Memories: Electronic Return to Jaffa." *Palestine-Israel Journal of Politics, Economics and Culture* 5 (1), unpaginated. Reprinted from *Al-Ahram Weekly*, February 19, 1998.

————. 2003. "Bourgeois Nostalgia and the Abandoned City." *Comparative Studies of South Asia, Africa and the Middle East* 23: 173–188.

————. 2008. *Mountain against the Sea: Essays on Palestinian Society and Culture*. Berkeley: University of California Press.

Tel-Aviv-Jaffa Municipality. 2012. *Statistical Yearbook*. Tel-Aviv: Tel-Aviv-Jaffa Municipality.

Tissot, Sylvie. 2007. *L'État et les quartiers: Genèse d'une catégorie de l'action publique* [The state and district: Genesis of a public action category]. Paris: Seuil.

Torfing, Jacob. 2005. "Discourse Theory: Achievements, Arguments and Challenges." In *Theory in European Politics: Identity, Policy and Governance*, edited by David Howarth and Jacob Torfing, 1–31. Basingstoke: Palgrave Macmillan.

Trouillot, Michel-Rolph. 1995. *Silencing the Past: Power and the Production of History.* Boston: Beacon.

Turner, Victor. 1975. *Dramas, Fields, and Metaphors: Symbolic Action in Human Society.* Ithaca, NY: Cornell University Press.

Wacquant, Loïc J. D. 2008. *Urban Outcasts: A Comparative Sociology of Advanced Marginality.* Cambridge: Polity.

Weber, Max. 1958. *The City.* Glencoe, IL: Free Press.

Webster, Chris, Georg Glasze, and Klaus Frantz. 2002. "The Global Spread of Gated Communities." *Environment and Planning B: Planning and Design* 29 (3): 315–320.

Williams, Raymond. 1985. *Keywords: A Vocabulary of Culture and Society.* New York: Oxford University Press.

Wimmer, Andreas, and Nina Glick-Schiller. 2002. "Methodological Nationalism and Beyond: Nation-State Building, Migration and the Social Sciences." *Global Networks* 2 (4): 301–334.

Wirth, Louis. 1938. "Urbanism as a Way of Life." *American Journal of Sociology* 44 (1): 1–24.

Yacobi, Haim. 2009. *The Jewish-Arab City: Spatio-Politics in a Mixed Community.* New York: Routledge.

Yacobi, Haim, and Shelly Cohen, eds. 2007. *Hafrada: Ha-Politika shel ha-Merhav be-Yisrae'l* [Separation: The politics of space in Israel]. Tel-Aviv: Xargol.

Yacobi, Haim, and Relli Shechter. 2005. "Rethinking Cities in the Middle East: Political Economy, Planning, and the Lived Space." *Journal of Architecture* 10 (5): 499–515.

Yiftachel, Oren. 1994. "The Dark Side of Modernism: Planning as Control of an Ethnic Minority." In *Postmodern Cities and Spaces,* edited by Sophie Watson and Katherine Gibson, 216–239. Oxford: Blackwell.

———. 2006. *Ethnocracy: Land and Identity Politics in Israel/Palestine.* Philadelphia: University of Pennsylvania Press.

Yiftachel, Oren, and Haim Yacobi. 2003. "Urban Ethnocracy: Ethnicization and the Production of Space in an Israeli 'Mixed City.'" *Environment and Planning D: Society and Space* 21 (6): 673–693.

Zreik, Raef. 2003. "The Palestinian Question: Themes of Justice and Power; Part II; The Palestinians in Israel." *Journal of Palestine Studies* 33 (1): 42–54.

Zukin, Sharon. 1987. "Gentrification: Culture and Capital in the Urban Core." *Annual Review of Sociology* 13: 129–147.

Zureik, Elia T. 1979. *The Palestinians in Israel: A Study in Internal Colonialism.* Boston: Routledge and Kegan Paul.

INDEX

and Palestinian-Israeli relations, 11; and theory of urban ethnic mix, 40; and violent history of Jaffa, 74

"What Is Social Justice and What Makes a Nation" (Vaanunu), 270–271

"White Night," 271

Williams, Raymond, 251

Wimmer, Andreas, 305n7

Wirth, Louis, 243

World Heritage Sites, 249

World War I, 303n5

Yacobi, Haim, 292, 308n2

"Yafa" (al-Hout), 97

Yafa Action, 90

Yafa Café, 88–94, 173, 282

Yafa iza Mukhatat al-Tahwid al-Jadid, 191

Yafa List: and circumstantial coalitions, 52, 290; and the Islamic Movement, 119; and Jewish-Arab relations in mixed towns, 128; key members, 314n22; and municipal elections, 310n24, 314n26; and Palestinian identity, 47–48; and relational analysis, 288; and the "stand-tall generation," 120–121

Yafa Municipality, 90

"Yafawiye hiye hawiye" (Jaffan is an identity), 130

Yafo, Minhal, 112

Yedi'ot aharonot, 13

Yedi'ot 'iryat Tel-Aviv, 75, 77

Yedi'ot Tel-Aviv, 77–78

Yefet Street, 194, 198–199, 258

Yiftachel, Oren, 292, 308n2

Yishuv, 39–40

Yonathan, Natan, 284

"Young Leadership," 48

youth movements, 48, 163

Zbeidi, Zakariyah, 89

zero-sum view of urban structure, 10, 20, 24, 65–66, 71, 173, 285

Zionism: and Abu-Ramadan's narrative, 231; and the Andromeda Hill project, 190–192; and the Arab Spring protests, 244, 247, 260–261, 263; and colonial paradigm, 292–293; and contrived coexistence, 8–9, 24–25; and cultural indeterminacy, 59–61, 94–96; and "erasure" of Palestinian past, 308n2; and gated communities, 194; and genealogy of mixed towns, 13–15, 17–18; and gentrification, 145, 163, 169, 172–174; and Hebrew education, 307n18; and Jaffa's counterculture, 276; and Jday's narrative, 219; and Jewish population of Jaffa, 49; and Jewish-Arab relations in mixed towns, 127; and *Miqra'ot Israel,* 307n18; and mixed cities, 22; and "muscle Jewry," 318n18; and Orientalist realism, 84; origins of, 325n5; and Palestinian-Israeli relations, 10–11; and the "stand-tall generation," 120–121; and stranger sociality, 56; and Tel-Aviv's relationship to Jaffa, 304n6; and theory of urban ethnic mix, 38–40; and urban Orientalism, 68–69, 71–72, 73; and violent history of Jaffa, 75–78, 77; and Yafa Café, 90–91, 93–94

Zman Tel-Aviv, 84

Zochrot (Remembering) Association, 62, 88, 278

Zreik, Raef, 127, 129

Zubeida, Hani, 257

DANIEL MONTERESCU is Associate Professor of Urban Anthropology at the Central European University in Budapest. He is author (with Haim Hazan) of *A Town at Sundown: Aging Nationalism in Jaffa*, a bilingual (Arabic-Hebrew) study of autobiographical narratives of elderly Palestinians and Jews in Jaffa; and editor (with Dan Rabinowitz) of *Mixed Towns, Trapped Communities: Historical Narratives, Spatial Dynamics, Gender Relations and Cultural Encounters in Palestinian-Israeli Towns*.